MW01486883

# Liberty as Independence

What does liberty entail? How have concepts of liberty changed over time? And what are the global consequences? This book surveys the history of rival views of liberty from antiquity to modern times. Quentin Skinner traces the understanding of liberty as independence from the classical ideal to early modern Britain, culminating in the claims of the Whig oligarchy to have transformed this idea into reality. Yet, with the Whig vision of a free state and civil society undermined by the American Revolution of 1776, Skinner explores how claims that liberty was fulfilled by an absence of physical or coercive restraint came to prominence. *Liberty as Independence* examines new dimensions of these rival views, considering the connections between debates on liberty and debates on slavery, and demonstrating how these ideas were harnessed in feminist discussions surrounding limitations on the liberty of women. The concept of liberty is inherently global, and Skinner argues strongly for the reinstatement of the understanding of liberty as independence.

Quentin Skinner is Emeritus Professor of Humanities at Queen Mary University of London. He was at the Institute for Advanced Study at Princeton between 1974 and 1979, and was Regius Professor of History at the University of Cambridge between 1996 and 2008. He is the author and editor of numerous books on Renaissance and Modern Intellectual History, and the recipient of many awards including the Wolfson Prize for History and a Balzan Prize. Previous publications include the two-volume study, *The Foundations of Modern Political Thought* (Cambridge, 1978), *Liberty before Liberalism* (Cambridge, 1998) and, most recently, *From Humanism to Hobbes: Studies in Rhetoric and Politics* (Cambridge, 2018).

# Liberty as Independence

*The Making and Unmaking of a Political Ideal*

Quentin Skinner

*Queen Mary University of London*

CAMBRIDGE
UNIVERSITY PRESS

Shaftesbury Road, Cambridge CB2 8EA, United Kingdom

One Liberty Plaza, 20th Floor, New York, NY 10006, USA

477 Williamstown Road, Port Melbourne, VIC 3207, Australia

314–321, 3rd Floor, Plot 3, Splendor Forum, Jasola District Centre,
New Delhi – 110025, India

103 Penang Road, #05–06/07, Visioncrest Commercial, Singapore 238467

Cambridge University Press is part of Cambridge University Press & Assessment,
a department of the University of Cambridge.

We share the University's mission to contribute to society through the pursuit of
education, learning and research at the highest international levels of excellence.

www.cambridge.org
Information on this title: www.cambridge.org/9781107027732

DOI: 10.1017/9781139226677

© Quentin Skinner 2025

This publication is in copyright. Subject to statutory exception and to the provisions
of relevant collective licensing agreements, no reproduction of any part may take
place without the written permission of Cambridge University Press & Assessment.

When citing this work, please include a reference to the DOI 10.1017/9781139226677

First published 2025

Printed in the United Kingdom by TJ Books Limited, Padstow Cornwall

*A catalogue record for this publication is available from the British Library.*

*A Cataloging-in-Publication data record for this book is available from the Library of Congress*

ISBN 978-1-107-02773-2 Hardback

Cambridge University Press & Assessment has no responsibility for the persistence
or accuracy of URLs for external or third-party internet websites referred to in this
publication and does not guarantee that any content on such websites is, or will remain,
accurate or appropriate.

# Contents

# Acknowledgements

My first thanks are due to Annelien De Dijn. It was Annelien who organised a conference in May 2017 at the Netherlands Institute for Advanced Study under the title 'Freedom: Liberalism, Republicanism and Beyond' to mark the twentieth anniversary of my book *Liberty before liberalism*. I also owe particular thanks to Annabel Brett for chairing the conference, which proved to be an inspiring as well as a highly enjoyable occasion. I learned a lot from the impressive and challenging papers that were delivered, as well as from the days of intense discussion that followed. It was this event that prompted me to start thinking again about the unruly history of liberty.[1]

I began by converting the talk I had given at the conference into a lecture, which I then tried out on some exacting but encouraging audiences. I first did so while serving, later in 2017, as Visiting Professor at the Neubauer Collegium in the University of Chicago, and I am very grateful to Jonathan Lear, as well as Gabriel Richardson Lear, for being such attentive and generous hosts. I presented more of my new material early in 2019 as Weinstein Fellow in the School of Law at Berkeley, and I owe special thanks to Kinch Hoekstra and David Lieberman for their invitation and for much valuable advice. But David died soon afterwards, and I continue to mourn the loss of a greatly valued friend.

The papers delivered at the 2017 conference were published by Cambridge University Press in 2022 under the title *Rethinking Liberty before liberalism*, edited by Hannah Dawson and Annelien De Dijn. I incorporated my new research into a reply-to-critics chapter, on which I have drawn in several places in the present book. The publication of the volume was celebrated in May 2023 with a further conference, this time held at King's College London and organised with memorable panache by Hannah Dawson. A further series of remarkable papers were presented on this occasion by Teresa Bejan, Richard Bourke, Cécile Laborde,

---

[1] Here I allude to Annelien De Dijn's book *Freedom: An unruly history*, to which I am also indebted. See De Dijn 2020.

Sophie Smith, Amia Srinivasan and Lyndsey Stonebridge. These two conferences above all shaped my thinking, and it was out of this process that *Liberty as independence* eventually emerged. I owe very many thanks to all the friends and colleagues who helped to guide me towards this path.

During the years when I was writing *Liberty as independence* I was still teaching at Queen Mary University of London. There I supervised a number of outstanding MA and PhD students, and I need to single out several who wrote dissertations on topics akin to my research on the concept of liberty, notably Lorenzo Sabbadini, Evangelos Sakkas and Max Skjönsberg, all of whom have influenced my work.[2] I am also most grateful to numerous colleagues at Queen Mary for support and encouragement throughout these years, particularly to Warren Boutcher, David Colclough, Andrew Fitzmaurice, Gareth Stedman Jones and Georgios Varouxakis. I am likewise indebted to several members of the wider community of scholars in London who study and teach intellectual history, especially Valentina Arena, Adrian Blau, Hannah Dawson, Angus Gowland, Dina Gusejnova, Niall O'Flaherty and Samuel Zeitlin.

I am much beholden to friends and colleagues in the wider world with whom I have discussed my recent work, many of whom have assisted me with information and advice, corresponded with me about aspects of my project, and in several cases read some or even all of my text in various versions and drafts. My warmest thanks to David Armitage, Richard Bourke, J. C. D. Clark, Cui Zhiyuan, John Dunn, Richard Fisher, Martin van Gelderen, Marco Geuna, Carlo Ginzburg, Lena Halldenius, Fred Inglis, Matthew Kramer, Cécile Laborde, Li Hansong, Liu Yuwei, Frank Lovett, Johnny Lyons, Melissa Lane, Noel Malcolm, Jeremy Mynott, Eric Nelson, Anthony Pagden, Kari Palonen, Markku Peltonen, Daniel Pick, John Pocock, Christopher Ricks, Isabel Rivers, John Robertson, Peter Stacey, Keith Thomas, John Thompson, James Tully and Richard Whatmore.

I need to add a special word of thanks to Philip Pettit. The seminar we gave at the Australian National University in 1994 on the topic of republican freedom was a crucial moment for me, and I also owe a very large debt to Philip's now classic sequence of books on the theory of liberty.[3] I am no less grateful to him for his unfailingly illuminating and encouraging conversations and correspondence over the years. I remember with particular pleasure our most recent talks when he and Tori McGeer spent a month in London during the summer of 2023.

---

[2] See Sakkas 2016; Skjörnberg 2016; 2019; 2021; 2022; 2023; Sabbadini 2016; 2020.
[3] See Pettit 1997; 2001; 2012; 2014.

As always, I reserve my most heartfelt thanks for Susan James. She has read every draft of this book, discussed it with me in the fullest detail, and shown endless patience with my project. At the same time she has brought to bear her profound and wide-ranging understanding of early modern philosophy, thereby improving my argument as well as saving me from misstatements and mistakes. The value of her support, and that of our children Olivia and Marcus and their families, remains beyond words.

I also owe many thanks for a large amount of institutional as well as personal support. I began teaching at Queen Mary University of London in 2008, retiring at the end of 2022. I remain much indebted to Philip Ogden, whose idea it was that I should join Queen Mary, and to all my colleagues in the School of History, who gave me such a warm welcome. These years turned out to be among the happiest and most fruitful of my academic life.

My research for this book was initially conducted at the British Library, but its closure in 2020 during the Covid pandemic left me even more reliant than usual on electronic resources. For some years intellectual historians have been much indebted to Jisc for bringing together the EEBO and ECCO databases as *Historical Texts*, but it was during the pandemic that I began to find this resource nothing less than indispensable. As always, however, I also owe many thanks to the British Library. The staff remain as courteous and efficient as ever, and every reader owes them additional thanks for their heroic response to the cyber attack suffered by the library in 2023. I was one of a large number of scholars whose ability to consult secondary materials was suddenly cut off, but was reinstated by the library's willingness to create an interim catalogue and keep its reading rooms open, all of which proved to be crucial to the completion of my book.

I am about to say something I have said before, but it remains important for me to repeat how greatly I appreciate the help and encouragement I have always received from Cambridge University Press. Liz Friend-Smith has again acted as my editor, and has done so with unfailing efficiency and kindness, from which I never cease to benefit. I am deeply grateful as always for her guidance and support. To Ruth Boyes as Senior Content Manager I am indebted for overseeing the process of production, and to Dino Costi I owe many thanks for compiling an exemplary index. To Mary Starkey I owe special thanks for her meticulous copy-editing, which has rescued me – not for the first time – from numerous confusions and mistakes. I am grateful to her not only for extensive advice, but also for a highly enjoyable correspondence. My warmest thanks to everyone for so much assistance and expertise.

# Conventions

## Abbreviations

| | |
|---|---|
| BL: | The British Library. |
| *ODNB*: | *The Oxford dictionary of national biography*, 60 vols. (Oxford, 2004). |
| n.p. | No stated place of publication. |

*Bibliographies*   These are simply checklists of the primary and secondary sources I quote in the text. They make no pretence of being systematic guides to the critical literature on the themes I discuss. The bibliography of primary sources lists anonymous works by title. Where a work was published anonymously but the name of the author is known I place the name in square brackets.

*Classical names*   I refer to ancient writers in their most familiar single-name style both in the text and in the bibliographies.

*Dates*   Generally I follow my sources, except that I date by the common era. The shift to the Gregorian calendar was not made in Great Britain until 1752, but throughout my text I treat the year as beginning on 1 January, not 25 March.

*Gender*   I try to use gender-neutral language wherever possible but occasionally I have felt obliged to follow the usage in my sources in order to avoid altering their sense.

*References*   I use the author-date system when quoting from primary as well as secondary sources. All references to journals in the bibliography of secondary sources are given in Arabic numerals. But when I refer in footnotes to sections of books I sometimes use Roman and sometimes Arabic numbering, depending

|                | on the preference shown by the author or editor of the work concerned. |
| -------------- | --------------------------------------------------------------- |
| *Transcriptions* | I modernise all spelling and punctuation, remove most italics and capital letters, and correct obvious typographical mistakes. My aim, without I hope sacrificing accuracy, is to make my sources as accessible as possible. |

# Introduction

My principal aim in this book is to outline and explain a major transformation in anglophone discussions about the meaning of liberty. I ask when and why it came about that one prevailing way of understanding what it means to be free was displaced by a strongly contrasting account that in turn became no less generally accepted. I argue that this shift mainly took place in the closing decades of the eighteenth century. Before that time it was widely agreed that what it means to be free is that you are not subject to the exercise of arbitrary power, and are consequently able to act according to your autonomous will and live as you choose.[1] Liberty was construed as independence. By the early nineteenth century this view had been replaced as a hegemonic ideology by the rival contention that liberty simply consists in not being restrained. According to the most exacting version of this argument, you are rendered unfree only if the restraint you suffer takes the form of an external impediment that physically prevents you from doing as you wish. But according to the version that came to be generally accepted, you are also rendered unfree if your choices are restricted by threats.[2] Liberty was now construed as an absence of either physical or coercive restraint.[3]

In recent years there has been a recrudescence of interest in the ideal of liberty as independence, and one result has been that most of the claims

---

[1] Here my analysis connects with Nyquist 2013, in which the exercise of arbitrary power is described as giving rise to 'political slavery', that form of servitude which is suffered under tyrannical government. On chattel and political slavery, and on the equation between the latter and living subject to arbitrary power, see also Reid 1988, pp. 38–59.

[2] But for the more exacting account see Carter 1999; Kramer 2003.

[3] Before I go further, it seems worth adding a word of warning about the terminology I use. Generally I treat 'freedom' as a synonym for 'liberty'. I refer to the second view of liberty I have singled out as the claim that liberty consists in not being restrained. However, this view has also been labelled the 'non-interference' conception, and this formula has recently gained widespread currency, largely due to the analysis in Pettit 1997, pp. 41–50. This being so, I sometimes make use of this terminology myself, while at other times I put the formulae together, speaking of the view that liberty consists in absence of interference (or hindrances) or absence of restraint (or impediments).

I have just summarised have become subjects of vigorous debate.[4] The bluntest reaction to the claims I am making has been that, in the historical period I single out, no such arguments about the meaning of liberty took place.[5] One of my chief aspirations in what follows is to contest this objection by providing a historical survey of the rival understandings involved, together with an explanation of why the ideal of liberty as independence was largely displaced by the view that liberty simply consists in not being restrained.

Why this displacement happened is also a question that has lately been much discussed. One favoured suggestion has been that the shift was closely connected with the rise of modern commercial society in the eighteenth century.[6] I propose a different explanation. We need to reflect, I suggest, on the implications of the fact that the American Revolution of 1776, as well as the French Revolution of 1789, were promoted and legitimised in terms of the claim that liberty consists in living as equal citizens in conditions of independence and self-rule. This was more than enough to arouse the conservative forces at work in British society at the time, prompting them to find a means of discrediting this demand for a more egalitarian form of society and state. It was panic about democracy, not the imperatives of commerce, that displaced the ideal of liberty as independence.[7]

Amid the scepticism and hostility provoked by recent attempts to revive this ideal of liberty, two objections have been raised that seem to me particularly worth singling out. Some historians (notably J. G. A. Pocock) have argued that the view of liberty animating the era of revolution at the end of the eighteenth century needs to be seen as a 'positive' one in which liberty was in effect equated with self-realisation, and more specifically with a life of virtuous public action.[8] The most usual objection, however, has been that the two allegedly rival views of liberty are not in fact analytically distinct. There is said to be no 'conceptual opposition' and hence 'no interesting disagreement' between them, and it has even been

[4] For a survey see Hammersley 2020, pp. 197–209. For early hostile reactions see Ghosh 2008, esp. pp. 132–5, 139–45.
[5] See Whatmore 2016, esp. pp. 109–10 and references there.
[6] See Pocock 2006, esp. pp. 13–17; Kalyvas and Katznelson 2008; MacGilvray 2011.
[7] Here I agree with Philp 1998 and De Dijn 2020.
[8] See Pocock 1975, p. 550, where he aligns himself with Hannah Arendt's view of freedom and – or as – political action (on which see Arendt 1968 ). See also Pocock 1985, pp. 40–4; Pocock 2006, p. 13–15; and, for a similar view, see Rahe 1994. For a defence of 'positive' liberty see Taylor 1991, and for discussions of Arendt's positive view see Beiner 1984 and Honohan 2002, pp. 111–14, 119–31. For a general discussion of positive liberty see Ivison 1997, pp. 2–10; for a critique of the concept see Skinner 2002d. For attempted genealogies of negative, positive and republican liberty see Spitz 1995, pp. 83–269 and Skinner 2016.

argued that it is a mere invention to suppose that they can be distinguished.[9] We are told that the alleged distinction between the two views of liberty I single out simply collapses,[10] and also that 'the dominating role' in political discourse has at all times been played by the idea of liberty as nothing other than absence of interference or restraint.[11]

I argue that both these objections reflect a failure to grasp what is involved in the assertion that liberty can be equated with independence. The proponents of this view are not denying that, if we say of someone that they are free to act, we are saying that they are unimpeded. What they wish to affirm is that the basic question to ask about liberty cannot be whether or not you are able to choose and act freely. The fundamental and logically prior question must be whether or not you are a free person, someone who is not subject to the arbitrary power of any other person or institution within civil society or the state.[12]

If you are a free person, your freedom will not necessarily be forfeited if restrictions are imposed on your choices. You may be prevented from acting in some specific way, but your standing as a free person may be unaffected.[13] If, on the other hand, you are not a free person, then – and this is the crucial point – you will never be in a position to choose and act freely. All your choices and actions will be the product not merely of your own will, but at the same time of the permission and hence the will of those to whom you are subject, whether that permission is silently or explicitly granted.

The restriction of your choices, in other words, is neither a necessary nor a sufficient condition of being unfree. Just as it is possible to remain a free person even if someone interferes with your choices, so it is possible to be unfree in the absence of any such interference or even any threat of it. Those who have the good fortune to be subject to a beneficent master or an enlightened despot may find their behaviour very little regulated or restrained. But so long as they are subject to the will of a master they remain incapable of acting autonomously, and hence remain unfree.

The defenders of the ideal of liberty as independence believe, in short, that what it means to be free is essentially to possess a distinctive status in social life. By contrast, those who defend the claim that liberty consists in absence of restraint think of it simply as a predicate of choices and

---

[9] Patten 1996, p. 25; Kalyvas and Katznelson 2008, pp. 4, 8, 10; Haakonssen 2007; Podoksik 2010, pp. 225–7. For further statements to the same effect see Larmore 2001, pp. 234–5; Goodin 2003, pp. 60–1; Kramer 2008, p. 56; McBride 2015, p. 351; Moen 2022. For a robust rebuttal see Lovett 2022, pp. 17–20.

[10] Straumann 2016, p. 9.     [11] Podoksik 2010, pp. 221, 240.

[12] Here I have changed my mind since I wrote about this issue in Skinner 1998. For helping me to improve my argument I am indebted to Pettit 1997, pp. 300–3 and Pettit 2002.

[13] This constitutes my answer to Talisse 2014. See Skinner 2022, pp. 242–3.

actions.[14] It is surely clear that these are not merely contrasting but rival approaches to thinking about the concept of liberty.

The recent revival of the view that liberty should be understood as independence has been due above all to the pioneering work of Philip Pettit, who has devoted a sequence of outstandingly important books to the subject.[15] I have been greatly influenced by his work, but it is worth registering that, when I refer to this ideal of liberty, I do so in terms somewhat different from those employed by Pettit and most of his followers. The contrast they generally draw is between liberty as non-interference and liberty as non-domination, the latter of which they treat in turn as a distinctively republican way of thinking about freedom and government.[16] They also focus on how the pivotal concept of arbitrary power should be understood, and here some of Pettit's followers have continued to adopt his initial suggestion that it needs to be equated with a capacity to act without being obliged to track the interests of those who will be affected.[17] One of my aims in what follows will be to show that it would be beneficial to pay more attention to the terms in which the so-called republican theory of liberty was originally articulated. As we shall see, it turns out to be significant that those who embraced the theory rarely spoke of non-domination, and never contrasted arbitrariness with the tracking of interests.[18] Still more important, few showed any inclination to describe themselves as republicans in their political allegiances. My suggestion here is that, if we wish to improve our understanding of liberty as independence, it will be worth paying more attention to the vocabulary and political circumstances in which the ideal was originally discussed.

The historical sources from which I draw my narrative also differ from those usually cited in recent discussions of liberty as independence. There has been a tendency to focus on a relatively small number of prominent authors and texts. But since my aspiration is to trace the formation of an ideology I have tried to cast my net more widely. I have drawn on novels,

---

[14] The point is especially well made in Pettit 2007. See also Pettit 2008 and Skinner 2008a. Cf. also Benn and Weinstein 1971. My argument thus needs to be distinguished from the claim that liberty consists in independence from interference, as argued in List and Valentini 2016. According to the theory with which I am concerned, liberty consists not in independence from interference but in independence from any arbitrary power or capacity to restrain or interfere.

[15] See Pettit 1997; Pettit 2001; Pettit 2012; Pettit 2014. For another series of discussions to which I am much indebted see Lovett 2010; Lovett 2018; and Lovett 2022.

[16] See Pettit 1997, pp. 51–73, and for a restatement Pettit 2014, pp. 28–54. On non-domination see also Lovett 2018.

[17] See Pettit 1997, pp. 36–7, 55–6; and cf. Arnold and Harris 2017.

[18] However, as Lovett 2010, pp. 236–7 rightly points out, some Roman writers, especially Cicero and Sallust, speak of *dominatio* by contrast with *libertas*.

sermons, newspapers, debates in Parliament and above all an extensive pamphlet literature. Most of the writers I discuss are relatively obscure, and many of them published anonymously. There were moments, however, when some celebrated authors joined the debate. Among the novelists, these included Smollett, Richardson and above all Fielding. Here, I argue, there is something to be said about the much-discussed phenomenon of 'the rise of the novel' in the middle decades of the eighteenth century. Why did these writers move away from using the novel to tell tales of romance and towards the project of chronicling the mores of contemporary civil society? Among literary scholars who have seen a political motivation for this development there has been a tendency, especially in the case of Fielding, to concentrate exclusively on his pro-Whig and anti-Jacobite political commitments.[19] But his aspiration to find a new use for the novel can in part be explained, I suggest, by his desire – fully shared by Smollett – to reflect less as a historian and more as a satirist on the contemporary social and political scene.[20] One of Smollett's as well as Fielding's concerns was to scrutinise how far the promise made in the constitutional settlement of 1688–9 to institute a free state and a peaceful civil society was being fulfilled, and how far this promise of equal freedom from dependence was being ignored and betrayed.[21]

A number of major political philosophers also contributed to the early modern debate about liberty, including Hobbes, Locke, Hume, Bentham and Wollstonecraft. It seems worth adding an introductory word about each of these canonical names, if only because my attempt to contextualise them sometimes has the effect of showing them in an unfamiliar light. Hobbes in his *Leviathan* of 1651 has rightly been seen as a pioneer in arguing that liberty should be defined as an absence of impediments or restraint. But it has tended to be assumed that this made him virtually the sole protagonist of a view that only came to be broadly accepted at the end of the following century.[22] As I show in Chapter 7, however, it was not long before Hobbes's distinctive analysis of liberty began to be widely discussed and embraced. By the beginning of the eighteenth century, due largely to the influence of Pufendorf and his disciples, Hobbes's political theory was being taught in a number of law schools in Switzerland and

---

[19] See, for example, Beasley 1982, pp. 203–8; Cleary 1984, pp. 207–72. In Watt's classic study of the rise of the novel (Watt 1957) the question is not discussed. On Fielding as a political journalist see McCrea 1981.

[20] On the satire of Fielding and Smollett see Paulson 1967, pp. 52–99, 165–79. See also Tavor 1987, who concentrates on Fielding's satirical concern with faulty reasoning.

[21] See Monod 2005, esp. pp. 277–81, 286–90.

[22] See, for example, Pettit 1997, pp. 43, 45; Elazar 2015, p. 418.

Germany by such jurists as Barbeyrac, Burlamaqui and Heineccius, and the works of all these writers soon became available in English. Pufendorf's *De iure naturae et gentium* appeared in 1703 as *On the law of nature and nations*, and was reprinted with Barbeyrac's commentary in 1729. During the 1740s Heineccius and Burlamaqui were also translated, and by the middle decades of the century there was a growing interest in their work among English legal theorists. These developments in turn raise a question about the 'great breakthrough' and the 'innovative and subversive definitions' that Jeremy Bentham is said to have produced in the 1770s when he insisted that liberty amounts to nothing more than an absence of restraint or constraint.[23] I argue that there was no such sudden breakthrough, and that the process by which this understanding of liberty came to be embedded in anglophone political theory was more gradual and more complex than has generally been recognised.

As in the case of Hobbes's *Leviathan*, the influence of John Locke's *Two treatises of government* in the eighteenth century has long been a subject of scholarly debate. Here the consensus has come to be that, although Locke's philosophical works were widely read, this is much less clear in the case of his *Two treatises*.[24] One prominent strand in the historiography of the American Revolution centres on the claim that a far greater influence on the colonists was exercised by the 'commonwealth' tradition of neo-Machiavellian republican thought.[25] Here it is arguable that two caveats need to be entered. We must take care not to mark too sharp a distinction, as Pocock has arguably done, between the figure of Locke as 'no kind of classical or Machiavellian republican' and the 'unmistakably Machiavellian' allegiances of the 'commonwealth' writers from the first half of the eighteenth century.[26] As we shall see in Chapters 2 and 3, Locke's views on liberty, subjection and arbitrary power were wholly in line with 'commonwealth' principles.[27] We also need to recognise that

---

[23] See Long 1977, p. 55; Pettit 1997, pp. 43–4; Elazar 2015, p. 418.

[24] For the extent to which Locke in eighteenth-century America was seen as the author of *An essay concerning human understanding* rather than *Two treatises of government* see Arcenas 2022, pp. 1–3, 19–24, 49–52. On the marginal role of the *Two treatises* at the time of the 1688 revolution and in the ensuing generation see Kenyon 1977, pp. 1, 17; Dunn 1980, pp. 62–7; Tully 1993b, pp. 253–66. See also Goldie 2006, pp. 47–50, although he rightly warns against overstatement. But see Ward 2004, pp. 1–18 on those who have supported a 'comeback' of Locke's *Two treatises*.

[25] See Bailyn 1967, pp. 22–54; Pocock 1975, pp. 423–552; Rahe 1994.

[26] Pocock 1975, pp. 424, 426–8, 467–77.

[27] Clark 2023 seeks to reinstate 'Lockean liberalism' and 'classical republicanism' as rival schools of thought, while treating both as unsatisfactory when it comes to explaining the American Revolution. A more satisfactory way forward might be to acknowledge that, in their accounts of tyranny and the liberty of subjects, these were not in fact rival schools of thought. The view of liberty and tyranny espoused by the anti-imperialists in the American colonies had been endorsed no less strongly by the 'liberal' John Locke than

there was one juncture at which Locke's *Second treatise* was extensively and admiringly invoked in English political debate. At the time of the Jacobite rebellion in 1745–6 a large number of pamphlets and sermons were published on the need to avoid arbitrary government, and during these years Locke's views on political liberty were quoted frequently and with deep respect. It is perhaps not surprising, however, that this episode has been overlooked, because the writers who quoted Locke with so much enthusiasm preferred in almost every instance not to acknowledge him.

Hume's place in the political debates of the same period has also been much discussed, and here too there may be room for some reassessment. Hume was always emphatic about what he liked to describe as his moderation and impartiality in handling political subjects.[28] Some commentators have agreed that he is 'remarkably detached', and have sought to mark a distinction between his scientific approach to the political issues of his time and the 'vulgar Whiggism' from which he distanced himself.[29] But this is arguably to accept him too much at his own estimation. If we survey the range of topics on which the pro-government Whigs of the 1730s and 1740s were most anxious to pronounce, we find that Hume almost never failed to support the pro-government cause.[30]

It needs no underlining that Mary Wollstonecraft is the only woman among the canonical figures I have singled out. An overwhelming majority of the texts I discuss were written by men, and it cannot be denied that, throughout the historical period on which I concentrate, the enjoyment of liberty in the sense of not being subject to arbitrary power was largely the preserve of a small male elite. These considerations have led some commentators to conclude that the ideal of liberty as independence is 'inherently conservative and elitist'.[31] This way of thinking about freedom is said to have 'a dark side', to be 'overtly oppressive', and to exhibit 'a pervading hostility to democratic tendencies'.[32] As I try to illustrate, however, Wollstonecraft is only the most celebrated of a number of eighteenth-century feminist writers who remind us that there is nothing inherently conservative or elitist about the ideal itself. Wollstonecraft fervently believed in liberty as independence, but always as the best means to win equality for women and create a more democratic society for all.[33]

---

by the classical republican writers singled out by Robbins and subsequently by Bailyn and Pocock.

[28] Hume 1741, p. iv.   [29] Forbes 1975, pp. 125–92; Skjönsberg 2021, pp. 138–9.

[30] Here I agree with Dickinson 1977, pp. 132–3 and Pocock 1985, p. 138.

[31] Maddox 2002, p. 430.

[32] Goodin 2003, pp. 56–7, 61–2; Brennan and Lomasky 2006, p. 222; Maddox 2002, p. 425.

[33] On Wollstonecraft's equation of liberty with independence see Halldenius 2015, pp. 19–32.

I have been stressing that this ideal of liberty has recently undergone a revival in anglophone political philosophy. But I do not mean to imply that this development followed a long period in which it was wholly overlooked. There is no doubt that the ideal was successfully banished to the margins of political debate at the end of the eighteenth century. But it continued to flourish among the pioneers of English socialism, and it subsequently played an important role in Marxist thought, as Marx's frequent references to wage-slavery remind us.[34] As I argue in my opening and closing chapters, the recent revival of interest is merely the latest attempt to reaffirm an ideal that has always had a presence in Western political thought.

The origins of this presence can largely be traced, I argue, to a specific range of classical sources, and above all to the jurists, historians and moral philosophers of ancient Rome. I accordingly begin by examining the provenance of the ideal of liberty as independence in this body of texts. But here I need to underline that my examination of these sources is deliberately circumscribed. I am exclusively concerned with the development of the so-called republican concept of liberty, not with the broader history of republicanism in Europe. Any engagement with this further and vastly larger question would require many additional lines of enquiry to be pursued, most obviously in ancient Greek and Hebrew traditions of thinking about self-government.[35] Furthermore, my engagement with the Roman republican sources is limited in itself. My aim is to highlight the concepts and arguments taken from these sources by the early modern writers on whom I chiefly concentrate. I make no attempt to provide a socio-political analysis of liberty in ancient Rome. Any such account would need to include (as many scholars have rightly pointed out) a discussion of how the republic, although notionally a *civitas libera* or free state, continued to be dominated by a senatorial oligarchy, and how the plebeians were always subjected to a paternalistic form of rule.[36]

I want to round off these opening remarks by underlining one element in the ideal of liberty as independence that seems to me of particular importance in relation to contemporary debates. Those who defended the ideal in the historical period I discuss took it for granted that to speak of liberty is at the same time to speak of slavery. Here they made a number of connections that have largely been lost to sight in contemporary

[34] See Gourevitch 2015; Leipold 2020; Leipold 2022.
[35] On the Greek contribution see Nelson 2004; De Dijn 2020, pp. 15–68. On Hebrew sources see Boralevi 2002; Nelson 2011. On ancient and modern liberty see Skinner 2012.
[36] See Maddox 2002; Kapust 2004; Ando 2010. For a full analysis of Roman republican constitutionalism see Straumann 2016.

discussions of liberty as absence of interference or restraint. It is true that, as we shall see in Chapter 8, some proponents of liberty as independence were rightly criticised for arguing that anyone subject to the power of others must be accounted a slave, thereby drastically understating the special horror of chattel slavery. But the insistence of these writers on equating subjection with servitude had the salutary effect of drawing attention to the fact that liberty can be undermined by many different forms of dependence.[37] As we confront the increasing disgrace of modern slavery, there is much to be learned from the distinctions to be found in these earlier debates.

I have already published two brief books that may be regarded as preliminary studies for this present work. One examined the evolution of Hobbes's thinking about the concept of liberty.[38] The other focused on the conception of liberty as independence as it was expounded at the time of the English civil wars in the mid-seventeenth century.[39] With this new work I have moved forward to the era of the Enlightenment. I begin with the revolution of 1688 in England, when the ideal of liberty as independence was promised to the people as the cornerstone of a new constitution. I go on to examine the fortunes of this view of liberty as it was propagated under the Whig oligarchy and subsequently challenged and set aside. I draw mainly on anglophone sources, but I like to think that there is nevertheless a sense in which the outcome is a study of a broader kind. Some concepts are inherently global, and liberty is undoubtedly one of them. The rejection of the ideal of liberty as independence was fundamental to the self-styled 'liberal' political theory that emerged at the end of the eighteenth century, and this development gave rise to some significant and enduring consequences that, for better or worse, have by now reached across the world. The question I finally address in my Conclusion is whether these consequences have in fact been for better or for worse.

---

[37] On the need for such a broad view see Watkins 2016.
[38] See Skinner 2008b. For a discussion and critique see Collins 2009.
[39] Skinner 1998. For an earlier sketch see Skinner 1990.

*Part I*

# Liberty and the Revolution of 1688

# 1    The Ideal of Liberty as Independence

## The Affirmation of the Ideal

On 30 September 1688 Prince William of Orange ordered the publication of a *Declaration* in which he announced his intention of mounting an invasion of England.[1] The text had been written for him by a group of English peers, and was primarily the work of the Earl of Danby.[2] They had already contacted William at the end of June to invite him, as they delicately put it, to contribute to their deliverance from the government of King James II.[3] The aim of the *Declaration* was to provide a justification for the invasion and the revolution that swiftly followed. The title page offered the assurance that William would 'appear in arms in the kingdom' with the sole aim of protecting the Protestant religion and 'restoring the laws and liberties of England, Scotland and Ireland'.[4] These laws and liberties are said to have been overturned by James II and a body of evil councillors, who are jointly blamed for depriving the people of their religion and civil rights. The charge laid specifically against the king is that, due to the violation of the promises made at his coronation, the inhabitants of the three nations can no longer be said to be living as free subjects with 'the free enjoyment of their laws and liberties'.[5]

To establish this basic claim, the *Declaration* goes on to provide an account of what it means to speak of liberty being undermined and lost. James II stands accused of insisting 'that he is clothed with a despotic and arbitrary power' to act according to his will, so that his subjects 'depend wholly on his good will and pleasure, and are entirely subject to him'.[6] But if you are rendered subject to, and hence dependent upon, the arbitrary will of someone else, you will have lost any 'free enjoyment' of your rights and liberties, which are now capable of being enjoyed only subject to the

---

[1] See *The Declaration* 1688, p. 8 on its publication 'by his Highness's special order'.
[2] Harris 2006, pp. 271, 279. For the background of radical Whiggery in the 1680s see Zook 1999, pp. 1–36.
[3] Williams 1960, p. 8.    [4] *The Declaration* 1688, p. 1.    [5] *The Declaration* 1688, p. 3.
[6] *The Declaration* 1688, p. 3.

will and pleasure of someone else.[7] You will, in a word, have lost your liberty. This charge is then repeatedly underlined. The king's evil councillors 'have subjected the honours and estates of the subjects, and the established religion, to a despotic power and to arbitrary government'. They have procured the surrender of town charters, so that local rights and privileges are now 'disposed of at the pleasure of those evil councillors'. They have undermined the administration of impartial justice, which has likewise been subjected 'to an arbitrary and despotic power'. They have 'disposed of all military employments' not merely in contempt of the law but with the aim of using the army 'to maintain and execute their wicked designs'. It has become apparent, in short, that the king and his evil councillors are planning 'to render themselves the absolute masters' of the people, who will soon be obliged 'to submit in all things to their own will and pleasure'.[8]

To say, however, that an entire people is being reduced to dependence on such an uncontrolled form of power is equivalent to saying that they are being transformed from free subjects into slaves. This is the conclusion towards which the argument of the *Declaration* is directed. The rulers of the state are turning themselves into masters under whom the people will be condemned to subsist in a condition of 'arbitrary government and slavery'.[9] If the king and his evil councillors now execute their wicked designs with the help of the army, the final outcome will be 'to enslave the nation'.[10] The English, the Scots and the Irish will all have lost their standing as free peoples and fallen into a condition of servitude.

To be delivered from this state of enslavement, the people will need to be fully secured in the possession of their rights and liberties, rather than holding them without any security under the mere will and allowance of an arbitrary and despotic prince. William's declared aim is accordingly 'to procure a settlement of the religion and of the liberties and properties of the subjects upon so sure a foundation that there may be no danger of the nation's relapsing into the like miseries at any time hereafter'.[11] The *Declaration* includes an account of the specific range of rights that must indispensably be secured if this goal is to be realised. There must above all be equal protection for 'the lives, liberties, honours and estates of the subjects'.[12] These and other rights and privileges have been established by ancient and immemorial custom, and have thereby come to form part of the fabric of the constitution, as well as being essential to public peace

[7] *The Declaration* 1688, p. 3.    [8] *The Declaration* 1688, pp. 4–5.
[9] *The Declaration* 1688, p. 8.    [10] *The Declaration* 1688, p. 5.
[11] *The Declaration* 1688, p. 8.    [12] *The Declaration* 1688, pp. 3, 5, 6.

and happiness. They must now be confirmed in such a way as to restore the security and happiness of the subject.[13]

As the authors of the *Declaration* emphasise, there are two immediate constitutional implications of these claims. One is that the rule of law must never be transgressed or annulled. The mere possibility of exercising discretionary power outside the law has the effect of taking away our liberty. The law provides the only security that the people can have against the use of such 'arbitrary proceedings' to undermine their rights.[14] The aim must therefore be that of securing to everyone 'the free enjoyment of all their laws, rights and liberties under a just and legal government'.[15] A closing 'Additional Declaration' reiterates that there is now an urgent need for such a legal framework to be given 'a secure re-establishment'.[16]

The other implication is that the people must be in a position to give their consent to whatever laws are enacted. Here the reason given is that, unless they are able to contribute the expression of their wills to the making of the laws, they will remain in a slavish condition of dependence upon the will of others. The only solution, as the *Declaration* ends by underlining, is for government to be conducted by a free Parliament in which everyone, by representation, may be said to have a voice. The effect will be to ensure that the people's representatives are at once 'freely elected' and are able 'to give their opinions freely upon all matters that are brought before them',[17] with the result that 'no laws can be made but by the joint concurrence of King and Parliament'.[18] This is why, as William ends by promising, 'we will refer all to a free assembly of the nation in a lawful Parliament'.[19]

The plans and aspirations announced in the *Declaration* were realised with remarkable speed.[20] William landed his forces in Devon on 5 November 1688 and arrived in London on 18 December. James II finally took flight five days later, and by the end of the month William was in charge of the government. A day of thanksgiving was appointed to celebrate England's deliverance 'from popery and arbitrary power', and the clergy dutifully responded by delivering and publishing a multitude of sermons under that title.[21] By 12 February 1689 the Convention Parliament had agreed the terms of a Declaration of Rights, which was presented to William and Mary on the following day together with an offer of the crown. The original intention had been to proclaim Mary

---

[13] *The Declaration* 1688, p. 3.   [14] *The Declaration* 1688, pp. 3, 6.
[15] *The Declaration*, 1688, p. 7.   [16] *The Declaration* 1688, p. 8.
[17] *The Declaration* 1688, p. 6.   [18] *The Declaration* 1688, p. 3.
[19] *The Declaration* 1688, p. 8.   [20] See Harris 2006, pp. 274, 305–7, 311–13.
[21] See, for example, Halley 1689; Patrick 1689; Tillotson 1689; Wilson 1689.

(daughter of James II) as queen, thereby preserving hereditary succession. But William refused to be a mere consort, while Mary was reluctant to be made queen alone, so the crown was offered jointly to both of them. They jointly accepted, and were immediately proclaimed king and queen of England.[22]

The Declaration of Rights closely follows the language as well as the aspirations of William's original *Declaration*, and its constitutional proposals were finally given statutory force in the Bill of Rights in December 1689.[23] The three basic complaints in William's *Declaration* were again given special prominence. The first was that the crown had been laying claim to an arbitrary and despotic form of power. The Bill of Rights now declared that 'the pretended power' of suspending laws or dispensing with them was illegal without the consent of Parliament.[24] This commitment was later supplemented in the Act of Settlement of 1701. One prerogative had always been that of appointing and dismissing judges *durante beneplacito regis*, at the king's pleasure, but the Act established that judges should instead hold their commissions *quamdiu si se bene gesserint*, so long as they properly upheld the law of the land.[25] A second anxiety had been that the crown might make use of the army to enforce its arbitrary and despotic policies. Here the Bill of Rights broke new constitutional ground[26] by responding that 'the raising or keeping a standing army within the kingdom in time of peace, unless it be with consent of Parliament, is illegal'.[27] Finally, William's original *Declaration* had underlined the need for a free Parliament and an independent judiciary, and here the last six of the thirteen specific requirements of the Bill of Rights were designed to secure these results.[28]

The language used in celebration of these changes speaks of deliverance from subjection and even of liberation.[29] The Proclamation of William and Mary as sovereigns on 13 February 1689 announced that God had vouchsafed to the people 'a miraculous deliverance',[30] a contention closely echoed in the Declaration of Rights, which affirms that God has been pleased to make William of Orange 'the glorious instrument of delivering this kingdom from popery and arbitrary power'.[31] The Bill of Rights rounded off by making two claims about the rights that had now been secured. The first reiterated the contention in William's original *Declaration* that they take the form of ancient liberties that have been

---

[22] Harris 2006, pp. 328, 334.    [23] Harris 2006, p. 349.    [24] Williams 1960, p. 28.
[25] Williams 1960, p. 59.    [26] As noted in Harris 2006, pp. 341–3.
[27] Williams 1960, p. 28.    [28] Williams 1960, pp. 28–9.
[29] On liberation see, for example, Stewart 1689, p. 4.
[30] *A Proclamation* 1689, London (single sheet).    [31] Williams 1960, p. 27.

tested by time and now need to be recognised as 'undoubted rights'.[32]
The Bill accordingly enacted that 'the rights and liberties asserted and
claimed in the said declaration are the true, ancient and indubitable rights
and liberties of the people'.[33] The second claim was that, because no one
can be said to enjoy the standing of a free person if their rights are held at
the discretion of anyone else, they must now be protected in such a way
that they cannot 'again be in danger of being subverted'.[34] The solution
adopted in the Bill was to lay it down that they cannot be changed or
revoked even by the statutory power of the king in Parliament. They must
'remain and be the law of this realm for ever' and be taken to be binding
on everyone 'in all times to come'.[35]

## The Republican Provenance of the Ideal

There was nothing unusual about the definition of civil liberty embodied
in William's *Declaration* and endorsed in the Bill of Rights. By the time of
the 1688 revolution, the view that liberty consists in absence of dependence on the arbitrary will of others, and hence consists in having an
independent will, had come to be almost universally accepted. One
major source from which this way of thinking had arisen was a body of
classical Roman works of history and moral philosophy, especially from
the close of the republican period.[36] Following the proliferation of translations of the Latin classics in the Renaissance, the relevant writings of
Cicero, Sallust, Livy and Tacitus had all become available in English by
the beginning of the seventeenth century, and were regularly reprinted
thereafter. Between them these writers provided an unprecedentedly
sophisticated analysis not merely of how to think about the meaning of
liberty, but also about the conditions under which it can be maintained
and lost.[37]

Among the Roman moralists it is Cicero who particularly draws attention to the nature of the liberty possessed by free citizens.[38] He initially
does so in his *Paradoxa stoicorum*, and later in his *De officiis*, the two
earliest of his works to be translated into English. Robert Whitinton's

---

[32] Williams 1960, pp. 28, 29.   [33] Williams 1960, p. 30.   [34] Williams 1960, p. 28.
[35] Williams 1960, pp. 30, 33.   [36] See Fontana 2009.
[37] On the ideal of *libertas* see Wirszubski 1950. On Sallust as an ambiguous republican see
Kapust 2011, pp. 32–52. On civil liberty in Sallust, Cicero and Livy see Arena 2012,
pp. 45–72. Jensen 2012 rightly reminds us that these writers were studied for many
reasons other than their views on liberty.
[38] I concentrate on the *Paradoxa*. As Kennedy 2014 argues, Cicero speaks differently in the
*De re publica* and *De legibus*. For Cicero on the *civitas libera* and non-domination
see Atkins 2018. For Cicero's view of political authority in *De legibus* and *De officiis* see
Straumann 2016, pp. 168–90.

version of the *Paradoxa* appeared as early as 1534, and was reprinted in 1540.[39] Whitinton also published the pioneering English translation of the *De officiis*, although this version was soon superseded by Nicolas Grimalde's more accurate edition, which first appeared in 1556 and went through six further printings before the end of the century.[40]

Cicero's discussion in the *Paradoxa* begins by drawing a contrast between a free person – specifically, for Cicero, a free man[41] – and the condition of a slave who lives in submission to the will of a master. As Whitinton's translation expresses the predicament of the slave, his state of subjugation leaves him 'lacking his own free will'.[42] The free man, by contrast, is able to think and act independently: he 'nothing saith, nothing doeth' except 'with his good will'.[43] He is consequently someone 'whose intentions all and singular, and all things that he goeth about, cometh forth from himself of free will and returneth the same way'.[44] This view is echoed in Book I of the *De officiis*, in which Cicero speaks (in Grimalde's translation) of those who possess 'a well-framed mind by nature'.[45] Such persons cannot fail to have 'a certain desire of sovereignty'[46] and will never be willing to submit themselves to the will of anyone else.[47]

Later in the *De officiis* Cicero notes the constitutional implications of his affirmation that, if I am obliged to live in dependence on the will of anyone else, I am thereby condemned to live as a slave. He concludes that this makes it impossible to live in freedom under any form of government in which the will of the ruler is capable of taking precedence over the law.[48] If this can happen, the citizens must already be living in subjection to the power of someone else, and hence in servitude. As soon as 'the laws be sunk by some man's might', one consequence is that liberty is lost.[49] The rule of a king will always bring with it 'the overthrow of law and liberty'.[50] A free man will only ever defer to the requirements of law, and hence to someone who 'justly and lawfully governeth' in the name of the common weal.[51]

---

[39] Cicero 1534.

[40] Cicero 1556. There were reprintings in every decade for the rest of the century. On Cicero in Tudor England see Jones 1998.

[41] When referring to free persons Cicero and Whitinton use masculine pronouns. See, for example, Cicero 1942, V. 36, p. 286; and cf. Cicero 1534, Sig. C, 3r.

[42] Cicero 1534, Sig. C, 4v.    [43] Cicero 1534, Sig. C, 3r.    [44] Cicero 1534, Sig. C, 3r.

[45] Cicero 1556, fo. 6r. Cf. Cicero 1913, I. 4. 13–16, pp. 14–16.    [46] Cicero 1556, fo. 6r.

[47] Cicero 1556, fo. 6r. The phrase Cicero uses is *nemini parere*, 'to submit to no one'. See Cicero 1913, I. 4. 13, p. 14.

[48] As Arena 2012 emphasises, Cicero's *De re publica* also has much to say on these issues. But this text was unknown – except in quoted fragments – until a palimpsest was uncovered in the nineteenth century.

[49] Cicero 1556, fo. 71v.    [50] Cicero 1556, fo. 141v.    [51] Cicero 1556, fo. 6r.

Cicero's *Paradoxa* also made an influential contribution to a further line of argument about the idea of liberty. Following the Stoics, Cicero marks a categorical distinction between liberty and licence, a distinction that was later to play a central role in Renaissance and early modern ways of thinking about different forms and sources of servitude.[52] The analysis in *Paradoxa* begins by asking (as Whitinton's translation puts it) 'For what is liberty?'[53] It appears that the freedom of action enjoyed by a free man must consist in having 'power and free choice to do what thou will'.[54] But here Cicero complicates this seemingly straightforward claim by introducing the Stoic paradox that 'only the wise man is free'.[55] The wise live as they wish, but they alone are able at the same time to follow 'right ways', to live 'in honesty' and to obey the law 'not for dread', but because they judge it 'to be most wholesome'.[56] The will of such people is grounded on having mastered their passions, as opposed to being mere slaves to their impulses. 'A free man', as Cicero summarises, is someone who knows how to 'govern his affections and desires',[57] and 'no man is free' except those of whom this can be said.[58] Everyone else is little better than 'a bondman of all folly',[59] and 'what bondage is there, if this may be esteemed a liberty?'[60] Such people are not merely in the same position as those who are obliged to obey a master. They are obliged to obey 'filthy and lewd masters' in the form of 'shame, infamy and villainous life', so that none of them can ever count 'in any wise as a free man'.[61]

Of still greater significance for the transmission of classical views about civil liberty were the histories of Sallust, Livy and Tacitus, all of whose major works became available in English at around the turn of the sixteenth century.[62] Henry Savile's translation of Tacitus's *Histories* was first published in 1591, followed by Richard Grenewey's version of the *Annals* in 1598.[63] Two years later Philemon Holland issued his enormous folio containing the whole of the extant books of Livy's *History*,[64] and in 1608 Thomas Heywood published his translations of Sallust's *Catiline* and *Jugurtha*.[65]

---

[52] See James 1997, pp. 1–25.     [53] Cicero 1534, Sig. C, 2v.     [54] Cicero 1534, Sig. C, 2v.
[55] Cicero 1942, V, p. 284: *Solum sapientem esse liberum*.     [56] Cicero 1534, Sig. C, 2v.
[57] Cicero 1534, Sig. C, 2r.     [58] Cicero 1534, Sig. C, 3v.     [59] Cicero 1534, Sig. C, 4v.
[60] Cicero 1534, Sig. C, 6v.     [61] Cicero 1534, Sig. C, 2r.
[62] On Livy, Sallust and Tacitus as inspirations for later republicans see Sellers 1994, pp. 69–89.
[63] See Tacitus 1591; 1598; and cf. Peltonen 1995, pp. 124–35 on these translations and their influence.
[64] See Livy 1600; on Holland's translation see Matthiessen 1931, pp. 182–216; Peltonen 1995, pp. 135–6.
[65] Sallust 1608. But Sallust's *Bellum Iugurthinum* had already been translated by Alexander Barclay in *c.* 1520.

Sallust begins his *Catiline* by taking up a theme that, a generation later, Livy was to handle at much greater length in the opening two books of his *History*. Both focus on the climacteric moment when Tarquinius Superbus, the last king of Rome, was removed from power and replaced by annually elected consuls. Both characterise this transition as a moment of liberation for the people of Rome. It is impossible, they agree, to survive as a free person under any monarchical form of rule. As Sallust explains, to live under a monarchy is to experience *dominatio*, itself the outcome of a corrupt lust for mastery.[66] The system of hereditary monarchy in Rome was at first ordained 'for protection of liberty and augmentation of territory'.[67] But it did not take long before it 'degenerated into pride and *dominatio*' and an aspiration to uphold 'licentious sovereignty'.[68]

Livy speaks even more feelingly about the evil character of monarchical rule. He thinks of kingship as an inherently capricious form of power under which the will of the ruler not only stands above the law but serves as law in itself. There can be no liberty under any such regime, and Livy more than once contrasts life under monarchy with 'the sweetness of liberty and freedom'.[69] We are told that, soon after the liberation of the people from Tarquin's tyranny, Brutus felt obliged to remind them of the oath they had taken to renounce monarchy. They had sworn 'that they should suffer none to be king, nor naught else in Rome from whence might arise any danger to their liberty'.[70] Livy adds that, when the Tarquins petitioned to return to the city, they were confronted by ambassadors sent to explain 'that the people of Rome were not under the regiment of a king, but were a free state'. They were 'fully settled in this purpose', and would 'set open their gates to enemies sooner than to kings'.[71]

The transition to living under annually elected magistrates is consequently treated as a moment of release from capricious tyranny and as the founding of a free state. The rule of law rather than the will of the king now formed the basis of government, and the requirements of the law were made known to everyone and equally imposed on all. Sallust adds that this achievement soon began to generate a distinctive attitude on the part of the people, imbuing them with what later came to be described as the spirit of liberty. Under the rule of their absolute kings there had been a jealous suspicion of talent and virtue, but now 'began every man to

---

[66] Sallust 1931, II. 2, p. 4.    [67] Sallust 1608, p. 17 (*recte* p. 7).
[68] See Sallust 1608, p. 17 (*recte* p. 7) and cf. Sallust 1931, VI. 7, p. 12. In stressing Sallust's emphasis on *libertas* and *dominatio* I differ from Walker 2006, who argues that Sallust is chiefly concerned with loss of liberty through acts of interference.
[69] Livy 1600, p. 13; cf. also p. 32.    [70] Livy 1600, p. 45.    [71] Livy 1600, p. 54.

estimate his own worth and to hammer his head on high designs'.[72] As a result, 'the city, having obtained this form of liberty in government, increased and prospered' with the unleashing of the people's energies and their 'desire of glory' after their escape from the slavish condition of living under kings.[73] Empowered by their freedom, 'it is incredible to report in how short a time' they thereafter 'advanced and augmented themselves and their state' to the heights of glory and greatness.[74]

Livy celebrates the same moment of liberation at the opening of Book II of his *History* in a passage that has sometimes been invoked as the founding moment in the creation of a distinctively republican way of thinking about freedom and free states:

> Now will I describe from henceforth the acts both in war and peace of the people of Rome, a free state now from this time forward: their yearly magistrates and governors: the authority and rule of laws more powerful and mighty than that of men. Which freedom of theirs, the last king's pride made more acceptable and welcome.[75]

Livy adds an ironic commentary on how this transition was experienced by those who had benefited from the previous regime. They now 'made moan and complained one to another that the liberty of others turned to their servitude'. Under the king, they said, it had been possible to 'obtain somewhat, as need required, were the cause right or were it wrong'. But the rule of law is 'deaf and inexorable'. The laws are 'more wholesome and commodious to the poor than to the rich and mighty', because they allow 'no release nor pardon if one chance to trespass and transgress'.[76]

More explicitly than Sallust, Livy offers a definition of the concept of liberty underlying his account. For Livy, as for Cicero, what it means to be free is to be guided by your independent will and not in any way subject to the will of others. When in Book I he describes the surrender of the Collatines to Rome, he notes that they were required to give an assurance that they were freely giving themselves up. The question asked by the Romans was 'Are the people of Collatia in their own power and at liberty to do what they will?'[77] Much later in the *History*, Livy offers the same definition when speaking about the possibility that the state of Greece, by means of the Aetolian association, might be restored 'to her lively and lightsome lustre'. This lustre is said to have consisted in 'true liberty', which Livy defines as the condition in which an individual or

[72] Sallust 1608, p. 17 (*recte* 7).   [73] Sallust 1608, pp. 17(*recte* 7) and 9.
[74] Sallust 1608, pp. 17 (*recte* 7) and 8.
[75] Livy 1600, p. 44. Lovett 2022, p. 11 invokes the passage.   [76] Livy 1600, p. 45.
[77] Livy 1600, p. 28.

a community 'dependeth not upon the will and pleasure of others', but is able to live in a state of independence.[78]

Livy, and later Tacitus, both summarise what liberty requires by speaking of the need to outlaw what they describe as arbitrary power.[79] By this they mean a power to act entirely according to one's own *arbitrium* or will, and thus entirely at discretion, without being subject to any form of control.[80] Livy provides several vivid illustrations at an early stage in his *History*. He first does so when speaking about the constitutional reforms introduced after the removal of the decemvirs. The new consuls ordered 'that all the acts of the Senate should be brought into the church of Ceres and presented unto the Aediles of the Commons, which aforetime were suppressed and smothered, yea and corrupted or perverted at the will and pleasure (*arbitrium*)[81] of the Consuls'.[82] We are told that it was only with the cancelling of this ability to act on a mere whim that 'both the Tribunes' power, and also the commons' freedom, were once well and surely grounded'.[83]

Tacitus speaks of arbitrary power in similar terms. He first does so at several points in the *Histories*, notably in the course of recounting the fall of Vitellius. There was a plan to ambush him and his troops, but without delay he decided 'to yield himself and his cohorts to the discretion (*arbitrium*)[84] of the conqueror', placing themselves entirely at his mercy.[85] Later Tacitus describes in the *Annals* how Tiberius cancelled the legal right of the people to vote in the election of magistrates. Although this was 'the first time that the election of magistrates was taken from the people', it was already evident that that by then 'all matters were swayed as best liked the prince (*arbitrio principis*)'.[86] Tacitus mournfully adds that 'neither did the people but with a vain rumour complain that their right was taken from them' by this move towards rule by mere *arbitrium* or sovereign will.[87]

Tacitus also shows a particular concern for the feelings of those who are obliged to live in dependence on arbitrary power. What they experience is not merely a lack of control over the conduct of their masters and rulers, but a sense of continual anxiety that stems from not knowing what may be

---

[78] Livy 1600, p. 907; cf. also p. 1025.
[79] As my examples show, I disagree with the line of argument in Clarke 2014.
[80] On arbitrary power as uncontrolled see Pettit 2012, pp. 56–60, 153–160; Lovett 2012; Lovett 2022, pp. 51–4.
[81] Livy 1922, III. 50. 13, p. 184.    [82] Livy 1600, p. 125.
[83] Livy 1600, p. 125. (Cf. Livy 1922, III. 55. 13, p. 184.) For a further example see Livy 1600, p. 145. (Cf. Livy 1922, IV. 8. 3, p. 284.)
[84] Tacitus 1931, IV. 2, p. 4.    [85] Tacitus 1591, IV. 2, p. 170.
[86] Tacitus 1598, I, 4, p. 8. On the *arbitrium principis* see Tacitus 1931, I. 15, p. 272.
[87] Tacitus 1598, I, 4, p. 8.

about to happen to them. Tacitus offers a memorable example in his *Histories* when describing the chaos that followed the death of Vitellius. The Gauls and Germans destroyed a number of Roman legions and the survivors were summarily ordered to leave camp and turn themselves loose. As a result they found themselves completely exposed to 'the mere will (*arbitrium*) of those whom they had made lords over life and death', and hence in a terrified state of uncertainty.[88]

This concern about the wilful character of monarchical rule is closely connected with a further claim about freedom and slavery. Living in servitude, as Tacitus repeatedly illustrates, has the almost inevitable effect of breeding servility. Anyone living in dependence on the arbitrary will of a master or ruler will find that they have no option but to take the greatest care to appease their superiors in the hope of avoiding harm. The outcome will almost certainly be a collapse into obsequious slavishness. Tacitus first develops this argument in the *Histories*, in which he concentrates on the servility of the common people. He accuses them of making it 'a received custom to flatter the prince whatsoever he be, framing acclamations at pleasure, and vainly endeavouring to show their good wills'.[89] He speaks with particular distaste about the reception of Otho in Rome, when the people received him with acclamations that were neither due to fear nor love, but merely to 'a delight in servility'.[90]

By the time he came to write the *Annals*, Tacitus was no less ready to accuse the entire political class of lapsing into slavishness.[91] Speaking once more about the reign of Tiberius, he observes that 'those times were so corrupted with filthy flattery' that former consuls as well as leaders of the Senate 'rose up and strove who should propound things most base and abject'.[92] Tiberius, we are told, used to reply (in Greek, and to himself) 'O men ready to servitude!'[93] Although he 'could of all things least suffer public liberty', he nevertheless abhorred 'such base and servile submission', which by that time was 'falling by little and little from unseemly flatteries to lewder practices'.[94] Tacitus wearily accepts, however, that it is hard to imagine how anything better could have been expected from a society in which the exercise of civic virtue had by that time become 'the ready broad way to most assured destruction'.[95]

As this analysis suggests, the classical republican ideal of the *liber homo* can be expressed in affirmative as well as negative terms. To be a free person is not to be dependent on the arbitrary will of anyone else, but it is

[88] Tacitus 1931, IV. 62, p. 118. My translation. Cf. Tacitus 1591, IV. 24, p. 216.
[89] Tacitus 1591, I, 2, p. 19.    [90] Tacitus 1591, I. 21, pp. 51–2.
[91] Tacitus 1598, I. 1, p. 2.    [92] Tacitus 1598, III. 14, p. 84.
[93] Tacitus 1598, III. 14, p. 84.    [94] Tacitus 1598, III. 14, p. 84.
[95] Tacitus 1591, I. 2, p. 2.

also to possess a distinctive status and standing in society. If you live in dependence on the will of others, all your actions will have the character of permissions, of allowances from your ruler or master that can be withdrawn without warning at any time. But if you are a free person, and hence your own master, you will be able to act as you choose and go your own way. Furthermore, if you live in a condition of dependence, you can hardly fail – in the words of Grenewey's translation – to become low and base, abject and submissive, ready to crouch and fawn. But if you are your own master, you will be able to stand up for yourself instead of being low and base, to act in an upright and straightforward manner instead of crouching and fawning, and to speak your mind without fear or favour instead of being abject and submissive.

The question that remains for the Roman historians is what kind of constitution will enable us to follow such a free way of life. They concede that even living under the most suitable constitution is never a sufficient condition of being able to act as a *liber homo*, a free person. It is obviously necessary to have some confidence and determination,[96] and in every classical as well as early modern society it is taken for granted that it is also necessary to be an owner of property as well as being a man of a certain age and class. The historians believe, however, that the constitutional question is of pivotal significance, and they answer it by focusing on two political implications of their views about freedom and enslavement, both of which were destined to exercise a profound influence. One is that, if we are to live in freedom, the force of law must always be greater than that of men.[97] If the will of men is more potent, the people will still be living in dependence on uncontrolled power and hence in servitude. The other implication is that, as Livy particularly emphasises, the voice of the people must always be heard in the making of laws. If law is simply imposed by the will of their rulers, this too will leave the people in a state of servitude, even if their rulers happen to govern them with benevolence.

This latter requirement, Livy acknowledges, was not at first met when the Tarquins were removed from power. Brutus proved to be 'more forward to procure and recover the liberty' of the people 'than he was afterward a sure maintainer and protector of the same' under consular rule.[98] The problem was not resolved until a large number of plebeians revolted against the new tyranny of the consuls and seceded from Rome. It was then agreed that the people 'should have certain sacred and inviolable magistrates of their own among themselves, such as might have

---

[96] As emphasised in Pettit 2012, pp. 84–5.     [97] Livy 1600, p. 44.     [98] Livy 1600, p. 44.

power to assist the commons against the Consuls'.[99] A system was established with a separation of powers under which the consuls and tribunes served as heads of the executive, while the Senate – later joined by the Council of the People – constituted the legislative element in government. The people were thereby granted a form of representation that guaranteed them a role in making the laws. As Livy underlines, the need to meet this requirement is an immediate implication of his views about civil liberty. Without such representation, the people would still have remained dependent on the will of others and hence in servitude.

Later in the history of the republic a different and more populist solution was sometimes proposed. A number of public speeches from the first century BCE survive in which the sole right of the people to wield sovereign power is affirmed.[100] However, the system adopted under the early republic was the one that later enjoyed the most widespread influence. It came to be generally agreed that the greatest political achievement of ancient Rome had been the creation of a mixed and balanced constitution in which the best features of monarchy, aristocracy and democracy were all granted a place and successfully put to work. As Livy had summarised, the achievement took the form of creating a free people living in a free state.[101]

Although the Roman historians celebrate this achievement, they are scarcely less preoccupied with the fragility of Roman *libertas* and its eventual corruption and decline. Sallust traces the source of Rome's moral decay to the acquisition of an empire and the resulting opportunities for unscrupulous political leaders to undermine the republic in their own interests. As Rome grew great, and 'mighty kings were by war subdued', there arose 'the ambitious desire of superiority'. This brought 'pride and cruelty, irreligion, and unconscionable sales of everything vendible', while ambition 'made us false and brazen-faced'.[102] Eventually 'the contagion grew strong and violent' and a form of government that had originally been 'most just and excellent' became 'most cruel and intolerable'.[103]

Livy no less that Sallust sees himself as a historian of decline, and traces its source to an even earlier date, when the decemvirs were appointed under the leadership of Appius Claudius.[104] They were granted supreme power without appeal for a year, and it was not long before 'favour and friendship' began to prevail in their decisions 'as much as equity and right

---

[99] Livy 1600, p. 75.    [100] Arena 2012, pp. 124–68.
[101] Livy in the two crucial passages only speaks of living in liberty. See Livy 1919, II. 1. 1, p. 218 and II. 15. 3, p. 268. But in both passages Holland speaks of the 'free state'. See Livy 1600, pp. 44, 54.
[102] Sallust 1608, p. 9.    [103] Sallust 1608, p. 10.    [104] Livy 1600, p. 109.

should have done', so that the people were once more 'plunged into servitude and thralldom'.[105] Eventually an uproar prompted the decemvirs to lay down their powers, so that 'freedom and concord were restored to the city again'.[106] But the fragility of the republican constitution had been exposed in a way that eventually helped to bring about civil war and the end of the free state.

By contrast with Sallust and Livy, Tacitus is a chronicler not of ascendancy and decline, but of the shocking consequences of republican collapse. Writing a century after Sallust and Livy, his *Annals* follows the consolidation of the early principate after the death of Augustus, while his *Histories* takes up the narrative after the death of Nero. The whole period is seen as bringing a return of capricious and tyrannical rule, and hence a return of enslavement and servility. Tacitus begins by tracing this development back to the moment when Augustus, 'entitling himself by the name of prince, brought under his obedience the whole Roman state'.[107] By that time, 'how many were there which had seen the ancient form of government of the free commonwealth?'[108] With memories of the republic fading, 'there was no sign of the old laudable customs to be seen', and as soon as equality was taken away 'every man endeavoured to obey the prince'.[109] The upshot was that, after Augustus died and his stepson Tiberius succeeded, 'the Consuls, the Senators, and Gentlemen ran headlong to servitude'.[110] Tacitus concedes that some of Tiberius's early pronouncements 'were masked with a colour of liberty', but his government soon became tyrannical, and 'in the end he burst into all wickedness, dishonesty and reproach'.[111] The freedom of the republican age had been entirely corrupted and lost.

**********

By the end of the sixteenth century, the earliest English translations of the Roman historians had begun to be supplemented by English versions of Italian humanist treatises on republican government. Francesco Patrizi's *De institutione reipublicae* was translated as early as 1576, and Gasparo Contarini's *De republica Venetorum* in 1599.[112] Most significantly, Edward Dacres produced the first English version of Machiavelli's *Discorsi* on Livy in 1636.[113] Meanwhile a number of tracts by English writers on the virtues of republicanism had also begun to

---

[105] Livy 1600, pp. 111–12.    [106] Livy 1600, p. 124.    [107] Tacitus 1598, p. 1.
[108] Tacitus 1598, p. 2.    [109] Tacitus 1598, p. 2.    [110] Tacitus 1598, p. 3.
[111] Tacitus 1598, p. 140.
[112] For Patrizi on liberty as independence see Skinner 1978, vol. 1, pp. 153, 156–61; and Hankins 2023, pp. 92–125. On Contarini see Pocock 1975, pp. 320–30.
[113] See Machiavelli 1636. For Machiavelli on liberty as independence see Skinner 2019, pp. 57–89. For a contrasting view see Pocock 1975, pp. 186–99.

appear: John Barston's *Safeguard of society* was published in 1576, Richard Beacon's *Solon his folly* in 1594 and Thomas Scott's *Vox populi* in 1620.[114] The celebration of republicanism as the best form of government finally reached the forefront of English political debate in 1649,[115] when the institution of monarchy was abolished and England was declared 'to be a commonwealth and free state'.[116] These unprecedented developments stood in urgent need of justification, and one way in which this ideological need was satisfied was by invoking and developing the accounts of civil liberty that the Roman historians and their heirs among the humanists of the Renaissance had so fully provided.[117]

The two most important writers who immediately came forward as official propagandists for the new commonwealth regime were Marchamont Nedham, editor of the government newspaper *Mercurius politicus*, and his friend and colleague John Milton.[118] Already famous as a poet, Milton was appointed secretary for foreign tongues to the Commonwealth Council of State in March 1649.[119] By then he had already published *The tenure of kings and magistrates*, in which he had asserted the right of the people to place their king on trial.[120] Nedham's first work in defence of the republic appeared as *The case of the commonwealth of England stated* in May 1650, and was later expanded and generalised in *The excellency of a free state* in 1656. The final months of the Interregnum saw the appearance of several more republican tracts, including those of William Sprigge and Henrey Vane,[121] but incomparably the most important was John Milton's *The ready and easy way to establish a free commonwealth*, which was published in February 1660, only weeks before the return of Charles II to the throne.[122]

Among these writers, it was Nedham and Milton who most powerfully articulated the republican case. Both unequivocally endorse the classical Roman understanding of liberty.[123] To be free, they agree, is not to be subject to, or dependent upon, the power of anyone else.

---

[114] See Peltonen 1995 on Barston, pp. 59–73; on Beacon, pp. 75–102; on Scott, pp. 229–70.

[115] See Worden 1994; Peltonen 2023.    [116] Gardiner 1906, pp. 385, 388.

[117] On these sources and the use made of them see Sellers 1998, pp. 7–77.

[118] On Nedham see Worden 1994. For contrasting accounts of Nedham and Milton see Worden 1995, pp. 156–80 and Peltonen 2023, pp. 113–16, 173–82, 208–12. On Milton's collaboration with Nedham see also Worden 2007. On Milton's republicanism see Dzelzainis 1995; Lovett 2005; Hamel 2013; Foxley 2023. On the republican writers of the 1650s see Skinner 1998, pp. 13–57; Scott 2004, pp. 233–314; Hammersley 2020, pp. 72–92. On Milton and republicanism in 1658–60 see Norbrook 1999, pp. 379–432.

[119] Dzelzainis 1991, p. xxvii.    [120] See Dzelzainis 1991, p. xxvii.

[121] For Sprigge and Vane see Scott 2004, pp. 159–60, 296, 308–9.

[122] A second and revised edition (from which I quote) appeared in March 1660.

[123] On Milton and Nedham (and also Harrington) on liberty see Scott 2004, pp. 151–69.

More specifically, they follow their classical authorities in speaking of civil liberty as the condition of not being subject to arbitrary power. Milton refers at the start of *The tenure* to the danger 'of committing arbitrary power to any' instead of ensuring that there are laws 'consented to by all' which serve to 'confine and limit the authority of whom they choose to govern them'.[124] As he later confirms, 'the root and source of all liberty' lies in being your own master.[125]

Nedham in *The case of the commonwealth* prefers to lay his emphasis on what it means to be deprived of liberty. This happens as soon as we are rendered subject to an 'arbitrary way of government' based on a ruler's 'own sword and will'.[126] This form of rule is the very definition of tyranny, under which a king is invested 'with an arbitrary power to do what he list' and is able to use it against any 'that dare but pretend unto liberty'.[127] As Nedham later adds, quoting Sallust, what takes away liberty in such circumstances is not necessarily that the ruler uses his power to your prejudice, but simply that you are living at his mercy, and thus that 'it is in his power to be wicked if he please'.[128]

Milton and Nedham likewise agree that, if you are unable to act according to your own will, this is equivalent to saying that you have been reduced to servitude. As Milton puts it in *The tenure*, those who are not their own masters are no better than 'slaves and vassals born', condemned to live under a lord whose government 'hangs over them as a lordly scourge'.[129] Nedham in *The case of the commonwealth* declares that living in dependence on 'the will of imperious tyrants' is equivalent to living 'in miserable slavery',[130] and goes so far as to say that Machiavelli in his *Discourses* speaks very aptly when he equates kingship with tyranny.[131] By the time Milton came to write *The ready and easy way* he was fully prepared to endorse this judgement. He speaks with pride about how the people of England succeeded in turning 'regal bondage into a free commonwealth', and with despair about how they now appear to be preparing themselves 'for new slavery' under the 'detested thralldom of kingship'.[132]

Echoing Tacitus, Milton adds that a further reason for finding monarchy detestable is that, by imposing servitude, it has the effect of making people slavish and servile. In *The ready and easy way* he compares the

---

[124] Milton 1991, p. 9.
[125] Milton 1991, p. 32. For Milton on liberty see Foxley 2013 and Foxley 2022.
[126] Nedham 1969, p. 6.     [127] Nedham 1969, p. 62.     [128] Nedham 1969, p. 64.
[129] Milton 1991, p. 32. For Milton on liberty and slavery see Skinner 2002a and Dzelzainis 2019.
[130] Nedham 1969, pp. 79, 113.     [131] Nedham 1969, p. 62.
[132] Milton 1660, pp. 6, 19, 21.

position of 'they who are greatest' in free commonweaths, who are never 'elevated above their brethren', with the position of kings in relation to their people. A king 'must be adored like a demigod', and cannot fail to create 'a dissolute and haughty court about him', thereby encouraging 'the multiplying of a servile crew, not of servants only, but of nobility and gentry, bred up then to the hopes not of public but of court offices'. The minds of these people are soon 'debased with court opinions, contrary to all virtue and reformation' and they end up as 'his servants and his vassals'.[133] To Milton, this renunciation of freedom in favour of 'the base necessity of court flatteries and prostrations' is a spectacle so lamentable that he can hardly bring himself to contemplate it.[134]

Milton and Nedham are careful to add that the freedom of action enjoyed by those who live independent lives cannot be equated with doing whatever they like. Both follow their Christian as well as their classical authorities in marking a categorical distinction between liberty and licence. Milton opens *The tenure* by affirming that 'none can love freedom heartly but good men' since 'the rest love not freedom but licence'.[135] Nedham in *The case of the commonwealth* cites Tacitus as well as Sallust and Livy for the view that 'liberty becomes the greatest vice' when people who are 'free and dissolute' confuse it with having the power 'to do even what they list'.[136] As he later explains in *The excellency of a free state*, 'true freedom' consists 'not in a licence to do what you list', but rather in living in accordance with wholesome laws under a system of government in which everyone is able to enjoy their rights.[137] Like Milton, Nedham is especially struck by Sallust's warning that it was due to the acquisition of an empire that Rome's liberty declined into ruinous licence, and this leads both of them to express forebodings about the imperialist foreign policy of the Cromwellian protectorate.[138]

When they turn to consider the constitutional implications of these claims, Milton and Nedham begin by following the classical republican line of argument. They agree that, if we are to live in freedom as members of civil associations, it is indispensable that the laws alone should rule. Nedham argues in *The case of the commonwealth* that 'a trampling of all laws underfoot' is always the first among 'the effects and consequences of tyranny'.[139] Later he asserts in a thunderous passage in *The excellency of a free state* that 'all standing powers have and ever do assume unto themselves an arbitrary exercise of their own dictates at pleasure, and

---

[133] Milton 1660, pp. 35–6.    [134] Milton 1660, p. 36.    [135] Milton 1991, p. 3.
[136] Nedham 1969, pp. 99–100.    [137] Nedham 1656, pp. 4–5.
[138] On Nedham and Milton on the incompatibility of empire and liberty see Armitage 2000, pp. 146–69; on this republican dilemma see Armitage 2002.
[139] Nedham 1969, p. 62.

make it their only interest to settle themselves in an unaccountable state of dominion', thereby bringing about 'inundations of arbitrary power and tyranny'.[140]

Milton in *The tenure* develops the point at greater length when discussing 'the danger and inconveniences of committing arbitrary power to any'.[141] The danger is so great that those who start by succumbing to it soon find themselves turning instead to making laws that are 'framed or consented to by all'. This enables them to 'confine and limit the authority of whom they chose to govern them', so that it is no longer men who rule, 'but law and reason abstracted as much as might be from personal errors and frailties'.[142] As he later adds, it is 'a rule undeniable, and fit to be acknowledged by all kings and emperors, that a prince is bound to the laws' and ought always to submit to their requirements.[143]

As soon as they shift, however, to asking how far the people should be included in the making of laws, Nedham and Milton part company with their classical sources. Livy had followed Polybius in arguing that the aim must be to create a mixed and balanced constitution in which monarchical and aristocratic as well as popular elements are included, but Nedham in *The excellency of a free state* rejects this solution out of hand. He lays it down as an undeniable rule that the people 'are the best keepers of their own liberties'.[144] They alone know 'what grievances are most heavy, and what future fences they stand in need of to shelter them from the injurious assaults of those powers that are above them'.[145] They need to ensure that those appointed to positions of supreme authority are not only 'persons of their own election', but also 'such as must in a short time return again into the same condition with themselves'.[146] The fact is that 'the right, liberty, welfare, and safety of a people' all depend on upholding a system of popular sovereignty.[147]

Milton in *The ready and easy way* argues no less unequivocally. He takes it to be obvious – and believes that 'all ingenuous and knowing men will easily agree with me' – that in England the members of the House of Commons constitute 'the only true representatives of the people', and should not be required to deal with a king and his mere creatures, who are 'nothing concerned with the people's liberty'.[148] We need to recognise that 'the happiness of a nation must needs be firmest and certainest in a full and free Council of their own electing, where no single person but

---

[140] Nedham 1656, p. 77.    [141] Milton 1991, p. 9.    [142] Milton 1991, p. 9.
[143] Milton 1991, p. 13.    [144] Nedham 1656, p. 24.    [145] Nedham 1656, p. 36.
[146] Nedham 1656, p. 36.    [147] Nedham 1656, p. 242.
[148] Milton 1660, pp. 40, 69–70. Hammersley 2020, p. 82 notes that here Milton finally endorses an 'exclusivist' republicanism.

reason only sways'.[149] It is within this council that sovereignty must reside, although it must also be understood that it is lodged there not by a transfer of the people's power, 'but delegated only, and as it were deposited' by the ultimately sovereign body of the people.[150]

The claim that the securing of liberty can never be achieved under a mixed form of government was destined to become central to revolutionary political theory a century later.[151] During the 1650s, however, the contention was forcefully challenged by James Harrington in his *Oceana* of 1656.[152] Harrington has no quarrel with the account that Milton, Nedham and other republicans give of the concept of liberty itself. He agrees that personal liberty consists in not being subject to the will of others, and thus that the vital question is always about who has control.[153] He also agrees that, although the liberty enjoyed by those who live free from arbitrary power consists in being able to act according to their independent will, this is not the same as saying that they are free to do anything they like. He too insists on a categorical distinction between liberty and licence. We need to recognise that 'the liberty of a man consists in the empire of his reason, the absence whereof would betray him unto the bondage of his passions', thereby depriving him of any genuine liberty.[154]

As soon as Harrington turns, however, to explain the constitutional implications of his account of liberty, he makes it clear that he is only willing to endorse one of the two claims put forward by the official spokesmen for the commonwealth. He agrees that the laws alone must rule. If we wish to live in liberty, we must follow Aristotle and Livy, both of whom had called for 'the empire of laws and not of men'.[155] But he rejects the claim that, if the people are to maintain their liberty, they must be the sole bearers of sovereign power. Rather, he identifies himself as a passionate follower of Machiavelli's account in his *Discourses* on Livy of the type of mixed constitution best suited to upholding civil liberty. For Harrington, Machiavelli is 'the only politician of later ages',[156] the sole

---

[149] Milton 1660, p. 33.

[150] Milton 1660, p. 44. On the extent to which Milton's was a democratic form of republicanism see Hamel 2013 (who stresses Milton's egalitarianism) and Foxley 2022 and Foxley 2023 (who sees more ambivalence).

[151] For a recent restatement of the claim see De Dijn 2020, ch. 4, pp. 184–227.

[152] On the distinctiveness of Harrington's republicanism see Hammersley 2013 and Hammersley 2019. On the contrast between Harrington and Milton see also Dzelzainis 2014. On Harrington as the paradigm English republican of the 1650s see Fink 1962, pp. 52–89, Pocock 1971, pp. 104–47 and Pocock 1977, pp. 43–76. For a critique of this view see Hammersley 2020, pp. 86–92.

[153] Harrington 1992, p. 20.     [154] Harrington 1992, p. 19.

[155] Harrington 1992, p. 8; cf. also pp. 19–20.     [156] Harrington 1992, pp. 9, 10.

political writer of modern times who has properly understood how to construct an enduring free state.[157]

Machiavelli had argued that liberty is impossible under princely government. To live under a prince is to live in dependence, and hence in servitude.[158] As Edward Dacres expressed the point in his pioneering translation of the *Discourses*, first published in 1636, that you can 'govern a multitude either by way of liberty or by way of principality'.[159] If freedom is to be upheld, it is not merely essential to live under a republican constitution; it is also essential to divide the exercise of sovereign power between the different ranks of the people. The sagest law-givers soon saw the defects in every pure form of government, and instead 'chose one that might partake of all', so that 'in one and the same city there was the principality, nobility and commonalty as parts of the governments'.[160] For Machiavelli, as for Livy, the best example is provided by republican Rome. After the expulsion of the Tarquins, Rome was able for a long time to flourish as a free state.[161] This was because, once the tribunes were established, they 'bore such sway and had such credit that they could always after mediate between the people and the Senate'.[162] It was only when the people ceased to be able to control the ambitions of the nobility that Rome eventually collapsed back into servitude.[163]

This is the type of constitutional system that Harrington lays out in detail in *Oceana*.[164] One component is the Senate, which for Harrington 'is no more than the debate of the commonwealth'.[165] Once the Senate has debated, it is essential 'to have another council to choose'.[166] The Senate represents the wisdom of the commonwealth, but the second assembly must represent its interest, and must therefore consist of the whole body of the people. Since they are too numerous to be brought together, however, 'this council is to consist of such a representative as may be equal, and so constituted as can never contract any other interest than that of the whole people'.[167] Once the Senate has proposed a piece of legislation, and the assembly has resolved on it, it is then necessary to have

---

[157] Harrington 1992, p. 155. But Nelson 2004, pp. 87–126 shows that Harrington's Machiavellianism was constructed out of Greek as well as Roman and Renaissance sources.

[158] For liberty as the antonym of slavery and servitude see Machiavelli 1636, pp. 85, 119–20, 259, 270.

[159] Machiavelli 1636, p. 84.     [160] Machiavelli 1636, p. 14.

[161] Machiavelli 1636, p. 88.     [162] Machiavelli 1636, p. 19.

[163] Machiavelli 1636, p. 156.

[164] Foxley 2023 sees the result as a fusing of aristocratic elements with a democratic republicanism.

[165] Harrington 1992, p. 23.     [166] Harrington 1992, p. 24.     [167] Harrington 1992, p. 24.

a third institution, that of the magistracy, to execute the laws that have been passed. As Harrington summarises, 'the commonwealth consisteth of the Senate proposing, the people resolving, and the magistracy executing, whereby partaking of the aristocracy as in the senate, of the democracy as in the people, and of monarchy as in the magistracy'.[168] He feels able to end on a triumphant note. 'Now there being no other commonwealth but this in art or nature, it is no wonder if Machiavel have showed us that the ancients held this only to be good.'[169]

## The Legal Provenance of the Ideal

Many contemporary political theorists have taken the line of argument so far traced to be a distinctively republican one, and in recent discussions it has come to be widely described as the republican view of liberty. But this is an unhistorical claim. While it is true that all English republican thinkers of the early modern period endorsed the view that liberty consists in having an independent will, the same view was no less emphatically upheld by a wide range of legal and political commentators who would have been horrified to find themselves described as republican in their political allegiances. These writers were far more deeply indebted to a different tradition of thinking about what it means to be free, one that originally stemmed from the corpus of Roman law as codified under Justinian, and especially from the analysis of the law of persons in the opening book of the *Digesta*.[170] As early as the middle of the thirteenth century this discussion was incorporated virtually word for word into one of the pioneering compilations of English common law, the massive treatise *De legibus et consuetudinibus Angliae*, and from that source a distinctive legal analysis of civil liberty soon became centrally established in English legal and political thought.

The *De legibus* used to be attributed to Henry de Bracton and dated to around 1260.[171] But recent scholarship has suggested that the work may have been compiled a generation earlier, and that Bracton was at most a part-author and final reviser of the text.[172] Among early modern English lawyers, however, there was never any doubt about Bracton's authorship, and after the *De legibus* was printed from a collation of the manuscripts in 1569 we find its authority increasingly cited, and with much reverence.[173] One section that came to be widely invoked was the opening discussion of the *status* of persons, in which Bracton had begun by quoting the pivotal

---

[168] Harrington 1992, p. 25.    [169] Harrington 1992, p. 25.
[170] On the compilation of the *Corpus iuris* see Stein 1999, pp. 32–7.
[171] The ensuing discussion of Bracton draws on Skinner 2022, pp. 235–40.
[172] See Brand 2010.    [173] I therefore continue to refer to Bracton as the author.

claim in the *Digesta* that 'the principal and briefest division of persons' is that 'all men and women are either *liberi homines*, free persons, or else they are *servi*, slaves'.[174] To which Bracton had added that we can equally well say – 'thereby resolving the plural altogether into the singular' – that 'every man or woman is either free or a slave'.[175]

What does it mean to be a slave? Quoting the *Digesta* again, Bracton lays it down that a slave is someone who, 'contrary to nature, but due to an institution of the law of nations, is subject to the power of someone else'.[176] Here he follows the *Digesta* in repudiating the Aristotelian category of natural slaves, while conceding that, under the *ius gentium* or law of nations, the institution of slavery is recognised by law. The condition of natural and equal freedom is obliterated in practice by a set of norms and institutions that allow some persons to hold others under their control with legal impunity. This explains why – as Bracton adds, again quoting the *Digesta* – 'when slaves are granted their freedom, they are said to be manumitted, that is, released from living under the hand of someone else'.[177]

If everyone is either a slave or a free person, and if a slave is someone subject to the power and hence the will of another person, then it follows that a free person must be someone who is not subject to the power of anyone else, but is capable of acting according to their independent will. Here Bracton quotes a dictum of the jurist Florentinus already cited in the *Digesta*, according to which the *libertas* enjoyed by such free persons consists in their being able 'to do as they please, provided that their actions are not prohibited by law or prevented by force'.[178] So far Bracton's analysis closely resembles that of the Roman moralists and historians. But at this point he introduces a further and crucial distinction already mentioned in the *Digesta* and later elaborated by such medieval glossators as Azo of Bologna. The classical Roman writers had not only spoken of slaves as persons subject to the will of others; they had generally agreed that anyone living in such a state of subjection can be described as living in servitude. By contrast with this expansive sense of what can be said to constitute enslavement, the jurists contend that, while a slave is someone subject to the will of someone else, the converse does not hold. There are several classes of persons who, although they meet this

---

[174] Bracton 1569, 6. 1, fo. 4v. Cf. *Digesta* 1902, I. V. 3, citing Gaius. All my translations from Bracton are taken from Skinner 2022.
[175] Bracton 1569, 6. 1, fo. 4v.
[176] Bracton 1569, 6. 3, fo. 4v. Cf. *Digesta* 1902, I. V. 4. 1, citing Florentinus.
[177] Bracton 1569, 6. 3, fo. 4v. Cf. *Digesta* 1902, I. I. 4, and 1.V. 4. 2.
[178] Bracton 1569, 6. 2, fo. 4v. Cf. *Digesta* 1902, I. V. 4. I have changed the singular into the plural.

condition, cannot be counted as living in servitude. The distinction, as Bracton expresses it, is between those who are able to act *sui iuris*, in their own right, and those who are required to live *in aliena potestate*, in the power of someone else.[179]

As Bracton observes, the most obvious instance of those who live *in aliena potestate* are slaves.[180] But there are several other categories of persons who, although not slaves, cannot be described as having full power to act in their own right. One is that of 'sons who have been born to parents living in a lawful and legitimate marriage'.[181] A second category consists of people 'who perform servile works while nevertheless remaining free',[182] so that we can speak of 'free persons who live under the power of masters' in the manner of servants rather than slaves.[183] A further category consists of women, and particularly of wives. Although they are not slaves, they are subject to their husbands and consequently among those obliged 'to live under the rod'.[184] Finally Bracton considers the case of persons 'who are under protection or guardianship', or else 'under the care of parents and friends'.[185] They may be able to follow their own wills in some domains of their life, but they cannot be counted as free persons in the fullest sense.[186]

The compilers of the *Digesta* had not failed to recognise that these considerations raise a further question about the concept of slavery. If it is possible to be subject to the will of someone else without being reduced to slavery, what else is needed to make someone a slave? They responded by citing a formulation owed to the jurist Marcianus. While rejecting the Aristotelian category of natural slavery, Marcianus had accepted that it is legally possible for slaves to be 'converted into being our property either by the civil law or the *ius gentium*'.[187] For example, adults can legally choose to reduce themselves to slavery by participating in their own sale.[188] Later in the rubric Modestinus is cited as agreeing with the view that free persons can legally become slaves by selling themselves.[189] Putting together the *dicta* of Marcianus and Modestinus, the view of slavery at which the *Digesta* arrives is thus that a slave is someone who is subject to the will and power of a master by virtue of being in his ownership. The crucial defining fact about slavery is not that slaves live in dependence on their masters, but rather that they are the property of those who have power over them.

---

[179] Bracton 1569, 9. 2, fo. 6r.     [180] Bracton 1569, 9. 3, fo. 6r.
[181] Bracton 1569, 9. 4, fo. 6r.     [182] Bracton 1569, 11. 1, fo. 7r.
[183] Bracton 1569, 11. 3, fo. 7v.    [184] Bracton 1569, 10. 3, fo. 6v.
[185] Bracton 1569, 10. 2, fo. 6v.    [186] Bracton 1569, 10. 2, fo 6v.
[187] *Digesta* 1902, 1. 5. 5.    [188] *Digesta* 1902, 1. 5. 5.    [189] *Digesta* 1902, 1. 5. 21.

It is of considerable historical importance that Bracton did not include these passages in his *De legibus*, and that it was rare for this omission to be rectified by later writers in either the republican or the common law tradition of thinking about civil liberty. As a result, later writers generally adopted the more expansive view of what can count as enslavement that the Roman moralists and historians had originally embraced when they applied the term *servus* to anyone living in subjection to the will and power of someone else. Among English republican writers, John Milton was a rare exception. He noted in his commonplace book that, if we wish to see 'what lawyers declare concerning liberty', we must turn to the *Codex* of Justinian.[190] And he argued in *The tenure* that to say of a subject that he is 'no better than the king's slave' would be to say that the subject must be 'his chattel or his possession that may be bought and sold'.[191] As we shall see, the failure of most early modern writers on civil liberty to endorse this definition eventually exposed them to much hostility and ridicule.

Bracton's analysis was of vital importance, however, in establishing the correlative claim that what it means to be a free person is not to be subject to the will of anyone else, and the constitutional implications of this argument soon began to be spelled out in English legal thought. One of the most influential reformulations of Bracton's basic distinctions can be found in the *De laudibus legum Angliae* of Sir John Fortescue, who became Chief Justice of the King's Bench in 1442 and composed his treatise in the late 1460s.[192] Fortescue introduces his analysis of the English constitution by drawing a distinction between two forms of monarchical rule, one of which he describes as 'royal' (*dominium regale*) and the other as 'politique' (*dominium regale politicum*).[193] Under royal government the king can 'change the laws of his realm at his pleasure' and 'charge his subjects with tallage and other burdens without their consent'.[194] Such rulers are said to 'subdue' their people in the same way that 'a hunter subdueth wild beasts living at their liberty' and brings them 'under his obedience'.[195] The law under such systems is 'no other thing but the pleasure of the king'.[196] As a result, the laws in royal governments sometimes merely 'procure the singular commodity of the maker' and 'redound to the hindrance and damage of his subjects'.[197]

---

[190] Milton 1953, pp. 410, 470.    [191] Milton 1991, p. 11.

[192] Lockwood 1997, p. xviii. Fortescue's text was published in a facing-page translation by Robert Mulcaster in 1567, after which it was reissued in 1573 and 1599, and reprinted with additional notes by John Selden in 1616. I quote from the 1616 edition. For a modern edition see Fortescue 1997.

[193] Fortescue 1616, fo. 25v. For Fortescue on law and the English constitution see Lobban 2007, pp. 7–14; for Fortescue on *dominium* see Burns 1985.

[194] Fortescue 1616, fo. 25v.    [195] Fortescue 1616, fos. 28v, 29r.

[196] Fortescue 1616, fo. 29r.    [197] Fortescue 1616, fo. 40r.

For Fortescue the main question is what constitutional arrangements will most readily prevent such an outcome. His reason for commending the laws of England is that they have established a 'politique' system with two features that serve to guarantee the freedom of the people. One is that the king 'can neither change laws without the consent of his subjects, nor yet charge them with strange impositions against their wills'.[198] The result is that they 'frankly and freely enjoy and occupy their own goods'.[199] The other commendable feature of English government is that the statutes 'proceed not only from the prince's pleasure, as do the laws of those kingdoms that are ruled only by regal government', but are made 'by the assent of the whole realm, so that of necessity they must procure the wealth of the people and in no wise tend to their hindrance'.[200] The special merit of this system is that the laws can always be 'quickly reformed' if necessary, 'but not without the assent of the commons and states of the realm, by whose authority they were first devised'.[201] Fortescue echoes Bracton's conclusion that kings 'ought to be under the law, because law makes the king'[202] and that 'there is no king', but merely a tyrant, 'where his will rules rather than the law'.[203]

Fortescue's view of the English constitution soon became widely accepted, and was later restated and influentially developed by Sir Thomas Smith, the first Professor of Roman Law at the University of Cambridge, in his *De republica Anglorum* of 1583.[204] Smith begins by speaking in general terms about the concept of a commonwealth, which he defines as 'a multitude of free men collected together and united by common accord and covenants among themselves'.[205] He notes that three different types of commonwealth have generally been distinguished – monarchy, aristocracy and democracy – but prefers to make a simpler distinction between just and unjust rule, and hence between monarchy and tyranny.[206] A king is someone who 'doth administer the commonwealth by the laws of the same' and 'doth seek the profit of the people as much as his own'. Any ruler who instead makes laws 'at his pleasure' and 'without the advice of the people' is not a king but a tyrant.[207] Here Smith gives the example of 'the prince of the Turks', who cannot be regarded as the ruler of a kingdom, but only as someone 'that hath under him an infinite number of slaves or bondmen among

---

[198] Fortescue 1616, fo. 26r. On personal liberty under English law during the period 1200–1600 see Baker 1995.
[199] Fortescue 1616, fo. 26r.   [200] Fortescue 1616, fo. 40r.
[201] Fortescue 1616, fo. 40r.   [202] Bracton 1569, 7. 5, fo. 5v.
[203] Bracton 1569, 7. 5, fo. 5v.   [204] See Dewar 1982, pp. 1–2, 8.
[205] Smith 1982, p. 57.   [206] Smith 1982, pp. 49, 51.   [207] Smith 1982, p. 53.

whom there is no right, law nor common compact, but only the will of the lord'.[208]

For Smith, however, the subjects of the sultan are to be counted as slaves not merely or even chiefly because they live wholly subject to his will, but rather because they are bondmen of the type discussed in the *Digesta*. When Smith turns at the end of his analysis to consider those who are not fully *sui iuris*, he includes a chapter on bondmen in which he examines what he calls 'this old kind of servile servitude and slavery'.[209] By this he means the type of system under which a bondman is 'bought for money', becomes 'the possession of his lord and master', and is 'received among his goods'.[210] The slaves described in the *Digesta* were the property of their masters, whereas in English law there was a progressive move away from chattel slavery to villeinage, then to 'servitude of lands and tenures' until 'by little and little' the institution of slavery was extinguished.[211]

When Smith shifts from his general discussion of forms of government in Book I to consider the case of England in Book II, his main concern is to explicate the distinctive form of mixed constitution under which the English live. The 'head governor' is the king or queen, 'in whose name and by whose authority all things be administered', but the actual government is conducted by the crown in Parliament.[212] As a result, 'the most high and absolute power of the realm of England is in the Parliament', which 'representeth and hath the power of the whole realm'.[213] Every subject is taken 'to be there present' either in person or by representation, so that 'the consent of the Parliament is taken to be every man's consent'.[214] Every law is thus enacted with the consent of the people, and can therefore be regarded as 'the prince's and whole realm's deed'.[215] By these means the power of the ruler and the liberty of the subject are fully reconciled.

**********

By the time of the accession of the Stuart dynasty in 1603, the belief that the upholding of civil liberty requires a mixed constitution embodying the supremacy of law had come to be widely shared. But this was a doctrine that James I was strongly inclined to contest. So it is hardly surprising that, by the time his son Charles I came to the throne in 1625, relations between the crown and Parliament had already come under strain. Nor did Charles I take a less elevated view of his regal authority, and within

---

[208] Smith 1982, p. 58.    [209] Smith 1982, p. 137.    [210] Smith 1982, p. 57; cf. also p. 138.
[211] Smith 1982, p. 137.
[212] Smith 1982, p. 77. For this commitment as an instance of 'monarchical republicanism' see Hoak 2007.
[213] Smith 1982, pp. 78, 79.    [214] Smith 1982, p. 79.    [215] Smith 1982, p. 78.

three years of his accession he found himself confronting a Petition of Right drawn up by Parliament in protest against his illegal conduct towards his subjects.

The Petition accuses the king of assuming a power to rule 'by command or direction' instead of governing 'according to the laws and statutes of this realm'.[216] He has instructed commissioners to require people to lend money to the crown. He has issued a 'special command' for the imprisonment of a number of subjects without any cause being shown. And he has authorised martial law to be used to bring offenders to trial and in some cases to put them to death.[217] But all these policies are grounded on the assumption that the mere will of the king can take precedence over the law, and are consequently 'not warrantable'.[218] There is a statute explicitly declaring that 'no person shall be compelled to make any loans to the king against his will'. There is a prohibition in Magna Carta on the imprisonment of freemen unless they are 'brought to answer by due process of law'. And the use of martial law in time of peace is 'wholly and directly contrary' to the laws of the realm.[219]

At the same time the Petition argues that the king's illegal actions have violated the fundamental rights of his subjects. A number of these rights have been tested by time until they have become part of the established laws and customs of the realm, and thus among the inherited freedoms of Englishmen.[220] The most essential are laid down in Magna Carta, in which it is 'declared and enacted that no freeman may be taken or imprisoned or be disseised of his freeholds' or 'in any manner destroyed' except 'by the lawful judgment of his peers or by the law of the land'.[221] As the Petition points out, however, the king's use of martial law has unlawfully destroyed the lives of subjects, while imprisonment without trial has unlawfully taken away their liberty and the imposition of forced loans has unlawfully disseised them of their property. Later in the same month, a Remonstrance presented in Parliament against the use of prerogative powers to impose taxation explicitly denounced the practice as 'a breach of the fundamental liberties of this kingdom'.[222]

We can already hear, echoing below the surface of these accusations, the litany voiced by opponents of the crown at the outbreak of civil war in 1642: that there are some rights so fundamental that they must be placed beyond the power of government to challenge, and that the most essential of these are the rights to life, liberty and property. These rights are capable of being equally exercised by everyone, and must be absolutely protected

---

[216] Gardiner 1906, p. 67.     [217] Gardiner 1906, pp. 67–8.     [218] Gardiner 1906, p. 67.
[219] Gardiner 1906, pp. 66, 67, 69.     [220] Gardiner 1906, pp. 67, 68, 69.
[221] Gardiner 1906, p. 67.     [222] Gardiner 1906, p. 73.

and secured if we are to retain our status as freemen and avoid falling into servitude. As the lawyer John Glanville summarised in his speech on behalf of the House of Commons when the Petition of Right was presented, there are certain 'lawful and just liberties' that must be recognised as part of our birthright and inheritance, because they are indispensable to upholding our standing as 'free subjects of this realm'.[223]

The Petition stops short of concluding that the king's elevation of his 'special commands' above the law is already reducing his free subjects to the condition of slaves. But if we turn to the Parliamentary debates of 1628 we find this accusation repeatedly voiced. Before the Petition was presented to the king, the two Houses set up a committee to investigate 'the rights and privileges of the subjects'.[224] The committee presented an extensive account, drawn up by Edward Littleton and John Selden, of the legal grounds on which the Petition was basing its claim about 'the liberty of the person of every free-man'.[225] John Selden began by stressing the need to enforce what he describes as a right 'so fundamental' as that of personal liberty.[226] Sir Edward Coke added some 'general reasons' in support of their case, one of which was that the king's assumption of unaccountable powers was having the effect of turning every subject into nothing more than a 'tenant at will of his liberty', thereby leaving him 'no certain estate'. But as Coke admonishes, 'it should be no honour to the king to be king of slaves'.[227] We need to remember that 'the Common law hath so admeasured the king's prerogative as he cannot prejudice any man in his inheritance, and the greatest inheritance a man hath is the liberty of his person'.[228] The general point of the Petition, as he ends by underlining, is to reaffirm 'our ancient undoubted and fundamental liberties'.[229]

The accusation that the king was setting himself up as a ruler of slaves was also voiced at several stages in the ensuing parliamentary debates. Sir Dudley Digges opened the discussion of the Forced Loan by reiterating what Coke had already said. Denouncing those who argue that 'he is no great monarch' who cannot take 'whatsoever he will', Digges retorted that any king who 'is not tied to the laws' but instead rules according to his will is nothing but 'a king of slaves'.[230] Sir Robert Phelips referred to Livy's cautionary tale of the decemvirs, warning that 'there's now a decemvir in

---

[223] Johnson et al. 1977, pp. 562, 564–5.
[224] The findings of the committee were published in 1642. See *A Conference* 1642.
[225] *A Conference* 1642, pp. 4, 30, 55.     [226] *A Conference* 1642, p. 30.
[227] *A Conference* 1642, p. 68.
[228] *A Conference* 1642, p. 69. For Coke on common law see Pocock 1987, pp. 30–55; for a contrasting account see Lobban 2007, pp. 33–51.
[229] *A Conference* 1642, p. 71. On Coke and Selden in 1628 see Pocock 1987, pp. 289–99.
[230] Johnson and Cole 1977, p. 66.

every county, and amongst that decemvir there's some Appius Claudius that seek their own revenges'.[231] Later he invoked Fortescue's distinction between 'royal' and 'politique' government, arguing that 'the condition of a freeman is to live where there is not *dominium regale* but *dominium regale politicum*'.[232] Sir John Eliot also drew the attention of the House to Livy's account of how a free people can fall into slavery, adding that Livy's explanation 'now reflects upon us'.[233] We need to remember that the very fact of being 'liable to the command of a higher power' is what takes away our liberty.[234] Towards the end of the session, several other members recurred to the threat of slavery and the urgent need to counter it.[235] Summarising their arguments, Sir Roger North put it to the House that their overriding duty was to halt the crown's encroachments on the liberty of subjects and thereby 'save ourselves and them that sent us from being slaves'.[236]

After one further turbulent session in 1629, Charles I ceased to summon Parliament and turned instead to a system of personal rule. This experiment lasted eleven years until the crown's worsening fiscal difficulties forced a recall of Parliament in 1640. The king then found himself faced with such vociferous opposition that it took less than two years before the wrangling descended into civil war. A number of different lines of attack were pursued, but the most threatening was the renewed charge that the king was arrogating to himself an uncontrolled and hence an illegal form of dominion over the people. The type of dominion in question now began to be widely described as arbitrary power.[237] Sir Robert Phelips had already used the term in 1628 in referring to Livy's account of the decemvirs, but it was first extensively employed in the impeachment of the Earl of Strafford. When John Pym presented his preliminary accusation in November 1640, he spoke of Strafford's arbitrary and confused government, making it clear that he was referring to the exercise of an 'unlimited' capacity to dispose of 'our lives, our persons and estates'.[238] Responding to Strafford's subsequent speech of defence, Pym reiterated that Strafford had endeavoured 'to introduce an arbitrary and tyrannical government', thereby seeking 'to subvert the fundamental

---

[231] Johnson and Cole 1977, p. 69.     [232] Johnson and Cole 1977, p. 109.
[233] Johnson and Cole 1977, p. 72.     [234] Johnson and Cole 1977, p. 72.
[235] See, for example, Johnson et al. 1977, p. 214.     [236] Johnson et al. 1977, p. 269.
[237] This is not to say that the term made its earliest appearance in anglophone political debate at this time. Jean Bodin had spoken of 'arbitrary power' when discussing the concept of justice in the concluding chapter of his *Six books of a Commonweal*, where he had defined it (in the words of Richard Knolles's translation of 1606) as the power of a judge to decide simply 'according to his own mind' and 'according to his own good liking'. See Bodin 1962, pp. 764–5.
[238] Kenyon 1966, p. 206.

law of England and Ireland'.[239] Pym underlined once more that, in speaking of arbitrary power, what he meant was a form of power 'loose and absolved from all rules of government'.[240]

As the parliamentary attack on the crown gathered momentum in 1641, the contention that Charles I was seeking to exercise just such an uncontrolled form of power was regularly repeated. When the Court of Star Chamber was abolished in July 1641, the principal accusation was that it had been used as 'the means to introduce an arbitrary power and government'.[241] When the session of 1641 culminated in the presentation of the Grand Remonstrance, the king's advisers were claimed to be bent on elevating 'the arbitrary power pretended to be in His Majesty'.[242] During the next and epoch-making year, the same vocabulary was adopted by some of the most prominent pamphleteers in favour of Parliament. The most combative was the radical lawyer Henry Parker, who published his *Observations* on the king's replies to Parliament in July 1642.[243] Parker accuses Charles I of opening a gap 'to as vast and arbitrary a prerogative as the Grand Seignior has in Constantinople'.[244] He focuses in particular on the right of the king to refuse assent to Bills presented to him by the two Houses of Parliament, which is said to subject the nation 'to as unbounded a regiment of the king's mere will as any nation under Heaven ever suffered under'.[245] Finally, the same objection was voiced in the Declaration of 2 August, in which Parliament finally announced that it was taking up arms. It was now said to be evident that the king's party was aiming to 'take away the law and introduce an arbitrary government', their aim being 'to destroy the Parliament and be masters of our religion and liberties, to make us slaves'.[246] This is why Parliament has decided to raise an army under the Earl of Essex, 'with whom, in this quarrel, we will live and die'.[247]

After the parliamentarian armies triumphed in the ensuing war, the defeated king was eventually put on trial for having levied war against his people. On 27 January 1649 the High Court of Justice sentenced him to death, and he was executed three days later. According to the charge against him, he had been 'trusted with a limited power' to govern 'for the good and benefit of the people, and for the preservation of their rights and liberties'. But instead he had engaged in 'a wicked design to erect and uphold in himself an unlimited and tyrannical power to rule according to

---

[239] Pym 1641, p. 2.     [240] Pym 1641, pp. 7, 19, 25.     [241] Gardiner 1906, p. 181.
[242] Gardiner 1906, p. 222.
[243] On Parker see Mendle 1995; Skinner 2002b, pp. 332–9; Cromartie 2016; Sabbadini 2016; Skinner 2018, pp. 197–207.
[244] [Parker] 1642, p. 17.     [245] [Parker] 1642, p. 8.     [246] Cobbett 1807, col. 1439.
[247] Cobbett 1807, col. 1440.

his will, and to overthrow the rights and liberties of the people'.[248] Less than two months later, Parliament went on to abolish the office of king, arguing that 'for the most part, use hath been made of the regal power and prerogative to oppress and impoverish and enslave the subject', and concluding that the office is 'unnecessary, burdensome and dangerous to the liberty, safety and public interest of the people'.[249] By this time, the distinctive vocabulary as well as the full range of arguments deployed in the *Declaration* of 1688 had become fully available, ready to be used in denunciation of the despotic and arbitrary rule of Charles I's son James II.

---

[248] Gardiner 1906, pp. 371–2. On justifying the regicide see Burgess 2004 and Peltonen 2023, pp. 39–56.

[249] Gardiner 1906, p. 385.

# 2 The Legitimacy of the Revolution Debated

## The Securing of Liberty Celebrated

The Declaration of Rights, the terms of which were agreed by Parliament on 12 February 1689, concluded with a stipulation that two new oaths of allegiance must now be taken.[1] After William and Mary accepted the crown on the following day, a Proclamation was issued declaring them to be king and queen, and adding that they were 'accordingly so to be owned, deemed, accepted and taken by all the people', who 'are from henceforth bound to acknowledge and pay unto them all faith and true allegiance'.[2] Two months later an Act was passed requiring that the oaths stipulated in the Declaration must be taken by all civil and ecclesiastical office-holders. Anyone failing to swear the oaths by the beginning of August would, after a six-month period of grace, be deprived of their offices.[3]

This development sparked an intense debate about the legitimacy of paying allegiance to the new king and queen, in the course of which some fundamental questions about civil liberty and political obligation were vociferously discussed.[4] A majority argued that the new regime ought definitely to be regarded as legitimate, and thus that everyone owed a duty of allegiance. Many chose to put this case in merely de facto terms.[5] Among these, some simply asserted that William was a successful conqueror. Edward Fowler, a London clergyman who later became Bishop of Gloucester, made the case in 1689 in his *Vindication* of those who had already sworn the oath of allegiance.[6] By the time his tract was printed, however, the same argument had been more weightily presented by Gilbert Burnet, the newly installed Bishop of Salisbury.[7] Burnet reminds

---

[1] Harris 2006, p. 346.  [2] See *A Proclamation* 1689 (single sheet).
[3] Harris 2006, p. 349.
[4] Goldie 1980a provides a comprehensive and indispensable guide.
[5] See Kenyon 1977, pp. 21–34 for a discussion, although he exaggerates when he speaks (p. 21) of 'the triumph of *de facto* theory' in legitimising the revolution of 1688.
[6] On Fowler see Goldie 1980a, p. 539. The argument was later developed by Charles Blount. See Blount 1693 and cf. Goldie 1980a, p. 532.
[7] See Kenyon 1977, pp. 29–31.

his readers that King William, faced with the question of his right to govern, decided 'to leave the matter to the determination of the peers and people of England, chosen and assembled together with all possible freedom, who did upon that declare him their King'. But he insists that William had no obligation to act in this way. He had made war on James II for abusing his powers, and with his victory he had won the right to take the crown and 'hold it in the right of his sword', although he magnanimously allowed the people to confer what was already his by right.[8]

A different line of de facto argument was pursued by William Sherlock, the dean of St Paul's, who caused a sensation in 1691 with *The case of the allegiance due to sovereign powers*,[9] in which he summarily asserted that the possession of political power in itself confers the right of dominion over a people.[10] He takes only a few pages to make the case before profusely illustrating it with biblical and historical examples. The specific claim on which he concentrates is that once our rulers 'are thoroughly settled in their thrones' they are automatically 'invested with God's authority, and must be reverenced and obeyed by all who live within their territories and dominions, as well priests as people'.[11] To establish that they are thoroughly settled, we only need to show that 'the whole power of the nation is in the hands of the prince', and that 'the great body of the nation has submitted to him'.[12] Where this is the situation, as it is in England, everyone must 'pay all the duty and allegiance of subjects'.[13]

Most commentators, however, clearly felt that a mere acceptance of the status quo evaded the central moral question that needed to be faced. They wished to show that, if we examine the circumstances under which it is legitimate for a people to remove a ruler from power, we shall find that the decision to remove James II in favour of William and Mary was undoubtedly justified. Many argued in turn that the decision can best be defended along the lines already laid out in William's *Declaration* of 1688 and in the Bill of Rights of 1689. As we have seen, both documents had argued that the free people of England possess a number of fundamental rights and liberties that have been enshrined in law over the centuries. Under the reign of James II, however, the people were reduced from the condition of freemen to that of slaves condemned to live in dependence on their sovereign's arbitrary will. This enforcement of tyranny made it fully justifiable to remove James II from the throne.

---

[8] Burnet 1689, pp. 20–1.
[9] For the debate about Sherlock's *Case* see Kenyon 1977, pp. 26–8; Goldie 1980a, p. 557; Parkin 2007, pp. 382–4.
[10] On the presence of this 'Hobbist' argument in debates about the revolution see Parkin 2007, pp. 378–409.
[11] Sherlock 1691, p. 5.    [12] Sherlock 1691, pp. 5, 9.    [13] Sherlock 1691, p. 8.

The effect was to liberate the people from servitude and re-establish their time-honoured standing as free subjects living in a free state.

This was the argument reiterated in such treatises as George Petyt's *Lex parliamentaria* of 1690,[14] Thomas May's *Epitome of English history* of the same year, Richard Ames's *Liberty or slavery* of 1692 and James Tyrrell's *Bibliotheca politica*, which appeared anonymously in 1694. George Petyt, who was a friend of Tyrrell's, particularly emphasises the role of Parliament in guaranteeing the rights and liberties of the people.[15] He sees it as entirely owing to Parliament that the people were in earlier times saved from becoming vassals and slaves, and were able to avoid having 'their lives, estates, and liberties given away, and disposed of, without their own assents'.[16] May and Ames are more preoccupied by the recent subversion of the ancient constitution. May agrees that time-honoured customs established the fundamental laws of the land,[17] but mainly focuses on how these laws came to be undermined. He traces this development to the success of Oliver Cromwell in replacing the rule of law with what May describes as 'arbitrary government displayed to the life', under which the people were reduced to 'absolute slaves'.[18] He then traces a parallel with the reign of James II, 'whose government was popery, slavery and arbitrary power' until the nation was happily delivered from servitude.[19] Ames focuses more specifically on the reign of James II and his 'arbitrary actions', and on his attempt to 'turn upside-down our laws, religion, and liberties'.[20] He too ends by rejoicing in the nation's deliverance, and the restoration of the people to the greatest freedom that anyone could hope to possess.[21]

It is to James Tyrrell, however, that we need to turn for the most systematic account of what he describes in the subtitle of his *Bibliotheca politica* as the ancient constitution of the English government.[22] Tyrrell had begun his studies at Oxford, where he became a friend of John Locke, and subsequently trained at the Inner Temple, where he was called to the bar in 1666.[23] His foremost concern in his *Bibliotheca politica*, as he describes it, is to explore 'dark labyrinths of law and history'.[24] What his exploration discloses is a familiar story about how the English constitution came into being and evolved. Like his friend George Petyt, who had

---

[14] This attribution has been questioned. But the title page of the first edition (although not the second) is signed 'G. P'.

[15] On their friendship see *ODNB*, vol. 55, p. 805.    [16] [Petyt] 1690, p. 111.

[17] May 1690, pp. 43, 171, 205.    [18] May 1690, pp. 6–7, 121.    [19] May 1690, title page.

[20] Ames 1692, pp. 12–13.    [21] Ames 1692, pp. 4, 13.

[22] On Tyrrell see Kenyon 1977, pp. 36–7, 47–50; Pocock 1987, pp. 187–8, 346–9, 354–5; Ward 2004, pp. 105–51.

[23] See *ODNB*, vol. 55, pp. 805–6.

[24] [Tyrrell] 1694, preface to the thirteenth dialogue, Sig. A, 2r (following p. 900).

explicitly denied that 'the fundamental law of government in this nation' was 'originally founded on any capitulation or compact',[25] Tyrrell thinks of the English as having inherited an ancient constitution that arose from deep and even immemorial roots.[26] There was never any agreement between rulers and subjects to uphold any antecedent rights. The rights and liberties enjoyed by the people as free subjects of the state were constructed within and by the state itself. They became established at an early stage in the history of the nation, and subsequently proved their value and efficacy over the course of time. Like the numerous authorities on the common law whom Tyrrell cites, he is anxious to emphasise that the history of the constitution has in consequence been less concerned with developing these rights and liberties than with reaffirming their time-honoured importance at moments when they were placed under threat.

These claims are debated in a sequence of thirteen dialogues by two figures called Meanwell and Freeman. Meanwell attempts in the third dialogue to mount a defence of absolute monarchy, but Freeman wins the argument by showing how the ancient constitution of England endowed the people with a number of rights and privileges that came to be established as 'the fundamental laws of the land' and were accepted as such by their kings.[27] One of these rights was that the people should be able to express their consent, through their representatives in Parliament, to the laws by which they are governed. Responding to Meanwell in the fifth dialogue, Freeman outlines the historical origins and development of this indispensable right of a free people.[28] But as Freeman has already made clear in the third dialogue, the most essential among the rights held by the English people is that of being secured in the possession of their lives, liberties and estates – a phrase used by Freeman at least a dozen times.[29] Later, in the ninth dialogue, in the course of arguing that the people can lawfully defend these rights by force, Tyrrell describes them as the fundamental rights of the people,[30] while adding that they are at the same time 'the immemorial rights and liberties of this kingdom'.[31]

Freeman shows that, although these rights have sometimes been challenged and endangered, they have always been successfully reaffirmed. The first major reaffirmation took the form of the Great Charter promulgated in 1215, which gave the people 'not any new grants, but rather confirmations of their ancient rights and liberties'.[32] Sir Edward Coke is cited for having shown that Magna Carta 'is for the most part declaratory

---

[25] Petyt 1690, preface (unpaginated).    [26] [Tyrrell] 1694, pp. 170, 666.
[27] [Tyrrell] 1694, pp. 187–8; cf. also p. 669.    [28] [Tyrrell] 1694, pp. 317–18.
[29] [Tyrrell] 1694, pp. 172, 176–7, 182, 185–7.
[30] [Tyrrell] 1694, p. 636; cf. also pp. 670, 680.    [31] [Tyrrell] 1694, p. 666.
[32] [Tyrrell] 1694, p. 321.

of the principal grounds of the fundamental laws of England', and Sir John Fortescue is praised for having emphasised that 'the same laws and customs' had already governed the English people.[33] The other major restatement came with the Petition of Right of 1628. This was 'no grant or concession of any new rights or privileges', but only 'a declaration of several ancient rights and liberties of the subjects which had been very much broken and infringed'.[34] The figure of Freeman concludes that, if we had not been so effective in defending this heritage, 'I doubt not but the people of England had been long before this time in the same condition, as to their liberties and properties, as some of our neighbouring nations', in which they live as slaves under arbitrary power 'and enjoy nothing but at their princes' pleasure'.[35]

Tyrrell is eager to emphasise that England has recently come very close to falling into just such a state of enslavement. When he turns to the reign of James II he announces that the question we must ask is whether, due to the king's 'notorious violation of the fundamental laws of this kingdom', he may be said to have 'discharged the nation from all allegiance to him'.[36] Tyrrell takes himself to have answered this question in his previous dialogues, and especially in the third, in which he had partially switched to a more contractarian style of argument. We cannot suppose, the figure of Freeman had there argued, that any people would voluntarily give themselves up 'to the absolute arbitrary power and will of a single person'.[37] This would be to enslave the whole nation, enabling their ruler 'to make a prey of them whenever he pleases'.[38] We need to recognise that 'such an absolute arbitrary power, in princes or states, can never consist with the main ends of civil society'.[39] Rather than allowing an entire people to be 'enslaved or destroyed by the boundless will of a tyrant', we must accept that the preservation of society from intolerable slavery requires either 'vigorous resistance' or else 'joining with some powerful neighbour prince or state, who shall interpose for their deliverance'.[40] Turning to the practical implications, Tyrrell concludes that 'I think it becomes any honest man to thank God' for the success of William III's intervention, which proved to be 'the only means (now miracles are ceased) which God hath been pleased to ordain by the course of his Providence for our deliverance'.[41]

**********

[33] [Tyrrell] 1694, p. 321.    [34] [Tyrrell] 1694, p. 336.
[35] [Tyrrell] 1694, pp. 178, 186; cf. also p. 665.
[36] [Tyrrell] 1694, preface to tenth dialogue, unpaginated (between pp. 689 and 691).
[37] [Tyrrell] 1694, p. 155.    [38] [Tyrrell] 1694, p. 155.    [39] [Tyrrell] 1694, p. 155.
[40] [Tyrrell] 1694, 'Advertisement' prefacing third dialogue, following p. 136, at Sig. T, 2r.
[41] [Tyrrell] 1694, pp. 189, 904.

While many defended the revolution of 1688 in historical terms, others argued that the legitimacy of the new regime needed to be vindicated on the basis of more abstract principles. These writers agree that, although life, liberty and property are undoubtedly among our fundamental rights, this is not because their value has stood the test of time and become part of the established laws and customs of the realm. Rather, it is because they form part of the *ius naturale*, the right of nature, rather than the mere *ius positivum* or positive law of particular states. They are, in a word, the natural rights that everyone would possess outside the bounds of political society, and that every state has a duty to uphold. They constitute the most essential liberties that need to be secured if we are to retain our standing as free persons while at the same time living as subjects of states. If these rights cease to be enforced by law, and come to be upheld merely at the will and pleasure of the prince, this has the effect of reducing us, contrary to the law of nature, to the condition of slaves. We then have a natural right to join in the removal of the tyrannical power that has reduced us to servitude.

This is not a line of argument we encounter in the *Declaration* of 1688 or the Bill of Rights of 1689. During the years that immediately followed, however, such claims became increasingly important, and those who developed them were able to draw on a venerable legal tradition of reflection about the rights of the people. The origins of this way of thinking can be traced as far back as the debates about popular sovereignty among the earliest glossators of Roman law. The source on which they had liked to focus was the *Lex regia* cited by Ulpian in Book I of the *Digesta*. According to this alleged law, the people were originally possessed of all political power, but chose to confer it upon their emperors. They thereby divested themselves of *omne ius*, the entirety of their right to govern, and accepted that 'whatever pleased their ruler must have the force of law'.[42] Some commentators, however, argued that the sovereignty of the people was never relinquished, but only delegated in such a way as to enable the grant of power to be revoked if the people felt there was due cause. This was the case originally put forward by Azo of Bologna in his *Lectura super codicem*, and he went on to draw the inference that the power of the whole people must be greater at all times than that of any ruler they may choose to appoint over themselves.[43]

Azo's claim was largely repudiated by the later legal tradition. It was aggressively revived, however, during the religious wars of the late sixteenth century by the so-called monarchomachs, the fighters against

---

[42] *Digesta* 1902, I. 4. 1.
[43] Azo of Bologna 1966, VIII. LIII. 2, p. 671. On the *Lex regia* and popular sovereignty see Lee 2016, pp. 25–39.

kings, who revived and endorsed Azo's defence of popular sovereignty.[44] The most influential statement of their case was put forward in the *Vindiciae contra tyrannos* of 1579, which was published in English at two highly significant moments, first in 1648 and again in 1689.[45] By this time the claims of the monarchomachs had been taken up by a number of spokesmen for the parliamentarian cause in England, most notably by Henry Parker in his *Observations* of 1642, in which he closely follows the *Vindiciae* in considering 'whether it be lawful to resist a prince which doth oppress and ruin a public state'.[46]

The author of the *Vindiciae* had begun by arguing that 'kings are made by the people'.[47] Parker similarly begins by affirming that 'power is originally inherent in the people', and was at first held and exercised in natural communities.[48] But it soon became evident that man was 'so untame and uncivil a creature' that nothing was sufficient 'to restrain him from mischief or to make him sociable'.[49] The people came to realise that without some king or magistracy 'to provide new orders, and to judge of old, and to execute according to justice, no society could be upheld'.[50] It is crucial to the thrust of Parker's argument, however, that the people never gave away their original sovereignty, and here he comments directly on the debate about the *Lex regia*. Taking Azo's side, he insists that the covenant made by a people with a king always takes the form of a delegation and concession of power with conditions attached.[51] As he states the case, 'at the founding of authorities, when the consent of societies conveys rule', the people 'may ordain what conditions and prefix what bounds it pleases', and whatever laws are established must in addition be 'agreeable to the dictates of reason' and 'ratified by common consent'.[52]

The *Vindiciae* had gone on to affirm that 'kings receive laws from the people' and that 'the whole body of the people is above the king'.[53] Again Parker agrees. We can now see 'that power is but secondary and derivative in princes', and that 'the fountain and efficient cause is the people'.[54] But if the people are responsible for giving the laws, what laws will it be best for them to give? Parker responds that it would be 'rebellious to nature' if any free people were 'to contribute its own inherent puissance merely to abet tyranny and support slavery'.[55] The aim of the people will naturally

---

[44] See Garnett 1994, pp. 109–110n. and p. 111n., and for an analysis of monarchomach theories see Skinner 1978, vol. 2, pp. 302–48 and Lee 2016, pp. 121–57.
[45] *Vindiciae* 1648. On the authorship see Garnett 1994, pp. lv–lxxvi.
[46] *Vindiciae* 1648, p. 46.    [47] *Vindiciae* 1648, p. 46.    [48] [Parker] 1642, pp. 1, 13.
[49] [Parker] 1642, p. 13.    [50] [Parker] 1642, pp. 2, 13.    [51] [Parker] 1642, p. 4.
[52] [Parker] 1642, p. 13.    [53] *Vindiciae* 1648, pp. 51, 63.    [54] [Parker] 1642, p. 2.
[55] [Parker] 1642, pp. 3–4, 7.

be to improve the security of the rights and liberties they had enjoyed outside the confines of the state. 'The charter of nature entitles all subjects of all countries whatsoever to safety by its supreme law', so that the main aspiration must be to ensure 'that the subject shall live both safe and free'.[56] Above all, it must be ensured 'by a special trust of liberty and safety' that the rights of the people to the enjoyment of their 'lives, liberties and possessions' are fully protected and upheld.[57]

What if a king becomes a tyrant, ruling at his mere discretion and thereby enslaving the people?[58] The *Vindiciae* had affirmed that 'subjects are the king's brethren and not his slaves', and thus that all such tyrants can and must be resisted and removed.[59] Once more Parker agrees. The transcendent rule must be that 'if the king will not join with the people, the people may without disloyalty save themselves' from the tyranny of their king.[60] They must stand ready to affirm that 'the state hath an interest paramount in cases of public extremity' to ensure 'its own necessary preservation'.[61] By acting to save the state, the people will merely be re-exerting the ultimate sovereign power they originally held and never gave up.

Parker's arguments were taken up by several other defenders of the parliamentarian cause in the 1640s,[62] and were subsequently developed by some of the republican writers in the 1650s as an ancillary element in their defence of free states. John Milton observes in *The tenure of kings and magistrates* that, when we speak of the natural condition of mankind, we are at the same time referring to a condition of freedom and independence. 'All men naturally were born free, being the image and resemblance of God himself', so that when they subsequently agreed to form themselves into communities and 'bind each other from mutual injury', they retained the 'authority and power of self-defence and preservation' that was 'originally and naturally in every one of them'.[63] These considerations show us 'that the power of kings and magistrates is nothing else, but what is only derivative, transferred and committed to them in trust from the people to the common good of them all, in whom the power yet remains fundamentally, and cannot be taken from them without a violation of their natural birthright'.[64] Milton draws the inference that every ruler 'holds his authority of the people', who retain the natural right to 'retain him or depose him, though no tyrant, merely by the liberty and right of free born men to be governed as seems to them best'.[65]

---

[56] [Parker] 1642, p. 4.    [57] [Parker] 1642, p. 5.
[58] On tyranny and enslavement in the *Vindiciae* and in Parker see Skinner 1978, vol. 2, pp. 324–37 and Skinner 2002a, pp. 292–8. See also Nyquist 2013, pp. 71–9, 184–92.
[59] *Vindiciae* 1648, p. 78.    [60] [Parker] 1642, p. 16.    [61] [Parker] 1642, p. 34.
[62] See Skinner 2018, pp. 197–202.    [63] Milton 1991, pp. 8–9.    [64] Milton 1991, p. 10.
[65] Milton 1991, p. 13.

The same line of argument was later deployed to vindicate the cause of William III. We find a number of anonymous pamphleteers speaking in these contractarian terms in 1689,[66] and they were soon joined by such leading political writers as Thomas Harrison in *Political aphorisms*,[67] William Atwood in *The fundamental constitution of the English government* and James Stewart in *Salus populi suprema lex*, in which William III's intervention is hailed as an act of national liberation rather than God-given deliverance.[68] All these writers defend the legitimacy of William and Mary's rule,[69] and largely do so on the grounds that James II had violated the compact of government designed to uphold the natural rights of the people.[70] Among these defences, by far the most important – as well as one of the earliest to appear – was John Locke's *Two treatises of government*, which was licensed for publication on 23 August 1689 and was probably in print before the end of the year.[71] The special significance of the *Two treatises* stems not so much from its immediate influence, although it was enthusiastically recommended by Atwood[72] and extensively plagiarised by Harrison.[73] Of greater importance is the fact that Locke not only presented the most sophisticated statement of the argument about the compact of government and the upholding of natural rights, but went on to exercise a distinctive influence in helping to solidify the Whig theory of the state, particularly in the mid-1740s.[74]

Locke opens the *Second treatise* by offering a restatement of the classical view of what it means to possess our liberty. He begins with an account of the natural condition of mankind, in which we are able to act as we think fit 'without asking leave or depending upon the will of any other man'.[75]

---

[66] See Goldie 1980a, item 20 (p. 533), item 72 (p. 542) and item 132 (p. 554).

[67] For this attribution see Goldie 1980a, p. 553 and Kenyon 1977, pp. 123–4, 209–10.

[68] Stewart 1689, p. 4.

[69] Stewart 1689, p. 4; [Harrison] 1690, p. 31 ; [Atwood] 1690, pp. 45, 85–7.

[70] Stewart 1689, p. 4; [Harrison] 1690, pp. 17, 19, 31; [Atwood] 1690, pp. 4–5, 9–10, 17–19, 31, 45, 61.

[71] The date of publication of the first edition is nevertheless given as 1690. See [Locke] 1690, title page (for date of licensing see facing page). I quote from this edition (first state), as this was the version read in the years immediately following the 1688 revolution. The second edition did not appear until 1694. See Laslett 1988, p. 127. Laslett established that the *Second treatise* was probably written between 1679 and 1681 (although others have since argued for a slightly later date). The text was then revised in 1688–9 to bring out its relevance to the revolution of those years. See Laslett 1988, pp. 46, 65, 123–6.

[72] As noted in Goldie 2006, p. 48. See [Atwood] 1690, pp. 3–4, 101.

[73] See, for example, [Locke] 1690, para. 4, p. 220 and cf. [Harrison] 1690, p. 2; [Locke] 1690, para. 135, p. 355 and cf. [Harrison] 1690, pp. 25–6; [Locke] 1690, para. 137, pp. 358–9 and cf. [Harrison] 1690, p. 3.

[74] My understanding of Locke's *Two treatises* is much indebted to two classic studies, Dunn 1969 and Tully 1980. For Locke on liberty see also Tully 1993a, pp. 281–323.

[75] [Locke] 1690, para. 4, p. 220.

As he subsequently adds, this is what it means to possess the status of a *liber homo*, a free person – or, in his preferred vocabulary, the standing of a freeman.[76] He speaks of freemen as those who are 'independent one of another'[77] as opposed to being 'subjected to the will or authority of any other man'.[78] A freeman is someone who possesses 'the liberty to dispose of his actions and possessions according to his own will'.[79] The freedom of action enjoyed by such freemen consequently takes the form (as Florentinus had originally said) of being able to live as they wish, 'to order their actions and dispose of their possessions and persons as they think fit', independently of the will and power of anyone else.[80]

Next Locke contrasts this state of liberty as independence with the condition of slavery. Whereas to be free is to be your own master,[81] what it means to be a slave is to live 'under the absolute arbitrary power of another'.[82] Locke frequently recurs to the claim that a slave is someone who is subject specifically to 'arbitrary' power.[83] He is also emphatic that it is possible for entire communities as well as individuals to fall into such a state of servitude. As an example he offers the case – as Livy had done – of 'the intolerable dominion of the *Decemviri*', which for a time enslaved the free people of Rome.[84]

When Locke explains what he means by arbitrary power, he aligns himself firmly with the classical understanding of the term. As we saw in Chapter 1, the early modern translators of Livy and Tacitus had made them speak of those who behave arbitrarily as acting merely at their own 'will and pleasure' – a phase that had already been repeated several times in the *Declaration* of 1688. Locke likewise equates arbitrary conduct with acting simply 'at pleasure'.[85] He characterises the dominion held by any ruler who is not constrained by standing laws as 'an arbitrary power depending on his good pleasure',[86] which is capable of being exercised in the form of 'extemporary dictates' not subject to any control.[87] Like the classical writers, however, Locke is also interested in the perspective of

---

[76] On the figure of the freeman see [Locke] 1690, para. 58, p. 276, para. 103, p. 322 and paras 117–18, pp. 339–40.

[77] [Locke] 1690, para. 103, pp. 322, 323.

[78] [Locke] 1690, para. 22, p. 241 and para. 54, p. 273.

[79] [Locke] 1690, para. 59, p. 277.    [80] [Locke] 1690, para. 4, p. 220.

[81] [Locke] 1690, para. 44, p. 263 and para. 172, p. 395.

[82] [Locke] 1690, para. 23, p. 242.

[83] [Locke] 1690, para. 85, p. 303, para. 189, p. 412 and para. 221, p. 441. For Locke on arbitrary power see Halldenius 2002.

[84] [Locke] 1690, para. 201, pp. 422–3.

[85] [Locke] 1690, para. 137, p. 359 and para. 138, p. 361.

[86] [Locke] 1690, para. 156, p. 378.

[87] [Locke] 1690, para. 131, p. 350, para. 136, p. 357 and para. 137, p. 359. On control see para. 6, p. 222 and para. 123, p. 345.

those who live in subjection to such uncontrolled power. He describes their predicament as that of confronting an 'inconstant, uncertain, unknown, arbitrary will',[88] and later speaks of the 'arbitrary and irregular commands' of those who hold this form of sway.[89]

There is one juncture, however, at which Locke appears to qualify this definition of civil liberty as absence of dependence on the arbitrary power of our rulers and fellow subjects. He is strongly in favour of granting our rulers an element of personal power in the form of prerogative right.[90] But he is insistent that, although the exercise of prerogative is discretionary, it is not 'an arbitrary power to do things hurtful to the people'.[91] Rather, it takes the form of a power 'to act according to discretion for the public good'.[92] No act can count as an exercise of prerogative unless it is wholly directed at 'public good and advantage', and thus at the benefit of the nation as a whole.[93]

The opening chapters of the *Second treatise* also introduce a further and pivotal claim about the condition of being a free person. Locke maintains that, if we consider 'what state all men are naturally in', we see that it is 'a state of perfect freedom to order their actions and dispose of their persons and possessions as they think fit'.[94] They not only have 'a title to perfect freedom' but 'an uncontrolled enjoyment of all the rights and privileges of the law of nature equally with any other man or number of men in the world'.[95] This is by no means to say, however, that everyone in this natural condition would be able to do whatever they want. As Locke immediately adds – invoking another classical distinction – 'though this be a state of liberty, yet it is not a state of licence'.[96] This is because 'the state of nature has a law of nature to govern it' and reason 'is that law', so that the requirements of natural law are at all times 'intelligible and plain to a rational creature'.[97] What this means is that 'the freedom then of man, and liberty of acting according to his own will, is grounded on his having reason', which enables him to know 'how far he is left to the freedom of his own will' as opposed to having 'an unrestrained liberty'.[98]

What then does reason teach us? Reason 'teaches all mankind, who will but consult it, that being all equal and independent, no one ought to harm

[88] [Locke] 1690, para. 22, p. 241.    [89] [Locke] 1690, para. 201, p. 422.

[90] For Locke on prerogative see Skinner 2009a.

[91] [Locke] 1690, para. 163, p. 386. On the compatibility of Locke's view of prerogative with his understanding of liberty as independence see Dawson 2022.

[92] [Locke] 1690, para. 160, p. 383.

[93] [Locke] 1690, para.159, pp. 382–3 and para. 167, p. 389.

[94] [Locke] 1690, para. 4, p. 220.    [95] [Locke] 1690, para. 87, p. 305.

[96] [Locke] 1690, para. 6, p. 222. For Locke on liberty and propriety see Kelly 2011, pp. 20–52.

[97] [Locke] 1690, para. 6, p. 222 and para. 12, p. 230.

[98] [Locke] 1690, para. 63, p. 281.

another in his life, health, liberty or possessions'.[99] These are the most essential of our rights in the state of nature, the 'just and natural rights' of which Locke speaks in the preface to the *Two treatises*.[100] He repeatedly underlines this claim as he develops his argument. When he refers to 'the rights and privileges of the law of nature', he specifies that everyone 'hath by nature a power' to preserve 'his life, liberty and estate'.[101] When any group of people decides to unite together in a political society, their reason for doing so will be to secure 'the mutual preservation of their lives, liberties and estates'. The power they place in the hands of their rulers 'can have no other end or measure' than to uphold and secure these basic natural rights.[102]

Locke speaks with marked irony of those who instead believe that – 'as some men would persuade us' – it is possible to create 'sacredness of customs' out of the mere passage of time.[103] Here he may be alluding to Tyrrell, towards whom Locke had become less friendly in the course of the 1680s.[104] He objects that private interests often sustain customs and privileges even 'when the reasons of them are ceased', and he ridicules the 'gross absurdities' that arise from 'the following of custom, when reason has left it'.[105] The natural rights we now enjoy do not owe their standing to the fact that they have become recognised over time as valuable elements in an ancient constitution. Rather, they need to be cherished because they are indispensable to the preservation of our standing as free persons, so that any attempt to take them away by reducing us 'to slavery under arbitrary power' will amount to a transgression of the fundamental rule of society.[106] The watchword must always be to regulate political associations 'not by old custom but true reason'.[107]

As Locke admits, however, many people are not guided by reason, so that in our natural condition we would soon find our rights jeopardised by the exercise of uncontrolled and arbitrary power. It is at this juncture that the parallels with the argument of the *Vindiciae contra tyrannos* become especially close. We would quickly discover that, with everyone our equal, and 'the greater part no strict observers of equity and justice', life would be 'very unsafe, very unsecure'.[108] This is the difficulty that makes people 'willing to quit a condition which, however free, is full of fears and continual dangers' and consent 'to join in society with others' for 'the

---

[99] [Locke] 1690, para. 6, p. 222.    [100] [Locke] 1690, preface, Sig. A, 3r.
[101] [Locke] 1690, para. 87, p. 305.
[102] [Locke] 1690, para. 123, p. 345 and para. 171, p. 394. On natural rights see also [Locke] 1690, para. 82, p. 301 and para. 115, p. 337.
[103] [Locke] 1690, para. 94, p. 314.    [104] See *ODNB*, vol. 55, p. 805.
[105] [Locke] 1690, para. 157, p. 379.    [106] [Locke] 1690, para. 222, p. 442.
[107] [Locke] 1690, para. 158, p. 380.    [108] [Locke] 1690, para. 123, p. 345.

mutual preservation of their lives, liberties and estates'.[109] Men came to recognise that they needed to accept a compact of government whereby they gave up the freedom of the state of nature in favour of submitting to the rule of law. They became willing to consent, as Locke puts it, to divest themselves of their natural liberty and put on the bonds of civil society in the name of attaining a more secure and peaceable way of life.[110]

But what if the government placed in power subsequently ignores the terms of the compact? Here Locke introduces some dark allusions to the conduct of James II. What if the people 'see several experiments made of arbitrary power', especially the favouring of the religion 'which is readiest to introduce it'?[111] What if the ruler is persuaded by flatterers, or else persuades himself, 'that as supreme magistrate he is uncapabable of control'?[112] Locke unhesitatingly endorses the monarchomach answer to these questions, and brings the *Second treatise* to a close with a hostile commentary on William Barclay's *De regno*, his treatise of 1600 'against the monarchomachs', in which he had specifically denounced the *Vindiciae contra tyrannos*. Locke agrees with the *Vindiciae* that the agreement of any people to submit themselves to sovereign power must always take the form of a revocable concession, never an alienation of their original power and rights. The rulers they establish 'have no manner of authority, any of them, beyond what is by positive grant and commission delegated to them'.[113] As a result, 'the community perpetually retains a supreme power of saving themselves from the attempts and designs of anybody, even of their legislators, whenever they shall be so foolish, or so wicked, as to lay and carry on designs against the liberties and properties of the subject'.[114] If their ruler 'sets up his own arbitrary will in place of the laws', thereby attempting 'to reduce them to slavery under arbitrary power',[115] there is an undoubted right to resist such tyranny, and Locke even attempts to show that Barclay himself cannot evade this conclusion.

There remains the question, as Locke puts it, of 'who shall be judge' of whether the tyranny of an arbitrary ruler is sufficiently oppressive to warrant an insurrection.[116] Here the *Vindiciae* had answered with caution, arguing that the people must leave it to the subordinate magistrates of the kingdom to decide the issue on their behalf.[117] Locke has a much more radical response: 'to this I reply, the people shall be judge'. Any ruler is merely deputed by the people and trusted to follow the rule of law, and 'having deputed him', the people must still have 'a power to discard him

---

[109] [Locke] 1690, para. 123, pp. 345–6.    [110] [Locke] 1690, para. 95, p. 316.
[111] [Locke] 1690, para. 210, p. 431.    [112] [Locke] 1690, para. 218, pp. 437–8.
[113] [Locke] 1690, para. 152, p. 373.    [114] [Locke] 1690, para. 149, p. 370.
[115] [Locke] 1690, para. 214, p. 435 and para. 222, p. 441.
[116] [Locke] 1690, para. 240, p. 269 (*recte* p. 465).    [117] *Vindiciae* 1648, p. 131.

when he fails in his trust'.[118] With this conclusion, Locke takes it that he has fully vindicated the promise made in his preface. His hope, as he had expressed it, was that his book would prove 'sufficient to establish the throne of our great restorer, our present king William' and 'to make good his title in the consent of the people', and would at the same time be sufficient 'to justify to the world the people of England, whose love of their just and natural rights, with their revolution to preserve them, saved the nation when it was on the very brink of slavery and ruin'.[119]

### The Betrayal of Liberty Denounced

Although the ideological forces ranged in support of the 1688 revolution were formidable, the new regime nevertheless found itself confronting immediate and outspoken hostility. The most intransigent opposition came from those who rejected the legitimacy of William and Mary outright and refused to take the new oath of allegiance. Some of these non-jurors simply felt that they could not abjure the oath of allegiance they had already sworn to James II, but the most unyielding rejected the basic idea that the liberty of the people should be an aim and end of government. They argued that the unswerving duty of every subject must be (as the word implies) to live in subjection to their rulers, so that there can never be any justification for resistance even to tyrannical government. James II must therefore have been unlawfully deposed, and the rule of William and Mary must be illegitimate.

Some defenders of the revolution professed to see in this argument nothing more than a disgraceful willingness to turn subjects into slaves. When the figure of Meanwell in the fourth dialogue of Tyrrell's *Bibliotheca politica* attempts to argue in these terms, Freeman incredulously retorts that 'if resistance be in no case lawful, though in never so great extremities', then 'all government whatsoever will not only be absolute but arbitrary'. As a result, 'the lives, liberties and estates of a free people or nation shall be in as bad or a worse condition than if they were slaves, if all means of defending themselves by their own resistance, or joining with those that would assist them, be wholly denied'.[120] Tyrrell is well aware, however, as he makes Freeman admit, that 'many men have carried these doctrines of passive obedience and non-resistance to so great a height' that their claims have by now become widely accepted,[121] and he feels the need to devote the whole of his fourth dialogue to attacking their case.[122]

---

[118] [Locke] 1690, para. 240, p. 269 (*recte* p. 465).
[119] [Locke] 1690, preface, Sig. A, 3r.    [120] [Tyrrell] 1694, p. 270.
[121] [Tyrrell] 1694, p. 291. On the supporters of divine right monarchy see Kenyon 1977, pp. 83–101.
[122] [Tyrrell] 1694, pp. 215–307.

One of the writers whom Tyrrell singles out is Abednego Seller, a clergyman from Plymouth, who had published a learned and highly successful work entitled *The history of passive obedience since the Reformation* in 1689.[123] Seller begins by arguing that 'from the infancy of the happy Reformation, the Church of England hath always believed and avowed' that the duty of every Christian is 'to obey his superior', even 'in things unlawful', and not to resist their authority 'in any case or upon any pretence whatsoever'.[124] He adds that this doctrine can never be unreasonable, 'since no government can be safe without it'. Any subject who doubts this eternal truth will soon find their fruitful land 'turned into a barren wilderness, and Paradise itself become a field of blood'.[125] Seller then devotes the whole of his *History* to citing a wide range of authorities in his support. He refers to passages from the Articles and Homilies of the Church of England, as well as quoting more than 100 witnesses, including Luther and Calvin, James I and Charles I, several prominent non-jurors and the compiler of *The whole duty of man*.[126]

Seller's defence of non-resistance provoked an immediate outcry,[127] but at the same time it gained him strong support, most conspicuously from George Hickes, a former chaplain to Charles II, who was soon to become a bishop in the short-lived non-juring Church.[128] Hickes dismisses the objections raised by Seller's critics by outlining what he takes to be the undoubted rights of any holder of sovereign power:

> The rights of a sovereign are that he is accountable to none but God, that he cannot be judged, deposed or deprived by his subjects, nor forfeit his government to them, that they have no power over him, nor any right to take the sword without commission from him, and therefore when he is once king he must continue to be so till he dies, or freely and voluntarily resigns.[129]

Having laid out what he describes as these eternal principles, Hickes concludes that 'from hence it follows, that the subject of such a sovereign prince cannot dispose of his crown, nor renounce his right to reign over them, nor transfer their natural and sworn allegiance from him without his consent'. We need to recognise in addition that 'it tends more to the safety of the community to bear a tyrannical king than to resist his tyranny and unhinge the government by force'.[130]

A more widespread and threatening line of opposition to the new regime soon began to be developed by those who, while accepting the

---

[123] For the attribution see Goldie 1980a, p. 556.     [124] [Seller] 1689, Sig. A, 2v.
[125] [Seller] 1689, Sig. A, 2v–3r.     [126] For the full list see [Seller] (1689), Sig. A, 5v–6r.
[127] For some of the responses see Goldie 1980a, pp. 531, 539, 542–3, 550, 559, 563.
[128] On Hickes see Goldie 1980a, p. 541.     [129] [Hickes] 1689, pp. 7–8.
[130] [Hickes] 1689, pp. 8, 10. For a similar line of argument see [Kettlewell] 1691.

legitimacy of the revolution, had come to feel that the government was failing to live up to the promises made when William and Mary were given the crown.[131] One of the principal objections of these self-styled real Whigs or commonwealthmen was that William III was maintaining a large standing army, although the Bill of Rights had condemned the use of such forces as a threat to liberty.[132] Robert Molesworth was one of the first to raise the alarm when he published his *Account of Denmark* in 1694, which he wrote on his return from an unhappy period as envoy to the Danish court.[133] He devoted much space to the revolution of 1660 in which the people of Denmark, with the aim of cancelling the oppressive powers of the nobility, had permitted all power to be granted to the crown. The immediate outcome was that the monarchy became 'absolute and arbitrary', with 'not the least remnant of liberty remaining to the subject'.[134] Molesworth contends that what has kept this tyrannical system in place ever since has largely been 'the maintenance of a great standing army, so that the people are contributors to their own misery' and forced to pay for their own enslavement.[135]

The argument became much more heated when William III continued to maintain a standing army after the end of the war with France in 1697. A year later the radical lawyer John Trenchard published a tract ominously entitled *An argument showing that a standing army is inconsistent with a free government and absolutely destructive to the constitution of the English monarchy*. Trenchard begins with the stark warning that, if we ask why so many unhappy nations 'have lost that precious jewel liberty, and we as yet preserved it', what we find is that 'their miseries and our happiness proceed from this: that their necessities or indiscretion have permitted a standing army to be kept amongst them, and our situation rather than our prudence hath as yet defended us from it'.[136] He allows that, if William III were immortal, it might be possible for us 'wholly to rely on his care and conduct'. But since he is not, 'we ought not to entrust any power with him which we don't think proper to be continued to his successors', because a standing army 'must in the hands of an ill prince (which we have the misfortune frequently to meet with) infallibly destroy our constitution'.[137] 'If we keep a standing army, all depends upon the uncertain and capricious humours of the soldiery, which in all ages have

---

[131] On the origins of this argument see Goldie 1980b and Goldie 1993.
[132] On the resulting debate in 1697–9 see Schwoerer 2019, pp. 155–87.
[133] *ODNB*, vol. 38, pp. 530–2. On Molesworth's writings see Robbins 1959, pp. 87–112, 121–4.
[134] [Molesworth] 1694, p. 43.    [135] [Molesworth] 1694, pp. 68, 116.
[136] [Trenchard] 1698a, p. 4.    [137] [Trenchard] 1698a, p. 6.

produced more violent and sudden revolutions than ever have been known in unarmed governments.'[138]

Writing at the same time, the Scottish politician Andrew Fletcher expressed himself with more forthright hostility. Fletcher had initially been an ardent supporter of William III, and had taken part in the invasion in 1688, but he deeply disapproved of the king's military policies.[139] He considered it sufficiently serious that the king had already impoverished England with a long and expensive war, and was still employing large numbers of mercenary troops.[140] If this policy is continued, then 'I desire to know where the security of the British liberties lies, unless in the good will and pleasure of the king'.[141] The truth is that 'to give him standing armies puts his power beyond control and consequently makes him absolute'.[142] But as we see only too clearly in Europe, where most princes employ such forces, the outcome is that 'all such governments are changed from monarchies to tyrannies'.[143] Nor can the power of refusing to pay for such troops 'be a sufficient security for liberty', because 'he that is armed is always master of the purse of him that is unarmed'.[144] We must never fail to remember that governments may be tyrannical even when they are not behaving tyrannically. 'All governments are tyrannical which have not in their constitution a sufficient security against the arbitrary power of the prince.'[145] Fletcher concludes with the dire warning that 'whether standing armies will enslave us, neither reason nor experience will suffer us to doubt'.[146]

A yet more serious accusation against the new regime was that it had begun to betray the constitutional settlement of 1688. The Bill of Rights had laid it down that a mixed and balanced constitution is indispensable to the maintenance of a free state. But the balance was being dangerously tipped in the direction of executive tyranny. This line of attack was not confined to radical critics of the government; it was no less vigorously pursued by a number of high Tories and Jacobites.[147] Many such voices were raised in protest,[148] the most fearless being that of the London printer William Anderton, who was tried and executed for treason after publishing his *Remarks upon the present confederacy* in 1693. Anderton chiefly denounces William III's disastrous military exploits in Europe, but in the central section of his tract he turns to ask about the condition of England under William's four years of tyranny.[149] He speaks of

---

[138] [Trenchard] 1698a, p. 27.     [139] Robertson 1997, p. xxxii.
[140] Fletcher 1997, pp. 12, 18.     [141] Fletcher 1997, p. 12.     [142] Fletcher 1997, p. 19.
[143] Fletcher 1997, p. 4.     [144] Fletcher 1997, p. 4.     [145] Fletcher 1997, p. 4.
[146] Fletcher 1997, p. 19.     [147] For a survey see Goldie 2006, pp. 43–7.
[148] See, for example, the high Tory tract *An answer to a letter* 1699 and the Jacobite tracts of 1692–3 cited in Goldie 1980a, items 121 and 142, pp. 552, 555.
[149] [Anderton] 1693, p. 18.

corruption 'in the elections of burgesses for Parliament all over the nation' and a continual stirring up of 'animosities and quarrels' in Parliament, which is being manipulated to be 'the more eager and emulous of serving him'.[150] The constitution of the Church and state have both been 'reversed and quite disjointed, our liberties and properties most unjustly invaded, and more instances of arbitrary power daily committed than in several of the former reigns'.[151] Anderton concludes that we are witnessing the dwindling of 'our liberties into slavery, our property into beggary, the honour and reputation of the English nation into the utmost contempt' and 'the constitution of our government broken'.[152]

The same year saw the publication of a more focused and equally scathing Jacobite attack in a tract entitled *The price of the abdication*. The author concentrates on the role of placemen in Parliament, whose behaviour 'precludes all means of vindicating the honour of the House of Commons from the odious names of pensioners', and at the same time 'heightens the suspicion that such are preferred before the innocent and uncorrupted'.[153] What hope can we now have 'of the freedom of future Parliaments?' We must remember that 'the direct opposite to freedom is bondage and slavery', and that 'if our Parliaments be denied the privilege of free and impartial debates', then the country will soon be 'reduced to absolute slavery'.[154]

A similar line of argument was pursued from the opposite end of the political spectrum by a number of the real Whigs or commonwealthmen.[155] Following his attack on standing armies, John Trenchard turned to the issue of political corruption in his *Free thoughts concerning officers in the House of Commons* in 1698.[156] He begins by observing that 'the freedom of this kingdom depends upon the people's choosing the House of Commons'. So long as this system operates 'free from external force or private corruption', then no measures will pass except those which the members think to be for the public advantage. This arrangement is nothing less than 'the fountain head from whence the people expect all their happiness'.[157] But a great danger to our freedom has now arisen from the growing number of placemen in Parliament. If this system is continued, we can never expect the House of Commons 'to act vigorously for the interest either of king or people'. Some members will 'servilely comply with the court to keep their

---

[150] [Anderton] 1693, p. 21.   [151] [Anderton] 1693, p. 30.   [152] [Anderton] 1693, p. 45.
[153] *The price of the abdication* 1693, pp. 7–8.   [154] *The price of the abdication* 1693, p. 8.
[155] On what it means to be a 'real Whig' see [Molesworth] 1721, p. vii. See also Goldie and Jackson 2007 on Whig Jacobites.
[156] See [Trenchard] 1698b. This tract was originally published as the preface to Fletcher's *History of standing armies*.
[157] [Trenchard] 1698b, p. 2.

places', while others will do the same to gain a place.[158] Meanwhile 'those gentlemen whose designs are for their country's interest will grow weary of the best form of government in the world, thinking by mistake the fault is in our constitution'.[159] The moral is that we must do 'as much as possible, to keep the Legislative and Executive parts asunder', or else we are in danger of losing our liberty.[160]

This was also the moment when John Toland, already notorious as a deist, came forward as a self-consciously independent Whig in *The danger of mercenary Parliaments*, which he published anonymously in 1698.[161] Toland argues along the same lines as Fletcher, but he writes with despair rather than indignation when contemplating the corruption of the constitution. After the revolution the people expected Parliament to serve its proper purpose of supporting the king's just prerogative, protecting the people in their rights and privileges, and acting as 'a check and curb to insolent and licentious ministers and a terror to ambitious and over-grown statesmen'.[162] By now, however, the people have become 'sadly sensible how wretchedly they have fallen short of their expected happiness', although they do not fully understand 'the true spring and fountain from whence all their misfortunes flow'.[163] This spring is 'no other than that bare-faced and openly avowed corruption which, like a universal leprosy, has so notoriously infected and overspread both our court and Parliament'.[164] We need to recognise, before it is too late, that designs are now being carried on 'for the total subversion of our most excellent constitution', and that those who are promoting this corruption 'are making us slaves'.[165]

Toland was at the same time instrumental in foregrounding the most radical of the constitutional questions raised by the settlement of 1688: is it ever possible to live free of corruption and arbitrary power under any form of monarchical rule? The year 1698 saw this question return to the centre of the political stage with the posthumous publication of Algernon Sidney's *Discourses concerning government*. Sidney's work appeared almost clandestinely, and was edited and printed anonymously. The caution was undoubtedly prudent, for the *Discourses* contains a strongly anti-monarchical restatement of the ideal of liberty as independence,[166] together with the claim that (as the anonymous editor puts it in the

---

[158] [Trenchard] 1698b, p. 3.     [159] [Trenchard] 1698b, p. 3.
[160] [Trenchard] 1698b, p. 4.
[161] On Toland see Jacob 1981, pp. 151–7; Champion 2003; Hammersley 2020, pp. 95–6, 105–10.
[162] [Toland] 1698a, p. 1.     [163] [Toland] 1698a, p. 3.     [164] [Toland] 1698a, p. 3.
[165] [Toland] 1698a, p. 8.
[166] See Pocock 1994 and for a full account see Hamel 2011, pp. 161–90.

preface) what is 'invincibly proved in the following Discourses' is that 'the happiness or infelicity of any people entirely depends upon the enjoyment or deprivation of liberty'.[167]

Early in his opening chapter Sidney asks himself how the concept of liberty should be understood. He answers with a definition that was subsequently much repeated: 'Liberty solely consists in an independency upon the will of another, and by the name of slave we understand a man who can neither dispose of his person nor goods, but enjoys all at the will of his master.'[168] As he later underlines, 'liberty consists only in being subject to no man's will', while 'dependence upon the will of another' is what denotes a slave.[169] He also points to a crucial implication: 'he is a slave who serves the best and gentlest man in the world, as well as he who serves the worst', because 'he must obey his commands, and depends upon his will'.[170] Liberty is independence, so the mere fact of living in subjection to someone else's will is sufficient to reduce you to servitude.

For Sidney, the next question is whether it is possible to live in freedom under a monarchy. He avows that 'nothing is further from my intention than to speak irreverently of kings',[171] and he concedes that, if a ruler is wholly bound by law, then a monarchy can resemble a free state. He is emphatic, however, that 'if there be no other law in a kingdom than the will of a prince, there is no such thing as liberty', and he goes on to argue that, because property 'is an appendage to liberty', it is 'impossible for a man to have a right to lands or goods if he has no liberty'.[172] Where a king's will is accepted as law, the creation of such an absolute monarchy entirely extinguishes the people's liberty.[173] They are not only turned into slaves, but condemned to a life of inescapable servility.[174] And because any absolute ruler 'will always seek such as are content to depend upon his will', the nation will be corrupted as well as enslaved.[175]

The form of government under which we have the best chance of avoiding corruption and servitude will always be what Sidney describes as the 'popular' style of rule that prevails in free states.[176] A free state with a popular government is one in which all political power originates with the people,[177] who are able to exercise 'the free use of their own understanding' to 'dispose of their own affairs as they think fit'.[178] The political power they create is conferred by their consent on elected magistrates,

---

[167] [Sidney] 1698, Sig. A, 2r. The preface is not included in Sidney 1990.
[168] Sidney 1990, p. 17.    [169] Sidney 1990, p. 402.    [170] Sidney 1990, p. 441.
[171] Sidney 1990, p. 188.    [172] Sidney 1990, pp. 402–3.    [173] Sidney 1990, p. 192.
[174] Sidney 1990, pp. 123, 252–7, 463.    [175] Sidney 1990, p. 257.
[176] On 'popular' government see Sidney 1990, pp. 189, 263 and the chapter headings at pp. 184, 195, 217, 251, 263 and 270. On the extent to which Sidney's republicanism can be regarded as democratic see Ashby 2022.
[177] Sidney 1990, p. 69.    [178] Sidney 1990, pp. 90, 263.

leaving the people with the right to change or remove their government if they choose.[179] They are thus 'governed only by laws of their own making',[180] and are never dependent on the will of anyone else.[181] The effect is to defend them 'from all manner of arbitrary power' and to fix a rule to which government actions must conform.[182] This is what it means to live in a 'commonwealth', and Sidney concludes by drawing a series of unflattering comparisons with what it is like to live under a king.[183]

The year 1698 was also the moment when John Toland initiated a campaign to give greater publicity to the republican cause. This is not to say that Toland was a republican himself. Like Molesworth and Trenchard, he was anxious to establish that the value of freedom from subjection can equally well be secured under a limited form of monarchical rule. He patriotically declares that the English owe it 'to his present majesty's glorious example' that they have discovered 'the secret of so happily uniting two seemingly incompatible things, principality and liberty' and he testifies that 'there's not a man alive that exceeds my affection to a mixed form of government' of the kind now established under William III.[184] Toland likes to present himself as a moderate, and in the outline of his political principles in the opening chapters of his *Anglia libera* of 1701 he puts forward his argument largely in the form of unacknowledged quotations from Locke's *Second treatise*.[185]

At the same time, however, Toland was largely responsible for giving renewed prominence to the English republican writers of the 1650s. He began by publishing a three-volume collection of John Milton's historical and political works in 1698, in which he not only included Milton's defence of Charles I's trial in *The tenure of kings and magistrates*, but also *The ready and easy way to establish a free commonwealth*. Here Toland gave the tract its full title, in which Milton had contrasted the excellence of republican government with 'the dangers and inconveniences of readmitting kingship to this nation'.[186] A year later Toland caused an outcry by publishing an adulatory biography of Milton, in which he spoke of him as 'a man eminent at home and famous abroad for his universal learning, sagacity and solid judgment, but particularly noted as well for those excellent volumes he wrote on the behalf of civil, religious and domestic liberty'.[187] One apoplectic critic responded that Milton's republican

---

[179] Sidney 1990, esp. pp. 90, 113, 189, 257, 263, 270.
[180] Sidney 1990, p. 17; cf. also p. 440.    [181] Sidney 1990, esp. pp. 439–46.
[182] Sidney 1990, p. 416.    [183] Sidney 1990, esp. pp. 132, 191, 262, 440.
[184] [Toland] 1700, preface, p. viii.
[185] See Toland 1701, pp. 2, 3 4; and cf. [Locke] 1690, paras 13, 95, 149, pp. 230, 316, 369.
[186] [Toland] 1698b, items 12 and 24, vol. I, p. iv.    [187] [Toland] 1699, pp. 5–6.

writings amount to nothing more than 'specious pretentions about liberty', which are 'equally destructive to religion and civil society'.[188] Nothing daunted, Toland went on to produce an edition of the most celebrated work of republican political theory from the 1650s, James Harrington's *The commonwealth of Oceana*. The work was reissued in 1700 with a laudatory preface by Toland hailing Harrington as 'a bright ornament to useful learning' and 'a hearty lover of his native country', whose *Oceana* provides us with a model of 'the most perfect form of popular government'.[189] With these editorial labours Toland called renewed attention to the fundamental question as to whether the ideal of equal liberty can ever be realised under a monarchy. This was the question that Milton and Harrington had raised, and it was destined to haunt the Anglo-American debate about liberty throughout the coming century.

[188] *Remarks on the life of Mr Milton* 1699, Sig. A, 3v–4r.    [189] Toland 1700, pp. vii, ix.

*Part II*

# Liberty as Independence: The Ideal Entrenched

# 3    Towards the Whig Idea of a Free State

## The Whigs and their Opponents

The airing of so many disagreements turned the decades following the revolution of 1688 into a period of unceasing political turbulence. With the death of Queen Anne in 1714, however, and the coming of the Hanoverian dynasty, a period of greater political stability ensued. The Whigs won a landslide victory in the general election of 1715 and soon began to entrench themselves in power. They succeeded in passing the Septennial Act in 1716, thereby extending the life of Parliaments from three to seven years and making parliamentary business correspondingly easier to manage. They won a further victory in the election of 1722, at which point Robert Walpole became first minister.[1] He narrowly avoided dismissal when George II came to the throne in 1727, but managed to retain his position and went on to win a further term of office in 1734. Walpole fell from power only after the general election in 1741, when he was forced to resign after a vote of no confidence.[2] But the leaders of the opposition were outwitted in the negotiations that followed, and it fell to Henry Pelham, Walpole's preferred successor, to form a new government.[3] The Tories were effectively excluded, and the Whigs quickly settled down into a further period of political supremacy, with Pelham continuing as prime minster until 1754.[4]

This is by no means to say that the Whig ascendancy went uncontested. On the contrary, the debates of the 1690s about the legitimacy of the revolution never came to an end. The Jacobites remained intransigent enemies of the Revolution Settlement, and within six months of winning the general election of 1715 the Whig government found itself confronting a rebellion aimed at placing the son of James II on the throne. A combination of military vacillation by the Scottish generals and the

---

[1] On political manoeuvring between 1716 and 1722 see Plumb 1967 and Champion 2005.
[2] On government and opposition between 1725 and 1742 see Foord 1964, pp. 161–200.
[3] On the negotiations of 1741–2 see Foord 1964, pp. 200–31.
[4] See Gerrard 1994, pp. 44–5; Brewer 1976, pp. 3–8.

greater strength of the Hanoverian army soon brought the rebellion to an end, but even after this failure the Jacobite threat remained.[5] There was a further attempted rebellion in 1719, and in 1721 the high Tory Bishop of Rochester, Francis Atterbury, committed himself to organising an uprising against the regime.[6] Meanwhile the most conservative among the Anglican supporters of the Tories continued to preach the need for passive obedience, thereby implicitly impugning the Revolution Settlement. A number of sermons were published in the immediate aftermath of the Jacobite rebellion in which it was strongly implied that there should have been no active resistance to the invasion,[7] and further sermons on the divine origins of political power and the duty of absolute submission were still being published more than a decade later.[8]

More serious was the fact that, as soon as Walpole managed to entrench himself in power, the attacks specifically directed against the Whig administration began to increase in intensity.[9] These years saw the rise to notoriety of a merciless group of satirists whom the government could do little to silence or match.[10] Jonathan Swift in his *Gulliver's travels* of 1726 lampooned Walpole as Flimnap, the lord high treasurer of Lilliput and the leader of a people entirely without stature. Livy had referred in his *History* (in Holland's translation of 1600) to the 'foolish flimflams' used by some speakers to distract the Senate,[11] and the figure of Flimnap is similarly viewed as foolish and absurd.[12] But he is also described as malicious and filled with enmity, and is shown to be treacherous and cruel.[13] John Gay went on to portray Walpole with no less hostility in his *Beggar's opera* of 1728 as Macheath, the corrupt and endlessly deceiving hero and villain of the piece. Soon after this, and most contemptuously of all, Walpole was mocked and dismissed by Alexander Pope in *The dunciad* as the man most likely to turn the whole of England into a land of dunces.[14]

The same years saw the re-emergence of a radical attack on the Whig administration from the real Whigs or commonwealthmen, who now liked to describe themselves as untainted Whigs by contrast with the court Whigs who were running and ruining the country.[15] Several of the most prominent commonwealthmen of the 1690s returned to the fray.

---

[5] See Colley 1982, pp. 25–50; Wilson 1998, pp. 93–106.
[6] On the Atterbury plot see Cruickshanks and Erskine-Hill 2004.
[7] See, for example, Mynors 1716; Bedford 1717.
[8] See, for example, *An excellent sermon* 1733; Southcomb 1735; Smith 1742.
[9] On opposition in Parliament see Foord 1964, pp. 111–59; on popular opposition see Wilson 1998, pp. 106–36.
[10] On Swift, Gay and Pope in the 1720s see Goldgar 1976, pp. 28–86.
[11] Livy 1600, p. 227.   [12] Swift 2003, pp. 39–40.   [13] Swift 2003, pp. 52, 62, 64, 66.
[14] Pope 2011, p. 289, ll. 599–604.   [15] See Trenchard and Gordon 1995, p. 120.

These included Robert Molesworth, who had followed his *Account of Denmark* with a translation of François Hotman's *Franco-Gallia* in 1711, the first English version of one of the most revolutionary monarchomach treatises from the period of the French religious wars. In 1721 Molesworth reissued his translation with a new introduction in which he offered what he described as a public profession of his political faith as a real Whig.[16] Meanwhile John Trenchard returned to political life in the years shortly before his death in 1723, becoming a member of Parliament and joining with Thomas Gordon to write their series of *Cato's letters*, which began to appear in *The London Journal* at the end of 1720 and were published as a four-volume book in 1724.[17]

These writers pursued several lines of attack, but they largely continued to focus on the same themes as in the 1690s. The basic principle on which they took their stand was that our greatest blessing, and the key to our happiness, lies in being able to live in a free state in which we enjoy 'the liberties of a free people'.[18] Trenchard and Gordon describe their aim in *Cato's letters* as seeking 'to maintain and explain the glorious principle of liberty, and to expose the arts of those who would darken or destroy them'.[19] A sequence of letters at the end of their second volume is wholly given over to what they describe as 'dissertations on liberty'.[20] Here they reiterate the familiar claim – drawing on Locke[21] – that liberty consists in having the power to act according to your independent will, and hence without being condemned to live 'at the mere mercy of another'.[22] A free person is 'sole lord and arbiter of his own private actions', and is able 'to think what he will, and act as he thinks', and live 'happily and independently'.[23] The contrast to which Trenchard and Gordon repeatedly return is between living in freedom and living in submission to any form of arbitrary power.[24]

Still following the same well-established train of thought, they next explain what it means to live under arbitrary rule. This is the condition of anyone who is subject to a form of power that can be exercised at the 'mere will and pleasure' – including 'the wanton and brutish pleasure' – of

---

[16] [Molesworth] 1721, p. vii.
[17] On Trenchard and Gordon see Robbins 1959, pp. 111–21; Hamowy 1990; Ward 2004, pp. 288–304; Higgins 2005.
[18] Trenchard and Gordon 1995, pp. 123, 179.
[19] Trenchard and Gordon 1995, p. 269. For their attack on the arts of selfish citizens see Burtt 1992, pp. 64–86.
[20] Trenchard and Gordon 1995, pp. 405–93.
[21] Locke's account of the freedom of the state of nature is paraphrased in Trenchard and Gordon 1995, pp. 406–7.
[22] Trenchard and Gordon 1995, pp. 427, 430.
[23] Trenchard and Gordon 1995, pp. 427, 429, 483.
[24] Trenchard and Gordon 1995, pp. 417, 426, 437–8, 443, 446–7, 451.

those who possess it.[25] To live under arbitrary rule is thus to live in circumstances in which 'all things must depend upon the humour of the prince'.[26] As they underline, citing Tacitus, what they are describing is a form of 'absolute discretion', and hence a form of 'power without control'.[27] The plight of those who live under such conditions is that they are condemned to 'a continual state of uncertainty and wretchedness' in which there is 'no settled rule of right or wrong'.[28] To live under such a government is to be wholly bereft of your freedom to act according to your own will, and is thus to live as a slave.[29]

If the mere fact of living under arbitrary rule has the effect of reducing us to servitude, the upholding of liberty must require that everyone be kept secure from the possibility of falling into such a state of dependence. It is not sufficient for liberty that our rulers should refrain from exercising arbitrary power or happen to exercise it with benignity. It is necessary that no such power should exist, so that we are able to live secure in the knowledge that there is nothing precarious about our enjoyment of liberty.[30]

For the real Whigs, the foremost constitutional question is accordingly how we can hope to avoid subjection and dependence while living as subjects of sovereign states. Here too they rehearse a familiar set of answers. The first requirement is that the laws alone should rule. If liberty is to be upheld, the people 'must have no masters but the laws'.[31] They must be governed entirely 'by fixed rules and known statutes', and nothing must be 'left to chance or the humours of men in authority'.[32] A second requirement is that, when a government enacts laws, it must be animated by a virtuous willingness to uphold the common good. Molesworth in the introduction to his *Franco-Gallia* of 1721 had laid much emphasis on the value of having a constitution in which 'the good of the whole is taken care of by the whole'.[33] We must have 'no interest but that of the public' and make sure to act 'for the public good'.[34] Trenchard and Gordon speak no less forcefully about the importance of public spiritedness[35] – which they describe as 'the highest virtue' – and about the indispensable need to cultivate this quality as a means 'to

---

[25] Trenchard and Gordon 1995, pp. 405, 433, 439.
[26] Trenchard and Gordon 1995, p. 475.    [27] Trenchard and Gordon 1995, pp. 550, 557.
[28] Trenchard and Gordon 1995, pp. 430, 437, 445.
[29] Trenchard and Gordon 1995, pp. 430–2, 438, 456.
[30] Trenchard and Gordon 1995, pp. 267, 426–35.
[31] Trenchard and Gordon 1995, p. 484.    [32] Trenchard and Gordon 1995, pp. 107, 186.
[33] [Molesworth] 1721, p. viii.    [34] [Molesworth] 1721, pp. xv, xxi, xxii.
[35] But not always consistently. See Trenchard and Gordon 1995, pp. 271, 418.

maintain the people in liberty, plenty, ease and security'.[36] One further requirement is that that the people must be able to give their consent to the requirements of the law. If they are unable to do so, the effect will be to impose the law on them by a will other than their own, thereby reducing them to the condition of slaves. If, however, they are able to express their consent through elected representatives, then the law will count as an expression of their will, so that they will remain free in obeying it.[37]

As these writers reflect on this range of requirements, they begin to express considerable fears about the extent to which the English constitution is being corrupted. Here Molesworth had already argued that the gravest danger arises from the maintenance of standing armies. Such forces will always 'be subservient to the will of a tyrant', and will thereby 'contribute towards the enslaving the nation'.[38] Trenchard and Gordon echo these anxieties, returning to the issue that Trenchard had singled out in his contributions to the debates of the 1690s. They observe with revulsion that 'all parts of Europe which are enslaved have been enslaved by armies', and that 'it is absolutely impossible that any nation which keeps them amongst themselves can long preserve their liberties'.[39]

The real Whigs are no less concerned about the Septennial Act of 1716 and the resulting decrease in the frequency of Parliaments. Molesworth explains that every real Whig 'looks upon frequent Parliaments as such a fundamental part of the constitution that even no Parliament can part with this right'.[40] He insists that the only sane choice, from the point of view of preserving our liberties, is between 'high Whiggism', which calls for annual elections, and 'low Whiggism', which asks for annual meetings of triennially elected Parliaments.[41] Trenchard and Gordon agree that the people 'cannot otherwise preserve their liberties' than by choosing representatives who are 'either so numerous that there can be no means of corrupting the majority, or so often changed that there can be no time to do it'.[42] This prompts them to issue a series of warnings about the threats to liberty posed by pensioners and placemen in government, whose numbers have been dangerously increased by the shift to septennial Parliaments. They treat it 'as a rule for all nations to consider' that 'the

---

[36] Trenchard and Gordon 1995, pp. 128, 130, 250–1. Taking Trenchard and Gordon as his chief example, Pocock marks a strong contrast between their 'commonwealth' preoccupation with civic virtue and a 'juristic' emphasis on rights. See Pocock 1985, pp. 39–41, 43–5. But Trenchard and Gordon repeatedly stress the rights of the people, especially their right to liberty, to hold property and to judge the conduct of their government. See Trenchard and Gordon 1995, pp. 405, 409–10, 416, 427.

[37] Trenchard and Gordon 1995, pp. 126, 484.  [38] [Molesworth] 1721, p. xxv.

[39] Trenchard and Gordon 1995, pp. 671, 682; cf. also p. 439.

[40] [Molesworth] 1721, p. xvi.  [41] [Molesworth] 1721, p. xvii.

[42] Trenchard and Gordon 1995, p. 421.

more bribery, the more mischief', and they warn that 'where government is degenerating into jobbing, it quickly runs into tyranny and dissolution'.[43]

\*\*\*\*\*\*\*\*\*\*

During the latter half of the 1720s a further and almost paradoxical line of attack on Walpole's administration began to win even greater prominence. A number of Tory writers began to appropriate the themes of the commonwealthmen in their attacks on the Whig regime.[44] Here the pre-eminent propagandist was Lord Bolingbroke, who had supported the Jacobite uprising in 1715 and after fleeing to France had briefly served as secretary of state to the Old Pretender.[45] Bolingbroke was permitted to return to England in 1723, although he was excluded from sitting in Parliament, and shortly afterwards he began his campaign against Walpole's government in *The Craftsman*, the newspaper he founded in 1726 with Nicholas Amhurst as editor.[46] Bolingbroke's first major contribution took the form of a series of articles published between September 1730 and May 1731 and eventually issued in book form as *Remarks on the history of England*. Meanwhile he went on to write *A dissertation upon parties*, which appeared in *The Craftsman* between October 1733 and December 1734 and as a book in the following year.[47]

Bolingbroke chiefly focuses in his *Remarks* on a number of claims about the English constitution that had been highlighted in the 1690s by Whig writers such as George Petyt and James Tyrrell. He argues that the basic principles of free government were already established under the Saxon constitution, in which political power was jointly wielded by the kings, lords and freemen. This arrangement ensured that 'the great affairs of state were directed by the whole body of the nation', in which the rights of the people were 'carried to a very great height'.[48] Bolingbroke then concentrates on the attempts of some kings to encourage faction and assume arbitrary powers, and the opposition of those who were still animated by a true sense of the public interest.[49] The spirit of faction became overwhelming in the Wars of the Roses, after which the early Tudors moved in the direction of absolute government.[50] But then came

---

[43] Trenchard and Gordon 1995, p. 197.
[44] On this development, and Bolingbroke's role in it, see the contrasting accounts in Burtt 1992; Gerrard 1994; and Skinner 2002c.
[45] Armitage 1997, p. xxvi.
[46] Armitage 1997, p. xxvii. For Bolingbroke's theory of party see Skjönsberg 2016. On Bolingbroke and the campaign against Walpole see Colley 1982, pp. 209–16; Skjönsberg 2021, pp. 77–110.
[47] Armitage 1997, p. xxvii.    [48] Bolingbroke 1752, pp. 43–5.
[49] Bolingbroke 1752, pp. 50–63, 96, 114–15.    [50] Bolingbroke 1752, pp. 74–99.

the stupendous reign of Queen Elizabeth, in which the excellence of the constitution was gloriously displayed.[51] The limitations 'necessary to render monarchy consistent with public liberty' were all observed, the queen 'asked nothing which would have been refused by the people', and the national interest was fully served. Supported by the people's sense of what conduces to the public good, the queen reigned as 'the head of the freest people on earth'.[52] Bolingbroke briefly concludes with the collapse into faction under the early Stuarts, the increasing exercise of arbitrary power and the eventual catastrophe of civil war, for which the tyrannical conduct of James I is largely blamed.[53]

With his *Dissertation upon parties* Bolingbroke focuses more specifically on the constitutional issues already emphasised by the real Whigs in the 1690s and again in the early 1720s. He begins by pronouncing that the old divisions between Whig and Tory are at an end. Almost everyone now agrees about the powers of the people, and about 'the real and permanent blessings of liberty', especially when they are 'diffused through a whole nation'.[54] He goes on to argue, in full agreement with the Whig analysis, that to speak of someone as free is to say that they are 'governed by their own will' as opposed to being 'exposed to the arbitrary will of other men', which is the condition not of subjects but of slaves.[55] To which he adds, closely following Trenchard and Gordon, that what it means to live under the arbitrary will of others is to live in submission to a form of power which is 'without control' and thus is capable of being exercised entirely 'at pleasure'.[56]

There are further echoes of the Whig analysis when Bolingbroke turns to consider how freedom can best be upheld. He first declares that 'true liberty' must be 'liberty stated and ascertained by law, in equal opposition to popular licence and arbitrary will'.[57] We must never do anything 'to let the arbitrary will of our prince loose from the restraints of law'.[58] If we become dependent on the mere will of our prince we forfeit our liberty, since 'private liberty cannot be deemed secure under a government wherein law, the proper and sole security of it, is dependent on will'.[59] The people must in addition be given a share, through their representatives, in the making of laws. This arrangement alone sustains 'that mixture of monarchical, aristocratic and democratical power' within the

---

[51] Bolingbroke 1752, pp. 120, 127–8.
[52] Bolingbroke 1752, pp. 128–9, 142, 147, 168–70.
[53] Bolingbroke 1752, pp. 194–5, 214, 217, 224, 252.    [54] Bolingbroke 1997, p. 107.
[55] Bolingbroke 1997, pp. 126–7. On slavery as the antonym of liberty see also pp. 85, 89, 112, 139 and 168.
[56] Bolingbroke 1997, pp. 89, 107, 126–7.    [57] Bolingbroke 1997, p. 112.
[58] Bolingbroke 1997, p. 170.    [59] Bolingbroke 1997, p. 170.

constitution 'on which the preservation of liberty depends'.[60] Bolingbroke also underlines a further claim he had already defended at length in his *Remarks*. The people must be imbued with a virtuous willingness to serve the public good. Here, as he puts it, 'the civil faith of the old Whigs' is 'consented to by the Country party', whose spokesmen have also 'drawn their pens in the cause of truth, virtue and liberty' against the 'ignoble asserters of corruption' among the court Whigs and their dangerous neglect of the common good in pursuit of self-interest.[61]

Bolingbroke's overriding concern is to lay bare the various forms of corruption employed by the court Whigs, whom he stigmatises as 'friends to the government and enemies to the constitution'.[62] Here too he closely follows the lines of attack already mapped out by the real Whigs. The government and its supporters plead for the maintenance of a standing army, although this wicked policy is known to be incompatible with public liberty.[63] They interfere with the integrity of parliamentary elections, although this is one of the essentials of British liberty.[64] And they jeopardise the security of our liberty by ignoring the fact that the plain intent of the constitution is that there should be frequent sessions of Parliament and frequent new Parliaments.[65] These policies are altering the balance of the constitution, undermining the independence of Parliament and thereby subverting 'the essence of our constitution and by consequence of our liberty'.[66] This final danger Bolingbroke takes to be the gravest of all. He attacks the power of the chief minister to award pensions and places to members of Parliament in return for supporting his policies, and later criticises the king for using the civil list to create 'a vast number of new dependents on the crown', thereby opening the way to 'universal corruption'.[67] Echoing Swift, Bolingbroke concludes that the English constitution, which has managed over so many centuries 'to resist the united efforts of so many giants', may be about to be 'demolished by a race of pigmies'.[68]

✳✳✳✳✳✳✳✳✳✳

Bolingbroke's warning was a dire one, but by the time he voiced it the Whig administration had become much more skilled at responding to its critics and enemies.[69] Towards the end of the 1720s a forceful counterattack was launched in a number of pro-government newspapers covertly

---

[60] Bolingbroke 1997, pp. 125, 135.    [61] Bolingbroke 1997, pp. 4, 8–9; cf. also p. 89.
[62] Bolingbroke 1997, pp. 91, 94.    [63] Bolingbroke 1997, pp. 10, 92–3.
[64] Bolingbroke 1997, pp. 101, 124.    [65] Bolingbroke 1997, pp. 103–4.
[66] Bolingbroke 1997, p. 169.    [67] Bolingbroke 1997, pp. 93–7 and 170–5.
[68] Bolingbroke 1997, p. 94.
[69] For a survey of the pro-government Whig case see Dickinson 1977, pp. 121–62. Browning 1982 prefers to speak of court Whigs. This is admittedly more elegant than

financed by Walpole.[70] William Arnall, who had trained as a lawyer and became the most highly paid of the ministerial writers, began contributing to *The Free Briton* in 1729 and also published several tracts in support of the regime.[71] These efforts duly won him a place in Pope's *Dunciad*, in which we are told that no one has been 'more active in the dirty dance'.[72] James Pitt, the most prominent of the pro-government Whig journalists after Arnall's death in 1736, regularly contributed to *The Gazetteer* in tones of uncritical support for Walpole's policies.[73] While many would doubtless have agreed with the Inn-keeper in Fielding's *Joseph Andrews* that *The Gazetteer* was likewise dirty and abusive, it was probably the most widely read newspaper of its time.[74]

The government also gained extensive support from the Anglican establishment, and especially from a number of clergymen who were willing to address legal and political issues when preaching at Assize courts. Thomas Coney, prebendary of Wells Cathedral, defended the government against all charges of misconduct in an uncritically loyal address to the Somerset Assizes in 1731.[75] James Bate, the rector of Deptford, used his sermon to the Kent Assizes in 1734 to denounce the opposition as cynical and seditious.[76] John Myonnet, the rector of Swayfield in Lincolnshire, when preaching at the Kingston Assizes in the same year, similarly attacked what he described as the groundless discontent being fomented by treasonous men.[77] Speaking more generally, George Osborne, the vicar of Battersea in London, underlined the duty of respect and 'the necessity of submission to the higher powers' when he too spoke at the Kingston Assizes in 1735.[78]

Nor did the Whig ministry lack for weighty political support. Sir William Yonge, one of the commissioners of the Treasury, published an outraged denunciation of *The Craftsman* in his *Sedition and defamation displayed* in 1731.[79] Lord Hervey, vice chamberlain of the royal household, produced a series of tracts in the early 1730s defending the probity and effectiveness of Walpole's government.[80] And David Hume frequently aligned himself with the ministerial cause in his *Essays moral*

---

speaking of pro-government Whigs, but my reason for preferring the latter formula is that the former was used at the time mainly as a term of denigration.

[70] For detailed accounts see Harris 1987 and Targett 1994.

[71] See especially [Arnall] 1731 and [Arnall] 1735. For Arnall's contributions (which were signed 'Francis Walsingham') see Horne 1980.

[72] Pope 2011, p. 259, l. 319.

[73] See Haig 1960. Pitt's contributions were signed 'Francis Osborne'. He is satirised as 'Mother Osborne' in Pope's *Dunciad*. See Pope 2011, p. 259, l. 312.

[74] Fielding 1999, p. 198.    [75] Coney 1731, pp. 12–15.    [76] Bate 1734, pp. 17–19.

[77] Myonnet 1734, pp. 17–22.    [78] Osborne 1735, pp. 2, 4.

[79] [Yonge] 1731. For the attribution see BL catalogue *sub* Pulteney 1731.

[80] On Hervey see Browning 1982, pp. 35–66 and Moore 2000.

*and political* of 1741 and 1742.[81] Hume proudly remarks in his introductory advertisement that, although his readers may condemn his abilities, they cannot fail to 'approve of my moderation and impartiality in my method of handling political subjects'.[82] Hume undoubtedly cultivated a moderate tone, but his claim to impartiality seems more questionable. He frequently echoes the arguments already developed by the pro-government Whig writers in the 1730s, and he no less frequently speaks firmly on their side of the case.

When these writers turn to mount their critique of Tory and Country party ideology, they like to make it clear that some of the opposition's arguments strike them as too absurd to take seriously. This was the attitude they preferred to adopt in the face of the continuing attacks on standing armies, and throughout the 1730s most of them chose to ignore the issue. There were two arguments, however, that the pro-government writers felt obliged to address with full seriousness and at considerable length. One was the claim that the preservation of free government depends on a virtuous willingness to place the good of the community above any considerations of private advantage. Bernard Mandeville had already won notoriety with *The fable of the bees* in 1714 for challenging this piety, and for arguing that private vices can be the source of public benefits.[83] When he reissued his fable in a revised and extended form in 1723 he went still further, adding a number of satirical comments on the concept of public virtue and the alleged value of 'public spiritedness', while mocking the hypocrisy of those who take themselves to be of a superior social class because of their willingness to forgo private advantage and act without seeming to pursue 'any visible interest of their own'.[84]

Mandeville's comments provoked outrage, but it was not long before a milder version of the same challenge began to be mounted by a number of pro-government Whigs.[85] Hervey produced the most searching response, which he published in 1732 as *The public virtue of former times and the present age compared.* He begins by conceding that, throughout the constitutional upheavals of the seventeenth century, the prevalence of a noble public spiritedness was of the utmost importance. The intention of the court was to engross all power, so that 'many violations were actually committed on the rights of the subject' and 'arbitrary measures'

---

[81] Hume 1741 and Hume 1742 appeared anonymously, but in 1748 Hume issued a third volume stating that it 'completes the former edition in two volumes octavo by David Hume Esq.'. See Hume 1748, title page.

[82] Hume 1741, p. iv.    [83] [Mandeville] 1714, title page.

[84] [Mandeville] 1723, pp. 31–4. On this development see Douglass 2023.

[85] For the pro-government Whigs on civic virtue see Burtt 1992, pp. 102–27.

were increasingly enforced. It was indispensable that there should have been men of 'unwearied vigilance, courage, and patience' ready to oppose the violence and stratagems adopted by the Stuart kings in pursuit of their tyrannical ends. Fortunately a large number of brave patriots had proved willing, at the cost of exposing 'their persons and estates to innumerable hardships and dangers', to do everything necessary to ensure that their fellow citizens and their posterity were not deprived of their birthright of liberty.[86]

Nowadays, however, there is no longer any need to exercise such qualities. 'We have now the most excellent laws to secure the rights of the people [and] to protect their persons and properties from all sorts of violence.' Under the rule of the Stuart kings these laws were not in being, but with the Revolution Settlement 'everything necessary to adjust and establish our liberty' has been achieved. No longer do we need to rely on the civic virtue of our fellow citizens to ensure that our rights and liberties are settled and maintained.[87] These happy effects are now guaranteed by the constitution itself, which functions as a machine in which the crown and executive, working with the concurrence of Parliament, serve as 'the grand spring that has kept the whole machine on work'.[88]

Hervey's contrast was soon reiterated by other supporters of the Whig regime. We encounter echoes of his argument in Bate's *Divine and human laws* of 1734,[89] in Myonnet's *Nature and advantages of civil liberty* of the same year,[90] and above all in Arnall's *Opposition no proof of patriotism* of 1735. Arnall asks how freedom can be undermined by corruption to such a degree that liberty is replaced by slavery.[91] He concedes that this can readily happen if 'one man or a few men' are 'invested with sovereign power', or if the government lies in the hands 'of despotic princes who rule by mere will'.[92] But this cannot happen in a nation that succeeds in 'preserving itself by laws of its own making, and power of its own keeping, or its own limiting'. Explaining why this is so, Arnall begins to write in tones strongly reminiscent of Mandeville. The great difference is that there will be 'numerous representatives and legislators who are themselves parties and sharers' in what is decided for everyone. Where this is so, the legislators will be 'interested in the preservation of the whole' and 'will for their own sakes preserve the whole'. Even if – perhaps especially

---

[86] [Hervey] 1732, pp. 4–5, 12–14, 23.     [87] [Hervey] 1732, p. 6.

[88] [Hervey] 1732, pp. 19, 30. See Bourke 2016, stressing that this mainstream Whig view of the British constitution embodies an element of popular sovereignty. For different perspectives on the relations between free citizens and the state in the early modern period see the chapters by Iain Hampsher-Monk, Antti Tahvanainen, Rosanna Cox and Lena Halldenius in Skinner and van Gelderen 2013, pp. 105–243.

[89] Bate 1734, pp. 12, 17–18.     [90] Myonnet 1734, pp. 8–12.

[91] [Arnall] 1735, pp. 22–3.     [92] [Arnall] 1735, p. 23.

if – they are activated exclusively by their own self-interest, 'it is not probable they will sacrifice themselves by sacrificing their own and public liberty'.[93] So long as power is 'naturally distributed and balanced' so that 'the governing and the governed are equally interested in the preservation of each other', the resulting system will serve in itself to ensure that the rights and liberties of the people are upheld.[94]

Hume follows a similar line of argument in his essay of 1741 *That politics may be reduced to a science*.[95] He begins by contending that 'all absolute governments must very much depend on the administration', and thus on the humour and temper of the specific individual in control. But a free government 'would be a most glaring absurdity if the particular checks and controls provided by the constitution had really no influence'. The intention lying behind these controls, and 'the real effect where they are wisely constituted', is to make it 'the interest even of bad men to operate for the public good'.[96] Hume goes on to refine this familiar Whig argument by using it to enunciate one of the scientific laws that can be derived, he believes, from a study of political life. 'So great is the force of laws, and of particular forms of government, and so little dependence have they on the humours and temper of men, that consequences as general and as certain may be deduced from them, on most occasions, as any which the mathematical sciences can afford us.'[97]

The other criticism that the pro-government writers were above all anxious to fend off concerned the award of pensions and places to members of Parliament in return for supporting the regime. The initial and brazen reaction of the government's supporters was simply to deny the charge. Hervey in his *Observations on the writings of The Craftsman* of 1730 disdainfully notes that the corruption of the times has become a fashionable theme, but insists that all such accusations are 'utterly false'. He claims that 'not one single instance' has ever been given 'of solicitation made or favour shown by the force of money'.[98] Bate speaks with no less scorn about how the opposition is fixated on 'a few pretended small errors of government'. Although we are told 'much of bribery and corruption by places and preferment', these are the merest calumnies propagated in 'the seditious pamphlets with which the world is daily pestered'.[99]

---

[93] [Arnall] 1735, pp. 24.    [94] [Arnall] 1735, p. 25.

[95] For a contrasting account see Forbes 1975, who claims (pp. 225, 229) that Hume is here questioning an 'all-pervasive' commonplace.

[96] Hume 1741, p. 29. This argument was much reiterated when the pro-government Whig case was restated in the mid-1740s. See, for example, Ballard 1746, pp. 10–11; Dobson 1747, pp. 29–31; Head 1747, pp. 9–15; Pendlebury 1746, pp. 45–52.

[97] Hume 1741, pp. 29–30.    [98] [Hervey] 1730, pp. 22–3.    [99] Bate 1734, pp. 17–18.

Later the pro-government writers developed a more challenging response. They began to call on the opposition to recognise the need to inject some realism into the argument. Hervey published a tract on *Ancient and modern liberty* in 1734 in which he pointed out that the opposition are in effect asking for government to be conducted without expense.[100] Writing in the following year, Arnall put the point more bluntly: 'Can there be any government without places?'[101] He answered that it is little better than 'a sort of frenzy' to 'traduce men in place because they are in place' without acknowledging that no government can hope to function 'without places and men to fill them'.[102] Hume closely echoes the argument in his essay on the independence of Parliament. He admits that the powers of the crown and executive cannot fail to be extensive, and that it is easy to describe their influence 'by the invidious appellations of corruption and dependence'. But this is to ignore the fact that 'some degree and some kind of it are inseparable from the very nature of the constitution, and necessary to the preservation of our mixed government'.[103] Still more worldly was the tone adopted by Samuel Squire, the vociferously Whig archdeacon of Bath, in his *Letter to a Tory friend*.[104] We need to recognise that 'the great work of government must go on', and that if those in charge find that 'saints are not to be had', then they 'must make use of sinners'.[105] We need to ask how many people are prepared to 'adhere to virtue without consideration of the reward'.[106] Rather than complaining, we ought to 'lament the hard necessity to which the iniquity of the times may have driven the government'.[107] 'These observations', Squire concludes, 'may be deplorable, but they are founded in truth.'[108]

### The Whig Victory

While the pro-government writers were anxious to defend the adminis-tration against its numerous enemies, they were much more concerned to lay out their own views about the ideal of a free state. When they turn to this task it becomes clear that they have two underlying purposes in mind. One is to establish that, whatever their enemies may say, the current regime has at no point betrayed the 1688 settlement. The principles of the Whigs now in power do not differ in any significant degree from the commitments of even the most exacting among the so-called real Whigs. Their further aim is to show that, as Samuel Squire insists in his *Letter to*

---

[100] [Hervey] 1734, pp. 2–3.    [101] [Arnall] 1735, p. 6.    [102] [Arnall] 1735, p. 22.
[103] Hume 1741, p. 89.    [104] See *ODNB*, vol. 52, pp. 19–20.    [105] [Squire] 1746, p. 22.
[106] [Squire] 1746, p. 23.    [107] [Squire] 1746, p. 24.    [108] [Squire] 1746, p. 24.

*a Tory friend*, while the opposition have merely shown 'perpetual discontent at every step and measure of the government', the Whigs in power have succeeded in putting their principles into practice, thereby creating a perfect model of the institutions of a free state.[109]

A number of pro-government writers began to develop this positive case in the course of the 1730s, but it was in the following decade that the greatest volume of Whig political commentary appeared. The spur was the threat of a new Jacobite rebellion, which finally materialised in July 1745 when Charles Edward Stuart, the grandson of James II, landed in Scotland and quickly raised a large military force. By early December the Jacobite army had marched as far south as Derby, with the route to London open and almost unguarded. The new year, however, saw the crisis turn to the decisive advantage of the Whig regime. The rebels hesitated, and in January decided to retreat. At first they managed to evade the pursuing English army under the Duke of Cumberland, but in April he inflicted a final and brutal defeat at the Battle of Culloden, and by September the Young Pretender had fled to a lifetime of exile.[110]

Meanwhile numerous defenders of the Hanoverian regime had already fought back with the pen as well as the sword. The years between 1745 and 1747 saw an unparalleled outpouring of propaganda in which the ministerial arguments of the previous decade were revisited and more extensively explored. A number of different groups came together to produce this reaffirmation of the pro-government case. But it is notable that, among those who focused on questions about civil liberty, it was the clerical writers who made by far the greatest contribution to the debate. They included many leading Dissenting ministers who were anxious to defend the Whig Toleration Act of 1689 against the danger of persecution that a return of the Catholic Stuarts to the throne might bring.[111] Hume in his essay *Of the parties of Great Britain* of 1741 had seen it as inevitable that 'Dissenters of all kinds' will always be enemies of the ruling Whigs, but four years later this had emphatically ceased to be the case.[112] Samuel Chandler, perhaps the most prominent Presbyterian minister in London, preached a much-publicised sermon at the Old Jewry in September 1745 on *The duty of good men*, in which he urged 'zeal and fortitude' in defence of the government.[113] He was followed by Andrew Richardson, a Scottish Presbyterian minister, who delivered two fiercely anti-Jacobite sermons on *A free and an arbitrary government* at the end of the year.[114] During the ensuing months the importance of combining civil liberty with loyalty to

---

[109] [Squire] 1746, pp. 5, 8, 59.    [110] For a detailed account see Riding 2017.
[111] On the high level of support from Dissenters see Clark 1994, pp. 166–7, 318–21.
[112] Hume 1741, p. 123.    [113] Chandler 1745, p. 21. On Chandler see *ODNB*, vol. 2, p. 8.
[114] On the date of publication see Richardson 1746, pp. 1–5.

the established regime became a dominant theme among Dissenting preachers. John Brekell, the pastor of the Presbyterian Church in Liverpool, published his *Liberty and loyalty* in 1746, in which he presented (in the words of his subtitle) 'a defence and explication of subjection to the present government'.[115] Later in the same year William Pendlebury, a Dissenting minister from Yorkshire, addressed his congregation on *The fatal consequences of arbitrary and despotic power*.[116] Another north country Dissenter, Joshua Dobson, published a sermon on religious and civil liberty in 1647 in which he praised 'the excellencies of our present happy constitution', and especially the fact that 'the powers and privileges of our Parliaments denominate us a free people'.[117]

It was among the Anglican clergy, however, that the most extensive support for the government was voiced during the ominous months before the return of peace in the spring of 1746. Some of the most conspicuous Whig prelates now took to the stage. Benjamin Hoadly's much-admired sermon of 1708 on *The happiness of the present establishment* was reprinted in Edinburgh in 1745.[118] Thomas Herring, the Archbishop of York, delivered and published a violent harangue on the wickedness of the rebellion later in the same year.[119] And William Warburton, who later became Bishop of Gloucester, undoubtedly helped his career along its path with two patriotic sermons on the political implications of 'the present unnatural rebellion' in 1745 and 1746.[120]

During the same period a large number of Anglican sermons on the dangers of popery and the virtues of the established government were preached up and down the country.[121] As in the 1730s, however, many of the most penetrating were presented not in churches but in the form of sermons preached at Assizes. Leonard Howard, chaplain to the Prince of Wales, spoke at the Surrey Assizes in the spring of 1745 on *The advantages of a free people*,[122] while the local rector, Reeve Ballard, gave a sermon on *The necessity of magistracy* later in 1745 and another on *The rule of obedience* in August 1746.[123] Still more notable were two addresses delivered in Carlisle Cathedral to coincide with the special Assizes set up in September 1746 to try the leaders of the rebellion. Erasmus Head, prebendary of the cathedral,

---

[115] Brekell 1746. On Brekell see Wicksteed 1849, p. 124.
[116] Pendlebury 1746. On Pendlebury see Wicksteed 1849, p. 124.
[117] Dobson 1747, pp. 29, 31.
[118] Hoadly 1745 [1708]. On Hoadly see Browning 1982, pp. 67–88.
[119] Herring 1745. On Herring see Browning 1982, pp. 89–116.
[120] See *ODNB*, vol. 57, pp. 268–74.
[121] See, for example, Barr 1746 (Lincolnshire); Bradford 1746 (Devonshire); Harris 1745 (Kent); Ibbetson 1746 (Yorkshire); Kerrich 1746 (Norfolk); Lane 1746 (Herefordshire); Wiche 1745 (Wiltshire).
[122] Howard 1745.     [123] Ballard 1745 and Ballard 1746.

began by discussing the importance of loyalty[124] and was followed by John Brown, at this time a young canon of the cathedral, who gave two remarkable sermons on *The mutual connexion between religious truth and civil freedom*.[125]

After the defeat of the rebellion, a Royal Proclamation commanded that 9 October 1746 should be observed as a day of thanksgiving to God for upholding the liberties of the people and rescuing them from popery and 'arbitrary principles'.[126] With this announcement the crown in effect called upon the established Church to voice its approbation for the government's handling of the crisis. The outcome was a dutiful outpouring of patriotic sentiment in scores of sermons, many of which were immediately published.[127] A majority simply asked for the duty of thanksgiving (a favourite title) to be fully acknowledged.[128] But a number of leading churchmen took the opportunity to speak about the political values safeguarded by the defeat of the Jacobite cause. They included Arthur Sykes, the prebendary of Winchester, and Isaac Maddox, the Bishop of Worcester, both of whom preached in their cathedrals on the appointed day about civil liberty and the benefits of free government.[129]

When these pro-government writers of the 1730s and 1740s outline their views about the character of a free state, they generally begin by asking how legitimate governments arise. Here one striking development was that even the clerical writers now exhibit nothing but disdain for the time-honoured answer that governments arise by divine right, and that our rulers must be treated as vicegerents of God to whom we owe unquestioning obedience. It is perhaps not surprising that the Dissenters were hostile to a doctrine so closely associated with Jacobitism,[130] but numerous Anglican spokesmen struck a similar note. John Brown impatiently objects that it is all too easy to 'dress up sordid fear and slavery in the garb of rightful obedience' and thereby 'exhibit the most diabolical tyranny under the appearance of divine right'.[131] Yet more impatiently, William Warburton waves aside what he describes as 'the jargon of indefeasible hereditary right for the king and passive obedience and non-resistance for the subject'.[132] Hume is left ruminating that most people by now appear to have 'divested themselves of all superstitious reverence'. 'The mere name of king commands little respect', and if

---

[124] Head 1747.    [125] Brown 1746. For Brown on liberty see Crimmins 1986.
[126] For the Proclamation see Maddox 1746, p. 7.
[127] Caudle 2012 estimates that fifty-nine such sermons were delivered.
[128] See, for example, Bellinger 1746; Clarke 1746; Kerrich 1746; Stevenson 1746.
[129] See Maddox 1746, esp. pp. 19, 30; Sykes 1746, esp. pp. 10–11, 25–6.
[130] See, for example, the denunciations in Brekell 1746, pp. 9, 13, 33 and Pendlebury 1746, p. 56.
[131] Brown 1746, pp. 9–10.    [132] Warburton 1745, p. 24.

anyone were to speak of the present king as God's vicegerent they would merely 'excite laughter in everyone'.[133]

Thinking about how legitimate governments arise, the pro-government writers are scarcely less anxious to repudiate the answer given by such Whig legal theorists as Petyt and Tyrrell at the time of the revolution and more recently restated by Bolingbroke. As we have seen, they had argued that the fundamental rights and liberties of the English people had originally been established under the ancient constitution and had subsequently been reaffirmed and more effectively guaranteed. To this contention Hervey responded as early as 1734 in his tract on *Ancient and modern liberty*. He largely ignores the cherished landmarks in the history of the ancient constitution, and goes so far as to dismiss Magna Carta as nothing more than an attempt by the barons to tyrannise over the king.[134] When he confronts Bolingbroke's paean of praise to Queen Elizabeth for promoting the glory of England and the liberty of her subjects he rejects it with scorn. 'Never were the reins of prerogative held with a stricter hand, or the yoke of slavery faster bound upon the people's necks.' They may have been 'driven where they ought to have chosen to go, yet they were still driven', so that they never enjoyed 'the least shadow of liberty'.[135] It is nonsense, in short, to talk about 'the liberty of old England'. Before the Revolution Settlement 'there was no such thing as liberty'; there was nothing more than a succession of shifts 'from one tyrant, or one kind of tyranny, to another'.[136] It was only from the ending of James II's despotic rule in 1688 that we can date 'the birth of real liberty in this kingdom'. With the passing of the Bill of Rights in the following year, 'all those disputable points of prerogative and liberty that had hitherto been insisted on either by the crown or the people' were at last placed on a legal footing and, as Hervey puts it, finally ascertained.[137]

Hervey's analysis was soon picked up and strongly endorsed by Hume. In his essay *That politics may be reduced to a science* he agrees that the English government was basically an absolute form of rule and never a free government until the middle of the previous century.[138] This being so, he adds in his essay *Of the parties of Great Britain*, there was no free and ancient constitution for the Stuarts to undermine. Before Charles I sought to establish that the privileges of the people were mere 'concessions of his predecessors, revocable at pleasure', no settled constitutional structure had existed. Rather, the framework of the English constitution 'had lain in a kind of confusion'. It was this arrangement that the ignorant

---

[133] Hume 1741, pp. 99–100.    [134] [Hervey] 1734, p. 10.
[135] [Hervey] 1734, pp. 23, 24.    [136] [Hervey] 1734, pp. 4, 5, 6, 8.
[137] [Hervey] 1734, p. 40. Courtville 1738, p. xiii speaks in the same terms.
[138] Hume 1741, p. 29.

and ambitious Charles I fatally attempted to alter to his selfish advantage, and it was out of the resulting civil war that the elements of a free constitution eventually began to emerge.[139]

The positive answer given by most pro-government writers to the question about the origins of government was that, if we wish to understand how free states arise, we must first ask about the natural condition of mankind. Here they frequently draw on Locke's account of the condition in which we would find ourselves if we were to live outside the confines of the state, and sometimes they simply copy out the relevant passages from his *Second treatise*.[140] A generation later Locke was to be denounced for betraying the cause of liberty with his defence of chattel slavery, but to many of the pro-government writers of the 1730s and 1740s he was a revered and much-cited authority on the idea of a free state. They fully endorsed his view that the natural condition of mankind would be one in which everyone would be equally endowed with what Locke had called their rights of nature.[141] John Myonnet had already spoken in 1734 about how, 'in a state of nature', everyone would be in possession of all their natural rights, and each person would be 'at liberty to follow his own private judgment'.[142] But it was among the pro-government writers of the mid-1740s that the terminology of natural rights rose to full prominence. Among the Dissenters, we find Pendlebury referring both to our natural rights and to 'that universal liberty which every man has a just claim to in a state of nature prior to that of civil policy'.[143] Among the Anglicans, one of the most startling interventions came from Francis Potter, vicar of Burford, in a sermon preached to the University of Oxford in 1745 in which he went so far as to challenge the principle of hereditary succession on the grounds that it is destructive 'of all the natural rights of a people'.[144] Samuel Squire likewise emphasised that 'all men are by nature equal and independent', so that it must be 'the natural right of all civil societies' to be able 'to choose their own forms of government'.[145] He added with his habitual confidence that this view of rights has been 'excellently well handled by Mr Locke' and 'is too evident to be denied'.[146]

Some of these writers take the further step of describing these natural rights as rights of mankind. Although this was not a term that Locke had used in the *Second treatise*, he had argued that everyone is born with 'an

---

[139] Hume 1741, pp. 124–5.
[140] See, for example, *Loyalty to our king the safety of our country* 1745, pp. 4–5; and cf. [Locke] 1690, para. 4, p. 220, para. 125, p. 346, para. 127, p. 347 and para. 137, pp. 358–9.
[141] On the rights of nature see [Locke] 1690, para. 65, p. 282 and para. 85, p. 303; on natural rights see para. 1, p. 217, para. 82, p. 301 and para. 115, p. 337.
[142] Myonnet 1734, pp. 5–6.    [143] Pendlebury 1746, p. 41.    [144] Potter 1745, p. 26.
[145] [Squire] 1746, pp. 38–9.    [146] [Squire] 1746, pp. 40, 46.

uncontrolled enjoyment of all the rights and privileges of the law of nature equally with any other man'.[147] So the step towards talking about the rights of mankind was not a large one to take, and we duly find it taken in a number of Anglican commemorative sermons in 1746.[148] It was among the Dissenters, however, that the terminology was employed with the fullest assurance. Writing in 1745, Chandler characterised the coming battle with the Jacobites as one in which the contest would be between 'property and the most servile dependence', and would consequently be about 'the most sacred rights of mankind'.[149] Writing after the suppression of the rebellion, Richardson similarly rejoiced in the fact that 'our rights and privileges as men and Christians' have been 'secured to us by our excellent constitution', and likewise refers to these privileges as 'the natural and civil rights of mankind'.[150]

The pro-government writers next argue that, if everyone is by nature free and in full possession of their natural rights, then the only means by which a legitimate government can be founded must be by the consent of those who submit to it. They agree, in other words, that there must be a compact between the people and their designated sovereign in which the people promise obedience on condition that their rights of nature are securely upheld. It is true that several of these writers urge us to acknowledge that, as Myonnet puts it, 'men must be presumed to have parted with some of their natural rights in exchange for the greater benefits of protection, peace and safety which they enjoy in a social life, and under government and laws'.[151] For most of them, however, it is important to underline that no such relinquishment takes place when a people consents to be governed. As Head summarises in *Loyalty recommended*, rather than giving up any of their natural rights they simply transfer them into the hands of the community for the benefit of all, so that the preservation of rights becomes the great end of government.[152]

Hume parts company with the pro-government Whigs at this point, arguing in his essay *Of the original contract* in 1748 that 'nothing can be a clearer proof that a theory of this kind is erroneous than to find that it leads us into paradoxes which are repugnant to the common sentiments of mankind'.[153] But this implicit defence of absolute sovereignty is exactly what most supporters of the Whig regime wished to disavow.

---

[147] [Locke] 1690, para. 87, p. 305.
[148] See, for example, Barr 1746, p. 5; Brown 1746, pp. 19, 26; Carr 1746, p. 10.
[149] Chandler 1745, p. 36.
[150] Richardson 1746, pp. 44, 47. See also Brekell 1746, p. 33.
[151] Myonnet 1734, pp. 6–7. See also Pendlebury 1746, p. 41.    [152] Head 1747, pp. 5–6.
[153] Hume 1748, p. 54. On Hume's critique of contract theory see Buckle and Castiglione 1991.

The Dissenters were particularly anxious to establish that, as Brekell puts it, no one can ever acquire 'authority to govern independently on the choice and consent of the people', which can be signalled only by way of 'national compact and agreement'.[154] Richardson agrees that free government must always 'be considered as founded on a contract between the king and people', who will always want to bring their rulers 'under the strongest, most solemn engagements to maintain them in their rights, their liberties and properties'.[155]

Among the Anglican writers we encounter even stronger resonances of Locke's contractual account of the origins of government. According to Erasmus Head, the only lawful means by which men can 'unite together for their mutual preservation' is to establish a 'common judge to decide all controversies' by 'settled standing laws' established 'by general consent'.[156] Arthur Sykes agrees that 'a right to dominion or sovereignty over a people' can only arise 'from consent or compact; and consequently can be no more than what is conveyed in the compact'.[157] That this requirement sets strict limits to the lawful use of sovereign power is further underlined by Reeve Ballard in *The rule of obedience*. 'What Mr Locke observes on this head' is something that 'the reason of every wise and unprejudiced person must bear testimony to the truth of'. This is that 'he who has the exercise of any power by any other means than those which the laws of the community prescribes has no title to be obeyed'.[158] The whole argument was finely summarised by Edmund Trott, chaplain to the Earl of Hadinton, in a sermon to the University of Oxford in 1746:

No supreme power in states can possibly be absolutely arbitrary over the lives, fortunes and religion of the people. For as it is only the joint power of every member of the society given up to that person or assembly of people which is the legislator, it can be no more than those persons enjoyed in a state of nature before they entered into society. For nobody can transfer to another more power than he has in himself, and nobody has an absolute arbitrary power over himself or any other. The power of government, in its utmost extent, is limited to the public good of society.[159]

Some of Trott's audience were no doubt impressed by the force of his rhetoric, but it is likely that others would have known that this entire passage was transcribed almost word for word from Locke's *Second treatise of government*.[160]

The pro-government writers next consider the nature of the power established by the compact of government. The type of rule we institute,

---

[154] Brekell 1746, p. 6.      [155] Richardson 1746, pp. 5, 10.      [156] Head 1747, p. 5.
[157] Sykes 1746, pp. 13, 14, 18.      [158] Ballard 1746, p. 3.      [159] Trott 1746, pp. 20–1.
[160] Trott 1746, pp. 20–1; cf. [Locke] 1690, para. 135, pp. 355–6.

they agree, will possess two distinctive characteristics, and in laying them out they are anxious to make it clear once more that their view of lawful government in no way differs from that of the so-called real Whigs. The first principle they reiterate is that the law alone must rule. As Erasmus Head puts it, although an original contract can be used to set up different forms of government, what must always be established is the supremacy of law. 'Sovereignty, or supreme power, in every community properly resides in the constitution and the laws made agreeable thereto.' He too quotes Locke without acknowledgement, arguing that 'arbitrary monarchy, which many have accounted the only genuine and proper government, is so far from being so, that it is really no form of it at all'.[161] The reason is that 'in this case one man is supposed to have a power of treating others just as he pleases, without their having any standing law, or common judge to appeal to for redress', an arrangement that amounts to the destruction of 'the very essence of civil society'.[162]

The Dissenters no less vigorously affirm the same commitment. According to Brekell, 'the laws and constitutions of a country' constitute 'the standing rules of civil and social life' so that 'every violation of these rules is proportionably an act of sedition against the majesty of the state'.[163] Richardson makes the distinction between legal and tyrannical rule the dominant theme of his two sermons of 1746 on free and arbitrary power. First he considers 'an absolute monarch' who makes 'his own arbitrary will the sole rule of government', and follows 'no other rule than his own mere will and pleasure'.[164] 'This sort of government', he maintains, 'destroys the mutual obligation betwixt prince and people, sets the one above all law and exposes the other to slavery without redress'.[165] His second sermon contrasts this form of power with 'free government', under which 'every man's property is secured by just and equal laws, and the king is appointed by the society to be the guardian and protector of the people's rights'.[166] The outcome is a type of rule 'founded upon justice' under which 'neither king nor people hold their rights on a precarious and uncertain tenure, but on just, wholesome laws' by which the society as a whole is preserved.[167]

The other cherished Whig principle reiterated by all these writers is that the body of the people must always be given a voice in making the laws by

---

[161] Head 1747, p. 9, quoting (somewhat approximately) [Locke] 1690, para. 90, p. 308.
[162] Head 1747, p. 9.    [163] Brekell 1746, p. 25.
[164] Richardson 1746, pp. 5–6. On arbitrary rule as government 'by mere will and pleasure' see also Head 1747, p. 9; Maddox 1746, p. 24; Sykes 1746, p. 10.
[165] Richardson 1746, p. 12. On arbitrary power as uncontrolled see also Potter 1745, p. 20; Ballard 1746, p. 8.
[166] Richardson 1746, p. 28.    [167] Richardson 1746, p. 38.

which they are ruled. If the liberty of the people is to be preserved, it is indispensable that there should be a mixed constitution under which they are able, by way of representation, to play an active role in government. As Leonard Howard warns in *The advantages of a free people*, our rights will inevitably 'hang by a slender thread where the government is arbitrary' and where 'the people are unconcerned in the making and repealing of laws'. It is only when the people play a part 'in making the laws which bind them' that we can speak of them as living in liberty.[168] His words were closely echoed by Arthur Sykes in his thanksgiving sermon of the following year, in which he describes the happy state of a people 'who can make their own laws; and can enjoy the labours of their own hands, and can provide for the common safety by what appears necessary to themselves'.[169] Erasmus Head adds the crucial point that, if the people take part in making the laws, the resulting enactments may be said to form an expression of the popular will, in consequence of which everyone will be acting 'consistently with the most perfect civil freedom' in obeying them.[170] Few phrases recur more frequently in the sermons of the Anglican divines than the dictum about the importance of being 'governed by laws of your own making' if you wish to retain your liberty under government.[171]

**********

The pro-government writers usually conclude by underlining that the constitution they have been anatomising gives rise to what they describe as 'free government', the government of a free state in which the people enjoy their liberty as a free people.[172] This generally leads them to offer an explication of the concept of liberty underlying their account. Here they fully endorse the understanding of the concept that had animated every strand of Whiggism since the revolution of 1688. If there is anything of special significance about their restatement of the case, it is only that they are the last political writers in the anglophone tradition who are able to present their analysis as if its validity is self-evident and unquestionable.

The account they offer pivots around the classical contrast between liberty and slavery. Here the spokesmen for the Anglican Church

---

[168] Howard 1745, p. 6.     [169] Sykes 1746, p. 11.     [170] Head 1747, p. 11.
[171] See, for example, Ball 1746, p. 21; Ballard 1745, p. 7; Barr 1746, p. 7; Potter 1745, p. 20; Warburton 1745, p. 19.
[172] On 'free government' see Hume 1741, pp. 10, 32–4, 49, 107, 123; Herring 1745, p. 25; Maddox 1746, p. 30; Pendlebury 1746, p. 45; Richardson 1746, pp. 5–7, 27–9, 31, 36. On the concept of a 'free state' see Hume 1741, pp. 35, 37, 42; Ibbetson 1746, p. 18; Pendlebury 1746, p. 52; Warburton 1746, pp. 32–4. On living as a free people see Howard 1745, p. 6; Maddox 1746, p. 20; Pendlebury 1746, p. 45; Richardson 1746, p. 10; Stevenson 1746, p. 23.

sometimes speak in almost rhapsodic terms. Leonard Howard begins *The advantages of a free people* by declaring that 'of all earthly possessions, liberty is the sweetest' before explaining that 'to know the value of liberty is to feel the pains of slavery'.[173] Edmund Trott in his address of 1746 to the University of Oxford likewise associated liberty with the good life and slavery with 'the moral death of the soul'.[174] The Dissenters prefer to speak more straightforwardly. Pendlebury simply contrasts those who are free with those who are enslaved, while Brekell describes the friends of slavery as the enemies of liberty.[175] Hume in his essay *Of the liberty of the press* begins in a comparably sober style, agreeing that 'the two extremes in government' are liberty and slavery.[176] But even he permits himself a more elevated tone when he adds that 'slavery has so frightful an aspect to men accustomed to freedom that it must steal upon them by degrees, and must disguise itself in a thousand shapes, in order to be received'.[177] Whether speaking soberly or rhapsodically, the point on which everyone agrees is that the antonym of liberty is slavery.[178]

Following the lead originally given in the *Digesta*, the pro-government writers next argue that, if we wish to understand the concept of liberty, what we most of all need to grasp is what it means to be a slave. Here the answer they invariably give is that a slave is someone who lives in submission to, and dependence upon, the arbitrary will of somebody else. Hervey already speaks in these terms in his tract of 1734 on *Ancient and modern liberty*. He begins by contrasting 'natural liberty' with 'the slavery of no liberty' and proceeds to define slavery as 'an absolute submission to the will of another'.[179] Hume in his essay of 1741 *Of the parties of Great Britain* similarly links 'subjection and slavery' while contrasting the subjection of slaves with the condition of liberty.[180] Discussing barbarian monarchies a year later in his essay *Of the rise and progress of the arts and sciences*, he again speaks of slaves as those who live subject to an arbitrary and unrestrained will, and hence under 'the dominion of another'.[181]

The pro-government writers of the mid-1740s frequently echo this line of thought. Leonard Howard in *The advantages of a free people* speaks of slaves as those who live with 'no rights nor liberties independent of

---

[173] Howard 1745, p. 5.    [174] Mays 1746, p. 22; Trott 1746, p. 20.

[175] Chandler 1745, p. 36; Pendlebury 1746, pp. 45–6, 58; Brekell 1746, p. 13.

[176] Hume 1741, p. 10; for further appositions of liberty/slavery see pp. 12, 13, 101, 150–1.

[177] Hume 1741, p. 17.

[178] For other examples see Blackwell 1746, p. 13; Head 1747, p. 16; Piers 1746, p. 12; Stevenson 1746, p. 23.

[179] [Hervey] 1734, p. 3. Browning 1982, p. 60 argues that Hervey contrasts liberty with acting 'under compulsion'. But Hervey's basic contrast – as in this passage – is always between liberty and submission to the will of others.

[180] Hume 1741, p. 120.    [181] Hume 1742, pp. 62, 63–4.

power'.[182] Christopher Mays, a Fellow of King's College Cambridge, refers in his thanksgiving sermon of 1746 to the state of enslavement introduced when we are made to live in dependence on 'the arbitrary pleasure' of a single ruler.[183] Arthur Sykes summarises by asking 'What is slavery?' and answering that it is 'a submission to a master whose will is not to be opposed'.[184] A number of these writers also stress that it is possible for an entire nation no less than an individual to be reduced to servitude. Chandler defines a tyrant as someone who 'regards his subjects but as slaves', that is, as 'ordained for the execution of his will and pleasure'.[185] Pendlebury agrees that 'a nation may be said to be enslaved when it is subject to the arbitrary will of any one man; or when one person or a number are invested with such authority, as to have it in their power to act without law or contrary to law'.[186] Maddox may be said to round off the discussion with his declaration that 'the pernicious maxims of arbitrary government' are 'incompatible with the safety or the very being of a free people'.[187]

To understand what it means to be a slave is at the same time to understand what it means to be a free person. You are a free person if no one possesses any arbitrary power to do you harm. A free person is consequently someone who is secure from any danger of suffering such mistreatment. As the Whig tradition had always argued, this is why the rule of law is of such paramount importance in relation to the mainten-ance of liberty. The pro-government writers fully endorse – and fre-quently allude to – Locke's contention that everyone's aim in joining together to form political communities will always be to establish 'stated rules of right and property to secure their peace and quiet' against any inroads from 'absolute arbitrary power'.[188] They no less warmly agree with Locke that 'where there is no law there is no freedom', and thus that the law 'ill deserves the name of confinement' when it hedges us in from bogs and precipices, preventing us from falling into the hands of those who might otherwise be capable of exercising arbitrary and enslaving power over us.[189]

Hervey already speaks in these terms at the outset of his tract of 1734 on *Ancient and modern liberty*. 'The best regulated and best concerted form of government' will always be the one that 'preserves mankind from the oppression consequent to an absolute submission to the will of another' by way of establishing a system of liberty under law.[190] Hume agrees in his essay of 1742 *Of the rise and progress of the arts and sciences* that 'from law

[182] Howard 1745, p. 5.    [183] Mays 1746, pp. 14–15.    [184] Sykes 1746, p. 15.
[185] Chandler 1746, p. 13.    [186] Pendlebury 1746, p. 46.    [187] Maddox 1746, pp. 19–20.
[188] [Locke] 1690, para. 137, p. 358. Cf. also para. 95, p. 316 and para. 219, p. 439.
[189] [Locke] 1690, para. 57, p. 275.    [190] [Hervey] 1734, pp. 3, 44.

arises security', and that where rulers 'are not restrained by any law or statute' we are left confronting 'a scene of oppression and slavery'.[191] The same line of argument was frequently reiterated during the crisis of the mid-1740s, not without a note of patriotic self-congratulation. The problem, as Pendlebury expresses it, is that 'where the sovereign reigns absolute without control, there can be no security given to the people for their rights'.[192] But in England the solution lies in the fact that we live in a free state, in which the liberty of the subject is well guarded, and 'every man's person and property is secured by the best laws'.[193] Francis Potter in his sermon of 1745 similarly identifies the danger as stemming from the fact that 'right indefeasible is power incontrollable', and offers the same reassurance. 'The peculiar happiness of these kingdoms' is that the people 'are governed by laws of their own making, under a king to whom they engage their allegiance upon a previous stipulation on his part to rule according to those laws'.[194] If the king 'attempts to substitute his own arbitrary will in the place of law, invades the rights of the people and aims at absolute monarchy, he ceases to be any king of theirs'.[195] Warburton sums up with his usual briskness, noting that the good fortune of the English is to be ruled 'by old, established, well known laws', as a result of which 'the people rest secure in the freedom of their persons and the enjoyment of their possessions from all encroachments of power'.[196]

If personal freedom consists in being independent of the will and power of anyone else, then it would appear that we can equally well describe the state of liberty as that in which we are able to act entirely according to our own will and power, and are consequently able to behave as we please. Some bold spirits duly embraced this conclusion. Christopher Mays declares that 'the true definition of liberty' is that everyone is able to 'think and do what he pleases', so long as 'nobody else is injured by it'.[197] Hume similarly remarks in his essay of 1748 *Of national characters* that the liberty enjoyed by every Englishman is now so great that everyone can act as he pleases and 'display the manners which are peculiar to him'.[198]

There are others, however, who introduce a strong note of caution at this point, insisting on a categorical distinction between liberty and licence. Here they sometimes seem to have in mind the biblical injunction that we must never use our liberty as a cloak for maliciousness.[199] But they usually appear to be alluding to the classical distinction between *libertas* and *licentia*, and the associated claim that true freedom of action is

[191] Hume 1742, p. 64.   [192] Pendlebury 1746, p. 48.   [193] Pendlebury 1746, p. 52.
[194] Potter 1745, p. 20.   [195] Potter 1745, p. 21.   [196] Warburton 1745, pp. 14–15.
[197] Mays 1746, p. 13.   [198] Hume 1748, p. 16.
[199] 1 Peter 2.16. See, for example, [Hervey] 1732, p. 26; Osborne 1735, p. 5.

always limited and controlled by reason and law. John Myonnet in his *Nature and advantages of civil liberty* warns that anyone who thinks of liberty as 'a power to act as they list, without fear or control' is gravely mistaken. No act is genuinely free unless it is 'bounded by reason' and thereby succeeds in avoiding licentiousness.[200] Thomas Blackwell, rector of St Clement Danes in London, similarly argued in his thanksgiving sermon of 1746 that we must never allow our liberty 'to degenerate into licentiousness', thereby making it 'instrumental not to the welfare but disturbance of civil society'.[201] A number of other thanksgiving sermons go much further, arguing that the near success of the Jacobite invasion was God's punishment for England's degeneration into a condition of uncontrolled licentiousness.[202]

There remains, however, a strong undercurrent of agreement about how the concept of liberty should be understood. For individuals and states alike, liberty is equated with the condition of being able to choose and act without being dependent on the will of anyone else. As Erasmus Head summarises – again quoting Locke without acknowledgement – a state of perfect liberty is thus a condition in which everyone is 'entirely free to order his person, actions, and possessions as he pleases, within the bounds and permission of the law of nature'.[203] To claim that you are free is to say that you are 'independent of any other'.[204] The thought we are left to ponder is that the act of insisting upon your liberty, whether as an individual or a state, would be to make a declaration of independence.

The proudest boast of the pro-government writers is that the ideal of the free state has been realised in Britain, making the English constitution the envy of the world. The ministerial propagandists of the 1730s already rise to exceptional heights of self-congratulation in proclaiming this achievement. Yonge celebrates 'our present happy establishment' as the source of 'the superior advantages this nation enjoys above all the kingdoms of the earth'.[205] Arnall similarly commends the excellence of the English constitution, in which the different parts 'are now in perfect unison', so that it has become 'the best framed of any upon earth to create and preserve liberty'.[206]

The Anglican supporters of the ministry frequently couple no less patriotic encomia with words of condolence to those who are still languishing under the enslaving yoke of popery in the tyrannical monarchies of Europe. When Thomas Coney preached at the Somerset Assizes in

---

[200] Myonnet 1734, pp. 4–5. See also [Arnall] 1731, p. 20; Howard 1745, p. 11.
[201] Blackwell 1746, pp. 13–14.
[202] See, for example, Clarke 1746, pp. 17–21; Richardson 1746, p. 24.
[203] Head 1747, p. 5; cf. [Locke] 1690, para. 4, p. 220.    [204] Head 1747, p. 5.
[205] [Yonge] 1731, pp. 1, 38.    [206] [Arnall] 1735, p. 21.

1731, he explained how the rule of law and 'the wise administration of a frugal government' have made the English 'a free nation' by contrast with the unhappy state of those countries in which 'the will of the prince is the rule of justice', and 'papal and arbitrary power' condemn the people to misery and servitude.[207] John Myonnet in his Assize sermon of 1734 further developed the theme. He too stresses that 'in some countries the arbitrary will of the prince is a law', and contrasts these regimes with 'our own constitution and government', which is 'so happily contrived as to contain all that is good in others with as little as possible of the bad'.[208] He concludes that 'among all the various forms of government in the world, that which we have the happiness to live under is the freest and the best, because it subjects us to the fewest inconveniences, and allows us the most and greatest privileges, that can possibly consist with the good of the whole'.[209]

When Hume published his essay *Of the rise and progress of the arts and sciences* in 1742 he mounted a similar contrast between free and arbitrary rule. He agrees that 'in a civilised monarchy' the prince 'is unrestrained in the exercise of his authority' and that the people depend on him 'for the security of their property'.[210] But at this point he suddenly loses patience with the self-entrancement of the English. He insists that in such monarchies the ruler 'is so far removed' from the people that 'this dependence is not felt'. To give the name of tyranny to this form of government is therefore nothing better than a high political rant.[211] He reiterates a francophile judgement he had already voiced in his essay *Of liberty and despotism*, in which he had concluded that 'private property seems to me fully as secure in a civilised European monarchy as in a republic; nor is any danger ever apprehended, in such a government, from the violence of the sovereign, no more than we commonly apprehend danger from thunder or earthquakes'.[212]

These remarks have sometimes been treated as the 'philosophical' moment at which Hume challenged the exaggerated language of the pro-government Whigs.[213] But Hume was never a consistent or even a coherent critic of so-called vulgar Whiggism. Several of his essays in 1741 strike a far more patriotic note. His essay *Of the parties of Great Britain* celebrates the fact that the British are 'living in a country of the highest liberty'.[214] He takes 'the sentiments of true Britons' to include 'their affection to liberty', and he equates 'an avowal of absolute monarchy' with 'a formal renunciation of all our liberties'.[215] He speaks

---

[207] Coney 1731, pp. 12, 21.    [208] Myonnet 1734, pp. 8–9.    [209] Myonnet 1734, p. 16.
[210] Hume 1742, p. 77.    [211] Hume 1742, p. 77.    [212] Hume 1741, p. 181.
[213] See, for example, Forbes 1975, pp. 143, 153.    [214] Hume 1741, p. 128.
[215] Hume 1741, pp. 129–30.

dismissively at the end of his essay *Of superstition and enthusiasm* about 'the small sparks of the love of liberty which are to be found in the French nation',[216] while in his essay *Of liberty and despotism* he not only contends that France 'never enjoyed any shadow of liberty', but concludes by contrasting the 'free government' of Great Britain with the 'state of servitude' prevailing in 'all the nations that surround us'.[217]

Whether or not Hume raised a coherent objection to the usual Whig pieties, all such doubts were soon swept aside by the patriotic outpourings that greeted the final defeat of Jacobitism in 1746. The official day of thanksgiving gave rise to the publication of scores of sermons in which a categorical distinction was drawn between free government and the enslaving effects of arbitrary power. Henry Piers, the vicar of Bexley in Kent, captured the prevailing mood in his sermon on *Religion and liberty rescued from superstition and slavery*, in which God was thanked for an unmerited act of merciful deliverance.[218] If He had not appeared in our favour, 'what could have prevented our liberty from being swallowed up in foreign slavery?' What could have stopped us from being subjected 'to lawless tyranny and arbitrary power?'[219] Isaac Maddox delivered a similar message in more measured tones in his thanksgiving address in Worcester Cathedral. He likewise treats it as an expression of God's undeserved mercy that 'our religious and civil enjoyments' have been saved from 'the dire effects of projected tyranny' and 'the exalted and unlimited claims of arbitrary authority'.[220] The rebellion was 'a French contrivance' designed to advance 'the pernicious maxims of arbitrary government', which are 'incompatible with the safety or the very being of a free people'.[221] As the Pretender's Declarations made only too clear, his intention was to rule in the French style by 'mere will and pleasure', regulating the exercise of civil authority not 'by the general course of the law', but instead 'by the most arbitrary and oppressive injunctions' and the 'haughty dictates of mere power'.[222]

It was generally agreed that the man who had done most to save England from this catastrophe was the Duke of Cumberland, whose courage was said to proclaim his noble birth and his membership of an illustrious house.[223] Cumberland's brutal victory at Culloden was widely celebrated, and by no one more memorably than Handel in *Judas Maccabaeus*, which he composed in the summer of 1746 and dedicated

[216] Hume 1741, p. 151.     [217] Hume 1741, pp. 178, 186–7.
[218] Piers 1746, pp. 8–9, 12.     [219] Piers 1746, pp. 12–13.     [220] Maddox 1746, pp. 5, 10.
[221] Maddox 1746, pp. 19–20.
[222] Maddox 1746, pp. 24–5. For the same argument see Bellinger 1746, p. 11; Mays 1746, pp. 13–14; Stevenson 1746, pp. 21–4.
[223] Blackwell 1746, pp. 6–8. For the same argument see Bradford 1746, pp. 4, 10; Kerrich 1746, pp. 21–3.

to the duke.[224] Judas begins by calling on his son to resolve on 'liberty or death', and after many travails the conquering hero returns to celebrate 'peace and liberty' gloriously restored.[225]

One of the most enduring outcomes of the return of peace was an increased sense of national unity. The defenders of the Whig regime in the 1730s had generally been content to address themselves to the people of England and the English nation.[226] But after the defeat of Jacobitism a broader sense of community was increasingly affirmed. With the rebellious Scots subdued, what now began to be celebrated was not the English but the British nation. Among spokesmen for the Anglican Church, William Warburton was one of many who took themselves to be addressing all Britons, whom he congratulates for being 'the most free and happy people upon earth'.[227] Samuel Kerrich in his thanksgiving sermon similarly speaks of 'the generosity of Britons' and their happiness,[228] while Leonard Howard refers with no less admiration to 'British courage and resolution' in the face of 'attempts to enslave us'.[229] Nor were these celebrations merely confined to London and other centres of power. When John Dupont delivered his sermon of thanksgiving to his rural community in Yorkshire in 1746, the title under which he chose to address his parishioners was *The peculiar happiness and excellency of the British nation considered and explained.*

It was among the Dissenters, however, that the most fulsome joy at Britain's deliverance from tyranny was expressed. Samuel Chandler in his thanksgiving sermon congratulated 'the friends of Great-Britain and the lovers of the religion and liberties of their country', while John Brekell saw the outcome as a triumph for 'noble spirit of humane Christian British liberty'.[230] William Pendlebury likewise rejoiced in the fact that we now possess 'all the privileges of free Britons'.[231] The goddess Liberty is now 'firmly established in her favourite land, which sits as Queen of the isles and mistress of the seas, enjoying every blessing in rich profusion that nature furnishes, or art and industry can procure'.[232] Andrew Richardson warmly agreed that 'liberty is the glory of the isle of Britain' and that 'no nation under heaven enjoys it so fully'.[233] Britannia was now fully ready to rule the waves.[234]

---

[224] Glover 2018, pp. 343–4.    [225] Morell 1754, pp. 7, 15.

[226] See, for example, [Arnall] 1731, p. 5; Coney 1731, p. 12: Myonnet 1734, p. 16. But there are already exceptions. See, for example [Yonge] 1731, p. 38 on the figure of the 'true Briton'.

[227] Warburton 1745, p. 18.    [228] Kerrich 1746, p. 23.    [229] Howard 1745, p. 10.

[230] Chandler 1746, p. 23; Brekell 1746, pp. 9, 35.    [231] Pendebury 1746, p. 55.

[232] Pendlebury 1746, p. 54.    [233] Richardson 1746, p. 20.

[234] On the emergence of 'Britain' and the concept of the British Empire in this period see Armitage 2000, pp. 170–98.

# 4     The Whig Vision of a Free Society

## Legal Equality and the Protection of Rights

As well as explicating the principles of free states, the pro-government Whigs were much concerned to trace the impact of these principles on the workings of civil society. When they speak of civil society they sometimes make it clear that they are thinking in Ciceronian rather than Aristotelian terms. The earliest English translation of Aristotle's *Politics* in 1598 had used 'civil society' interchangeably with 'commonwealth' and 'state', and this soon became a standard usage.[1] But a different tradition of Renaissance political theory had employed the term to refer to what Cicero had described as the habitual dealings of citizens with one another,[2] and hence as a means of referring to the various groups and communities governed by states.[3] This is evidently what Reeve Ballard has in mind when he speaks in *The rule of obedience* about the need to identify 'the best model of civil government' for preserving 'the welfare of all civil society'.[4] Erasmus Head in *Loyalty recommended* similarly describes how 'every member of civil society' in Britain is subject to the 'sovereignty or supreme power' of the state.[5] Distinguishing state from society even more clearly, John Brekell asserts in *Liberty and loyalty* that the extent to which we are obliged to obey our rulers depends on the extent of 'their usefulness to civil society'.[6]

When the pro-government writers reflect on the impact of the state on civil society, they do their best to place their emphasis on the benign effects of state power. As they like to argue, free states will always confer many blessings on their people, and nowhere is this more evident than in Britain.

---

[1] Aristotle 1598, Sig. C, 4r and pp. 2, 33, 61. Ehrenberg 1999, pp. xi and 3 claims that to speak of 'civil society' in the classical understanding of the term is to refer to 'a politically organised commonwealth'.

[2] See Cicero 1942, II. 16. 68, vol. I, p. 248 on what pertains *ad usum civium* in a *societas civilis*.

[3] See, for example, Goslicki 1598, p. 75; Vaughan 1600, Sig. D, 8v. This is also the sense in which Fielding speaks of 'civil society' in *Tom Jones*. See Fielding 2005, p. 580.

[4] Ballard 1746, p. 11.    [5] Head 1747, p. 11.    [6] Breckell 1746, p. 33.

The country is not only mightily blessed with a happy and excellent constitution,[7] but also with a mild, cautious and equitable government committed to implementing the most cherished Whig principles.[8]

Among these principles, the most fundamental was said to be that the laws alone must rule. With the successful implementation of the 1688 settlement, the Whigs took it that this crucial requirement had at last been met, and the significance of their achievement was celebrated in many of the Assize sermons delivered at the time of the Jacobite rebellion in 1745. Reeve Ballard in his sermon at the Kingston Assizes stressed that under English law 'the meanest appellant will find as sure a redress for injuries received as the most powerful' and that 'our laws are even and equal to both'.[9] Leonard Howard developed the argument at greater length in his address to the Surrey Assizes in the same year. ''Tis the voice of law, no threat of man above us, that an Englishman must hearken to.' The law now 'protects the meanest person under it from any wrong or injury', and 'the peasant's plea is as valid as the prince's, and equally regarded by our constitution'. Nowadays everyone can 'demand, and have a right to, justice against the most powerful adversary'. As a result 'we are as free as we can wish or desire', because 'no man of power can with impunity hurt us nor remove our landmark'.[10]

Because the laws alone rule, no one is any longer obliged to live in subjection to the arbitrary will and power of any fellow subject. Among the numerous thanksgiving sermons delivered after the defeat of the Jacobite rebellion in 1746, this was taken to be one of the most important reasons to offer thanks for victory. William Lane, preaching in Hereford Cathedral, rejoiced that the people had succeeded in preserving a form of government under which 'the very meanest is under no fear of violence and oppression from the greatest'.[11] John Dupont similarly praised the laws of England for being 'framed with such unprejudiced prudence and impartiality that they countenance no wickedness or oppression', but instead manage to uphold 'the rights, privileges and properties of every order of men, from the prince to the peasant, on the firm basis of invariable justice'.[12] The patriotic case was eloquently summarised by Arthur Sykes in the sermon of thanksgiving he delivered in Winchester Cathedral. 'It is certain that we are blessed with the enjoyment of the greatest liberty', since no one is exposed to 'arbitrary pleasure' or unbridled power in the sovereign, nor in 'any of the powerful and great ones in the land'. The laws are able to ensure 'the security of every man's

---

[7] Potter 1745, p. 22; Ballard 1746, p. 5.     [8] Harris 1745, p. 2; Piers 1746, p. 21.
[9] Ballard 1745, pp. 7–8.     [10] Howard 1745, pp. 7, 8, 9.     [11] Lane 1746, p. 28.
[12] Dupont 1747, pp. 13–14.

common rights' and 'an equal protection of their persons' from any such arbitrary oppression or injustice.[13]

There is one further observation about the rule of law that the pro-government writers are particularly eager to underline. Because civil society is now wholly regulated by law, those involved in the administration of justice have become experienced servants of the legal system. As a result, there are no longer any corrupt juries or incompetent magistrates, and the decisions of the courts are made strictly in accordance with the relevant evidence and the requirements of the law. We already find John Arnall in his attack on *The Craftsman* in 1731 insisting that 'the utmost wisdom and integrity' is shown in making appointments to the courts of judicature, so that public justice has never been better administered.[14] Hervey in his tract of 1732 on public virtue similarly urges his readers to reflect that nowadays 'there are no illegal Courts of Justice to keep us in awe', and that 'our property is not subject to the arbitration of Privy Counsellors and flatterers, nor are our lives at the mercy of corrupt judges and juries'. We not only have 'the best laws' but at the same time 'the best magistrates'.[15] By the time Hervey came to write his tract on ancient and modern liberty in 1734 he felt sufficiently confident to rephrase these contentions as a series of rhetorical questions: 'Was the law ever more equitably administered? Did men of greater abilities or fairer characters ever preside in the Courts of Justice? Were the sentences and decisions of the law, either in the first trials, or in the extreme resort, ever less complained of?'[16] Hervey draws to a close by assuring his readers that what he has been describing is nothing other than the happy condition in which everyone is now able to live.[17]

Not surprisingly, this was one of the claims most often repeated in the Assize sermons of the same years. Thomas Coney points to the 'due and regular dispensation of justice' throughout the land, in which Justice 'takes her residence with our commissioners of the peace'.[18] James Bate commends 'the wise contrivance and happy administration of our civil and religious laws',[19] while John Myonnet insists that 'all imaginable care is now taken' to ensure 'the due execution of the law'.[20] Hume is no less admiring in his essay of 1741 *Of the liberty of the press*. He praises the government for maintaining 'a watchful jealousy over the magistrates to remove all discretionary powers'. He also notes the care now taken to ensure that 'no action must be deemed a crime but what the law has plainly determined to be such' and 'no crime must be imputed to a man

---

[13] Sykes 1746, p. 28.    [14] [Arnall] 1731, p. 6.    [15] [Hervey] 1732, pp. 7–8.
[16] [Hervey] 1734, p. 62.    [17] [Hervey] 1734, p. 64.    [18] Coney 1731, pp. 14–15.
[19] Bate 1734, p. 12.    [20] Myonnet 1734, p. 12.

but from a legal proof before his judges', who in turn 'must be his fellow subjects'.[21]

When the government case was restated in the mid-1740s these claims were widely reiterated. Leonard Howard speaks of local magistrates as 'shields in our land to secure and relieve the injured and oppressed',[22] while Reeve Ballard heaps praise on England's 'fit and able magistrates' for their 'equal administration of justice'.[23] Arthur Sykes reassuringly adds that it is no longer possible for 'those who are trusted with the execution of our laws' to 'control, dispense or put a stop to their regular courses'.[24] Sometimes the clergy challenged their congregations to admit that these encomia cannot possibly be undeserved. 'Can the time be named', John Barr demanded of his Lincolnshire parishioners, 'when abler and more inflexible magistrates filled the Bench, or the laws themselves were more equally executed?'[25] Everyone is exhorted to recognise that the answer should be evident to all.[26]

A closely associated benefit emphasised in the Assize sermons of these years was that, because the law is now imposed equally and fairly on everyone, no one can hope to get away with behaving as if it does not apply to them. We already find George Osborne arguing in his sermon of 1735 that 'the law is open to the lowest subject, and the highest are not exempted from its cognisance'.[27] Hume usually liked to express some scepticism about such optimistic generalisations, but in his essay of 1741 *On the liberty of the press* he agreed that England can now be described as a country in which the constitution acts 'to secure everyone's life and fortune by general and inflexible laws'.[28] Erasmus Head likewise argued in his Assize sermon of the following year that nowadays every British citizen, 'howsoever they may differ in rank, fortune, or office', is equally obliged to obey the law, 'and no one more exempt than another'.[29] Nobody stands above the law.

**********

A further achievement celebrated by the pro-government writers was that, when they refer to the equal protection of every member of civil society, what they chiefly have in mind is that everyone is fully secure in the exercise of what Locke had described as 'the rights and privileges of the law of nature', and especially the right of everyone to the preservation of 'his life, liberty and estate'.[30] The thanksgiving sermons of 1746

---

[21] Hume 1741, p. 13.   [22] Howard 1745, p. 7.   [23] Ballard 1746, p. 9.
[24] Sykes 1746, p. 11.   [25] Barr 1746, p. 8. See also Herring 1745, p. 13.
[26] For further examples see Bradford 1746, p. 28; Clarke 1746, p. 4.
[27] Osborne 1735, p. 25.   [28] Hume 1741, p. 14.   [29] Head 1747, p. 11.
[30] [Locke] 1690, para. 87, p. 305.

frequently echo the cherished list. Gilbert Benet speaks of the right to 'life, liberty, and property';[31] John Dupont agrees that the basic purpose of law is to 'guard the lives, liberties and properties of the subject';[32] Christopher Mays singles out 'freedom and security in property',[33] while Thomas Blackwell refers more specifically to 'English liberty and English property'.[34]

Sometimes these reflections led to an engagement specifically with Locke's discussion of basic rights. Andrew Richardson in *A free and an arbitrary government compared* pays special attention to the guarding and defending of our lives, echoing Locke's account in chapter 3 of the *Second treatise*. If we imagine life outside political society, we shall come to see that, in such a condition, 'out of the law of self-preservation arises another, that of self-defence, which gives a man, when attacked by a thief, a robber, or a murderer, a right to defend himself against the unjust or cruel invader of his property or life; which, if he cannot do without taking away the life of the injurious person, he may justly kill him in self-defence'.[35] But as soon as we decide to unite with others in 'a well regulated society', in which our government engages 'to defend its members in their lives and fortunes against unjust aggressors', this right of self-defence is relinquished into the hands of society, which 'may reasonably inflict the proper punishment' in the name of upholding the underlying right to life.[36] One of the fundamental obligations of the state becomes that of guarding this basic right.

A similar account, even more clearly indebted to Locke, can be found in Erasmus Head's Assize sermon of 1746. Head agrees that everyone in the state of nature may be said to possess a natural right to defend themselves from 'attacks and ravages' and to protect their life 'against the invasion of any other'.[37] If this right were generally exercised, however, 'the weaker would always be forced to submit to the stronger, and a smaller to a greater number', so that the safety of most people's lives would be rendered very precarious.[38] Quoting Locke, Head goes on to treat the recognition of this danger as the reason why people proved willing 'to unite together for their mutual preservation' and gave up this 'right of self-defence and revenge into the hands of the community',

---

[31] Benet 1746, pp. 28–9.
[32] Dupont 1747, p. 15. See also *Loyalty to our king* 1745, p. 5.
[33] Mays 1746, p. 13. On 'liberty and property' see also Bradford 1746, p. 13; Nichols 1746, p. 31; Piers 1746, p. 12.
[34] Blackwell 1746, p. 7.     [35] Richardson 1746, p. 8. Cf. [Locke] 1690, para. 18, p. 238.
[36] Richardson 1746, p. 10.
[37] Head 1747, p. 5. Here Head, like Locke, is drawing on the legal maxim *vim vi licet repellere*. For a discussion of the maxim see Skinner 1978, vol. 2, pp. 125–7, 200–6.
[38] Head 1747, p. 5.

thereby constituting for themselves 'the common judge to decide all controversies' and assure their right to life.[39]

A majority of the pro-government writers were more interested in pointing out that the successful protection of everyone's right to life has been one of the greatest achievements of the Whig regime. Coney in his Assize sermon of 1731 boasts that citizens are no longer exposed to 'rapine and violence',[40] while Hervey in his tract of 1732 on public virtue agrees that 'we now have the most excellent laws' to protect our lives 'from all sorts of violence'.[41] Preaching before the University of Oxford in 1737, George Fothergill more emphatically adds that England is now living under a constitution 'so happily situated' that 'we may be as secure as anything human can secure us' in our properties as well as our lives.[42] Speaking more generally, Hume in his essay of 1741 *On liberty and despotism* likewise refers appreciatively to the improvements in the 'domestic management' of almost every state in recent times, specifically mentioning the greater security of life now enjoyed as a result of the decline in the number of highwaymen throughout Europe.[43] By the time of the celebratory sermons of the mid-1740s it had come to be widely agreed that 'the private security of every man's life and fortune' had at last been fully assured.[44]

If we turn to the second element in the triad of basic natural rights – the right to personal liberty – we at first find its importance almost taken for granted. The Habeus Corpus Act, which made it illegal for subjects to be detained in prison without due cause shown, had been passed as early as 1679 as *An Act for the better securing the liberty of the subject*,[45] and subsequent attempts to circumvent its provisions by demanding excessive bail had been expressly forbidden by the Bill of Rights in 1689.[46] This was the moment when, as Howard affirms in *The advantages of a free people*, 'the noble struggle for liberty at the glorious Revolution' finally ended in victory.[47] Since that time it has been possible to say, as John Breckell concludes in *Liberty and loyalty*, that 'the throne of these realms now stands upon the principle of liberty'.[48]

The moment when the right to personal liberty received the fullest attention was after the defeat of the Jacobite rebellion in 1746. There was much celebration of the fact that the government had succeeded in preventing this basic right from being fatally undermined by the return of despotic and arbitrary rule. Speaking in his thanksgiving sermon after the

---

[39] Head 1747, p. 5. Cf. [Locke] 1690, paras 19, 87, 91, pp. 239–40, 305–6, 309–11.
[40] Coney 1731, p. 14   [41] [Hervey] 1732, p. 6.   [42] Fothergill 1737, p. 35.
[43] Hume 1741, pp. 182–3.   [44] Herring 1745, pp. 14, 24–5; Trott 1746, p. 20.
[45] Kenyon 1966, pp. 430–2.   [46] Williams 1960, p. 28.   [47] Howard 1745, p. 10.
[48] Breckell 1746, p. 36.

return of peace, Samuel Kerrich rejoiced that the people were now protected once more 'from lawless violence and disorder', with no fear of being arbitrarily deprived of their freedom and 'dragged to noisome prisons for no faults by you committed'.[49] William Lane similarly expressed relief that the country had preserved a form of government under which no one suffers 'any other outward restraint' than the laws impose.[50] Writing a year later, the anonymous but intensely patriotic author of *An essay on liberty* felt able to conclude that personal liberty is now so deeply respected that 'imprisonment without cause, trial without evidence' have both become inconceivable.[51]

The pro-government writers have much more to say about the third element in the famous triad, the right to have one's private property protected and preserved. Here too they are eager to give thanks not merely for the special excellence of the British constitution, but also for the scrupulous way in which the rights of property are upheld. Archbishop Herring calls on his congregation to acknowledge that, under the present regime, 'their property stands upon the basis of the laws', so that 'their goods and possessions are guarded from all violence and outrage'.[52] The Dissenters speak in equally patriotic terms about the success of the government in protecting everyone's lands and goods. Richardson writes about the privilege of living 'under a free government, where every man's property is secured by just and equal laws'.[53] Pendlebury echoes his praise for the British state, in which property is fully secured, so that 'the fruit of his labours a man may safely call his own'.[54]

As with the values of life and liberty, the protection of private property suddenly assumed special importance at the time of the Jacobite uprising in 1745. Writing at the outset of the rebellion, Warburton laments the looming threat to the constitution under which everyone has for so long been able to rest secure in the enjoyment of their possessions.[55] The anonymous writer of *Liberty and property* warns that the holding of private property might even become impossible for Protestant subjects under a popish king. 'What property can they enjoy under such a prince?' The present king 'secures religion and property by good and wholesome laws', but 'zealous Papists detest a prince that pays any regard to Protestants, or so much as permits them to enjoy either liberty or property', because they consider 'their very goods, chattels and estates to be heretical'.[56] One of the recurrent themes in the thanksgiving sermons preached after the return of peace was that, as William Lane expressed it, the people had

---

[49] Kerrich 1746, p. 21.    [50] Lane 1746, p. 28.
[51] *An essay on liberty and independency* 1747, p. 26. See also Brekell 1746, pp. 35–6.
[52] Herring 1745, p. 14.    [53] Richardson 1746, p. 28.    [54] Pendlebury 1746, p. 52.
[55] Warburton 1745, p. 15.    [56] *Liberty and property* 1745, pp. 5, 19–20, 50.

managed to stave off any such disaster and uphold 'that happy constitution of government by which our persons and estates are so securely guarded'.[57]

These anxieties about private property led some pro-government writers to sound a rare note of warning to the government. They are especially eager to point out that, under the constitution established by the revolution of 1688, there can be no question of imposing taxes on the goods and incomes of the people by the exercise of discretionary sovereign power. Myonnet already puts the case in his *Nature and advantages of civil liberty* in 1734. One reason he gives for concluding that, 'among all the various forms of government in the world, that which we have the happiness to live under, is the freest and the best' is that the crown 'can indeed make no laws, nor impose any taxes' on the people 'without their consent first had by their representatives in Parliament'.[58] Richardson similarly argues that one reason for condemning absolute monarchy is that, because no one 'can be certain of his prince's humour, which is the chief rule he is directed by in levying his taxes, so no man can know by what he has in his possession today, how much of his estate or goods the king shall take, and how much he shall leave against to-morrow'.[59] Soon afterwards the anonymous author of *An address to the electors of Great Britain* of 1747 reminded his readers, in a tone of some alarm, that the need to avoid such uncertainty remains one crucial reason for wishing to curb the executive. We must always make sure that there are enough independent members of Parliament to remind the government that 'no power on earth can exact a shilling but by their previous direction and consent'.[60] In a free state there can be no taxation without representation, and it will always be an act of tyranny to question this right.

Some of these writers refer not to the protection of property but rather to our properties. Sometimes they make it clear that they are still speaking simply about our goods, possessions and estates.[61] But at other times they recur to the more radical claim that Locke had taken from the Leveller writers of the 1640s. Richard Overton had argued in *An arrow against all tyrants* that the natural condition of mankind includes not only a right to enjoy our natural liberties but a right of self-ownership. As Overton had formulated the claim, 'everyone, as he is himself, so he hath a self-propriety, else could he not be himself'. I may therefore be said to have a natural right to 'enjoy myself and my self-propriety'.[62] The loss of liberty suffered by those who live in dependence on the will of others is

---

[57] Lane 1746, p. 28.     [58] Myonnet 1734, pp. 8–10.     [59] Richardson 1746, pp. 29–30.
[60] *An address to the electors of Great Britain* 1747, p. 19.
[61] See, for example, Mays 1746, pp. 13, 21; [Squire] 1746, p. 26.
[62] [Overton] 1646, p. 3.

equated with a loss of the 'natural propriety, right and freedom' to live as men as opposed to living as slaves.[63]

Echoing Overton's argument, Locke had laid it down in the *Second treatise* that 'every man has a property in his own person' of a kind that 'nobody has any right to but himself'.[64] Everyone has 'a liberty to dispose or order freely as he lists his person, actions, possessions and his whole property' without being 'subject to the arbitrary will of another'.[65] He is partly speaking about how the work of one's hands creates property in the sense of producing an increase in lands and goods that one thereby gains a right to hold. But he is no less preoccupied with the right to protect one's person against acts of interference or the use of force and violence by others.[66] He repeatedly insists that nobody's person is 'at the disposal' of anyone else.[67] Rather, it is the right of everyone that their person should be secured against 'injuries and attempts' from any of their fellow subjects.[68] Everyone may thus be said to have a right to remain free from injury,[69] and anyone attempting to violate this right is exercising 'force without right upon a man's person'.[70]

The pro-government writers of the next generation are especially anxious to underline that one of the greatest benefits conferred by the government is that no one lives in danger of suffering any such injury or disturbance. Myonnet already speaks in these terms in *The nature and advantages of civil liberty* in 1734. When we are preserved 'in the undisturbed exercise of all our civil and religious rights', one great benefit is that 'no man is invaded either in his person or property'.[71] The happy outcome of living in security from any such disturbance is that 'as the Scripture expresseth it, we may sit down every man under his own vine, and under his own fig-tree'.[72] Howard closely follows Myonnet's line of thought in his tract of 1745 on *The advantages of a free people*. One of the elements in 'our happiness in this country of liberty' is that 'to any invader of our rights, any insulter of our persons' we can offer 'the plea of the Apostle, and can say with him that we are free born', and can be sure that our plea will be heard by the law. This in turn means that everyone 'can sit down without disturbance or molestation under the vines and the fig-trees which their ancestors or their own industry have planted'.[73]

---

[63] [Overton] 1646, pp. 5, 6.     [64] [Locke] 1690, para. 27, p. 245.

[65] [Locke] 1690, para. 57, pp. 275–6.

[66] [Locke] 1690, para. 221, p. 441 and para. 226, p. 447.

[67] [Locke] 1690, para. 57, pp. 194, 221.

[68] [Locke] 1690, para. 87; cf. para. 205, p. 425.     [69] [Locke] 1690, para. 10, p. 227.

[70] [Locke] 1690, para. 186, p. 410; cf. para. 17, p. 237. On self-ownership see Pateman 2002; Shanks 2019, pp. 320–9; Sabbadini 2020, pp. 63–94 and 189–219.

[71] Myonnet 1734, pp. 12–13.

[72] Myonnet 1734, pp. 12–13. See also Osborne 1735, p. 24.     [73] Howard 1745, pp. 6–7.

The exotic evocation of vines and fig trees soon became a mantra in Whig discussions about how to ensure that the property we possess in our person can be secured.[74] William Pendelbury agrees that the opportunity for everyone to 'sit unmolested under his own vine and his own fig-tree' is one of the infinite advantages that we reap from living in a free state.[75] Edward Yardley recurs to the image in rounding off his thanksgiving sermon of 1746. Before the rebellion of the previous year 'we sat every one under our own vine and our own fig-tree', and there were laws in force to take action 'when rapine and violence disturbed the peace of society'. 'Thus were our possessions secured, and our persons protected from injury' under a mild and equitable government.[76] With the suppression of the uprising and the return of peace, these are among the special blessings we can again expect to receive.[77]

### The Spirit of Liberty

One other leading concern of the pro-government writers was to promote and celebrate the idea that the enjoyment of personal freedom brings with it a distinctive spirit of liberty, and hence a characteristic way of interacting with our fellow citizens. Sir William Yonge may be said to have set the scene for this part of the discussion when he proclaimed in his tract of 1731 on *Sedition and defamation displayed* that 'the spirit of liberty is the distinguishing characteristic of a true Briton, and to that we owe the superior advantages this nation enjoys above all the kingdoms of the earth'.[78] The same claim was later repeated by the author of the *Essay on liberty*, who attributes the increasing greatness of the British people not merely to the excellence of their constitution, but also and more fundamentally to 'that spirit of liberty, that natural jealousy of all encroachments upon our freedom, which diffuses itself through all ranks of people in these islands'.[79]

The suggestion that there is a distinctive spirit of liberty particularly occupied the Dissenters, among whom there was a strong theological grounding for their interest. They frequently discuss the passage from the Epistle to the Romans (8.21) in which St Paul speaks of being delivered 'from the bondage of corruption into the glorious liberty of the children of God'. John Barret, one of the most prominent English

---

[74] For further examples see Ballard 1745, p. 9; Herring 1745, p. 14; Wiche 1745, p. 7; Bradford 1746, p. 28.
[75] Pendlebury 1746, pp. 51–2.    [76] Yardley 1746, p. 42.    [77] Yardley 1746, pp. 41, 51.
[78] [Yonge] 1731, p. 38.
[79] *An essay on liberty and independency* 1747, pp. 8, 22. See also *National spirit considered as a natural source of liberty* 1758.

Presbyterian theologians of the later seventeenth century, had com-
mented at length on the passage in his treatise of 1678 on *God's love to
man, and man's duty towards God.* Discussing the covenant of grace, he
had described God as the spirit of truth, power and grace, but also as the
spirit of liberty. 'Where the spirit of the Lord is, there is liberty', and where
we follow God's 'free spirit' we shall find ourselves upheld, quickened and
cheered.[80]

A similar view was put forward by a number of Dissenters in the early
1740s. Thomas Barnard, a Dissenting minister in Berkshire, addressed
the topic in a sermon of 1743 on *Tyranny and slavery in matters of religion.*
The freedom he describes takes the form of ensuring that we do not 'pay
too great submission to, or have too great dependence on, any man'. We
must never allow anyone 'in an arbitrary manner to prescribe to us what
we shall believe'. We must never 'rely on any man, though ever so famous
for learning or piety, any further than we can see the truth of their
assertions'. We need to recognise that 'it is part of the liberty wherewith
Christ has made us free' that we are 'in subjection to none but him'.[81]
John Brekell later wrote in like-minded terms in his *Liberty and loyalty* of
1746 when discussing the doctrines of passive obedience and non-
resistance. He dismisses those who continue to preach this creed as
a gloomy set of men who appear to be incapable of reasoning for themselves and whose opinions are 'shocking to common sense'.[82] He
denounces them as 'friends of tyranny' who are 'formed for the most
abject and ignominious slavery', and condemns them for having thereby
lost 'all the noble spirit of humane Christian British liberty'.[83]

Of greater significance were the classical sources for the claim that the
pro-government writers wanted to make. As we saw in Chapter 1, Sallust
in particular had argued that living in a free state encourages a thirst for
glory and a readiness to devote one's energies to high designs.[84] Taking
up this line of argument, the Whig writers tend to associate this spirit with
two particular virtues. Because the citizens of free states can develop their
talents as they wish, they are especially likely to acquire a distinctive kind
of courage and self-confidence. Bate in his Assize sermon of 1734 already
praises the bravery of his fellow countrymen,[85] while Pendlebury
describes 'the British spirit' as ardent and 'panting for glory'.[86]
Speaking more generally, Christopher Mays in his thanksgiving sermon
explains how liberty inspires men 'with generosity, with courage, with
magnanimity, and many virtues which are not to be found in abject

---

[80] Barret 1678, p. 279.    [81] Barnard 1743, p. 16.    [82] Brekell 1746, pp. 9–10.
[83] Brekell 1746, pp. 10, 13.    [84] Sallust 1608, p. 17 (*recte* p. 7).    [85] Bate 1734, p. 22.
[86] Pendlebury 1746, p. 53.

slaves'.[87] In his essay of 1742 on the arts and sciences Hume had already spoken with admiration of this distinctive spirit in free states. There you see greater curiosity, together with emulation in every accomplishment, so that 'genius and capacity have a fuller scope and career' than they can ever hope to attain under absolute monarchies.[88]

The other and related virtue said to be characteristic of free citizens is that, because they know that any gains they make will never be arbitrarily taken away from them, they tend to become especially active and industrious. Pendlebury thinks it obvious that, whereas 'slavery enervates both mind and body', liberty promotes not merely a generous but a 'lively and active spirit'.[89] This is the special quality that Richardson characterises as 'the spirit of British liberty'.[90] Under a free government, where 'every man in every rank of life may have as much property secured to him by law as he can justly and honestly acquire', the effect is that people acquire 'a cheerful unconstrained turn of mind' which in turn 'quickens and sharpens their invention'.[91] We may say that 'a spirit of liberty breathes in their behaviour'.[92] This outlook was rapturously celebrated by James Thomson in the climax to his narrative poem of 1736 on the history of liberty. The reawakening of the spirit of liberty in Britain to combat the arbitrary power of the Stuarts, together with the triumphant re-establishment of liberty by the immortal Nassau in 1688, are taken to have laid the foundations for Britain's current glory and wealth, with the result that 'plenty flows and glad contentment echoes round the whole'.[93]

As always, the contrast is with the depressing consequences that are said to follow from a consciousness of living under arbitrary power. As soon as you become aware that you are subject to the will of others in any domain of your life, you are almost certain to develop an abject spirit of slavishness.[94] Hume in his essay on the arts and sciences notes that, if a man wishes to prosper under absolute monarchy, he will be obliged to exhibit complaisance and learn how 'to render himself agreeable'. Under such regimes there will always be 'a long train of dependence from the prince to the peasant', which will in turn 'beget in everyone an inclination to please his superiors'.[95] This antithesis between independence and servility is particularly emphasised by the Dissenters, and in Richardson's tract on free and arbitrary government the contrast is used to introduce a general discussion of the psychological effects of enslavement. One of the

---

[87] Mays 1746, p. 22.    [88] Hume 1742, p. 66.    [89] Pendlebury 1746, p. 49.
[90] Richardson 1746, p. 22.    [91] Richardson 1746, pp. 28–9, 31.
[92] Richardson 1746, p. 40.    [93] Thomson 1736, pp. 58–9, 63.
[94] Richardson 1746, p. 41. This was a long-standing claim about the effects of arbitrary and despotic power. See Skinner 1998, pp. 87–96 and Skinner 2008a, pp. 94–8.
[95] Hume 1742, pp. 126–7.

horrors of slavery, Richardson argues, is that it tends to 'cramp and benumb the mind'.[96] When the people 'have no security for anything, no certain laws for holding their possessions' we can expect them to have 'an unbecoming terror on them in the presence of their superiors', or else 'to sink into a fawning slavish complaisance'.[97]

Richardson illustrates these observations by sketching a picture of life under the rule of an absolute prince:

> His subjects fear him, but they cannot love him. His favourites secretly despise him while they cringe before him. An abject spirit of flattery and dissimulation reigns through his whole Court. His courtiers who bow before him in a supple manner put on stately airs towards their inferiors. As they themselves hang on their monarch's will for their lives and fortunes, so in their turn they assume dominion over the persons and estates of others, who again are ready to oppress their dependents. Thus cruelty and oppression rages through all the ranks of life, superiors always bearing hard on those below them.[98]

Enlarging on his theme, Richardson offers a general view of the social consequences of absolute power:

> Such is the malign influence of arbitrary government that it foments pride and insolence in the great, sinks down the poor into mean-spiritedness, breeds in them a dejected sullen mood, overwhelms them with slavish terror, or, by driving them to despair, provokes them to mutiny and sedition, while it communicates a selfish spirit to all ranks and orders. No man being secured in his property, everyone is on self-defence, tries every art to secure himself, and his thoughts are swallowed up in his own private interest. This looses the bond of social love, weakens the kind affections, raises envy, provokes murmuring, spreads universal corruption through a land, renders it a scene of horror and confusion, and all this in proportion to the rigorous exercise of arbitrary power.[99]

Here Richardson seems consciously to echo Milton's account in *The ready and easy way* of how it comes about that servitude leads to dejection as well as servility.

A further serious consequence to which Richardson alludes is that, if subjects as well as rulers can exercise arbitrary power, this can readily undermine the security of the state. William Logan, an Edinburgh lawyer, had already voiced this warning in a tract entitled *Scotland's grievance*, which was first published in 1721 and reissued after the defeat of the rebellion in 1746. Logan begins by explaining that the most prevalent type of land-holding in Scotland permits overlords to exercise civil and criminal jurisdiction over their tenants. Not only can they 'authoritatively determine' what happens to their lands and goods, but they can also

---

[96] Richardson 1746, p. 32.    [97] Richardson 1746, p. 39.    [98] Richardson 1746, p. 41.
[99] Richardson 1746, pp. 41–2.

impose capital punishment.[100] As a result, much of Scotland is currently marked by what Logan condemns as 'the slavish dependence of the people upon their great men'.[101] This is a dangerous as well as an iniquitous arrangement, especially in the Highlands and Islands, where overlords can require their vassals to follow them in times of war and 'attend them on all occasions when called, under the most severe penalties'.[102] The problem is not simply that these heads of clans are in a position to muster large armies, but that they 'are always on the side of popery and slavery'. They represent a standing threat to the entire nation because their tenants, due to 'their slavish subjection and unlimited obedience', will follow them blindly 'even against the king and government'. Nothing, in short, does more to 'threaten the quiet of our excellent constitution' than these 'slavish dependencies'.[103] The British Parliament took the threat so seriously that one of its decisions in the immediate aftermath of the Jacobite uprising in 1745 was to abolish almost the entire Scottish system of heritable jurisdictions and feudal tenures.

**********

The promise held out by the pro-government writers was a double one. If you live in a free state, you can be certain that any gains you make in life will remain securely in your hands. And if you enjoy this sense of security, this will quicken your ambition and make you willing to work industriously, thereby contributing to the general growth of prosperity. The ministerial writers of the Walpole era had already made this argument central to their defence and celebration of the regime. It is our free way of life, Yonge had contended in 1731, to which we owe 'the flourishing state of our trade' and 'the increase of riches to the nation', which are indisputably reflected in 'the low interest of money and the prosperous state of public credit'.[104] Writing three years later, Hervey argued still more confidently that the state of liberty in which the people of England now live serves to explain why the country is basking in wealth and peace, with 'her commerce so unrivalled, so unobstructed, and so flourishing, that the imports and exports were never higher, nor our credit in greater prosperity'.[105]

As the country shifted into celebratory mood in the mid-1740s these claims were restated with overweening confidence. Preaching in his Yorkshire parish on the day of thanksgiving in 1746, The Reverend Nicholas Nichols proclaimed that one consequence of defeating the rebels had been 'the revival of our public credit' and 'the free exercise of

---

[100] [Logan] 1746, pp. 4, 11.     [101] [Logan] 1746, title.     [102] [Logan] 1746, p. 8.
[103] [Logan] 1746, pp. 4, 12.     [104] [Yonge] 1731, p. 17.
[105] [Hervey] 1734, pp. 57, 60–1.

our trade', the volume of which had already made us 'not only rich and flourishing', but 'generous and hospitable' as a people.[106] We now have unparalleled opportunities to get wealth, in addition to having 'the liberty to use and enjoy it as we please'.[107] Preaching in Cambridge on the same day of thanksgiving, Christopher Mays pointed to the virtuous circle that can now be discerned. We enjoy 'a government so well constituted' that 'it yields quietness and peace at home, it secures our properties from unjust invasions, and both these together encourage industry, labour and commerce', which in turn 'bring back plenty, strength and security'.[108] As Nichols had rhetorically asked, 'what change can there possibly be but for the worse?'[109]

The same line of reasoning was more soberly followed by a number of Dissenters writing in support of the government. Andrew Richardson rejoices in the fact that, because 'every man's private property' is 'secured under a free government', this serves as 'a great encouragement to trade and industry, which tend to advance the wealth and riches of a nation'. As a result, 'a free government has a happy tendency to make trade flourish, industry prevail, to set all hands to work', so that 'free countries are the proper seats of cheerful industry and plenty'.[110] Joshua Dobson in his tract of 1747 on religious and civil liberty agreed that, due to 'the excellencies of our present happy constitution', the industry of the people has been encouraged, so that 'our commerce flourishes' and we have become 'a rich, numerous, valiant and free people'.[111]

An associated benefit is that free states naturally become the leading centres for the practice and appreciation of the arts and sciences. Hume in his essay of 1741 *Of liberty and despotism* notes the widespread belief 'that the arts and sciences could never flourish but in a free government'. He wonders, however, if this conclusion may not stem from 'too great a partiality in favour of that form of government which is established amongst us'. As a counter-example he offers the case of France, which has 'never enjoyed any shadow of liberty, and yet has carried the arts and sciences nearer perfection than any other nation of the universe'.[112] Richardson was one of several patriotic commentators who offered a vigorous riposte. Wherever free governments are established, he replied, the effect is to improve the security and wealth of the community, which in turn 'tends to the encouragement of the useful arts and the liberal sciences'. This enlargement of opportunities quickens and sharpens the inventive powers of the people, while the growth of opulence provides an

---

[106] Nichols 1746, pp. 26–7.    [107] Nichols 1746, p. 28.    [108] Mays 1746, p. 21.
[109] Nichols 1746, p. 28.    [110] Richardson 1746, p. 29.
[111] Dobson 1747, pp. 31–2, 47.    [112] Hume 1741, pp. 177–8.

opening for 'bright and penetrating geniuses to furnish out instruction and entertainment for them'.[113] By the time Hume came to write his essay *Of commerce* in 1752, he had become willing to endorse this view about how social improvements come about. 'The greatness of a state, and the happiness of its subjects', he now agrees, are 'inseparable with regard to commerce'. The more that 'private men receive greater security in the possession of their trade and riches from the power of the public', the more the public 'becomes powerful in proportion to the opulence and extensive commerce of private men'.[114]

The focal points of commerce and civilised pursuits were of course the great cities, which increasingly came to be viewed with admiration and pride. This is not to say that urban life was universally approved. Erasmus Jones published a celebrated diatribe in 1740 in which he named 'luxury, pride and vanity' as 'the bane of the English nation', particularly condemning London for 'the tradesmen's expensive manner of living' and the shameless licentiousness of social life.[115] Others expressed economic as well as moral doubts. The same year saw the publication of William Webster's best-selling tract *The consequences of trade as to the wealth and strength of any nation*, in which he addressed the undoubted decline of the woollen and cloth industries. He particularly deplored the export to France of raw wool instead of woollen manufactures, going so far as to speak of 'the danger we are in of becoming a province to France'.[116] A year later Hume joined the chorus of concern in his essay *Of liberty and despotism*, in which he first began to complain about the rising level of public debt and the increase in taxation required to service it. He concluded that this source of degeneracy is 'an inconvenience, that nearly threatens all free governments, especially our own at the present juncture of affairs', so much so that we may 'be reduced, by the multiplicity of taxes, to curse our free government, and wish ourselves in the same state of servitude with all the nations that surround us'.[117]

The mood of the times, however, was generally one of buoyancy, and this gave rise to numerous celebrations of urban life. By the time Hume came to write his essay of 1752 *Of refinement in the arts* he too was speaking enthusiastically about how men 'flock into cities' and 'love to receive and communicate knowledge', thereby ensuring that 'industry, knowledge and humanity are linked together by an indissoluble chain'.[118] Meanwhile the Renaissance genre of panegyrics on cities had been revived, the most celebrated example being Mary Chandler's poem in

---

[113] Richardson 1746, pp. 31–2.    [114] Hume 1752, p. 255.    [115] [Jones] 1740, title page.
[116] [Webster] 1740, pp. 3–4.    [117] Hume 1741, pp. 186–7.
[118] Hume 1752, pp. 271–2.

praise of the glories of Bath.[119] The city is admired for its wealth, especially the comely order of its buildings and the grandeur of its palaces.[120] But it is also praised as a 'blest source of health', justly famous for curing the 'effects of luxury and ease'.[121] The people are elegant and cosmopolitan, and 'all mankind's epitome you view' in the stately pleasure rooms presided over by Beau Nash, where blooming virgins kindle amorous fires.[122] The city also affords many opportunities for self-improvement, and its bookshops provide the means to acquire and learn from the works of the wise and the great.[123] Most impressively, Bath holds an honoured place in the history of liberty. It was there that the great Nassau received a successful cure, thereby becoming the progenitor of 'heroes like William, ready to defend fair liberty oppressed and trampled laws'.[124]

London above all became an object of wonder and pride, and it was not long before Dr Johnson was declaring that to be tired of London is to be tired of life. Preaching in St Paul's Cathedral to the lord mayor and aldermen in 1747, Angel Chauncy assured the assembled dignitaries that the city had by now attained such heights that 'she hath scarce any superior, and few equals upon the face of the whole earth; few that can compare with her as to the splendour and pomp of her buildings, the extent and opulence of her trade, the number and dignity of her inhabitants'.[125] London was above all praised as a place in which there are unparalleled opportunities for advancement, so that the talents and energies of the industrious can hope to receive their greatest reward.

No one illustrated this scale of values more memorably than Hogarth in his sequence of engravings of 1748 on *The effects of industry and idleness*, which traces the contrasting lives of two London apprentices. An anonymous 'explanation' of the prints, published in the same year, recounts how the industrious apprentice managed to succeed. We learn that the spirit which is 'necessary to thrive in a mercantile state' involves 'a saving, careful disposition' and 'a scheme of emulation' together with 'sanguine ambitious hopes'.[126] The industrious apprentice duly cultivates these qualities, with the result that he is able not merely to prosper, but to marry his master's daughter, to inherit his business and to end up (in Hogath's final print) riding in his coach as lord mayor of London. The city itself is held out for our admiration at the same time, and we are informed of many good designs that are being carried forward, all of them

---

[119] On Chandler see Shuttleton 2003. The poem was first published in 1733 and in an extended form (from which I quote) in 1738.
[120] Chandler 1738, pp. 11–12.    [121] Chandler 1738, pp. 4, 6.
[122] Chandler 1738, pp. 13–14.    [123] Chandler 1738, p. 15.    [124] Chandler 1738, p. 13.
[125] Chauncy 1747, p. 17.    [126] *The effects of industry and idleness* 1748, p. 23.

'agreeable to the rules of religion and virtue' as well as beneficial to national wealth.[127]

The trajectory traced by the pro-government writers begins and ends with a celebration of happiness.[128] They start by congratulating the British on living under a happy constitution, happy in the sense of being well suited to its purposes. Due to the freedom it guarantees, everyone is able to cultivate their talents and enjoy an opportunity to win success and fulfilment. This in turn has the effect of bringing happiness in the sense of joy and contentment, which has enabled the British to become a happy and glorious people. The ministerial writers of the 1730s had already mapped out this trajectory,[129] but it was amid the euphoria following the defeat of the Jacobite rebellion that it was celebrated with the greatest confidence. Joseph Clarke in his thanksgiving sermon rejoiced that we are now 'the freest and the happiest people'.[130] Andrew Richardson expressed the conviction that, due to our happy constitution, we can now hope to achieve 'great abundance of everything that can make life joyous and delightful', thereby continually increasing 'the stock of private and public happiness'.[131] Arthur Sykes, preaching in Winchester Cathedral on the day of thanksgiving, resoundingly concluded that we are now 'blessed with the enjoyment of the greatest liberty, and in consequence with the greatest happiness of any nation upon earth'.[132] Among the rights secured to the British people by their constitution, everyone agreed that the list includes not merely life and liberty but the pursuit of happiness.

---

[127] *The effects of industry and idleness* 1748, pp. 19–21.

[128] On happiness as the goal of life as the defining feature of the Enlightenment see Robertson 2020, pp. 1–8. On the figure of the happy man in this period see Røstvig 1954–8.

[129] See, for example, Bate 1734, p. 11.      [130] Clarke 1746, p. 4.

[131] Richardson 1746, pp. 43, 48.      [132] Sykes 1746, p. 10.

*Part III*

Liberty as Independence: The Ideal Betrayed

# 5    The Persistence of Dependence

### The Plight of Women and Slaves

By the mid-1740s the pro-government Whig writers had forged a patriotic image of Britain as a free state presiding over a civil society in which everyone is able to enjoy a life of liberty. After the defeat of the Jacobite rebellion in 1746 this view of Britain's uniquely happy condition was emphatically reaffirmed, and in the general election of the following year the voters added their endorsement. The Pelhamite administration that had taken over in 1742 was returned to power with a decisively increased majority, leaving the Whig oligarchy in undisputed control.[1] A year later, Montesquieu in his *Spirit of the laws* felt able to congratulate the British on having constructed a beautiful system of government in which the laws of the constitution had established what he described as an extreme political liberty.[2]

Within less than thirty years this entire Whig vision had fallen victim to a combination of lethal ridicule and revolutionary attack. The onslaught may be said to have advanced in two distinct phases. The first took the form of a complete rejection of the optimistic Whig vision of the relationship between civil society and the state; the second involved nothing less than a dismantling of the Whig view of the state itself and the theory of liberty on which it was based. The first line of attack focused on the central claim advanced by the Whigs about the civil society they had created. As we saw in Chapter 4, their greatest boast was that, due to their implementation of the principles of 1688, the rule of law had at last been comprehensively achieved. Britain was now governed exclusively by laws that were 'equal and even' in their application, and under which the rights of every subject were 'equally regarded', so that no one was now obliged to live in subjection to any exercise of arbitrary power, whether by the state or any of their fellow citizens.[3]

---

[1] Foord 1964, pp. 265–7.    [2] Montesquieu 1989, part 2, book 11, ch. 6, p. 166.
[3] Howard 1745, pp. 7–9. On how liberty can be undermined by forms of domination and subjection permitted and enforced by social norms see Tully 2005; Coffee 2013; Coffee 2015; and Thompson 2018.

The most obvious way in which these claims were manifestly self-deceiving and false stemmed from their failure to acknowledge the persistence of slavery. As we saw in Chapter 1, when Sir Thomas Smith addressed the issue of enslavement in *De republica Anglorum* in the 1580s, he traced a development from the owning of bondsmen towards the employment of villeins, after which chattel slavery was 'by little and little extinguished' in England.[4] But the holding of slaves was never explicitly forbidden under English law,[5] and the number of slaves owned by Englishmen rose sharply after the Royal Africa Company began trading in the 1660s. The company mainly existed to export slaves to the American colonies and the West Indies, but some slaves were brought by their owners to England, and by the opening decades of the eighteenth century there were large numbers living in such major slave-trading ports as Bristol, Liverpool and especially London.[6] By the middle decades of the century some contemporary estimates were suggesting that up to 30,000 slaves were living in London alone.[7]

If the Whigs had reflected on the legal implications of this development they would have been obliged to admit that, according to their own principles, such a complete deprivation of liberty needed to be declared illegal at once. But the question of whether slavery and the slave trade should be abolished was scarcely even mentioned by English political writers during the first half of the eighteenth century. The only significant exception was Edward Trelawny, governor of Jamaica between 1738 and 1752, who published a tract in 1746 entitled *An essay concerning slavery*. This took the form of a dialogue between a sugar planter and an officer with whose views, Trelawny tells us, he is in agreement.[8] The officer criticises John Locke for appearing to allow slavery,[9] and expresses his surprise, grief and torment at the fact that 'the generous free Briton, who knows the value of liberty, who prizes it above life, who loves and enjoys it' is nevertheless willing for vile lucre to 'make a traffic of liberty' and 'be instrumental in depriving others of a blessing he would not part with but

[4] Smith 1982, p. 137. Some early eighteenth-century legal judgments continued to invoke this distinction. See Olusoga 2021, p. 120.

[5] On slavery and common law see Brewer 2021. See also Olusoga 2021, pp. 117–18 on the lack of legal clarity on the issue.

[6] Olusoga 2021, pp. 83–6. For a full account see Chater 2011.     [7] Olusoga 2021, p. 85.

[8] [Trelawny] 1746, p. 27.

[9] [Trelawny] 1746, p. 9. *The fundamental constitutions of Carolina* (1669), of which Locke was taken to be one of the authors, had endorsed the institution of slavery, with enslavers being granted the power of life and death over their slaves. On Locke and Carolina see Armitage 2004. On the problem of slavery in Locke's political thought see Farr 1986; Bernasconi and Mann 2005; Farr 2008.

with life'.[10] Speaking in his own voice in the introduction, Trelawny adds that slavery is without doubt 'contrary to the law of God and nature' and assures his readers that he wishes 'with all my heart that slavery was abolished entirely'.[11] But at the same time he makes it clear why the issue was so little discussed. The unthinkable result, he argues, 'would be a ruin to thousands whose wealth is wholly or chiefly invested' in the slave economy of the West Indies.[12] For the moment at least, the only question to be considered is 'how to render so valuable a possession safe and secure'.[13]

The predicament of women, and especially of wives, provided a further glaring instance in which the claim that no one living under English law was at the same time living in dependence on the arbitrary will of anyone else was obviously untrue.[14] This objection had already been raised in the aftermath of the revolution of 1688, when the supporters of the new regime began to publish their assurances that England was now a free state in which liberty was equally guaranteed to all. They suddenly found themselves confronted with an unprecedented barrage of criticism from women writers who managed to insist that their voices must be heard.[15] Judith Drake reacted at once in her *Essay in defence of the female sex* in 1696, pointing to the process by which women were still being required to 'give up their liberty and abjectly submit their necks to a slavish yoke'.[16] A few years later the same objection was vehemently reiterated in several responses to a sermon published in 1699 by the Dissenting preacher John Sprint under the title *The bride-woman's counsellor*. Sprint argued that the duty of wives is to cultivate a complete and willing submission to their husbands' authority. The author of *The female advocate* – who signed herself simply as Eugenia – immediately responded that this is to plead for nothing less than tyranny and enslavement, while the requirement of willingness means that the tyranny 'extends farther than the most absolute monarchs in the world'.[17] The demand is not merely that 'the woman must be a slave' but also 'a good easy tractable slave' who can be trodden underfoot with impunity.[18] A similar argument was developed in the following year by Mary Chudleigh in *The ladies defence*, a dialogue in verse in which the figure of Melissa responds to a demand for complete

---

[10] [Trelawny] 1746, p. 27. Lay 1737 also called for abolition, but his tract was never published in Britain.
[11] [Trelawny] 1746, Sig. A, 3r–v.    [12] [Trelawny] 1746, Sig. A, 3v.
[13] [Trelawny] 1746, Sig. A, 2r.
[14] On marital subjection see Sommerville 1995, pp. 79–113.
[15] See Broad 2014. For selections from their writings see Ferguson 1985, pp. 201–83.
[16] [Drake] 1696, p. 21.
[17] *The female advocate* 1700, pp. 12, 28. On Eugenia see Broad 2017, pp. 71–4.
[18] *The female advocate* 1700, pp. 17, 31, 40.

obedience by objecting that this would leave her in a state of bondage to her husband and 'a slave to his imperious will'.[19]

A more systematic statement of the case appeared in the 1706 Preface to Mary Astell's *Some reflections upon marriage*, which had first been published six years before.[20] Astell begins by observing 'that the custom of the world has put women, generally speaking, into a state of subjection' to the power of men.[21] She asks how this custom can be reconciled with the fundamental Whig tenet that 'arbitrary power is evil in itself, and an improper method of governing rational and free agents'.[22] If this is true in the case of kingdoms, how does the law come to permit the evil in the case of families, in which it is 'thought a wife's duty to suffer everything without complaint'? Turning to Locke's *Second treatise*, she quotes his declaration that 'the perfect condition of slavery' is that of someone 'subjected to the inconstant, uncertain, unknown arbitrary will' of someone else.[23] But this condition, she objects, is precisely that of women in Britain, so that slavery appears to be highly applauded and held to be necessary in their case while being wholly condemned in the case of men.[24] The question that demands an answer is: 'If all men are born free, how is it that all women are born slaves?'[25]

The same attack was forcefully renewed in the face of the increasingly complacent accounts of the impartiality of the law that the pro-government writers began to produce in the 1730s. One of the most powerful responses appeared in an anonymous tract of 1739 entitled *Woman not inferior to man*,[26] in which the author speaks of 'the tyrannical usurpation of authority' exerted by men over women,[27] and complains of 'the defect of justice' involved in this exercise of power.[28] Men have caused violence to take the place of justice, and 'all the authority which men have exerted over us hitherto' has been 'an unjust usurpation on their side'.[29] The outcome is that all women, and especially wives, have good reason 'to envy the lesser misery of a bond-slave' by comparison with their own condition, in which

[19] [Chudleigh] 1701, pp. 3, 5. On Chudleigh see Broad 2017, pp. 76–8.
[20] Springborg 1996, pp. xxxi–xxxii.
[21] Astell 1996, p. 10. For Astell on liberty see Sowaal 2017. On Astell see also Pateman 1988; Sommerville 1995; Springborg 1995.
[22] Astell 1996, p. 17.
[23] Astell 1996, p. 18; cf. [Locke] 1690, para. 22, p. 241. For Astell on Locke see Goldie 2007.
[24] Astell 1996, pp. 18–19. On Astell's call for equality as a demand for parity see Bejan 2019.
[25] Astell 1996, p. 18.
[26] *Woman not inferior to man* 1739. Based on the English translation (1677) of François Poulain de la Barre.
[27] *Woman not inferior to man* 1739, p. 2.    [28] *Woman not inferior to man* 1739, p. 7.
[29] *Woman not inferior to man* 1739, pp. 8–9.

they are forced to live 'in subjection and absolute dependence on the men'.[30] Speaking more positively, the author of *Beauty's triumph* of 1745 insists that 'there is no other difference between men and us than what their tyranny has created'.[31] Women are not inferior in intellectual capacity, and men are not better qualified to govern.[32] This being so, it is the merest injustice to exclude women 'from that power and dignity we have a right to share with them'. Men need to recognise 'how little reason they have to triumph in the base possession of an authority which unnatural violence and lawless usurpation put into their hands'.[33]

Meanwhile a remarkable series of examples showing how the law continued to uphold these injustices had been provided by Sarah Chapone in *The hardships of the English law in relation to wives*, first published in 1735.[34] One of the propositions Chapone illustrates is 'that the estate of wives is more disadvantageous than slavery itself'.[35] She takes the case of a cruelly treated wife who escapes to her brother's house. He appeals to her husband to let her stay there or else to treat her with common humanity. The only consequence is to reveal 'how unavailing is reason and soft persuasion when opposed to insolent power and arbitrary will'.[36] The husband insists on his legal 'right to control' and declares that 'it was an invasion of his prerogative royal for his wife to pretend to expostulate'.[37] His wife is carried home again, where she dies within a month, having been unable to gain any redress from the law. It will be objected, Chapone observes, that such cases are rare, and that in England most wives have no reason to complain.[38] As she insists, however, this is to misunderstand what is needed if women are to enjoy their liberty. It is not sufficient that no mistreatment should take place; it is also necessary that they should be protected by law from the possibility of any such mistreatment. If they lack this protection they are condemned to live 'in the condition of a slave', because there remains someone who has it in their power to tyrannise over them with impunity if they choose.[39] There can be no liberty without independence.

## The Maladministration of Justice

The 1740s saw the emergence of a further and devastating line of attack on the Whig vision of civil society in Britain. This was the juncture at which the hypocrisy and self-deception underlying the Whig account

---

[30] *Woman not inferior to man* 1739, pp. 18, 35.    [31] *Beauty's triumph* 1745, p. 10.

[32] *Beauty's triumph* 1745, pp. 21, 29.    [33] *Beauty's triumph* 1745, p. 10.

[34] See [Chapone] 1735. On Chapone see Broad 2015. On Astell and Chapone see also Dawson 2023, pp. 239–50.

[35] [Chapone] 1735, pp. 4, 6.    [36] [Chapone] 1735, p. 7.    [37] [Chapone] 1735, p. 7.

[38] [Chapone] 1735, p. 46.    [39] [Chapone] 1735, p. 46.

began to attract the satirical attention of a number of leading literary figures. It was at this moment that Henry Fielding came forward in the preface to *The history of the adventures of Joseph Andrews* in 1742 to announce in mock-Miltonic tones that he had invented a new species of satirical writing 'hitherto unattempted in our language'.[40] Fielding deprecates the prevailing use of the novel to tell stories of romance that contain 'very little instruction or entertainment'.[41] As the full title of *Joseph Andrews* informs us, he thinks of himself as writing a history, confining himself 'strictly to nature' in presenting his narrative and making sure that everything is 'taken from my own observation and experience'.[42] Fielding is keen to add, however, that he is at the same time writing a comedy, indeed nothing less than 'a comic epic poem in prose'.[43] His concern is thus with the ridiculous, and hence above all with hypocrisy.[44] This he takes to be most dangerous type of affectation, aiming as it does 'to avoid censure by concealing our vices under an appearance of their opposite virtue'.[45] The hypocrite is the worst of all the corrupters of religion and virtue, which 'are rightly called the bands of civil society'.[46] Fielding's chief aspiration, he tells us, is accordingly to strike his readers with surprise and pleasure by uncovering and satirising the numerous hypocrisies of the times.[47]

By the end of the decade, when Fielding published *The history of Tom Jones*, he felt obliged to recognise that this new kind of writing had by then gained a favourable reception for 'two or three authors' who had lately written in the same style.[48] One was Tobias Smollett, who had published *Roderick Random* in 1748, in which he had inveighed in his preface against the writers of romances and their thousand exaggerations and extravagancies, while insisting that his own narrative at no point deviates from the facts.[49] All the peculiarities of disposition he records 'appear as nature has implanted them', so that he 'brings every incident home to life', while at the same time giving himself 'an ample field for wit and humour'.[50] The

[40] Fielding 1999, pp. 49, 54. Cf. Milton 1998, p. 121, l. 16 on 'things unattempted yet in prose or rhyme'. But Fielding fails to acknowledge that Defoe in the preface to *Moll Flanders* (1722) had already criticised romances and claimed to be writing a history. See Defoe 1989, p. 37.

[41] Fielding 1999, p. 49.

[42] Fielding 1999, pp. 50–1, 54. Subsequently he speaks in the same terms at many points in *Tom Jones*. See Fielding 2005, pp. 73, 109, 137, 354.

[43] Fielding 1999, p. 49. On Fielding's use of classical models see Power 2015.

[44] Fielding 1999, pp. 51–3.    [45] Fielding 1999, pp. 52–3. Cf. Fielding 2005, p. 117.

[46] Fielding 2005, pp. 117, 423.    [47] Fielding 1999, pp. 52–3. Cf. Fielding 2005, p. 117.

[48] Fielding 2005, p. 428. For the date of publication of *Tom Jones* (February 1749) see Keymer and Wakely 2005, p. xi. Ten years later Sterne similarly claimed in *Tristram Shandy* that he was writing 'as an historian'. See Sterne 2003, p. 288.

[49] Smollett 1995, p. 5.    [50] Smollett 1995, pp. 3, 5.

other writer whom Fielding clearly had in mind was Samuel Richardson. Although Richardson was far from being a satirist in the manner of Fielding or Smollett, he was no less a critic of the hypocrisies they exposed, and in his *Clarissa* of 1748 he explicitly associated himself with Fielding's view of the novelist as a chronicler of civil society. He subtitled his work *The history of a young lady*, and expressed the hope in his postscript that his readers might gain from his work 'the pleasure that every person of taste receives from a well-drawn picture of nature'.[51]

Among the many achievements of this remarkable trio of 'new writers' was that they succeeded in creating a mirror-image of the civil society that the Whigs claimed to have established. More ruthlessly and effectively than any other commentators, they uncovered and illustrated the lies and delusions on which the Whig analysis was based. This is an aspect of their achievement that has not perhaps received as much attention it deserves, and I next want to concentrate on the force of the critique they were able to produce.

One of the most frequent targets of the new writers was the Whig contention that the administration of justice in Britain deserves the highest praise. As we saw in Chapter 4, the pro-government writers consistently argued that there are no longer any corrupt juries or incompetent Justices, and that the decisions of the courts are made in strict conformity with the relevant evidence and the requirements of the law. They constantly assure their readers that nowadays Britain not only has 'the best laws' but at the same time 'the best magistrates'.[52]

By the time the new writers began to address this claim, numerous pamphleteers had already reacted to it with incredulous rage. The shocking truth, as the author of *The law-suit* had argued in 1738, is that many country magistrates can hardly read or write, and that packed juries are regularly willing to perjure themselves.[53] If all Englishmen who have been undone by law were to hang out signs about their unjust treatment, 'we should see one at almost every door'.[54] The author of *English liberty* complained even more bitterly about 'the tyrannical and unconstitutional power of Justices of the Peace',[55] and some legal experts also spoke with remarkable frankness about the ignorance of local magistrates. Michael Dalton in his treatise on *The country Justice* included an appendix listing the penalties for offences against statutes, together with a note explaining that it had been included 'for the better help of such Justices of the Peace as have not been much conversant in the study of the laws of this realm'.[56]

---

[51] Richardson 1985, title page and p. 1499.    [52] [Hervey] 1732, pp. 7–8.
[53] *The law-suit* 1738, pp. 3, 26.    [54] *The law-suit* 1738, preface.
[55] *English liberty in some cases worse than French slavery* 1748, pp. 3, 6, 9, 11.
[56] Dalton 1746, title page and appendix. The 1746 edition was the finally revised version of Dalton's text, which originally appeared in 1705.

Among the new writers, Richardson has much to say in his *Pamela* of 1740 about the potentially dangerous powers of local magistrates. The heroine Pamela is a servant of barely sixteen years of age who lives in the household of Squire B. of Bedfordshire. He soon reveals himself to be a determined sexual predator whose advances she is constantly forced to negotiate and fend off. She writes to her parents about the possibility of swearing to the local constable that she feels in sufficient danger to ask that the squire should be bound over to keep the peace. But she immediately reflects that there is no prospect of being favourably heard by the local Justice, since that position is occupied by the squire himself.[57] As she complains to him, 'You are a Justice of Peace, and may send me to gaol if you please and bring me to a trial for my life.'[58] She objects that 'most hardly do you use the power you so wickedly have got over me', while acknowledging that 'to expostulate with such an arbitrary gentleman I know will signify nothing'.[59] Soon afterwards she confides to her journal that she does not see 'how can I help being at his beck', given that 'I am so wholly in his power'.[60] She feels nothing better than his slave, although she resolves to maintain the defence of her virtue, which is dearer to her than life.[61]

Fielding is likewise much concerned with the ignorance as well as the prejudices displayed by those who served as Justices. But he is initially content in *Joseph Andrews* to treat the problem at the level of farce. Joseph's friend Parson Adams, becoming lost at night in his travels, hears cries for help from a woman who turns out to be Joseph's intended bride, Fanny. She is being attacked by a group of men, but when the parson attempts to save her he in turn is overwhelmed. The group then resolve to carry Fanny and the parson before the local Justice on a charge of robbery and assault. The Justice is at dinner with some friends, and is already drunk, but he immediately orders Fanny and the parson before him. The depositions of the accusers are taken, and without troubling to read them the Justice instantly orders his clerk to prepare a mittimus that will enable him to send the two accused directly to gaol. Before anyone can protest that he lacks any such powers, one of his dinner guests recognises Parson Adams and is able to assure his host that, despite appearances, he is a clergyman and a gentleman. This brings the legal proceedings to an immediate halt. The Justice now assures his guest that, 'if he is a gentleman, and you say he is innocent, I don't desire to commit him', adding that 'nobody can say I have committed a gentleman since I have been in the Commission'.[62] Parson Adams is asked to give his

---

[57] Richardson 2001, p. 60.     [58] Richardson 2001, p. 58.     [59] Richardson 2001, p. 235.
[60] Richardson 2001, p. 238.     [61] Richardson 2001, pp. 191, 192.
[62] Fielding 1999, pp. 169, 170.

version of the story, after which the Justice declares that he believes every syllable of it, notwithstanding everything that his accusers have deposed against him on oath. By this time the accusers have felt it wise to make their escape, and further carousing brings the evening to an end.[63]

Smollett is no less scornful about the maladministration of justice, but he is more interested in illustrating the venality of magistrates. He first makes his attitude plain in recounting one of Roderick Random's early escapades in London. After a night on the town Roderick and his friends end up at a brothel, where one of them is robbed. When they complain, the brothel-keeper responds by summoning the constable and accusing them of defamation and riot. They are carried off as prisoners to the Round-House, but there the constable is able to sort everything out. He explains that their accuser 'has kept a notorious house in the neighbour-hood these many years, and although often complained of as a nuisance, still escapes through her interest with the Justices, to whom she and all of her employment pay contribution quarterly for protection'.[64] The safest course, the constable advises, will be to keep the whole matter out of the grasping hands of the magistrates and instead permit him to serve as umpire in their dispute. This is duly agreed, at which point the constable fines each party three shillings, with the proviso that the money should be spent in buying a bowl of punch. We are assured that in their ensuing drinking they drowned all animosities.[65]

By the time Fielding came to portray the administration of justice in *Tom Jones* he had become a magistrate himself, and was now inclined to reflect on the corruption and ignorance of local Justices in much graver tones. He regretfully observes that 'many arbitrary acts are daily commit-ted by magistrates'.[66] Referring specifically to the notoriously draconian game laws, he sarcastically adds that in matters of such high importance 'many Justices of Peace suppose they have a large discretionary power', and in exercising it they sometimes commit felonies themselves.[67] He concludes that 'the common fault' of magistrates is that they are 'apt to conclude hastily from every slight circumstance, without examining the evidence on both sides'.[68]

The plot of *Tom Jones* revolves around the households of two neigh-bouring landowners, Squire Allworthy and Squire Western, both of whom are Justices of the Peace. We are shown Western in action in his official role at the moment when his daughter Sophia is planning to run away from home. She wants her maid, Mrs Honour, to accompany her, and Mrs Honour ingeniously manages to do so, without having to leave

---

[63] Fielding 1999, p. 170.  [64] Smollett 1995, p. 96.  [65] Smollett 1995, p. 96.
[66] Fielding 2005, p. 171.  [67] Fielding 2005, p. 318.  [68] Fielding 2005, p. 534.

behind any of her possessions, by getting herself summarily dismissed. She seizes her chance during an argument with the maid employed by Western's sister, in which she describes Mrs Western as an ugly old cat, knowing that this judgement will immediately be reported to the old cat herself. Just as she had expected and hoped, Mrs Western's furious response is to insist that her brother should dismiss Mrs Honour at once. Far surpassing his sister in violence, Western not only agrees to her demand but swears twenty oaths that, in his capacity as a Justice, he will have Mrs Honour committed at once to Bridewell, the dreaded House of Correction. Mrs Western warmly welcomes his decision, 'earnestly desiring her brother to execute justiceship' on Mrs Honour's ill-bred insolence.[69]

Fortunately, Western's legal clerk has a qualification which, the authorial voice notes, 'no clerk to a Justice of Peace ought ever to be without, namely some understanding of the law of this realm'.[70] The clerk whispers to the Justice that he would be exceeding his authority if he were summarily to send Mrs Honour to prison. The reason is not merely that she made no attempt to breach the peace, but also that, as he levelly adds, 'you cannot legally commit anyone to Bridewell only for ill-breeding'.[71] Mrs Western refuses to be convinced, and immediately names 'a certain Justice of the Peace in London' who 'would commit a servant to Bridewell at any time when a master or mistress desired it'.[72] Western, however, finds himself reflecting that on two occasions he has already had information lodged against him in the King's Bench court for abusing his powers as a magistrate, and has 'no curiosity to try a third'.[73] He accordingly rescinds his decision, and his sister is 'obliged to content herself with the satisfaction of having Honour turned away'.[74]

At two moments in *Tom Jones* we are also able to observe Squire Allworthy in action as a magistrate. One is when his gamekeeper's daughter Molly becomes involved in an altercation in the churchyard, in the course of which a visiting musician is struck on the head. Next day he lodges a complaint with Allworthy, and Molly is summoned before him, at which point he can hardly fail to notice that she is pregnant. He demands to know the name of the father, but Molly resolutely refuses to tell him. Allworthy's instant reaction is to write a mittimus so that the constable can commit her to Bridewell.[75] Tom Jones, who admits to a shocked Allworthy that he may be the father himself, manages by means of his confession to secure Molly's release, and nothing more is

[69] Fielding 2005, p. 318.    [70] Fielding 2005, p. 318.    [71] Fielding 2005, p. 318.
[72] Fielding 2005, p. 319.    [73] Fielding 2005, p. 318.    [74] Fielding 2005, p. 319.
[75] Fielding 2005, pp. 167–8.

heard about Allworthy's initial judgment. Allworthy appears to think that he has behaved magnanimously in sparing Molly, but no one points out that he would have been acting far beyond his powers if his initial judgment had been carried out.[76] He ought to have known that his instructions to the constable were against the law. The signatures of at least two Justices of the Peace were required before an unmarried woman could be committed to the House of Correction, and no such committal could legally take place until at least a month after the birth of the illegitimate child.[77]

Still more disquieting is Allworthy's behaviour when he presides at the trial of the local schoolmaster, Benjamin Partridge, who has been accused of adultery by Mrs Wilkins, the maid to Allworthy's sister. Allworthy calls Partridge and his wife before him, and Mrs Wilkins presents her charge. The innocent and unworldly Partridge enters a plea of not guilty, but his name forewarns us that he is going to be fair game. His wife responds by unleashing a torrent of accusations against him, including cruelty, drunkenness and frequent adulteries. These are said to have included an affair with one of their own servants, Jenny Jones, to which Partridge is alleged by his wife to have confessed. She ends by expressing her willingness 'to take my bodily oath that I found them a bed together'.[78] Asked by Allworthy to respond, Partridge admits to his confession, but insists that he made it only to gain some domestic peace, and continues to protest his innocence of all charges against him.

Without hesitation Allworthy promises justice to Partridge's wife. Turning to Partridge, Allworthy tells him that he is 'sorry to see there was so wicked a man in the world'. He assures Partridge that the lies he has told are 'a great aggravation of his guilt' and exhorts him 'to begin by immediately confessing the fact, and not to persist in denying what was so plainly proved against him'.[79] Partridge pleads for Jenny Jones to be called as a witness in his defence, but it emerges that she has left home with a recruiting officer and no one knows her present whereabouts. Allworthy resolves the difficulty with no less dispatch than before. He first argues 'that the evidence of such a slut as she appeared to be would have deserved no credit'.[80] He then adds that, had she been present, he feels sure that 'she must have confirmed what so many circumstances, together with his own confession, and the declaration of his wife, that she had caught her husband in the fact, did sufficiently prove'.[81] Allworthy concludes that he is convinced of Partridge's guilt, and the trial ends with

---

[76] Except for the authorial voice. See Fielding 2005, p. 171.
[77] As noted by Keymer and Wakely 2005, p. 910.     [78] Fielding 2005, p. 92.
[79] Fielding 2005, p. 92.     [80] Fielding 2005, p. 93.     [81] Fielding 2005, p. 93.

the cancellation of Partridge's annuity and an exhortation from Allworthy to repentance.

During the trial scene, the reader is assured by the authorial voice that Allworthy is a man with a tender regard for legal procedure and justice.[82] But he turns out to be disgracefully ignorant of the law. He should have known – and numerous legal dictionaries were available to inform him – that in English law wives and husbands are forbidden to give evidence against one another.[83] We are constantly assured by the authorial voice that Allworthy is patient and careful as well as sagacious and wise.[84] But on both occasions when we see him discharging his role as a magistrate he wholly repudiates the Whig ideal of acting in strict conformity with the relevant evidence and the requirements of the law.[85]

**********

A further boast of the pro-government writers about the administration of justice had been that, because the law is imposed equally and impartially on everyone, even the highest in the land 'are not exempted from its cognisance' and nobody stands above the law.[86] Here it was even easier for the exponents of the new kind of writing to satirise the wishful thinking involved. Fielding in particular repeatedly illustrates the extent to which it seemed self-evident to many members of the ruling orders that a number of laws simply do not apply to them, and that they can also hope to rely on manipulating the law to serve their own interests.

The initial butt of Fielding's satire is the figure of Lady Booby in *Joseph Andrews* and her treatment of the hero of the novel. First Joseph finds himself obliged to fend off her amorous advances, for which he is angrily dismissed.[87] Lady Booby then suffers a further fit of pique when she learns that Joseph is planning to marry in the parish where her son has his estate, and that Parson Adams has begun to announce the banns. The parson is summoned to her presence and informed that she forbids any further announcements to be made. He explains that, because the couple have lived in the parish for more than a year, they have a legal right to be married in the parish church. Lady Booby responds by making it clear that the provisions of the law are of no interest to her. She informs the parson that 'it is my orders to you that you publish these Banns no more', and that if he

---

[82] Fielding 2005, p. 93.
[83] See the section on marriage in Wood 1738, pp. 57–63, esp. p. 59. Wood's guide was first published 1720; the 1738 version was the sixth edition.
[84] For these descriptions see Fielding 2005, respectively at pp. 223, 58, 128 and 251.
[85] See Tavor 1987, p. 123 on the frequent but mistaken perception that Mr Allworthy 'really is all-worthy'. See also Keymer and Wakely 2005, pp. xxxi–xxxiv.
[86] Osborne 1735, p. 25. See also Head 1747, p. 11.    [87] Fielding 1999, pp. 80, 85.

dares to do so she will ensure that he is dismissed.[88] She then sends for a lawyer, who assures her that her orders will undoubtedly be carried out, as 'the laws of this land are not so vulgar' as 'to permit a mean fellow to contend with one of your ladyship's fortune'.[89]

Later, in *Tom Jones*, Fielding similarly satirises Squire Western's reaction to the Profane Oaths Act that came into force in 1746. The Act imposed fines and even imprisonment on anyone found guilty of cursing and swearing, further specifying that the fines should be doubled in the case of members of the gentry.[90] The Act additionally required the clergy to read out these provisions from the pulpit four times a year, and we are told that Western's curate 'put the laws very severely into operation'.[91] This policy should have caused some difficulties for the squire, who is almost incapable of expressing himself without cursing and swearing at length. But his response is to insist that his privileges 'as a free-born Englishman' mean that the law simply does not apply to him.[92] The curate does not dare to argue the point, with the result that, as the authorial voice ruefully comments, 'the magistrate was the only person in the parish who could swear with impunity'.[93]

Subsequently we learn that Western's sister is no less high-handed, and that the squire is even more hypocritical. After his daughter Sophia runs away from home, the squire discovers that she has sought refuge with her cousin, Lady Bellaston, at her house in London. Reminding his sister that he has a legal right of access to his daughter, Western proposes to enforce it by taking out a warrant against Lady Bellaston. One might have expected Mrs Western to object that the squire's plan is unnecessarily heavy-handed, but instead she lectures him on the absurdity of supposing that the law has any application in the case of a person of such rank. 'Do you really imagine, brother, that the house of a woman of figure is to be attacked by warrants and brutal Justices of the Peace?'[94] There can be no question of permitting the law to intervene. 'Justices of Peace indeed! Do you imagine any such event can arrive to a woman of figure in a civilized nation?'[95] The squire is reduced to expostulating (with many curses) that this is not the law of England as he recognises it.[96] As he proudly boasts, he has heard his Lordship declare at the Assizes 'that no one is above the law'.[97] We are left to reflect that Western has either forgotten what he thought about the law on profane oaths, or else is wholly unmoved by his own hypocrisy.

---

[88] Fielding 1999, p. 281.     [89] Fielding 1999, p. 282.
[90] See *An act more effectually to prevent profane cursing and swearing* in Pickering 1765, pp. 442–9.
[91] Fielding 2005, p. 272.     [92] Fielding 2005, p. 271.     [93] Fielding 2005, p. 272.
[94] Fielding 2005, p. 709.     [95] Fielding 2005, p. 709.     [96] Fielding 2005, p. 710.
[97] Fielding 2005, p. 710.

The effect of imposing the rule of law equally on everyone, according to the pro-government writers, is that no one is left dependent on the mere will of anyone else in respect of their most essential rights. Everyone is equally secured by the law in the enjoyment of their life, liberty and property, and especially the property that everyone may be said to possess in their person. As we have seen, a number of the pro-government writers were especially keen to underline the success of the regime in upholding the first of these rights. The security of everyone's life was now said to be fully established,[98] so that even the humblest no longer have any need to fear rapine and violence.[99] We can all look forward to 'an uninterrupted enjoyment of life and liberty'.[100]

The more satirical among the new writers like to make it clear that these contentions are not merely ludicrously but dangerously out of line with everyday experience. When Joseph Andrews is dismissed by Lady Booby he has no option but to set out on foot for his native village. He is instantly attacked, robbed, thrown into a ditch and left for dead.[101] When Roderick Random begins his long walk from Scotland to England he is at once held up at gunpoint and narrowly avoids being killed.[102] When Tom Jones arrives at the end of his journey from Somerset to London he is accosted by an armed highwayman and has to save himself by wresting the pistol from his assailant's grasp.[103] The open road, proverbially a space of freedom, is shown to be a site of continual menace. Far from being protected by the law against any danger to their lives, these characters are all obliged to use their native strength to survive. Joseph Andrews and Tom Jones both carry cudgels, and both are prepared to put them to almost lethal use.[104] Roderick Random comes so close to death at the hands of an armed antagonist that he eventually decides to learn some skill at swordplay, although he is nearly murdered as a result.[105] The claim that the security of everyone's life is fully established in British society is repeatedly exhibited as a dangerous fantasy.

The second element in the Whig triad, the right to personal liberty, was held by pro-government writers to be no less safe and respected. They regularly celebrated the fact that Britain is governed by a system of laws under which liberty is 'preserved entire', so that no one can be imprisoned or held under forcible restraint by any power except that of a court of law.[106] Whether this further article of faith was any less a fantasy was a question much canvassed by the new writers, and by no one more extensively than Richardson in *Pamela* and later in *Clarissa*. He first

---

[98] Herring 1745, pp. 14, 24–5.
[99] Coney 1731, p. 14; Fothergill 1737, p. 35; Lane 1746, p. 28.     [100] Trott 1746, p. 20.
[101] Fielding 1999, pp. 88–9.     [102] Smollett 1995, p. 45.     [103] Fielding 2005, p. 598.
[104] Fielding 1999, p. 270; Fielding 2005, pp. 439–41.
[105] Smollett 1995, pp. 60–1, 363–4.     [106] Brekell 1746, pp. 35–6.

considers the issue in the course of examining the plight of servants. When Pamela persistently refuses Squire B.'s sexual advances, he arranges for her to be forcibly carried off to his estates in Lincolnshire, where she is kept prisoner for nearly two months.[107] She repeatedly refers in her journal to this violation of her personal freedom, speaking of her bondage and misery, the heavy restraint placed upon her movements, and a confinement so close and oppressive as to make her weary of life.[108] Pamela is not given to thinking of herself as someone possessed of natural rights, but she explicitly uses the language of freedom and servitude as she describes her predicament, lamenting that she is no longer 'a free person' but is being treated as 'a sordid slave'.[109]

Richardson recurs to the theme in *Clarissa*, in which one of his principal aims is to show that a lack of security for personal liberty can arise in the highest ranks of society. Clarissa is attracted to the handsome and dashing figure of Mr Lovelace, but her family insist that she must marry the rich Mr Solmes.[110] When Clarissa resolutely refuses him, she is imprisoned by her family as a means of forcing her compliance. She is eventually confined to her room under the hostile eye of a servant, who has special orders to keep her under lock and key.[111] She becomes, as she records, a prisoner who is not only made to suffer a hard confinement, but has seen her personal freedom sacrificed to the ambitions of her family.[112] Her sole consolation is that she is far from being 'such a poor slave' as to agree to change her mind simply because of the violence she has suffered.[113] The impatient Lovelace condemns her family for 'an arbitrariness that had few examples even in the families of princes', and eventually solves the problem by persuading Clarissa to run away with him.[114]

The third and final item in the Whig list of essential rights was agreed to be that of holding one's property with complete security. As we have seen, at this point the pro-government writers like to speak not merely of lands and goods, but also about the properties of individuals, arguing in Lockean vein that these include 'whatever a man may justly call his own', including 'all the constituent parts of himself'.[115] When the new writers think about property in the sense of lands and goods they have no complaints about the success of the Whig regime in securing this further natural right. But when they reflect on the property that everyone may be said to possess in their person they are much less happy with Whig complacencies. Here their principal concern is with the predicament of

---

[107] Richardson 2001, pp. 92, 97, 181, 239.
[108] Richardson 2001, pp. 119, 145, 161, 180–1.     [109] Richardson 2001, p. 139.
[110] Richardson 1985, pp. 55–8.     [111] Richardson 1985, pp. 62–3, 118–21, 151.
[112] Richardson 1985, pp. 123, 170, 198.     [113] Richardson 1985, p. 307.
[114] Richardson 1985, p. 168.     [115] Richardson 1746, p. 7; Head 1747, pp. 4, 6.

women, whose right to live free from molestation and violence is seen as very far from secure. The kind of threat that women are prone to face is vividly illustrated in *Joseph Andrews* when the beautiful Fanny, the hero's betrothed, happens to encounter the figure of Beau Didapper.[116] The terms in which Fielding describes the Beau make it clear that he is mocking one of the leaders of the pro-government Whigs, Lord Hervey.[117] First Didapper and then his servant attack and molest Fanny, and only the sudden appearance of Joseph enables her to be saved.[118] Nor are servants alone in facing this danger. When Sophie Western in *Tom Jones* takes refuge from her father in London, she is immediately pestered by the attentions of Lord Fellamar. After she rejects his advances, he decides to follow the advice of Lady Bellaston and entrap Sophia into marrying him by raping her. As he gets ready to pounce, he asks pardon for 'freedoms which nothing but despair could have tempted me to take'.[119] Sophia is saved only because her father, pursuing her to Lady Bellaston's house, bursts in upon the scene in the nick of time, and after violently insulting Lord Fellamar carries Sophia home.[120]

With Richardson, the danger posed by men who are prepared to violate young women is turned – not without some prurience – into one of his central themes. Pamela's master, Squire B., not only refuses to recognise her property in her person, but persistently refers to her as his own property. He declares that he has a right to be 'free with you', and objects that 'you have robbed me' in refusing to submit to his liberties.[121] Pamela is eventually allowed a happy ending of sorts when Squire B. sees the error of his ways and agrees to marry her. Not so Clarissa. When she decides to leave her parents' house and submit to Lovelace's protection, she finds him resolved on 'a still bolder freedom', and indignantly repulses him.[122] Lovelace complains that his 'innocent liberties' are being refused, and when Clarissa removes herself from the house in which he has virtually imprisoned her, he objects that she has robbed him of 'the dearest property I had ever purchased'.[123] He responds by staging a plot that enables him to drug and rape her.[124] Clarissa falls into a lingering decline, and after writing forgiving letters to her family she dies a willing death.[125]

---

[116] Fielding 1999, pp. 298–9.
[117] As noted in Beasley 1982, p. 77. See also Smallwood 1989, pp. 109–10. Fielding 2005, p. 307 describes the Beau as a 'little person or rather Thing'. Pope in *An epistle to Dr Arbuthnot* had described Hervey as 'that thing of silk'. See Pope 2011, p. 187.
[118] Fielding 1999, pp. 298–9.    [119] Fielding 2005, p. 701.
[120] On the misconduct of Lady Bellaston see Smallwood 1989, pp. 43–4.
[121] Richardson 2001, pp. 57, 58, 305.    [122] Richardson 1985, p. 7–5.
[123] Richardson 1985, pp. 619, 736.    [124] Richardson 1985, pp. 883, 998–1013.
[125] See Richardson 1985, pp. 1371–7 for her letters and p. 1362 on her death.

## The Spirit of Servility

The Whig vision of civil society culminates in the claim that the British are distinguished by their spirit of liberty, which is said to be manifested in their independence, their ambition and industriousness, and their willingness to devote their energies to high designs. These are the qualities that have brought prosperity to the whole nation, a prosperity magnificently reflected in the splendour of its cities and the greatness of its trade. By contrast, the enslavement suffered by the unfortunate subjects of absolute and tyrannical monarchies is said to bring with it an abject spirit of servility that no one can hope to avoid.

This was the self-image that the new writers sought above all to contest and reject. As they repeatedly illustrate, the British people may not be living under absolute monarchy, but most of them are nevertheless condemned to an ignominious life of dependence and servitude. One obvious instance is that of the entire servant class, a point already made with great bitterness by a number of servants themselves. Robert Dodsley in *The footman's friendly advice* of 1730 had addressed his fellow servants as 'brothers in servitude'.[126] The advice he had offered them is that they must learn submission in the face of every rebuke, but at the same time he had warned that they can expect to be despised and degraded, faced with imperious menaces, and treated with harshness and severity.[127] The anonymous author of *The footman's looking-glass* of 1747 went much further, complaining of cruel and inhuman behaviour, and of masters who act as if their servants are not their fellow creatures and treat them as slaves.[128]

Among the new writers, it is Fielding who most frequently echoes these claims about the plight of servants, strongly agreeing that they have little hope of justice, no security for their rights, and consequently find themselves reduced to acting with servile obsequiousness as the only means to survive. At an early stage in *Tom Jones* we are introduced to the figure of Mrs Wilkins, the maid to Squire Allworthy's sister. We are told that she has become a 'truly great politician', and has perfected the indispensable skill of seldom speaking 'either to her master or his sister till she had first sounded their inclinations, with which her sentiments were always strictly consonant'.[129] Mrs Wilkins's dependence is in turn shown to have a malign effect on her behaviour towards her supposed inferiors. Here Fielding invokes the language habitually used by pro-government Whigs to condemn despotic power, explaining that it is 'the nature of such persons as Mrs Wilkins to insult and tyrannize

---

[126] Dodsley 1730, p. 15.    [127] Dodsley 1730, pp. 6, 12.
[128] *The footman's looking-glass* 1747, pp. 21, 27.    [129] Fielding 2005, p. 56.

over little people', this being 'the means which they use to recompense to themselves their extreme servility'.[130]

Later Fielding paints a similar picture of Sophia Western's maid Mrs Honour. As her name tells us, she misses honour. She is incapable of any settled loyalty and is wholly attached to furthering her own interests.[131] But as Fielding invites us to reflect, how could it be otherwise?[132] Mrs Honour provides an answer herself in the course of explaining to Tom Jones why she is no longer in a position to offer him and Sophia any help. She has agreed to enter the service of Lady Bellaston, who has conceived a detestation for Sophia, and she does not dare to do anything that Lady Bellaston might dislike. Tom needs to understand, as she explains, that 'servants may be damned' and that 'it signifies nothing what becomes of them, though they are turned away and ruined'.[133] How can they hope to be other than compliant and submissive?

The new writers are also keen to emphasise that many other people, although more socially elevated than servants, live in such precarious circumstances that they too are obliged to cringe before their masters. As usual it is Smollett who addresses the underlying injustice with the greatest vehemence. When Roderick Random first arrives in London he aspires to gain a position that he believes to be in the gift of a member of Parliament. We are alerted to his naïveté, however, by the fact that the member is called Mr Cringer, who duly proves to be living in a state of shameful subservience. Roderick eventually gains admission to his house, but he is made 'to dance attendance every other morning' at an extremely early hour because Cringer is himself obliged to attend the levées of Lord Terrier at break of day.[134] After a long period of what he condemns as 'servile dependence', Roderick discovers that Cringer is merely pretending to be a man of influence and has nothing to offer him or anyone else.[135] Nor is this the only period in which, despite his standing as a gentleman, Roderick is reduced to following a way of life in which he is unable to avoid behaving with servility.[136] When he is employed for eight months as a footman, he declares that the time spent in that humiliating role amounted to nothing better than servitude.[137] Reduced to a slavish station in life, he found himself beginning to behave in abject ways as 'my spirit began to accommodate itself to my beggarly fate'.[138]

---

[130] Fielding 2005, p. 47.    [131] See Fielding 2005, pp. 310, 532, 716–17, 804.
[132] On Fielding and feminist debate see Smallwood 1989.    [133] Fielding 2005, p. 711.
[134] Smollett 1995, pp. 74, 80.    [135] Smollett 1995, pp. 80, 82.
[136] Smollett 1995, pp. 143, 221.    [137] Smollett 1995, p. 231.
[138] Smollett 1995, p. 143.

Fielding illustrates the same problem in *Tom Jones* with his portrait of Squire Western's curate, Parson Supple, who is wholly dependent on the good will of the squire for his advancement. Western does not scruple to point out the implications of the parson's predicament; when he dares to speak up for Sophia after she flees from her father's house to escape the marriage he wants for her, Western becomes not merely enraged but threatening. 'You take her part then, do you? A pretty parson truly, to side with an undutiful child. Yes, yes, I will gee you a living with a pox. I'll gee un to the Devil sooner.' The parson is reduced to a grovelling apology and silence.[139] With considerable fellow-feeling, Mrs Honour explains his dilemma to Tom Jones:

To be sure I wishes that parson Supple had but a little more spirit to tell the squire of his wickedness in endeavouring to force his daughter contrary to her liking; but then his whole dependence is on the squire, and so the poor gentleman, though he is a very religious good sort of man, and talks of the badness of such doings behind the squire's back, yet he dares not say his soul is his own to his face.[140]

As Fielding signals, the parson's predicament leaves him with no option but to be supple.

Far from being a land imbued with the spirit of liberty, the whole of British society is shown to be little more than a teetering ladder of dependence. Smollett likes to illustrate the true situation in his most farcical style. During his seafaring days Roderick encounters an uncle who promises to gain him renewed employment as a ship's surgeon. He then explains the reason for his confidence:

The beadle of the admiralty is my good friend; and he and one of the under-clerks are sworn brothers, and that under-clerk has a good deal to say with one of the upper-clerks, who is very well-known to the under-secretary who, upon his recommendation, I hope will recommend my affair to the first secretary; and he again will speak to one of the lords on my behalf.[141]

By this stage in his adventures, Roderick confides, he 'could not help smiling at the description of my uncle's ladder', since by now he 'knew the world too well to confide in such dependence myself'.[142]

The same image had already been invoked by Fielding in *Joseph Andrews*. He too wishes to present us, as he puts it, with 'the picture of dependence like a kind of ladder'.[143] As soon as the day dawns, a footman begins by serving the squire's personal attendant, who in

---

[139] Fielding 2005, pp. 703–4.   [140] Fielding 2005, pp. 712–13.
[141] Smollett 1995, p. 237; cf. also p. 388.   [142] Smollett 1995, p. 237.
[143] Fielding 1999, p. 177.

turn serves the squire. At this point the ladder comes into view: 'The squire is no sooner equipped than he attends the levée of my Lord; which is no sooner over than my Lord himself is seen at the levée of the favourite, who after his hour of homage is at an end appears himself to pay homage to the levée of his sovereign.'[144] As Fielding observes, 'the question might only seem whether you would choose to be a great man at six in the morning or at two in the afternoon'. Despite the universality of dependence, however, almost all of those standing on the ladder 'think the least familiarity with the persons below them a condescension, and if they were to go one step further, a degradation'.[145]

These depressing reflections sometimes induce in the new writers a feeling of misanthropy, and they occasionally seem to suggest that the only route to happiness might be to give up humankind altogether. Defoe had already entertained the thought when recounting Robinson Crusoe's reflections on his early years of living on his island. He comes to believe that it might be 'possible for me to be more happy in this forsaken solitary condition than it was probable I should ever have been in any other particular state in the world'.[146] What is he being denied, he asks himself, other than 'all the wickedness of the world', and why is he not better off in solitude?[147] A similar question is raised in *Joseph Andrews* when Fielding interrupts his narrative to insert the story of Mr Wilson's life. Mr Wilson recounts his rake's progress through a ruinous youth of gambling and debauchery until the redemptive moment when he meets and immediately marries his wife. By then he has come to realise 'that the pleasures of the world are chiefly folly and the business of it mostly knavery'.[148] He and his wife decide to withdraw from the 'noise, hatred, envy and ingratitude' they encounter every-where in urban life, and go to live in retirement 'with little other conver-sation than our own', finally gaining contentment by abandoning the world.[149]

For Fielding, as for Smollett, there is a milder version of retreat that they eventually wish to recommend. They both ground it on a strong distaste for urban life. As we saw in Chapter 4, cities such as London and Bath had become widely admired not merely for their splendour and opulence, but also for the dignity of their inhabitants and the usefulness of their lives. But Roderick Random decides after only a few days in London that the city must be where the devil has set up his throne, and

---

[144] Fielding 1999, p. 177.    [145] Fielding 1999, pp. 177–8.    [146] Defoe 2001, p. 91.
[147] Defoe 2001, p. 102.    [148] Fielding 1999, p. 231.    [149] Fielding 1999, pp. 231, 234.

throughout his time there he repeatedly reflects on the corruption, the caprice and the barbarity of the urban world.[150] Nor does Bath suit him any better. He finds the town full of scoundrels, and dismisses the celebrated Beau Nash as a ludicrous figure prone to aggression and insolence.[151] Fielding similarly warns us in *Tom Jones* that London is a place of affectation and vice, where the men are addicted to gambling and the women to what he describes as intrepid indecorousness.[152] He too finds Bath no more acceptable. Whereas Mary Chandler in her eulogy had spoken of blooming virgins and serious pursuits, Fielding repeatedly associates the place with prostitution and regards it as given over to vanity and deceit.[153]

The idea of a happy ending is explicitly connected with abandoning urban life and withdrawing into rural retirement. Once Roderick Random gets married he immediately bids farewell to his London friends and travels back to Scotland. He has suddenly become rich as a result of his final seafaring adventure, a lucrative shipment of slaves from Guinea to South America. He has nothing to say about the horrors of the slave trade; what alone matters for him is that his profits enable him to buy back his family's estate. There he settles down in the place from which he originally started out, drawing his story to a close by declaring that 'if there be such a thing as true happiness on earth, I enjoy it'.[154]

Fielding brings *Tom Jones* to an end on a strikingly similar note. He recalls the pivotal moment when his hero was banished by Squire Allworthy from his house, Paradise Hall in Somerset.[155] The end of the novel is a story of paradise regained. Tom Jones finally marries his beloved Sophia Western in London, but within two days they return to Somerset, where they settle down, raise a family and become beloved by all. The authorial voice ends by assuring us that no couple can be imagined who enjoy greater happiness.[156] They live in untroubled independence, not subject to the arbitrary will of any ruthless employers or haughty grandees, and they possess the fullest possible security for their lives, liberties and estates.

As the new writers repeatedly point out, such a way of life was possible only for a very small and very fortunate elite. Furthermore, they hint at a deeper problem raised by the ideal itself. If it is to be attained, it will be necessary – at the very least – to outlaw slave-holding in Britain, to guarantee equality for women under the law, and to provide some security

---

[150] Smollett 1995, pp. 78–9, 119–20, 141–2.   [151] Smollett 1995, pp. 322, 334.
[152] Fielding 2005, pp. 37, 615, 651–2.   [153] Fielding 2005, pp. 189, 437, 464, 475.
[154] Smollett 1995, p. 432.   [155] Fielding 2005, p. 91.   [156] Fielding 2005, p. 874.

of employment for all. But how can such a series of transformations be achieved in the absence of revolutionary social and economic change? The underlying moral to which the new writers point is not so much that the Whigs have failed to attain their goals, but rather that their goals may be unattainable.

# 6    The Continuing Use of Arbitrary Power

## The Despotic Potential of Public Debt

The middle decades of the eighteenth century saw the emergence of a further and yet more serious line of attack on Whig complacencies. The focus at this juncture was less on hypocritical claims about civil society and more on the failure to acknowledge that the standing of Britain as a free state was beginning to be dangerously undermined. One pressing anxiety centred on the growth of public debt as a threat to liberty as well as prosperity. The national debt had originally been created in 1694 when a group of city traders agreed to lend £1,200,000 to the government in return for being incorporated as the Bank of England.[1] The sum was raised within ten days and used to improve England's military and especially naval capabilities,[2] thereby forging a close link from the outset between the accumulation of state debt and the waging of imperial wars by fiscal military states.[3]

This new method of financing government was first put to intensive use after the outbreak of the War of the Spanish Succession in 1701, in which the Grand Alliance confronted the forces of Louis XIV. When the conflict finally came to an end in 1713, the cost of Marlborough's land campaigns, together with the subsidies paid to Britain's allies, had caused the national debt to spiral to unimagined heights. According to contemporary estimates, the figure had risen by 1716 to at least £45,000,000.[4] After Walpole came to power in 1721, however, the level began to stabilise. The Whig administration took care to keep out of continental wars, and a decade later the debt had grown by only a small percentage. According to a startlingly exact calculation published in 1731, the total sum owed in

---

[1] Dickson 1967, pp. 54–5.

[2] On public borrowing and war expenditure see the table in Dickson 1967, p. 10.

[3] As argued in Brewer 1989, pp. 29–63.

[4] See [Pulteney] 1727, p. 5. The author of *The present state of the national debt* 1740, p. 6 suggests a figure close to £54,000,000 for the same date. But modern estimates are lower. According to Dickson 1967, p. 80 the figure in 1714 was £40,357,011; according to Brewer 1989, p. 30 it was £36,200,000.

the previous year had been £47,436,924.10s.7d.[5] By 1742, when
Walpole fell from power, the figure had risen by only a similar percentage,
and stood at £48,915,074.16s.9d.[6] Two years earlier, however, the War
of the Austrian Succession had broken out, and Britain's decision to enter
the conflict on the side of Austria against France soon brought spiralling
military costs as before. By the end of the war in 1748 the price of
blockading the French sea coast, together with subsidies paid to the
Austrian regime, had helped to raise the debt to alarming heights. When
the economist Andrew Hooke published his *Essay on the national debt* in
1750, he estimated that the figure had by then reached £80,000,000.[7]

This was the moment when a number of commentators began to voice
the fear that these developments could hardly fail to bring national ruin.
Here they drew on several lines of argument originally put forward by
those who had opposed the establishment of the Bank of England in 1694.
One purely economic objection had been that, as the author of *Some
considerations* had expressed it, the bank will be 'pernicious to the whole
commerce and manufacture of this kingdom by draining the money out of
the channel of trade'.[8] An associated objection had been that, as John
Briscoe had argued in his *Discourse* on the Bank of England, the issuing of
bonds 'will be a means to carry out our wealth' and place it in foreign
hands, thereby impoverishing as well as endangering the security of the
kingdom as a whole.[9]

Some of these early critics also raised serious political concerns, and no
one more trenchantly than the author of *Some considerations* in 1694.
A future king with despotic leanings could easily use the funds to overthrow the laws of the kingdom, thereby 'trampling upon the people's
liberties'. He would only need 'to introduce his own creatures to be the
chief managers of the Bank by furnishing them with money out of the
exchequer to outbid all others in purchasing of shares', thereby putting
'all or most of the money in the kingdom at his own command'. With this
arrangement in place, what might such a ruler not attempt and accom-
plish 'against our rights, laws and liberties?' A king 'who has engrossed the
money of the nation into his own hands' would be in a position to

---

[5] *The national debt* 1731, p. 17.
[6] *The present state of the national debt* 1744, pp. 1–2. But again these contemporary figures
may be too high. Dickson 1967, p. 210 estimates that there was a net decrease of over
£6,000,000 under the Walpole regime.
[7] Hooke 1750, pp. 27, 46–7. The same figure had already been given in Henriques 1749
(single sheet) and was later endorsed in *An inquiry* 1753, p. 4. But again modern
estimates are lower. The figure in 1749 according to Dickson 1967, p. 232 was
£70,441,296; according to Brewer 1989, p. 30 it was £76,100,000.
[8] *Some considerations* 1694, p. 17. See also Briscoe 1694, p. 13.     [9] Briscoe 1694, p. 13.

maintain as large a military force as he pleased, and nothing would then hinder him from 'making himself absolute and reducing us to be slaves'.[10]

The same objections resurfaced in 1720 after Parliament accepted a proposal from the South Sea Company to assume responsibility for easing the national debt. This at first caused the company's shares to boom, but the bubble burst almost immediately, precipitating mass bankruptcies.[11] The government was ferociously denounced, and it was at this moment that Trenchard and Gordon began to publish *Cato's letters*, devoting their opening sequence of articles to attacking 'the execrable arts of stock-jobbers' and their destruction of so many livelihoods and so much trade.[12] They reiterated the economic arguments originally raised against the founding of the bank, especially the danger that industry and commerce might become increasingly marginalised.[13] But they also recurred to the constitutional anxieties that had initially been expressed. As they solemnly warned, the engrossing of too much money by the crown would enable wild wars to be waged and standing armies to be maintained, and these are the readiest means to convert liberty into servitude.[14]

This concern was strongly underlined by the parliamentary opponents of Walpole's regime. When Walpole's rival and enemy William Pulteney published *A state of the national debt* in 1727 he again spoke of the need 'to preserve the liberties of this kingdom in opposition to all endeavour to entail upon us a succession of endless debts', and concluded that current government policies will be bound to end in 'poverty and slavery'.[15] A decade later the author of *The present state of the national debt* recurred to earlier suggestions about how this disaster might easily arise. The danger is that the size of the debt allows the crown 'a greater weight in the constitution than it was ever able to acquire by the chimerical notions of prerogative'.[16] The king is now becoming 'the steward of all the public money', and the chief minister is gaining a correspondingly greater influence in the disposal of offices of state. A venal administration could easily betray the country by managing 'to corrupt the honesty of her representatives and to undermine the foundations of her liberty'. Suppose a chief minister wielding so much power also had the backing of 'a strong standing army to overawe the collective body of the nation'. Then we should have to ask ourselves 'by what means the people of Britain can assert their liberties'.[17]

---

[10] *Some considerations* 1694, pp. 5–6.   [11] Dickson 1967, pp. 90–121.
[12] Trenchard and Gordon 1995, p. 41.   [13] Trenchard and Gordon 1995, p. 47.
[14] Trenchard and Gordon 1995, pp. 41–2, 57.   [15] [Pulteney] 1727, p. 82.
[16] *The present state of the national debt* 1740, pp. 19–20.
[17] *The present state of the national debt* 1740, pp. 20–1.

After the addition of more than £30,000,000 to the national debt in the course of the 1740s these anxieties began to be expressed in nothing less than apocalyptic terms.[18] Trenchard and Gordon's warnings gained a new audience with the reprinting of *Cato's letters* in 1748, and again in 1754 and 1755. But the most alarmed and influential assessment of the situation was produced by David Hume in his essay *Of public credit* in 1752, in which he condemned the ever-increasing mortgaging of public revenues as 'a practice which appears ruinous beyond the evidence of a hundred demonstrations'.[19] The outcome of such reckless borrowing will be 'certain and inevitable', and will take the form of 'poverty, impotence and subjection to foreign powers'.[20]

The appearance of this essay, so intensely critical of Whig policies, constituted a notable departure for Hume. As we have seen, in his early political essays of 1741–2 he had almost invariably supported the pro-government Whig cause. Already in 1748, however, he had announced a departure from Whig orthodoxy in his essay *Of the original contract*, and he now carried his criticism of the Whigs much further, adopting a stance earlier associated almost exclusively with enemies of the Walpole regime. His essay on public credit begins by reiterating the economic objections to the national debt that earlier critics had already raised. He first observes that 'the taxes which are levied to pay the interests of these debts are a check upon industry, heighten the price of labour, and are an oppression on the poorer sort'.[21] He adds that 'as foreigners possess a share of our national funds, they render the public in a manner tributary to them, and may in time occasion the transport of our people and our industry'.[22] But Hume is even more worried about the political implications of continually allowing the debt to rise. He argues that the injury thereby done to commerce and industry 'is trivial in comparison of the prejudice that results to the state considered as a body politic'. 'The ill there', he concludes, 'is pure and unmixed, without any favourable circumstance to atone for it', and it is an ill 'of a nature the highest and most important'.[23]

Hume is reticent about explaining what he means by saying that the debt is placing the entire body politic in jeopardy. But he was much more forthright when he published an extended version of his argument in his

---

[18] I arrive at this figure by comparing *The state of the national debt* 1744, p. 1–2 with Hooke 1750, pp. 27, 46–7.

[19] Hume 1752, p. 124. On Hume and public debt see Forbes 1976; Pocock 1985, pp. 125–41; Hont 2005, pp. 325–53; Whatmore 2023, pp. 25–32.

[20] Hume 1752, p. 125.    [21] Hume 1752, p. 131.    [22] Hume 1752, p. 131.

[23] Hume 1752, pp. 131–2.

*Essays and treatises* of 1764.[24] During the intervening years Britain had played a leading role in the Seven Years War, fighting the French in Canada as well as Europe in an imperial conflict of unprecedented scale.[25] The cost was likewise unprecedented, and by the time the Treaty of Paris brought the war to an end in 1763 the national debt had risen to £140,000,000.[26] When Hume rewrote his essay at this juncture, he felt able to warn his readers that 'the seeds of ruin' in Britain have by now been 'scattered with such profusion as not to escape the eye of the most careless observer', and in a new section of his essay he laid out the reasons for his despair.[27]

Hume begins with the assumption that the propertied classes in Britain can be regarded as a natural bulwark against any attempt by the government to exercise arbitrary and despotic power. But as the national debt continues to rise, and as state bonds are increasingly held by foreign investors, a dangerous amount of national wealth will fall into the hands of men 'who have no connections in the state', and 'who can enjoy their revenues in any part of the world in which they choose to reside'.[28] If this process continues, 'the several ranks of men which form a kind of independent magistracy in a state' will disappear in Britain, and everyone in authority will derive their influence 'from the commission alone of the sovereign'. Once this happens, 'no expedient remains for preventing or suppressing insurrections but mercenary armies', and 'no expedient at all remains for resisting tyranny'. Parliamentary elections will be 'swayed by bribery and corruption alone', and 'the middle power between the king and people being totally removed, a horrible despotism must infallibly prevail'.[29] The income of every citizen will lie 'entirely at the mercy of the sovereign', thereby ushering in 'a degree of despotism which no oriental monarchy has ever yet attained'.[30] This is the fatal outcome 'to which Great Britain is visibly tending', and he concludes that the country is already travelling along 'the beaten road to power and tyranny'.[31]

Hume's original essay of 1752 gained him many admirers,[32] but by the time he published these further reflections in 1764 his argument had been anticipated by several other writers on the debt crisis. The author of *The herald or patriotic proclaimer* of 1758 had already expressed a similar fear

---

[24] On Hume's expansion of his argument in 1764 see Hont 2005, pp. 327–8, 342–8.

[25] See Marston 2001, pp. 9 and 29–79.

[26] This contemporary estimate has been endorsed by modern scholarship. See Perceval 1763, p. 4; and cf. Brewer 1989, p. 115.

[27] Hume 1764, vol. 1, p. 391.    [28] Hume 1764, vol. 1, pp. 391–2.

[29] Hume 1764, vol. 1, p. 392.    [30] Hume 1764, vol. 1, p. 393.

[31] Hume 1764, vol. 1, pp. 394, 398n.

[32] See, for example, the prefatory advertisement to *An inquiry* 1753 on 'the ingenious Mr Hume'; and cf. *The herald* 1758, vol. 1, pp. 74 and 77 and vol. 2, p. 17.

that state debt 'creates a property and dependence that throws a civil power into the hands of ministers which may endanger liberty'.[33] Four years earlier, the anonymous author of *A supplement* had expressed the same anxiety at greater length, attacking the principle of bypassing the people's representatives and handing funds directly to the crown. He demands to be told if a single instance can be given 'of a country retaining its liberty after the principal direction of the purse of the people was got into the hands of those who already had the supreme direction of the force of society'.[34] He insists that no one can be a genuine Whig 'who does not think it his duty, upon all suitable occasions, to hazard his life in support of a government of laws in opposition to the insolent domination and arbitrary will of any man, be he or they ever so much elated by their brief authority'. He concludes that 'no man consequently can be a Whig who is not zealous to preserve the principal power over the money of the people in the hands of their representatives, this being the only valid means by which a government of laws can be maintained'.[35] By the time the Seven Years War was brought to an end by the Treaty of Paris in 1763, it was generally agreed that the level of public debt had become dangerously unsustainable, and that a new and rigorous fiscal policy would need to be immediately pursued.

### Arbitrary Imprisonment and Arbitrary Taxation

The opening years of George III's reign in the early 1760s saw the re-emergence of a yet more serious criticism of Britain's self-image as a free state.[36] As a number of critics began to object, the truth is that arbitrary and despotic forms of legal power were still being exercised to the obvious detriment of the people's liberties. The first occasion on which this accusation led to a widespread outcry was after the terms of the Treaty of Paris were announced to Parliament in April 1763. The agreement negotiated by the government of Lord Bute was widely felt to have been too generous to France and Spain, and the ministry came under fierce attack. One of the most vehement denunciations of Bute's diplomacy was mounted by John Wilkes, the Whig member of Parliament for Aylesbury. As soon as Bute came to power in 1762 Wilkes began publishing an anti-government weekly journal, *The North Briton*.[37] When George III gave his assent to the terms of the Treaty of Paris Wilkes immediately devoted issue 45 of *The North Briton* to a denunciation of the treaty and the king's

---

[33] *The herald* 1758, vol. 2, p. 19.    [34] *A supplement* 1754, p. 14.
[35] *A supplement* 1754, p. 15.
[36] On the collapse of the Whig oligarchy see Brewer 1976, pp. 8–25.
[37] Brewer 1976, p. 154.

acceptance of it. Taking personal offence, the king ordered general warrants to be issued for the arrest of Wilkes and his publishers on a charge of seditious libel. Wilkes was summarily imprisoned, and was then brought before the Court of Common Pleas to answer the accusation against him.[38]

Defending himself in court, Wilkes did not hesitate to claim that he had been made the victim of an arbitrary, despotic and tyrannical exercise of power. He declared that his grievances were 'of a kind hitherto unparalleled in this free country'.[39] The question to be resolved, he argued, is 'of such importance as to determine at once whether English liberty be a reality or a shadow'.[40] He called for the final extirpation of 'inhuman principles of Star Chamber tyranny', so that 'henceforth every innocent man, however poor and unsupported, may hope to sleep in peace and security in his own house, unviolated by King's messengers and the arbitrary mandates of an overbearing secretary of state'.[41] Underlining his contempt for north Britons, he went on to express the hope that the outcome of his trial 'will teach Ministers of Scottish and arbitrary principles that the liberty of an English subject is not to be sported away with impunity in this cruel and despotic manner'.[42]

Wilkes was immediately released on the grounds that the charge against him was insufficiently serious to affect his immunity as a member of Parliament. The verdict prompted widespread celebrations of 'Wilkes and liberty' and 'the downfall of the jackboot'.[43] Soon afterwards, when the House of Commons voted against a motion challenging the legality of general warrants, this in turn gave rise to further attacks on the use of such despotic powers. The House of Commons was reminded that it had on an earlier occasion 'declared the said warrants to be arbitrary and illegal'.[44] Their continuing use was now denounced as 'an unconstitutional and illegal exercise of an uncontrolled power' which was not merely 'grounded on no sound principles or authorities of law', but was 'incompatible with personal freedom' and an infringement of 'the rights of the subject in the most essential article of liberty'.[45] Wilkes had succeeded in raising once more the fear of arbitrary power and the outrage it so readily aroused.

*********

By the time the Wilkes case was settled the Tory Lord Bute had been ousted as first minister and replaced by the Whig George Grenville.

---

[38] Brewer 1976, pp. 121, 166–7.    [39] Wilkes 1763 (single sheet).
[40] Draper 1763, p. 24.    [41] Draper 1763, p. 24.    [42] Wilkes 1763 (single sheet).
[43] *Wilkes and liberty* 1763, p. 1. On the reaction of the Wilkites see Brewer 1980.
[44] *A defence of the minority* 1764, p. 26.    [45] *A defence of the minority* 1764, pp. 16–17.

The new administration at once set about trying to address some of the fiscal and economic difficulties that Bute had failed to resolve.[46] One pressing problem was the increasingly high cost of protecting the American colonies, but the most serious issue was the price of having waged an imperial war against the French in North America as well as in Europe for nearly nine years. As we have seen, these years of international conflict had added hugely to the national debt, and Grenville did not fail to recognise that some major changes and retrenchments were urgently required.

Grenville initially outlined his plans for dealing with the problem to the parliamentary Committee on Ways and Means at the beginning of 1764. One of the resolutions he put forward concerned the need to find better means of 'securing and encouraging the trade of his Majesty's sugar colonies in America'.[47] This proposal duly came into force as the Sugar Act, which was passed in April 1764. The Act reduced customs duties on molasses by a half, the aim being to discourage smuggling and improve the collection of dues. A further resolution was that, in order to help 'towards defraying the necessary expenses of defending, protecting and securing the British colonies and plantations in America', it would now be proper for the government 'to charge certain stamp duties in the said colonies'.[48] Grenville's further suggestion was thus that, in addition to the new indirect tax imposed with the aim of improving the regulation of trade, a form of direct taxation should be introduced into the colonies to increase revenues, and specifically to help with the cost of maintaining British garrisons there.

This further resolution was not immediately enacted, as it was decided 'to allow time for the colonists to petition against it'.[49] But the mere warning early in 1764 that such a change might be imminent was enough to cause outrage as well as alarm in the colonies, and a grave objection to Grenville's proposal soon began to be raised. It was urged that, since the colonies had no representation in the British Parliament, the imposition of direct taxes without their consent would constitute a clear instance of exercising an arbitrary and hence an enslaving form of power.

The provenance of this argument among the colonists has long been a matter of scholarly debate. Perhaps the most influential recent claim has been that its line of descent can be traced from the classical republican tradition through to the so-called commonwealthmen of the early eighteenth century.[50] The influence of this tradition of thought was undoubtedly significant, but the attack on British colonial rule in America arose

---

[46] For details see Draper 1996, pp. 194–212.    [47] Cobbett 1813a, col. 1427.
[48] Cobbett 1813a, col. 1427.    [49] Cobbett 1813a, col. 1428.
[50] As Wootton 1994, pp. 8–19 notes, the pioneer here was Caroline Robbins, with her emphasis on the roles of Molesworth, Trenchard and Gordon. See Robbins 1959,

more generally out of an engagement with the Whig theory of the state as it had been articulated in 1688 and further developed by the pro-government writers of the 1730s and 1740s. As we saw in Chapter 4, one of the claims put forward by these propagandists had been that, after the revolution of 1688, the exercise of arbitrary power had been rendered illegal under the British constitution. The laws alone were said to rule, and these laws were enacted in Parliament with the consent of the people, who consequently remained free in obeying them. This form of represen-tation was said to guarantee to everyone the standing of free persons who are not dependent on the mere will of others, but are fully in possession of their civil liberty. The most pressing objection raised by the colonists was thus that, in planning to impose taxation without representation, the British government was betraying one of its own most cherished consti-tutional principles.

This objection was first officially put forward in May 1764, when the citizens of Boston appointed delegates to represent them at a coming meeting of the Massachusetts General Assembly. A committee of five was set up to explain what they expected of their delegates.[51] One member was Samuel Adams, who was later to play a radical part not merely in the Massachusetts Assembly but in the Congress of 1775 that eventually voted to issue the Declaration of Independence. Adams and his fellow committee members strongly objected to the provisions of the Sugar Act, and their first request was that their delegates should petition for it to be repealed. They then went on to express their apprehension 'that these unexpected proceedings may be preparatory to new taxations upon us' of a kind that that would annihilate 'our charter right to govern and tax ourselves', and would take away 'our British privileges, which, as we have never forfeited them, we hold in common with our fellow subjects who are natives of Britain'.[52] This prompted them to conclude by raising a question that was to resonate throughout the ensuing debate. 'If taxes are laid upon us in any shape without our having a legal representation where they are laid, are we not reduced from the character of free subjects to the miserable state of tributary slaves?'[53]

The earliest tract of major significance to take up this potentially revolutionary cry was the work of James Otis, one of the delegates elected by the citizens of Boston to represent them at the Massachusetts Assembly. Otis published *The rights of the British colonies asserted and proved* in Boston in July 1764. The tract rapidly became the most

---

pp. 87–124. This line of argument was further developed in Bailyn 1967, pp. 35–54 and in Pocock 1975, pp. 424–8, 467–76.
[51] For this text see Bailyn 1965, pp. 471–4.    [52] Bailyn 1965, p. 473.
[53] Bailyn 1965, p. 473.

celebrated and widely discussed of all the denunciations of the British government prompted by the threat of direct taxation, and it went through at least five reprintings within the next year.[54] Otis begins with some general reflections on the origins and character of legitimate government. He first makes it clear that, as he puts it, he is not 'in favour of the original compact' as imagined by writers such as Locke.[55] Otis stands closer to Hobbes and Pufendorf in considering government to be a natural necessity for humankind. 'Such is the nature of man, a weak, imperfect being, that the valuable ends of life cannot be obtained without the union and assistance of many' under some form of sovereign power.[56] When Otis turns, however, to the issue of freedom under government, he begins to reveal himself as a follower of Locke.[57] The aim of government, he lays down, is 'above all things to provide for the security, the quiet, and happy enjoyment of life, liberty and property'.[58] The supreme form of power required to bring about these ends 'is originally and ultimately in the people'.[59] They admittedly form too large a body to rule, so that in practice they need to govern by 'deputation, proxy or a right of representation'.[60] But so long as the wills of the citizens are represented, they may be said to consent to the laws by which they are governed and hence to obey freely.[61]

This leaves the question of what can be done if a government imposes its will on the people without their consent. Otis is clear that in these circumstances there must be a right of resistance. God 'has given to all men a natural right to be free, and they have it ordinarily in their power to make themselves so if they please'.[62] If our rulers verge towards tyranny they must be opposed, and he warns that 'if they prove incorrigible they will be deposed by the people'.[63]

When Otis turns to the case of the American colonies he at first appears to concede that, although any decision by the British government to tax them without representation would have the effect of turning them into slaves, it would nevertheless be their duty to offer 'a most perfect and ready obedience'.[64] If we return, however, to the general principles outlined by Otis at the beginning of his tract, we find him drawing his argument to a close with a long series of quotations from Locke's *Two treatises* in which the right of resistance to any such exercise of arbitrary

---

[54] Bailyn 1965, p. 409.
[55] Otis 1965, p. 419; cf. also pp. 423, 439. For Otis's views on the state of nature and formation of government see Somos 2019, pp. 52–75.
[56] Otis 1965, p. 425.    [57] For Otis's use of Locke see Arcenas 2022, pp. 33–7.
[58] Otis 1965, p. 425.    [59] Otis 1965, p. 424.    [60] Otis 1965, p. 427.
[61] Otis 1965, pp. 426–7, 466.    [62] Otis 1965, p. 426.    [63] Otis 1965, p. 427.
[64] Otis 1965, pp. 447, 448.

power is unequivocally affirmed. 'The legislative being only a fiduciary power to act for certain ends, there remains still in the people a supreme power to remove or alter the legislative when they find the legislative act contrary to the trust reposed in them.'[65] Any government which attempts to reduce the people to slavery 'by invading the property of the subject and making themselves arbitrary disposers of the lives, liberties and fortunes of the people' may thus be said to have 'put themselves into a state of war with the people, who are thereupon absolved from any further obedience'.[66]

Turning to the colonies, Otis first draws on the argument of his opening section to provide a list of requirements that any government of a free people must be sure to meet. Among the principles he singles out are that the legislative must never act 'by extempore arbitrary decrees'; that 'the supreme power cannot take away from any man any part of his property without his consent in person or by representation'; and thus that no taxes can be levied on the people except 'by their consent in person or by deputation'.[67] These considerations bring Otis to the central question he wishes to raise. How can it be argued 'that all the northern colonies, who are without one representative in the House of Commons, should be taxed by the British Parliament'?[68] He goes on to propose a solution that he earnestly hopes will somehow be adopted, although he hardly succeeded in persuading anyone to take it up. He argues that such a policy of taxation can never be equitable until 'the Parliament shall think fit to allow the colonists a representation in the House of Commons', so that they will be in a position to give their consent to it.[69] Once this is done, 'the equity of their taxing the colonies will be as clear as their power is at present of doing it' without consent.[70]

Otis ends on a more bellicose note. He declares that 'the very act of taxing exercised over those who are not represented appears to be depriving them of one of their most essential rights as freemen, and if continued seems to be in effect an entire disenfranchisement of every civil right'.[71] Here he adds an argument that was subsequently much repeated. Once this barrier of liberty is broken down everything will be lost, because 'if a shilling in the pound may be taken from me against my will, why may not twenty shillings; and if so, why not my liberty or my life?'[72] Otis's answer, given in the form of a quotation from Locke, is that any community 'perpetually retains a supreme power of saving themselves from the

---

[65] Otis 1965, p. 434. Cf. [Locke] 1690, para. 149, pp. 369–70.
[66] Otis 1965, pp. 434–5. Cf. [Locke] 1690, para. 222, pp. 441–2.    [67] Otis 1965, p. 446.
[68] Otis 1965, p. 446.    [69] Otis 1965, p. 465; cf. also p. 445.
[70] Otis 1965, pp. 445, 465.    [71] Otis 1965, p. 447.
[72] Otis 1965, p. 461. For a repetition of the argument see Priestley 1993, p. 140.

attempts and designs of anybody, even of their legislators, whenever they shall be so foolish or so wicked as to lay and carry on designs against the liberty and property of the subject'.[73] He ends in effect by telling the British that they have been warned.

A further and almost equally celebrated argument along similar lines was published by Stephen Hopkins, governor of Rhode Island, in November 1764 under the title *The rights of colonies examined.* Hopkins is less bold than Otis in confronting the constitutional questions facing the colonists. He accepts that it is necessary for them to be subject to 'some supreme and overruling authority with power to make laws and form regulations for the good of all, and to compel their execution and observation', and he thinks it obvious that this power is vested in the British Parliament.[74] He is more lucid than Otis, however, in articulating the view of freedom and government underlying the defence of the colonists that he and Otis wish to mount. The opening words of Hopkins's tract introduce the concepts of liberty and slavery as antonyms. 'Liberty is the greatest blessing that men enjoy, and slavery the heaviest curse that human nature is capable of.'[75] What then is slavery? 'Those who are governed at the will of another, or of others, and whose property may be taken from them by taxes or otherwise without their own consent and against their will, are in the miserable condition of slaves.'[76] What then is liberty? Hopkins regards it as fully sufficient to quote Sidney's *Discourses concerning government*: 'Liberty solely consists in an independency upon the will of another; and by the name of slave we understand a man who can neither dispose of his person or goods, but enjoys all at the will of a master.'[77] As Hopkins subsequently adds, even if the master on whose will a slave depends may happen to be benign, the slave will none the less have been deprived of his liberty. 'For one who is bound to obey the will of another is as really a slave though he may have a good master as if he had a bad one.'[78] The question is not how much arbitrary power the master exercises, but how much he could exercise if he chose.

Hopkins leaves no doubt about the constitutional moral he wishes to draw. He takes it to be beyond argument that every colony forms a separate part of the British Empire, so that 'British subjects in America have equal rights with those in Britain' and possess them not 'as a grace and favour bestowed', but 'as an inherent indefeasible right'.[79] But if that is so, they cannot be taxed unless they are represented. Anyone who can be 'taxed at pleasure by others' without being able to withhold

---

[73] Otis 1965, p. 434. Cf. [Locke] 1690, para. 149, pp. 369–70.
[74] [Hopkins] 1965, p. 512.     [75] [Hopkins] 1965, p. 507.
[76] [Hopkins] 1965, pp. 507–8.     [77] [Hopkins] 1965, p. 508. Cf. Sidney 1990, p. 17.
[78] [Hopkins] 1965, pp. 516–17.     [79] [Hopkins] 1965, p. 511.

their consent 'cannot possibly have any property, can have nothing to be called their own'.[80] But 'they who have no property can have no freedom, but are indeed reduced to the most abject slavery'.[81] Hopkins ends with an assurance that the colonies 'have as little inclination as they have ability to throw off their dependency'.[82] But the possibility has none the less been raised.

## The Revolutionary Response

Despite the many signs of alarm and hostility in the colonies, George Grenville went on to present his plan for a Stamp Act to the Ways and Means Committee of the House of Commons in February 1765, after which the proposed Act was passed by both Houses almost without debate and received the royal assent on 22 March.[83] The Act required that all forms of printed materials in the colonies – including newspapers and legal documents – should make use of stamped paper manufactured in London, on which a tax would be collected by local distributors in each colony, with payment being required in English currency. Hitherto the British government had never imposed any such direct taxes in the colonies, in which the rate had always been set locally by individual state legislatures, but it was now announced that the new legislation would come into force on 1 November 1765.[84] With this attempt to solve a local economic problem by exercising an almost unthinking imperialism, the Whig government unleashed a decade of wrangling that culminated in a revolutionary war in which Britain was defeated and the colonies were lost.

The wrangling began in earnest with an attempt by the Whig government to dismiss the objection that there can be no lawful taxation without representation. Thomas Whately, the secretary to the treasury, published an official response entitled *The regulations lately made concerning the colonies*, in which he defended the government's decision by invoking the concept of virtual representation.[85] Whately has sometimes been credited with developing this doctrine,[86] but he was drawing on

---

[80] [Hopkins] 1965, p. 517.    [81] [Hopkins] 1965, p. 516.    [82] [Hopkins] 1965, p. 522.

[83] Cobbett 1813b, col. 40.

[84] Draper argues that the ensuing conflict should therefore be seen as a contest for power. See Draper 1996, pp. 243-67, 356-8 and 392-7, stressing physical violence rather than the war of words in 1765, 1768 and 1773. Draper's claim seems true in a sense, but it risks underestimating how important it was for the colonists to succeed in legitimising their struggle.

[85] [Whately, Thomas] 1765. On Whately see Bailyn 1965, pp. 601-3; Christie 1998; Nelson 2014, pp. 82, 94; Cornish 2020.

[86] See Greene 2010, pp. 69-71.

a constitutional theory that (as we saw in Chapter 1) can be traced at least as far back as Sir Thomas Smith's account of the English Parliament in his *De republica Anglorum* of 1583. According to Smith, whenever Parliament acts, it is as if the whole people act. 'Every Englishman is intended to be there present, either in person or by procuration', so that 'the consent of the Parliament is taken to be every man's consent'.[87] Smith's argument was later much developed by the parliamentarian theorists in the English civil wars, and especially by Henry Parker in his defence of the sovereignty of Parliament in his *Observations* of 1642. Parker reiterates that the reason why Parliament cannot fail to serve the interests of the people is that it is 'virtually the whole kingdom itself';[88] so that its decisions are those of 'the whole body of the state'.[89]

Whately recurs to the same view at the end of his tract on the government of the colonies. 'The fact is', he insists, 'that the inhabitants of the colonies *are* represented in Parliament.'[90] 'They do not indeed choose the members of that assembly', but 'neither are nine tenths of the people of Britain electors' and 'the colonies are in exactly the same situation'.[91] All the colonists 'are virtually represented in Parliament, for every member of Parliament sits in the House not as a representative of his own constituents, but as one of that august assembly by which all the commons of Great Britain are represented'.[92] So the colonists are represented 'in the same manner as the inhabitants of Britain are', and 'they enjoy, with the rest of their fellow-subjects, the inestimable privilege of not being bound by any laws, or subject to any taxes, to which the majority of the representatives of the commons have not consented'.[93]

It was not difficult, however, for the colonists to produce a conclusive rebuttal of this defence. One of the earliest and most influential among the many tracts in which Whately's argument was demolished was Daniel Dulany's *Considerations on the propriety of imposing taxes on the British colonies*, which first appeared in October 1765 and went through five editions before the end of the year.[94] The son of a lawyer in Maryland, Dulany had been educated in England, where he trained at the Inner Temple and was called to the bar in 1746. Returning to Maryland, he practised as a lawyer, served in the legislative assembly, and by 1765 had become a member of the Governor's Council and secretary of the

---

[87] Smith 1982, pp. 78–9.     [88] [Parker] 1642, p. 28.
[89] [Parker] 1642, pp. 37, 39, 45. On virtual representation in the English revolution see Nelson 2014, pp. 72–5; Skinner 2018, pp. 196–7, 203–5; in the American Revolution see Nelson 2014, pp. 80–3.
[90] [Whately] 1765, p. 108. Italic added.     [91] [Whately] 1765, pp. 108–9.
[92] [Whately] 1765, p. 109.     [93] [Whately] 1765, p. 112.     [94] Bailyn 1965, p. 599.

colony.[95] He was consequently able to speak both as a lawyer and a politician in addressing the claim of the British government that, as he phrased it, 'the colonies, being exactly in the same situation with the non-electors of England, are therefore represented in the same manner' as those who do not possess the franchise in England.[96]

Dulany finds two disabling weaknesses in this argument. He first objects that the exercise of imperial power looks inherently questionable as soon as one reflects on the fact that the colonists are living in their own distinctive space. The right to be an elector in Britain is annexed to 'inhabitancy in some particular places'. But this means that 'the inhabitants of the colonies are, as such, incapable of being electors'. Even if every colonist possessed the requisite freehold, it would still be true that 'not one could vote, but upon the supposition of his ceasing to be an inhabitant of America and becoming a resident of Great Britain'.[97]

A second objection is that, as Dulany willingly admits, the electors in Britain 'may be justly deemed to be the representatives of the non-electors, at the same time they exercise their personal privilege in the right of election'. The reason is that the electors 'are inseparably connected in their interests with the non-electors', and can therefore serve as representatives of both.[98] Again, however, Dulany sees an obvious contrast with the colonies. There might easily be cases in which 'not a single actual elector in England might be immediately affected by a taxation in America imposed by a statute which would have a general operation and effect upon the properties of the inhabitants of the colonies'.[99] Furthermore, 'even acts oppressive and injurious to the colonies in an extreme degree might become popular in England', if only because 'the very measures which depressed the colonies would give ease to the inhabitants of Great-Britain'.[100]

The only possible inference is that 'not one inhabitant in any colony is or can be actually or virtually represented by the British House of Commons'.[101] The effect of the Stamp Act will be to impose a tax without leaving them any means of granting or withholding their consent. Dulany then reminds his readers that the colonists have no less a right than any other British subjects to claim exemption from taxes levied in this way. 'They derive this right from the common law, which their charters have declared and confirmed, and they conceive that when stripped of this right, whether by prerogative or by any other power, they are at the same time deprived of every privilege distinguishing free-men from slaves.'[102]

---

[95] Bailyn 1965, pp. 603–4.    [96] [Dulany] 1965, p. 615.    [97] [Dulany] 1965, p. 614.
[98] [Dulany] 1965, p. 612.    [99] [Dulany] 1965, p. 615.    [100] [Dulany] 1965, p. 615.
[101] [Dulany] 1965, pp. 618–19.    [102] [Dulany] 1965, p. 632.

The only conclusion to be drawn is that the imposition of the Stamp Act will have the effect of reducing the colonists to servitude.

The Stamp Act finally came into force on 1 November 1765, only a few days after the publication of Dulany's tract. By that time the Grenville administration had been unseated and replaced by a government led by the Marquis of Rockingham, which had taken control in July 1765.[103] The new administration was soon obliged to recognise that there was no possibility of enabling the Stamp Act to be successfully implemented. Before it had even come into force, the local stamp distributors in the colonies had been so widely harassed and threatened that they had resigned en masse. Faced with this difficulty, and with increasing levels of violence, the Rockingham ministry decided to annul the previous administration's decision, and in March 1766 the Stamp Act was rescinded.[104]

This decision, however, was far from being an offer of peace to the colonists, since the government at the same time passed the Declaratory Act. This affirmed that, although the Stamp Act had been rescinded, the British Parliament nevertheless continued to hold full power 'to make laws binding the British colonies in North America in all cases whatsoever'.[105] The right to reimpose the Stamp Act had in no way been altered or given up. A still more inflammatory series of decisions was made after the Rockingham Whigs fell from power and were succeeded by the ministry of William Pitt in July 1766. A year later Charles Townshend, as chancellor of the exchequer, brought in a new series of Acts relating to the colonies that came to be known collectively as the Townshend duties.[106] The first was the New York Restraining Act, forbidding the New York Assembly from passing any bills until the colony complied with the Mutiny Act of 1765 requiring them to pay for the quartering of British troops.[107] There followed the Revenue Act, which imposed a number of import duties to be levied locally on goods entering American ports, together with the Customs Act, which created a Board of Commissioners to collect the new revenues. The board was established in Boston, and in the following year a number of local courts were created to ensure that the new arrangements were fully enforced.[108]

These developments prompted further rebuttals, one of the earliest and most important of which was the work of John Dickinson. Like Dulany, Dickinson had been born in Maryland and received his legal training in London. Returning to the colonies in 1757, he was admitted to the

---

[103] Brewer 1976, pp. 80–1.     [104] Cobbett 1813b, col. 206.
[105] Cobbett 1813b, cols. 177, 203.     [106] Thomas 1987, p. 26.
[107] Thomas 1987, pp. 8, 80.     [108] Thomas 1987, pp. 18–35.

Pennsylvania bar and began practising in Philadelphia.[109] A decade later he rose to fame with his *Letters from a farmer in Pennsylvania*, which were published in newspapers towards the end of 1767 and as a book in March 1768.[110] Dickinson begins by expressing surprise and alarm that 'little notice has been taken of an Act of Parliament as injurious in its principle to the liberties of these colonies as the Stamp Act was: I mean the act for suspending the legislation of New York.'[111] If the people of that colony 'may be legally deprived in such a case of the privilege of making laws, why may they not, with equal reason, be deprived of every other privilege? Or why may not every colony be treated in the same manner, when any of them shall dare to deny their assent to any impositions that shall be directed?'[112] As soon as we seriously consider these questions, we see that 'a dreadful stroke is aimed at the liberty of these colonies: for the cause of one is the cause of all. If the Parliament may lawfully deprive New York of any of its rights, it may deprive any or all the colonies of their rights.'[113]

The issue was raised again in Letter VII, in which Dickinson notes that some people seem to think that the impositions now being demanded are 'of no consequence because the duties are so small'.[114] But this is a fatal error, failing as it does to recognise that the British Parliament has begun to act in 'the mode suited to arbitrary and oppressive governments'.[115] Dickinson asks us to consider 'Who are a free people?' His answer is 'not those over whom government is reasonably and equitably exercised, but those who live under a government so constitutionally checked and controlled that proper provision is being made against its being otherwise exercised'.[116] As long as the British government can act as it pleases, the colonists will not be living as a free people. Dickinson concludes with a question from Locke's *Two treatises*. 'What property have we in that which another may by right take, when he pleases, to himself?'[117]

Dickinson's uppermost concern, however, is with a more general feature that the New York Act and the Revenue Act share with the Stamp Act: they all seek to impose direct taxes to be collected within the colonies. Here he reaffirms an important contrast that Otis had sought to dismiss in his tract 1764. Otis had refused to draw any distinction between a claim by the British Parliament 'to tax our trade' and a claim

---

[109] On Dickinson see Draper 1996, pp. 304–8.
[110] [Dickinson] 1768. Dickinson's decision to present himself in the persona of a farmer appears to allude to Trenchard and Gordon 1995, p. 268 (on Cincinnatus).
[111] [Dickinson] 1768, p. 7.      [112] [Dickinson] 1768, p. 9.      [113] [Dickinson] 1768, p. 10.
[114] [Dickinson] 1768, p. 75.      [115] [Dickinson] 1768, p. 71.
[116] [Dickinson] 1768, pp. 75–6.
[117] [Dickinson] 1768, p. 76. Cf. [Locke] 1690, para. 140, p. 363.

'to tax the lands and everything else'.[118] Dickinson insists on a strong distinction between indirect taxes in the form of dues imposed to regulate trade and direct taxes imposed within the colonies to defray the cost of government.[119] This is the issue to which he turns in Letter II. He begins by declaring that 'I have looked over every statute relating to these colonies from their first settlement to this time'.[120] He finds that in every instance before the Stamp Act they were 'calculated to preserve or promote a mutually beneficial intercourse between the several constituent parts of the Empire'.[121] While some of these statutes imposed duties on trade, the aim was always 'to restrain the commerce of one part that was injurious to another, and thus to promote the general welfare'.[122] With the Stamp Act, however, and with several provisions of the Townshend Acts, payments are being demanded for the first time not as a method of regulating trade but solely 'for the purpose of raising a revenue'.[123] What all these Acts have in common is thus that they are designed 'to raise money upon us without our consent'.[124] So the question we are left confronting – as Dickinson states it at the end of Letter II – is 'whether the Parliament can legally take money out of our pockets without our consent'.[125]

The question is finally answered in Letter VII, in which Dickinson reiterates the main argument that Otis and others had already advanced: that legally there can be no taxation without representation. Dickinson draws Letter VII to a close by making the case in his most impassioned style:

> These duties, which will inevitably be levied upon us, and which are now levying upon us, are expressly laid for the sole purpose of taking money. This is the true definition of taxes. They are therefore taxes. This money is to be taken from us. We are therefore taxed. Those who are taxed without their own consent, given by themselves, or their representatives, are slaves. We are taxed without our own consent given by ourselves, or our representatives. We are therefore – I speak it with grief, I speak it with indignation – we are slaves.[126]

Perhaps due to his Quaker allegiances, Dickinson later refused to sign the Declaration of Independence. But while he may have doubted if there is any right to overthrow tyranny by force, he was in no doubt that the colonists were living in servitude.[127]

**********

---

[118] Otis 1965, p. 450.    [119] A point already made in [Dulany] 1965, p. 637.
[120] [Dickinson] 1768, pp. 13–14.    [121] [Dickinson] 1768, p. 14.
[122] [Dickinson] 1768, p. 15.    [123] [Dickinson] 1768, p. 17.
[124] [Dickinson] 1768, p. 22.    [125] [Dickinson] 1768, p. 26.
[126] [Dickinson] 1768, pp. 76–8.
[127] On Dickinson's Quakerism and his politics see Calvert 2008.

The extent and seriousness of colonial opposition had by this time become well known in London, where the pamphlets of Otis, Hopkins, Dulany and Dickinson were all reprinted almost as soon as they appeared in the colonies.[128] Faced with this mounting hostility, the British government decided to step back. After Pitt resigned on grounds of ill-health in October 1768, the short-lived ministry led by the Duke of Grafton was succeeded by that of Lord North, who became first minister in January 1770. The new administration was almost immediately confronted by a further crisis in the colonies that had arisen from the unpopular decision to station British troops in Boston to deal with disturbances arising from the enforcement of Townshend's revenue Acts. A confrontation between British soldiers and a hostile crowd on 5 March 1770 led to the Boston massacre, the fatal shooting of five people in the crowd.[129] Anxious to avoid further disturbances, the government moved rapidly to repeal several provisions of the Townshend Acts. The duty on tea continued to be imposed, but no attempt was made to enforce the New York Restraining Act, and most of the tariffs imposed by the revenue Acts were withdrawn.[130]

For a time there ensued a change of tone in the argument between the colonists and the British government.[131] It was beginning to seem obvious to some patriots that relentless denunciations of Parliament were not helping to mend relations with Great Britain, and they began to strike a more eirenic and constructive note. They developed what came to be known as the dominion theory, according to which the American colonies held the standing of independent states bound to Britain only through the person of the king as head of the British Empire. With this commitment they were able to bypass the debate about the extent of parliamentary jurisdiction over the colonies. They claimed that Parliament had no such jurisdiction at all, a position that freed them to propose that the colonists should give up arguing with Parliament and appeal for the relief of their grievances directly to the king.[132]

One writer who put forward this line of argument was the North Carolina lawyer James Iredell in his essay *To the inhabitants of Great Britain* in 1774. But the most influential exponent of the dominion theory was James Wilson, who had emigrated in 1766 from Scotland to Philadelphia, where he studied law with John Dickinson and followed him into legal practice. Wilson published his *Considerations on the nature*

---

[128] Bonwick 1977, pp. 38–9.    [129] Thomas 1987, pp. 180–2.
[130] Thomas 1987, pp. 196–214.
[131] On this 'pause in politics' see Thomas 1987, pp. 214–32.
[132] See Nelson 2014, pp. 29–65, an analysis to which I am much indebted. On pro-monarchism in the colonies see also McConville 2007.

*and the extent of the legislative authority of the British Parliament* in 1774,[133] a work that was later to encourage Alexander Hamilton to take up a similar stance.[134]

Wilson opens his *Considerations* with a paean of praise to the British constitution in the celebratory style of the pro-government Whigs. The constitution is said to embody 'the principles of justice and freedom', thereby providing for 'the enjoyment of those rights to which we are entitled by the supreme and uncontrollable laws of nature', as well as by the fundamental principles of the constitution.[135] For the upholding of liberty, however, it is not sufficient that there should be no interference with our rights. If there is any such possibility, then we remain subject to the will of those who have power to interfere should they choose, and thus in the condition of slaves.[136] Fortunately, the special glory of the British constitution lies in the fact that it provides many securities for liberty. One is that the people elect their representatives. This power 'has ever been regarded as a point of the last consequence to all free governments', and 'the independent exercise of that power is justly deemed the strongest bulwark of the British liberties'.[137] A further guarantee stems from the fact that 'the interest of the representatives is the same with that of their constituents', so that 'they cannot betray their electors without at the same time injuring themselves'.[138] This explains why the British House of Commons has always 'resisted with vigour every arbitrary measure repugnant to law', and has thereby 'checked the progress of arbitrary power'.[139] A further security is provided by the right of frequent elections, which gives the British people a regular opportunity to show their trust in their representatives or punish their perfidy.[140] By means of these safeguards, 'the first maxims of jurisprudence are ever kept in view – that all power is derived from the people, that their happiness is the end of government'.[141]

Wilson next switches, however, to the more critical style characteristic of his teacher John Dickinson. The American colonists enjoy none of these securities. They do not elect any of their alleged representatives in the British Parliament; it is not clear that these alleged representatives share their interests; and if they do not, the colonists have no power to punish them.[142] How then can we rely on them 'for the security of our liberties, of our properties, of everything dear to us in life, of life itself?'[143]

---

[133] See Wilson 1774. But Wilson's work was actually written in 1768 as a response to the Townshend Acts. For an even earlier statement of the dominion theory see Nelson 2014, p. 253 on William Hicks's *Considerations* of 1766.

[134] Nelson 2014, pp. 54–6, 58–60.    [135] Wilson 1774, p. 2.    [136] Wilson 1774, pp. 3–4.

[137] Wilson 1774, p. 5.    [138] Wilson 1774, p. 7.    [139] Wilson 1774, pp. 13–14.

[140] Wilson 1774, p. 11.    [141] Wilson 1774, p. 9.    [142] Wilson 1774, p. 15.

[143] Wilson 1774, p. 18.

To Wilson the answer is obvious: we cannot rely on them, from which it follows 'that the colonies are not bound by the acts of the British parliament, because they have no share in the British legislature'.[144] To believe otherwise 'is repugnant to the essential maxims of jurisprudence, to the ultimate end of all governments, to the genius of the British constitution, and to the liberty and happiness of the colonies'.[145]

By contrast with Dickinson, however, who had rested his case at this point, Wilson next puts forward his positive proposal about how a rapprochement with Great Britain might be reached. He first notes that 'every subject, so soon as he is born, is under the royal protection and is entitled to all the advantages arising from it'.[146] Furthermore, the king's duty of protection remains equally incumbent on him wherever in the British Empire they may happen to live.[147] The colonists ought therefore to stop arguing with Parliament and appeal directly to the king to preserve their rights. The Americans need to recognise that 'to the king is intrusted the direction and management of the great machine of government', so that 'he therefore is fittest to adjust the different wheels, and to regulate their motions in such a manner as to cooperate in the same general designs'.[148] The best and indeed the only way to preserve 'the connection and harmony between Great Britain and us, which it is her interest and ours mutually to cultivate', will consequently be to rely on 'the operation of the legal prerogatives of the crown' to bring peace and prosperity to Britain and the colonies alike.[149]

\*\*\*\*\*\*\*\*\*\*

James Wilson's plan for reconciliation was a constructive one, but his political timing could hardly have been more unfortunate. By the time he published his *Considerations*, the temporary lull in the political storm had come to an abrupt end. The change in the political weather began as early as the spring of 1773, when Lord North's administration decided to take action against the smuggling that had increasingly developed in the colonies as a means of evading the import duty on tea. In May 1773 the government passed what came to be known as the Tea Act.[150] The British East India Company was granted the right to sell its tea directly to the colonies, thereby avoiding export duties and making its price more competitive. New York and Philadelphia simply refused to accept the tea, but in Boston every chest was emptied into the harbour in a celebrated act of defiance in December 1773.[151] The British government responded with what came to be known as the Intolerable Acts in April 1774. Among

---

[144] Wilson 1774, p. 19.    [145] Wilson 1774, p. 19.    [146] Wilson 1774, p. 31.
[147] Wilson 1774, p. 32.    [148] Wilson 1774, p. 33.    [149] Wilson 1774, p. 34.
[150] Thomas 1991, p. 11.    [151] Thomas 1991, pp. 14–16, 18–22.

other penalties, the port of Boston was closed and the right of Massachusetts to elect its governor was withdrawn and assigned to the crown.[152]

The year 1774 proved a climactic one in the breakdown of relations between the colonies and the British government. This was when widespread debates about the need for revolution began to take place across the colonies.[153] This was also when a number of British observers began to argue that, in addition to reflecting on the legal grievances of the colonists, the British now needed to ask themselves if it might not be in their own economic interests to grant them independence.[154] Meanwhile a new phase in the pamphlet war erupted in the colonies, in which a much more bellicose style of patriot writing began to re-emerge. Rather than offering further suggestions for negotiation, one of the principal aims of the patriots was now to itemise the despotic and impoverishing policies that the British were pursuing, while prefacing these lists of grievances with accounts of the principles of liberty and natural right that were being hypocritically violated.

Here the way had already been shown by Samuel Adams, who had continued to give full rein to his pugnacity even during the period of relative calm in the early 1770s. Towards the end of 1772 Adams published a tract entitled *A state of the rights of the colonists*. He begins with a restatement of the Whig theory of freedom and government, which concludes with a section entitled 'the rights of the colonists as subjects'. Here Locke is quoted for the view that 'the Legislative has no right to absolute, arbitrary power over the lives and fortunes of the people', and 'cannot justly assume to itself a power to rule by extempore arbitrary decrees'.[155] Nor can it 'justly take from any man any part of his property, without his consent in person or by his representative'.[156] Rather, 'it is bound to see that justice is dispensed, and that the rights of the subjects be decided by promulgated, standing, and known laws, and authorised independent judges'.[157] These are declared by Adams to be 'some of the first principles of natural law and justice, and the great barriers of all free states'.[158]

Adams then provides a list of infringements of rights in which two of his complaints specifically inculpate the king. The quartering of British troops in Boston is not merely 'a violation of their rights as freemen' but of 'the charter or compact made between the king of Great Britain and the

---

[152] Thomas 1991, pp. 62–87.    [153] As shown in Norton 2020.
[154] See, for example, [Cartwright] 1774 and Tucker 1774.
[155] [Adams] 2003, p. 239. Cf. [Locke] 1690, para. 135, p. 355 and para. 136, p. 357.
[156] [Adams] 2003, p. 239. Cf. [Locke] 1690, para. 138, p. 360.
[157] [Adams] 2003, p. 239.    [158] [Adams] 2003, p. 239.

people of this province'.[159] The king is also blamed for 'the frequent alteration of the bounds of the colonies', the effect of which is to subject people to living 'under a constitution to which they have not consented'.[160] Apart from these grievances, however, Adams chiefly directs his attack against the British Parliament. The two Houses are said to have 'assumed the power of legislation for the colonists in all cases whatsoever without obtaining the consent of the inhabitants, which is ever essentially necessary to the right establishment of such a legislative'.[161] They have exerted their assumed powers 'in raising a revenue in the colonies without their consent, thereby depriving them of that right which every man has to keep his own earnings in his own hands until he shall in person, or by his representative, think fit to part with the whole or any portion of it'.[162] Furthermore, the revenues arising from these unconstitutionally imposed taxes have now been committed by Parliament to be managed by agents who are 'arbitrarily appointed and supported by an armed force quartered in a free city'.[163] Finally, it is proposed that 'the men on whose opinions and decision our properties, liberties and lives in a great measure depend receive their support from the revenues arising from these taxes', a decision that will 'if accomplished complete our slavery'.[164]

A similar approach was adopted by Thomas Jefferson in his *Summary view of the rights of British America* of 1774. Like Adams, Jefferson begins and ends with a statement of some fundamental Whig principles. The British need to recognise that the grievances of the colonists have arisen because of 'many unwarrantable encroachments and usurpations attempted to be made by the legislature of one part of the empire upon those rights which God and the laws have given equally and independently to all'.[165] It needs above all to be admitted that the colonists began by exercising 'a right which nature has given to all men' of 'establishing new societies, under such laws and regulations as to them shall seem most likely to promote public happiness',[166] and that they are now acting as 'a free people claiming their rights'.[167]

Turning to the plight of the colonists, Jefferson again writes in much the same style as Adams. The British Parliament has been responsible for 'a series of oppressions' which it has 'pursued unalterably through every change of ministers', thereby evincing 'a deliberate and systematical plan of reducing us to slavery'.[168] The Stamp Act and the Townshend Acts

---

[159] [Adams] 2003, p. 244.     [160] [Adams] 2003, p. 251.     [161] [Adams] 2003, p. 241.
[162] [Adams] 2003, pp. 241–2.     [163] [Adams] 2003, pp. 244–5.
[164] [Adams] 2003, pp. 245–6.     [165] [Jefferson] 2003, p. 258.
[166] [Jefferson] 2003, p. 258.     [167] [Jefferson] 2003, p. 275.
[168] [Jefferson] 2003, pp. 263–4.

between them reveal a 'connected chain of parliamentary usurpation' which is now reducing a free people to being the slaves of tyrants.[169] If more legislation of the same kind is passed, the measure of despotism will soon be filled up.[170] The entire conduct of the British Parliament towards the colonies has amounted to nothing more than a sequence of 'acts of power, assumed by a body of men, foreign to our constitutions and unacknowledged by our laws'.[171]

Jefferson differs from Adams only in his readiness to blame the king at least as much as Parliament. One of his objections is that 'for the most trifling reasons, and sometimes for no conceivable reason at all, his majesty has rejected laws of the most salutary tendency'.[172] A further objection is that 'with equal inattention to the necessities of his people here has his majesty permitted our laws to lie neglected in England for years'.[173] Finally, and 'in order to enforce the arbitrary measures before complained of', the king has also 'sent among us large bodies of armed forces, not made up of the people here, nor raised by the authority of our laws', failing to recognise that, 'did his majesty possess such a right as this, it might swallow up all our other rights'.[174] Jefferson ends with a strong hint that it may now be necessary for the presence of such illegal forces to be resisted with force.

The arbitrary powers that were so much condemned in the pamphlet literature of 1774 were experienced with particular harshness in Massachusetts, especially after the closure of the port of Boston. As Jefferson complains in his *Summary view*, the effect of the closure was that 'a large and populous town, whose trade was their sole subsistence, was deprived of that trade and involved in utter ruin'.[175] So it is not surprising that it was in Massachusetts that resentment against the British finally broke out into war. The first shots were fired, in a much-celebrated moment, at Lexington and Concord on 19 April 1775, after Paul Revere's midnight ride had alerted the local militia to the approach of British troops.[176] Thereafter the patriot pamphleteers began to con-centrate on justifying armed resistance,[177] while the Congress began to move increasingly towards the conclusion that the injuries they were suffering gave them the right, and even the duty, to throw off the yoke of despotism under which they were being forced to live.

---

[169] [Jefferson] 2003, pp. 264, 265.    [170] [Jefferson] 2003, p. 267.
[171] [Jefferson] 2003, p. 268.    [172] [Jefferson] 2003, p. 269.
[173] [Jefferson] 2003, p. 269.    [174] [Jefferson] 2003, pp. 273–4.
[175] [Jefferson] 2003, p. 265.    [176] Thomas 1991, pp. 226–8.
[177] See, for example, *Resistance no rebellion* 1775; *A declaration by the representatives of the united colonies [on] the causes and necessity of their taking up arms* 1775.

One important medium in which these revolutionary sentiments began to circulate was that of paper money. Paul Revere, a successful engraver as well as a hero of the revolution, designed a number of Massachusetts bills in 1775 in which a soldier is shown holding a copy of Magna Carta in one hand while brandishing a sword in the other. The inscription around his head reads: 'Issued in defence of American liberty.' Perhaps the most remarkable of these designs was a dollar bill that began to circulate in Maryland in July 1775. The figure of America is shown holding a cap of liberty while trampling on a scroll inscribed 'slavery'. America is presenting Britannia with a petition from the Continental Congress, while behind Britannia stands George III, who is setting fire to an American city while stamping on a copy of Magna Carta.[178] The revolutionary moral of the story is now explicitly underlined. America is still negotiating, but an army behind her is marching towards Britannia under the banner of liberty.

A final contribution to the stiffening of resolve to resist the British by force was made in the opening weeks of 1776, when two epoch-making tracts were published in which the revolutionary plan to fight for independence was explicitly recommended and justified.[179] The first to appear was Thomas Paine's *Common sense*, in which repudiation of British government was treated as the obvious course of action that the colonies now needed to take. Paine's tract was published in New York in January 1776 and gained immediate fame, selling over 100,000 copies within the next three months.[180] Paine announces his revolutionary credentials at the outset, sweeping aside the familiar Whig contention that we can speak of living in a free state so long as the law alone rules and there is some popular control over who makes the law.[181] One implication of this argument is that it must be possible to live as a free citizen under a limited form of monarchy. Jefferson had already begun to question this assumption, but Paine rejects it with brutal emphasis. He begins by declaring that the institution of monarchy is unworthy of anyone's allegiance, and ought to be cast off by any people unfortunate enough to find themselves living in subjection to such a tyrannical form of rule. 'A thirst for absolute power is the natural disease of monarchy', and in Britain the monarchy amounts to nothing better than 'the remains of monarchical tyranny', which 'contributes nothing towards the freedom

---

[178] Kelleher 2022, pp. 17–19.
[179] On this republican turn see Nelson 2014, pp. 31, 108–45.
[180] Kuklick 2000, p. x.
[181] For a different perspective see Clark 2018, pp. 146–52, in which *Common sense* is treated simply as an anti-monarchical tract. For a contrasting interpretation of Paine's views see Whatmore 2023, pp. 223–51.

of the state'.[182] The inescapable truth is that 'the will of the king is as much the law of the land in Britain as in France'.[183] As for hereditary succession, this is nothing more than a further evil that 'opens the door to the foolish, the wicked, and the improper', and consequently 'hath in it the nature of oppression'.[184] Monarchy joined with hereditary succession, Paine concludes, have at all times laid the world 'in blood and ashes'.[185] It is time to build with new republican materials instead of enduring ancient tyrannies.[186]

Having established that the colonies need to fight for their independence, Paine devotes the rest of his tract to addressing some practical difficulties that need to be faced if a successful republic is to be set up. He puts forward a number of constitutional proposals, centring on the creation of a continental congress that would exercise full sovereignty. The members would act democratically as representatives of the people without any division or separation of powers, and their authority would extend to the election of a president on the basis of an annual rota. Paine draws *Common sense* to a close by offering military advice on how to win the war that now needs to be fought. He takes it that the land forces available to the colonists are sufficient, but he has a number of suggestions to make about how to build a navy strong enough to defeat the British and uphold the security of the new nation in time of peace.[187]

The other and arguably even more important work that appeared very soon afterwards was *Observations on the nature of civil liberty*, first published in London in February 1776.[188] The author was Richard Price, who had by then been serving for nearly twenty years as minister to the Presbyterian chapel at Newington Green in London.[189] Price's tract caused almost as great a sensation as *Common sense*, reaching a fifth edition within a single month. Whereas Paine had issued a call to arms of unprecedented vehemence, Price reverts to a line of argument already much invoked by patriot writers in the colonies. He begins by restating a number of familiar Whig principles of government, after which he applies them to the case in hand. Like Adams, Jefferson and others, he is anxious to insist that the principles he is enunciating are those which true English Whigs have always professed. When he published the fifth edition of his *Observations* in March 1776, he added a new preface in which he went so far as to insist that his views on freedom and government

---

[182] Paine 2000, p. 6.    [183] Paine 2000, p. 7.    [184] Paine 2000, pp. 13–14.
[185] Paine 2000, p. 15.    [186] Paine 2000, p. 6.    [187] Paine 2000, pp. 31–4.
[188] The preface to the first edition is dated 8 February 1776. The fullest analysis of Price's views on liberty remains Thomas 1977, pp. 151–213. On Price and his critics after 1776 see Miller 1994, pp. 373–99.
[189] Thomas 1991, p. xii.

are in no way different from 'those taught by Mr. Locke and all the writers on civil liberty who have been hitherto most admired in this country'.[190]

Price begins by laying out the general idea of liberty in four divisions – physical, religious, moral and civil liberty – but immediately adds that 'there is one general idea that runs through them all', the idea of self-government.[191] 'To be free is to be guided by one's own will; and to be guided by the will of another is the characteristic of servitude.'[192] For Price, the contrast is always between liberty and enslavement. If we find ourselves obliged 'to look up to a creature no better than ourselves as the master of our fortunes, and to receive his will as our law', this is as much as to say that we are nothing more than 'the miserable slaves of arbitrary power'.[193] So far as we lose the power of self-government, 'so far slavery is introduced', and 'nor do I think that a preciser idea than this of liberty and slavery can be formed'.[194]

Next Price explains that, within the four divisions he has introduced, his sole concern will be with the idea of civil liberty, that is, the freedom we are capable of enjoying in our capacity as citizens of states.[195] But as he develops his argument he makes it clear that, when he describes his general idea of liberty as that of self-government, he is referring to the government not merely of one's own self but also of the state.[196] He lays it down that 'civil liberty is the power of a civil society or state to govern itself by its own discretion or by laws of its own making without being subject to the impositions of any power in appointing and directing which the collective body of the people have no concern and over which they have no control'.[197] Although he speaks more circumspectly than Paine, Price is no less insistent that 'all civil government, as far as it can be denominated free, is the creature of the people', and thus that there must be some question about the legitimacy of monarchy.[198] As Price expresses his doubt, if there is any will 'distinct from that of the majority of a community which claims a power in making laws for it', then to that extent 'slavery is introduced'.[199] The contrast between free and enslaved states is then heavily underlined. Liberty 'is too imperfectly defined when it is said to be a government by laws and not by men', for 'if the laws are made by one man, or by a junto of men in a state, and not by common consent, a government by them does not differ from slavery'.[200] We need to recognise that 'in every free state every man is his own legislator'.[201]

The implications of this analysis for a proper understanding of political representation are then spelled out. Here Price unequivocally supports the American colonists in their claim that they are being taxed without

---

[190] Price 1991, p. 20.   [191] Price 1991, p. 22.   [192] Price 1991, p. 26.
[193] Price 1991, p. 29.   [194] Price 1991, pp. 22, 23.   [195] Price 1991, pp. 23, 30.
[196] Price 1991, p. 22.   [197] Price 1991, p. 22.   [198] Price 1991, pp. 22, 23.
[199] Price 1991, p. 23.   [200] Price 1991, p. 24.   [201] Price 1991, pp. 23–4.

representation, but at the same time introduces a more radical view of what it means to be represented. As we have seen, the British government at the time of the Stamp Act crisis had sought to insist that the colonists were represented in the same way as the vast majority of British subjects. While admitting that the majority have no vote in determining who will serve as their representatives, the government had insisted that everyone can nevertheless be sure that those who are elected will follow their duty to legislate for the good of the nation as a whole, with the result that everyone's interests will equally be served.

Some colonial spokesmen, including Daniel Dulany, had been inclined to accept that this defence of virtual representation might be applicable to Britain, and had merely objected that the colonists lack the requisite communality of interests. Price counters by insisting that virtual representation violates the most fundamental principle on which a genuinely free state must be based. If I am to be free in obeying the law, it is indispensable that I should personally give my consent to whatever laws are proposed. Political representation is not a matter of representing the interests of the people but of voicing and enacting their will. Price accordingly takes it to be obvious 'that civil liberty, in its most perfect degree, can be enjoyed only in small states where every independent agent is capable of giving his suffrage in person'.[202] He allows, however, that if we are unable to vote on public measures individually, then it may be sufficient for our wills to be voiced by representatives.[203] These must be elected by the whole community, in which every independent person must be given a right to vote, and they can only be granted the powers of delegates, who remain subject to whatever instructions they receive from the people.[204] Only by these means can the people be assured that the law will at all times reflect their common consent, so that a genuinely free government will result.[205]

There is thus said to be an exact parallel between the freedom of individuals and the freedom of states. Just as individuals enjoy their civil liberty only to the extent that they are secure from dependence on the will of others, so a state can only be called free if it is 'guided by its own will or (which comes to the same) by the will of an assembly of representatives appointed by itself and accountable to itself'.[206] By contrast, 'every state that is not so governed, or in which a body of men representing the people make not an essential part of the legislature, is in slavery'.[207] As Price later summarises, 'a free government loses its nature from the moment it becomes liable to be commanded or altered by any superior power'.[208]

---

[202] Price 1991, p. 24.    [203] Price 1991, p. 24.    [204] Price 1991, p. 25.
[205] Price 1991, p. 24.    [206] Price 1991, p. 26.    [207] Price 1991, p. 26.
[208] Price 1991, p. 45.

Price next observes that one obvious instance of such an enslaved state would be a community living in subjection to the legislature of another. He sees it as 'an immediate and necessary inference' from his argument 'that no one community can have any power over the property or legislation of another community that is not incorporated with it by a just and adequate representation'.[209] As he has already explained, the reason is that a state, like an individual, can be accounted free only 'when it is governed by its own will'.[210] But 'a country that is subject to the legislature of another country, in which it has no voice, and over which it has no control, cannot be said to be governed by its own will'.[211] Any such country 'is in a state of slavery', to which Price adds that 'it deserves to be particularly considered, that such a slavery is worse, on several accounts, than any slavery of private men to one another'.[212]

A further inference is that, because our natural rights are inalienable, and because our civil liberty is one such right, any state that finds itself in a condition of enslavement to arbitrary power has a natural right to free itself from the tyranny being imposed on the people. Here Price speaks for colonial independence in the strongest terms:

Had our ancestors in this country been so mad as to have subjected themselves to any foreign community, we could not have been under any obligation to continue in such a state. And all the nations now in the world who, in consequence of the tameness and folly of their predecessors, are subject to arbitrary power, have a right to emancipate themselves as soon as they can.[213]

These considerations lead Price directly to address the case of the American colonies, and here he issues a call to arms scarcely less militant than that of Paine. He begins by quoting the Declaratory Act of 1766, which had laid down that 'this kingdom has power, and of right ought to have power to make laws and statutes to bind the colonies, and people of America, in all cases whatever'.[214] By this stage in the argument he feels able to respond with mere contempt. 'Dreadful power indeed! I defy anyone to express slavery in stronger language.'[215] This is simply to declare 'that we have a right to do with them what we please'.[216] And if this is their predicament, then they are living in circumstances 'destructive of everything that can distinguish a free man from a slave'.[217] The only possible conclusion is that the British are undoubtedly enslaving the colonists, who have a natural right to liberate themselves from such oppressive tyranny. As Price ends by declaring, the moment has now

---

[209] Price 1991, p. 30.  [210] Price 1991, p. 30.  [211] Price 1991, p. 30.
[212] Price 1991, p. 30.  [213] Price 1991, p. 33; cf. p. 25.  [214] Price 1991, p. 37.
[215] Price 1991, p. 37.  [216] Price 1991, p. 38.  [217] Price 1991, pp. 38, 44.

been reached at which there can only be one outcome, which is that the dispute will have to be settled by the sword.[218]

It was only a matter of weeks after the publication of Paine and Price's tracts that Congress found itself confronted, after much wrangling and delay, with a formal proposal that the colonies should declare themselves, as a matter of right, to be independent states. After much debate over the motion, and the exact wording of the proposed declaration, the motion was eventually passed on 2 July, and the Declaration of Independence was published two days later.[219]

To a remarkable extent the Declaration follows the format as well as the arguments of the patriot tracts that Adams, Jefferson and others had published in the early 1770s.[220] First of all, a familiar Whig vision of legitimate government is yet again laid out. We are all endowed with a number of inalienable rights, which governments are instituted to secure. If any government becomes destructive of these ends, it is the right of the people to abolish and replace it in such a way as to effect their safety and happiness. If any government evinces a design to reduce the people to living under absolute despotism, they have not only a right but a duty to throw it off and provide anew for their security. There follows a list of specific grievances, partly directed against the British Parliament, but mostly targeting George III in a style reminiscent of Paine and the earlier attacks on the king by Adams and Jefferson. George III is again accused of refusing to give his assent to wholesome laws, neglecting to pass laws of pressing importance, forcing compliance with his measures, invading and violating the rights of the people, obstructing the administration of justice, making the colonists dependent on his mere will, subjecting them to jurisdictions to which they have not consented, and illegally sending large bodies of armed forces to the colonies.[221] To these offences the Declaration is now able to add that this history of repeated injuries and usurpations has culminated in war. This being so, they solemnly declare that the colonies 'are absolved from all allegiance to the British crown, and that all political connection between them and the state of Great Britain is and ought to be totally dissolved'.[222]

---

[218] Price 1991, p. 37.    [219] Armitage 2007, pp. 34–5, 165.
[220] See Nelson 2014, pp. 63–5. But Armitage 2007, pp. 38–42 argues that the emphasis on independence reflects the influence of Emer de Vattel's *Law of nations* (1758).
[221] The fourth and seventh of these eight accusations echo Adams 1772, while the remainder echo Jefferson 1774.
[222] Armitage 2007, p. 170. For the full text see Armitage 2007, pp. 165–71.

*Part IV*

# A New View of Liberty

# 7   The New View and its Provenance

## The Continental European Sources

The publication of Paine and Price's inflammatory tracts, together with the Declaration of Independence, provoked an instant counter-revolutionary reaction in Britain. Some critics responded largely in tones of outrage and resentment. The colonists were denounced as disloyal and rebellious children, incapable of recognising the debt of gratitude they owed to their generous mother country.[1] The British supporters of the colonists were attacked with no less ferocity as fanatical anarchists and traitors.[2] Price was singled out as the most obnoxious and pernicious among the criminal sowers of sedition,[3] and his views on liberty were denounced as repugnant and disgusting, futile and frivolous, filled with gross errors and mad with misguided zeal.[4]

The more reflective opponents of the colonists and their supporters began at the same time to develop several lines of attack on their views about liberty and independence. One took the form of a restatement of the high Tory claim that all rulers are directly ordained by God, so that they cannot under any circumstances be removed from power. The anonymous author of *Strictures on a sermon* denounced the fomenters and defenders of the American Revolution for failing to recognise that all government is 'originally of divine institution', and that all rulers must be treated as ministers of God. The basic obligation of subjects is 'patiently to abide in their several stations and be subject to them that have the rule over them'.[5] The same case was more fully restated by John

---

[1] *Cursory remarks* 1776, p. 10; *A letter to the Rev. Dr Richard Price* 1776, p. 5 ; *A dialogue on the principles of the constitution* 1776, p. 1.

[2] *The duty of the king and subject* 1776, p. 3; *A letter to the Rev. Dr Richard Price* 1776, pp. 6, 8; Shebbeare 1776, p. 1. On European imperialism and the liberal view of liberty see Hesse 2014.

[3] *A letter to the Rev. Dr Richard Price* 1776, pp. vi, 6, 21; *Cursory remarks* 1776, p. 2; Dodd 1777, pp. v, vii.

[4] *A letter to the Rev. Dr Richard Price* 1776, p. 8; [Lind] 1776, pp. i, x; *The duty of the king and subject* 1776, p. 3; Dodd 1777, p. v.

[5] *Strictures on a sermon* 1776, pp. 5, 9, 16, 25.

Coleridge in a sermon preached to his parishioners in Devonshire in the following year.[6] We must never fail to remember that 'all power is of God',[7] and that 'man was never designed by God to enjoy absolute liberty'.[8] Rather, it is God's will that everyone 'should obey all lawful commands for conscience sake'.[9] Coleridge ends by calling for an end to conflict and war, and for 'a spirit of peaceable and just submission' to be cultivated by everyone living in British provinces throughout the globe.[10]

This high Tory response, however, appears to have exercised little influence. The majority of Price's critics preferred to engage directly with his views on civil liberty and self-government. They clearly saw that, if the imperial cause was to be effectively defended, the entire structure of thinking about the meaning of liberty on which the American colonists and their British admirers were relying would have to be destroyed. They found the machinery for this work of destruction readily available in a long-standing tradition of monarchist legal thought. As we saw in Chapter 2, the pivotal contention that the people must give up their natural liberty and submit to monarchical power can be traced as far back as the debates in the early Italian communes about the *Lex regia*. According to this alleged act of legislation, cited by Ulpian in Book I of the *Digesta*, the Roman people relinquished and transferred their sovereign power to their emperors, thereby granting the will of their rulers the force of law. As we also saw, however, some jurists argued that this transfer had been a mere delegation of the people's sovereignty, not in any way an alienation of their original freedom and power. The scene was thus set for a continuing debate about the relationship between the authority of government and the liberty of the governed.

The claim that the people never alienate their original freedom and sovereignty was generally repudiated in the later Roman law tradition, but it was revived during the religious wars of the later sixteenth century by the monarchomach or 'king-fighting' writers, first in France and soon afterwards in the Netherlands. Very soon, however, this led to a furious counter-attack from the defenders of absolute monarchy. A growing number of legal writers responded that the people have no alternative but to submit to an absolute form of sovereign power if they are to have any prospect of living together in security and peace. With this view of political obligation came a corresponding view about the concept of liberty. If we cannot carry over our natural independence into our lives as subjects of states, then the only liberty left to us must take the form of the freedom of action we continue to enjoy in consequence of the limited

---

[6] Coleridge 1777, title page.    [7] Coleridge 1777, pp. 5, 7.    [8] Coleridge 1777, p. 9.
[9] Coleridge 1777, p. 10.    [10] Coleridge 1777, p. 14.

extent to which we are shaped and restrained by sovereign power. To be free is not to be independent of subjection, which is an impossibility; to be free is simply to be unimpeded and unrestrained.

This was the tradition of legal thinking on which the enemies of the American revolutionaries and their English supporters were able to draw in formulating their pro-imperial case. This was when, and this was why, the new view of liberty as absence of restraint or interference suddenly rose to a position of centrality in English political debate. This explanation, however, is not an uncontentious one. Some have seen the new view as a creation of utilitarian political philosophy, particularly in the hands of Jeremy Bentham, William Paley and their followers in the 1770s and 1780s.[11] Others have taken a broader perspective and associated the emergence of the new view with the rise and development of commercial society in the course of the eighteenth century. They have argued that the established view of liberty as independence, which had largely described the condition of propertied male elites, could not fail to give way to a view of freedom based instead on markets. It was due to 'the spread of market norms and practices' that the established view of liberty was at first confronted and finally overcome.[12]

There is something to be said in favour of both these explanations. The new view of liberty may well have been especially attractive to proponents of market values,[13] and it was undoubtedly espoused and popularised by the early utilitarians. But both these lines of argument arguably suffer from the same deficiency. They fail to see that the new view of liberty long pre-dated the eighteenth-century rise of commercial society and the emergence of utilitarian political thought. As a result, both explanations fail to provide an answer to the main historical puzzle that needs to be solved. What caused the tradition of legal thinking in which the new view of liberty was embedded to ascend so suddenly to a position of ideological dominance in less than twenty years between the late 1770s and the 1790s?

The answer, I shall next seek to show, is that the new view of liberty was widely espoused as a means of fending off the republican and democratic potential of the established view that liberty consists in independence. As the promoters of the new view rightly feared, the revolutionaries in America and France were determined to establish that absolute sovereignty inevitably leads to enslavement, and thus that it is possible to live in

---

[11] See Long 1977; Pettit 1997, pp. 41–50, Rosen 2003, pp. 245–55; Pettit 2014, pp. 13–16; Elazar 2015, pp. 418, 431.
[12] MacGilvray 2011, pp. 2, 15, 17.     [13] As argued in MacGilvray 2011, pp. 115–46.

freedom only under conditions of independence and self-rule.[14] These commitments were more than sufficient to arouse the anti-egalitarian forces at work in late eighteenth-century British society, and to prompt them to find a means of discrediting this demand for a more democratic form of state. This is what principally serves to explain the sudden rise of the new view of liberty to a central position in public debate during the closing decades of the eighteenth century.[15] It is to the provenance of this way of thinking among the anti-monarchomach jurists in continental Europe, and to the growing influence of their arguments in Britain with the recrudescence of Toryism after 1760, that we accordingly need to turn if this pivotal development is to be understood.

**********

The earliest concerted attack on the monarchomach view of popular sovereignty was mounted in France towards the end of the sixteenth century. A group of legal writers, including François Grimaudet, Pierre Gregoire, Jacques Hurault and Louis Servin, as well as the Gallicised Scotsman William Barclay, produced a series of replies to the radical Huguenot writers whom Barclay in his *De regno* of 1600 was the first to label as monarchomachs or fighters against kings.[16] What these seditious writers fail to understand, Barclay argues, is that although 'the people are able to constitute a king', there is 'no element of right left to the people once a king has been accepted and inaugurated'.[17] Barclay rests his case almost entirely on the *Lex regia*, quoting the *Digesta* to the effect that 'the people transfer the entirety of their *imperium* and power'.[18] He goes on to argue that, in this exemplary case, the transfer takes the form of a gift or grant,[19] and concludes that the effect of such a relinquishment of power must be to leave kings 'with no superior but God alone'.[20] It is consequently beyond doubt that all kings 'hold legal superiority over the whole body of the people and not merely over their individual subjects'.[21]

Soon afterwards the monarchomachs were criticised in similar terms by Hugo Grotius in his *De iure belli ac pacis* of 1625, in which he frequently appears to be thinking specifically about the revolt against Spanish rule in his native Netherlands.[22] As soon as he turns in Book I to explicate the

---

[14] On whether anything less than democratic self-rule can hope to secure liberty as independence see Bellamy 2007; Celikates 2013; De Dijn 2020.

[15] As already argued in De Dijn 2020, pp. 3–4.

[16] See Skinner 1978, vol. 2, pp. 300–1. Books III and IV of Barclay's *De regno* directly target the *Vindiciae contra tyrannos*. See Barclay 1600, pp. 105–338. On the anti-monarchomachs see also Burns 1993.

[17] Barclay 1600, 2. 2, p. 114.    [18] Barclay 1600, 2. 4, p. 127.

[19] Barclay 1600, 2. 4, pp. 124–5.    [20] Barclay 1600, 2. 4, p. 131.

[21] Barclay 1600, 2. 4, p. 127.

[22] On Grotius and Dutch republicanism see Tuck 1993, pp. 153–69.

concept of *imperium*,[23] Grotius dismisses out of hand any suggestion that sovereignty must be an inalienable property of the body of the people. He laments the damage already done by this gravely mistaken belief, which involves a failure to recognise that any free people can always decide to deliver themselves up to one or more persons, wholly transferring the right to rule themselves without retaining any part of it.[24] There can be no doubt, in other words, that absolute monarchy needs to be recognised as a legitimate form of rule.[25]

A still weightier defence of absolute sovereignty appeared in England soon after the execution of Charles I with the publication of Thomas Hobbes's *Leviathan* in 1651. Hobbes argues that our primary goal in establishing any form of government will always be to improve our security, and goes so far as to assert in the conclusion that he wrote the work 'without other design than to set before men's eyes the mutual relation between protection and obedience'.[26] The first message he aims to convey is that there can be no hope of any such security if we continue to subsist in our natural condition of liberty outside the state. The reason is that there is 'a general inclination of all mankind' to pursue 'a perpetual and restless desire of power after power that ceaseth only in death'.[27] From this it follows that 'if any two men desire the same thing, which nevertheless they cannot both enjoy, they become enemies', and will 'endeavour to destroy or subdue one another'.[28] The only possible outcome of living in our natural state would be to generate a condition of endless war, 'and such a war, as is of every man, against every man'.[29]

The moral drawn by Hobbes is that we have no alternative but to relinquish what he describes as 'the liberty of man' and subject ourselves to an absolute form of sovereign power with the strength to guarantee security and peace.[30] This transformation is brought about when we come together as one person by agreeing, each with each, to confer all our power and strength upon a sovereign who is thereby authorised to act as the representative of the commonwealth or state. The state is envisaged as a person 'by fiction' brought into being by the generative act of the multitude in agreeing to submit to sovereign power. With this act, they

---

[23] Grotius speaks interchangeably of *imperium* and *summa potestas*. See Grotius 1718, I. III, pp. 14, 17, 19, 20. For Grotius on sovereignty and community see Brett 2002.
[24] Grotius 1718, I. III, p. 20.
[25] For discussions of this passage see Tuck 1979, pp. 77–80; Tuck 1993, pp. 192–4; Lee 2016, pp. 262–8.
[26] Hobbes 2012, vol. 3, *A review and conclusion*, p. 1141.
[27] Hobbes 2012, vol. 2, ch. 11, p. 150.    [28] Hobbes 2012, vol. 2, ch. 13, p. 190.
[29] Hobbes 2012, vol. 2, ch. 13, p. 192.
[30] Hobbes 2012, vol. 2, ch. 21, p. 326 and ch. 26, p. 418.

agree to conform their wills to the will of the state as expressed by their sovereign, who is said to 'bear' or 'carry' the person of the state.[31]

Once this transformation has taken place, we live entirely subject to the will of our sovereign as representative of the state. The law takes the form of the sovereign's commands, and we are tied to the performance of our covenants by fear of punishment.[32] Hobbes allows that our subjection is not complete, as there are certain rights that 'cannot by covenant be transferred'.[33] Basically, however, such freedom as we continue to enjoy depends on what Hobbes describes as the silence of the law.[34] As he explains in his chapter on the liberty of subjects, 'in cases where the sovereign has prescribed no rule, there the subject hath the liberty to do or forbear according to his own discretion'.[35] The power of the law to restrain us from acting is in this instance set aside, so that we are left unrestrained and hence at liberty. 'The liberty of a subject lieth therefore only in those things which, in regulating their actions, the sovereign hath pretermitted.'[36]

We are thus to understand, as Hobbes lays down at the start of chapter 21, that liberty can be defined as nothing more than an absence of impediments or restraints.[37] My liberty is not taken away if someone is merely in a position to impede my capacity to act at will.[38] My liberty is lost only when my power to act at will is in fact impeded or restrained, and Hobbes adds that the impediment must be sufficient to make it impossible for the relevant power to be exercised.[39] Liberty simply means 'absence of opposition', and specifically an absence of 'external impediments of motion'.[40] Hobbes concludes with a rhetorical flourish that 'there is written on the turrets of the city of Lucca in great characters at this day the word LIBERTAS, yet no man can thence infer that a particular man has more liberty, or immunity from the service of the commonwealth there, than in Constantinople. Whether a commonwealth be monarchical or popular, the freedom is still the same.'[41]

---

[31] Hobbes 2012, vol. 2; ch. 16, pp. 244, 248 and ch. 17, pp. 260, 262. On state personality in Hobbes see Runciman 2003 and Skinner 2018, pp. 341–83.

[32] Hobbes 2012, vol. 2, ch. 17, p. 254.

[33] Hobbes 2012, vol. 2, ch. 21, p. 336. Hobbes itemises these inalienable natural rights at pp. 336–40. For contrasting views on Hobbes's understanding of natural rights see Tuck 1979, pp. 119–42 and Brett 1997, pp. 205–35.

[34] Hobbes 2012, vol. 2, ch. 21, p. 340.    [35] Hobbes 2012, vol. 2, ch. 21, p. 340.

[36] Hobbes 2012, vol. 2, ch. 21, p. 328.

[37] See Hobbes 2012, vol. 2, ch. 21, p. 324 on being impeded or restrained (or hindered or stopped). For Hobbes's development of this theme see Skinner 2008b.

[38] This is the point that seems to be overlooked in Kapust and Turner 2013, in which they claim that Hobbes does not reject the 'republican' view of liberty but merely criticises its misuse.

[39] Hobbes 2012, vol. 2, ch. 21, pp. 324, 326.    [40] Hobbes 2012, vol. 2, ch. 21, p. 324.

[41] Hobbes 2012, vol. 2, ch. 21, p. 332.

Among English republican writers of the 1650s Hobbes's argument was at once ridiculed and dismissed. As James Harrington observes in *Oceana*, Hobbes's conclusion is based on an equivocation. 'To say that a Lucchese hath no more liberty or immunity from the laws of Lucca than a Turk hath from those of Constantinople, and to say that a Lucchese hath no more liberty or immunity by the laws of Lucca than a Turk hath by those of Constantinople, are pretty different speeches.'[42] The truth is that in Constantinople 'the greatest bashaw is a tenant as well of his head as of his estate', liable to lose either or both 'at the will of his lord'. But in Lucca the meanest citizen 'is a freeholder of both', and is 'not to be controlled but by the law', which is 'framed by every private man unto no other end (or they may thank themselves) than to protect the liberty of every private man'.[43]

Among the supporters of monarchy, however, Hobbes's argument was much more favourably received. An influential legal and political tradition soon developed in which the works of Grotius as well as Hobbes were invoked to support a systematic defence of the legitimacy of absolute monarchical power. Here the pivotal role was played by Samuel Pufendorf, whose *De iure naturae et gentium* was first published in Lund in 1672 and quickly achieved widespread fame.[44] Among Pufendorf's immediate successors, three in particular rose to comparable prominence: Jean Barbeyrac, who became professor of law at Lausanne in 1711; Johann Heineccius, a pupil of Christian Thomasius at the University of Halle, who became professor of jurisprudence there in 1718; and Jean-Jacques Burlamaqui, who received a professorship of law from the Academy of Geneva in the early 1720s and lectured there for the rest of his academic career.[45]

Thomasius was one of the earliest popularisers of Pufendorf's work, but his own treatise on natural jurisprudence received little attention in England.[46] By contrast, Pufendorf's *De officio* was translated by Andrew Tooke as *The whole duty of man* as early as 1691. This version was reprinted in 1698 and 1705, revised in 1716 and reissued in 1735 with the inclusion of Barbeyrac's notes to his French translation of 1707.[47] Meanwhile an English translation of Pufendorf's *De iure naturae et gentium* by Basil Kennett had appeared in 1703 as *On the law of nature and nations*.

---

[42] Harrington 1992, p. 20.    [43] Harrington 1992, p. 20.

[44] On Pufendorf and his followers see Haakonssen and Seidler 2016, pp. 388–95.

[45] I focus on the convergent views of these writers about the meaning of liberty. But see Tierney 2014, pp. 291–303 for their disagreements about natural law and Dawson 2013 for Pufendorf's affinities with Locke.

[46] On Pufendorf and Thomasius see Hunter 2001, pp. 5–7, 237–44.

[47] See Tully 1991, pp. xii, xiv–xxxvii.

This text was even more frequently reprinted, and in the fourth and corrected edition of 1729 it was supplemented with the extensive annotations added by Barbeyrac to his French translation of 1712. The reception of this strand of juristic thinking in anglophone political theory culminated in the publication of Heineccius and Burlamaqui's works in London during the middle decades of the century. Heineccius's *Elementa iuris naturae et gentium* of 1738 was translated by George Turnbull in 1741 as *A methodical system of universal law* and reprinted in 1763. Burlamaqui's *Principes du droit naturel*, first published in 1747 just before his death, was translated by Thomas Nugent as *The principles of natural law* in 1748. Finally, Burlamaqui's *Principes du droit politique*, posthumously assembled from his lecture notes, was also translated by Nugent and appeared as *The principles of politic law* in 1752, with a further edition in 1776.

None of these jurists has any quarrel with the basic premise of the Whig theory of the state developed in England during the same period. They agree that, to understand whether and how far it may be necessary to live in subjection to human law, we first need to ask what it might be like to live outside the legal order of the state. They acknowledge that many political writers will want to call an immediate halt at this point by replying that the state is not a human creation, but is wholly and directly ordained by God. But most of the jurists reject this objection out of hand. Barbeyrac in his notes on Pufendorf's *Law of nature and nations* lists many commentators who adopt this stance, but only to dismiss them as pitiful, perverted and weak.[48] Burlamaqui more equably replies that anyone who reads Grotius or Pufendorf will soon be convinced 'that men have established civil societies not in consequence of a divine ordinance, but of their voluntary motion', and have done so as a means of fulfilling their most basic purposes.[49] The correct starting point, as Pufendorf had proposed in his discussion of law in Book II of *The law of nature and nations*, must therefore be to ask about the natural condition of mankind, and more specifically 'what kind of rights attend men in a state of nature'.[50]

Pufendorf is not much interested in whether such a condition of mere nature ever existed. His reason for invoking it is to arrive at a representation of our condition 'abstracting from all the rules and institutions' that are supplied by human invention, and especially from

---

[48] Pufendorf 1729, p. 656, note (a).    [49] Burlamaqui 1752, I. 16. 16–17, pp. 42–3.
[50] Pufendorf 1729, II. 2. 2, p. 105. See also Heineccius 1763, vol. I, 7. 183, p. 129 and Burlamaqui 1752, I. 2. 2, pp. 7–8 and I. 3. 19, p. 17. On Pufendorf's view of the state of nature and the law of nature see Hont 2005, pp. 166–76; Hunter 2001, pp. 171–80; and Hunter 2023.

any 'civil conjunctions and societies'.[51] Burlamaqui goes further, explaining that the underlying aim of his enquiry is not to pursue historical questions at all. These can never hope to yield anything better than 'mere conjectures', whereas 'the point of importance, and that which is particularly interesting to mankind, is to know whether the establishment of government, and of a supreme authority, was really necessary', or 'whether they could not live happy without it'.[52]

The distinguishing feature of the state of nature, these jurists agree, is that it would be a condition – as Hobbes had said – of 'natural liberty', a phrase they repeatedly use.[53] Like Hobbes, they do not deny that such a condition would be one of independence. A free person, as Pufendorf explains, is someone who is 'perfectly in his own power and disposal', not in any way 'controlled by the pleasure or authority of any other'.[54] To live in natural liberty is 'neither to be subject to one another, nor to acknowledge a common master'.[55] Heineccius closely follows this analysis, describing our natural condition as 'a state of equality' in which 'there is no superior or inferior', and thus as 'a state of liberty', in which there would be 'no place for empire or subjection'.[56] Burlamaqui offers a similar account, while converting it more systematically into the vocabulary of natural rights. He begins by reaffirming that our condition of natural liberty would be 'a state of equality and independence'.[57] He goes on to infer that Nature 'was willing that those on whom she has bestowed the same faculties should have all the same rights'.[58] The term 'natural liberty' accordingly designates 'the right which Nature gives to all mankind of disposing of their persons and property' in whatever manner they choose.[59]

What would it be like to live in a condition of natural liberty? Here the jurists are haunted by Hobbes's portrayal of man's natural life as 'solitary, poor, nasty, brutish and short'.[60] As they ponder his pessimistic analysis they are at first inclined to reject it outright. What Hobbes forgets, Pufendorf complains, is that the state of nature would be governed by the laws of nature, which are at the same time the dictates of reason and an expression of the will of God.[61] 'Man has not only the rash cry of his lusts, but also the sober voice of reason' to which he can attend, 'from all of

[51] Pufendorf 1729, II. 2. 1 and 4, pp. 102, 109.
[52] Burlamaqui 1752, I. 2. 8, pp. 10–11 and I. 3. 1, p. 11.
[53] Pufendorf 1729, II. 2. 3–4, pp. 108–9; Heineccius 1763, vol. I, 7. 183, p. 129 and vol. II, 1. 6, pp. 4–5; Burlamaqui 1752, I. 3. 15, p. 15 and I. 3. 22–3, p. 18.
[54] Pufendorf 1729, II. 2. 3, p. 106.     [55] Pufendorf 1729, II. 2. 1, p. 102.
[56] Heineccius 1763, vol. II, 1. 5–6, pp. 4–5.
[57] Burlamaqui 1752, I. 1. 2, p. 2 and I. 3. 2, p. 12.     [58] Burlamaqui 1752, I. 6. 3, p. 38.
[59] Burlamaqui 1752, I. 3. 15, p. 15.     [60] Hobbes 2012, vol. 2, ch. 13, p. 192.
[61] Pufendorf 1729, II. 1. 1, p. 96 and II. 2. 9, p. 113.

which we conclude that the natural state of man' would be 'not war but peace'.[62] But while Pufendorf is a critic of Hobbes he is in some respects a disciple, and as he reflects further on the state of mere nature he moves towards a conclusion closer to that of Hobbes in *Leviathan*.[63] He praises Hobbes for painting 'the inconvenience of such a state',[64] and he concedes that it would undoubtedly be 'extremely miserable'.[65] Burlamaqui agrees that, if we were to attempt to live in our natural state, we would soon decline into 'the most frightful, the most melancholy of situations' in which our highest goals would have no prospect of being realised.[66]

When the jurists turn to consider the nature of these goals, they sometimes conclude that the foremost end to which mankind can and ought to aspire is that of achieving the greatest happiness. Burlamaqui speaks of the right given by nature to all mankind to act in the manner they judge 'most convenient to their happiness',[67] and when he asks about the purpose of civil association he answers that it must always be that of enabling mankind to attain, 'with greater certainty, that happiness to which they all do naturally aspire'.[68] Pufendorf prefers to stress that there is a more significant target we need to set ourselves if the greatest happiness is to be achieved. As he expresses it, our fundamental aim should be to ensure that we live in safety.[69] Like Hobbes, Pufendorf has little to say about the promotion of happiness, and prefers to summarise by quoting Hobbes on the supreme importance of 'common peace and security'.[70]

While safety and security are the basic goals, the jurists agree that there would never be any hope of attaining them in our natural state. Once again Pufendorf supplies the fullest and most influential explanation, and here too he shows himself a close student of Hobbes. He agrees with 'what Mr Hobbes observes', namely 'that all have a restless desire after power' and are willing to engage in an endless 'competition for riches, honour, command, or any other prerogative and power above others'.[71] These proclivities would be sure to produce 'contention, enmity and war', and hence a state of perpetual violence in which every competitor would be able to attain his hopes only 'through the death or defeat of his rival'.[72]

The same pessimistic view was fully endorsed by the next generation of writers on natural jurisprudence. Heineccius argues that the disposition

---

[62] Pufendorf 1729, II. 2. 9, pp. 113–14.
[63] For Hobbes and Pufendorf on the need to submit to state power see Palladini 1990, chs. 1 and 2; Palladini 2008; Hunter 2001, pp. 171–2, 180–5.
[64] Pufendorf 1729, II. 1. 1, p. 96.    [65] Pufendorf 1729, II. 2. 1, p. 102.
[66] Burlamaqui 1752, I. 3. 19, p. 17.    [67] Burlamaqui 1752, I. 3. 15, p. 15.
[68] Burlamaqui 1752, I. 1. 3, p. 2.
[69] Pufendorf 1729, VII. 2. 1, p. 635 and VII. 4. 3, p. 661.
[70] Pufendorf 1729, VII. 6. 13, p. 701.    [71] Pufendorf 1729, VII. 1. 4, p. 627.
[72] Pufendorf 1729, VII. 1. 4, p. 627.

of even a small number of wicked and profligate men, with their 'insatiable lust of power and wealth', would be enough to render the lives of everyone intolerable.[73] Burlamaqui goes further, insisting that 'the greatest part of mankind, abandoned to themselves, listen rather to the prejudices of passion than to reason and truth'. This being so, the state of nature would be filled with evils and perpetual troubles, especially 'in cases where there happened to be any clashing of interests or passions' among self-interested men.[74] He even suggests that this condition cannot properly be described as a state of liberty, as the prevalence of these passions would soon cause it to 'degenerate into licentiousness'.[75]

If we cannot hope to live securely in our natural state, how can we hope to attain the security we need? There is general agreement that there can only be one solution. We must relinquish our standing as free persons, as *liberi homines* capable of acting according to our independent will. This is the juncture at which these writers cease even to mention the idea of liberty as independence except to denounce it. They now shift to arguing that, if there is to be any prospect of living together in peace, it is this false and dangerous ideal that must be altogether given up. The only liberty we can hope to enjoy is civil liberty, the liberty of subjects.[76]

Here Pufendorf shifts into arguing in his most minatory style. We must renounce any concern for natural liberty, divest ourselves of it, abandon it completely.[77] So intensely does he feel the need for this act of relinquishment that he finds it difficult to view it as a choice. We are not so much 'led to it by the bias of nature', as Aristotle misleadingly suggests, as driven to it with a force that amounts 'almost to necessity'.[78] Burlamaqui later writes in very similar terms. It was 'absolutely necessary for the order, tranquillity and preservation of the species' for everyone to 'renounce that arbitrary disposal which he had of his own person and actions, in a word, his independence'.[79] Like Pufendorf, he scarcely regards the act as a choice. Mankind is 'under an absolute necessity of quitting this state of independence and of seeking a remedy against the evils of which it was productive'.[80]

---

[73] Heineccius 1763, vol. II, 6. 103, p. 89.
[74] Burlamaqui 1752, I. 3. 5–7, pp. 12–13, I. 3. 11, p. 14, I. 3. 20, p. 17 and I. 4. 2, p. 22.
[75] Burlamaqui 1752, 1. 3. 19, p. 17.
[76] See Spector 2010 on natural and civil liberty, which he sees as two distinct conceptions of 'republican' liberty. But as we saw in Chapter 6, for writers such as Price there is no distinction: civil liberty is simply natural liberty protected by law. By contrast, the jurists I am considering agree that natural liberty (that is, independence) must be repudiated in favour of civil liberty (that is, the extent to which subjects are able to live free of restraint).
[77] Pufendorf 1729, VII. 1. 4, p. 626, VII. 2. 20, p. 651 and VII. 4. 3, p. 661.
[78] Pufendorf 1729, VII. 1. 4, p. 626.
[79] Burlamaqui 1752, I. 3. 22, p. 18 and I. 6. 8, p. 39.    [80] Burlamaqui 1752, I. 3. 9, p. 14.

The act of giving up our natural liberty is at the same time taken to be the act of joining with others to submit our wills to a sovereign authority endowed with sufficient powers to restrain us from behaving with the violence that would otherwise be endemic and unavoidable. Here the argument is again developed in dialogue with Hobbes. Pufendorf congratulates him for giving us 'a very ingenious draught of a civil state', but he has two criticisms to make.[81] One is that the state should not be regarded merely as a person 'by fiction', but rather as 'one moral person' to whom distinctive obligations can be attributed.[82] The other is that the process by which this person is brought into existence must involve two distinct covenants rather than the all-encompassing act of authorisation envisaged by Hobbes. The first covenant must take the form of a social compact that has the effect of converting the multitude into a unified whole; the second must then take the form of a political covenant that endows the state with a particular form of government.[83]

Pufendorf is in full agreement with Hobbes, however, that the covenant by which political authority is instituted must involve a complete subjection of everyone's individual will to the will of an absolute sovereign. He first reminds us that our basic aim is to attain the fullest possible security. He then argues that this outcome can be achieved only by 'a union of wills' in which 'each member of the society submits his will to the will of one person or of one council' whose decisions 'shall be deemed the will of all'.[84] Later he confirms that 'a state then is a moral body conceived to act as one will', which is 'produced by the agreement of all persons to submit their own private wills to the will of one man, or one assembly of men' and thereby 'conform themselves to the will of the state'.[85] Once this union is complete, 'there at last arises what we call a commonwealth or state, the strongest of all moral persons or societies'.[86]

The jurists of the next generation strongly endorse this line of argument. Heineccius agrees that the act performed by 'those who unite into a civil state' by renouncing their natural liberty is that of constituting 'what is called supreme or absolute sovereignty or empire'.[87] Burlamaqui

---

[81] Pufendorf 1729, VII. 2. 13, p. 645.
[82] Pufendorf 1729, VII. 2. 6, p. 639. On Pufendorf's view of state personality see Holland 2017, esp. pp. 65–103. On this central issue, as Holland stresses, Pufendorf rejects Hobbes's account. Holland is correct to point out (pp. 8–12) that I gave a misleadingly Hobbesian account of Pufendorf's treatment of state personality in Skinner 2009b. But I agree with Palladini and Tuck that, on the issues of freedom and political obligation, Pufendorf is in part a disciple as well as a critic of Hobbes. See Tuck 1979, pp. 156–62; Palladini 1990; and Palladini 2008.
[83] Pufendorf 1729, VII. 2. 7, p. 639. On the two compacts and Pufendorf's associated criticisms of Hobbes see Hunter 2001, pp. 185–8, 192–4.
[84] Pufendorf 1729, VII. 2. 5, p. 638.    [85] Pufendorf 1729, VII. 4. 2, p. 661.
[86] Pufendorf 1729, VII. 2. 5, p. 638.    [87] Heineccius 1763, vol. II, 7. 127, p. 119.

writes in still more forceful terms. 'When mankind renounced their independence and natural liberty', they did so 'by giving masters to themselves',[88] thereby placing themselves 'under the dependence of a person' who was 'invested with an uncontrollable power'.[89] They did so not merely to avoid the evils of the state of nature, but also 'in hopes that, under the protection and care of their sovereign, they should meet with solid happiness'.[90] These are the only means by which 'a regular state and perfect government is formed'.[91]

This form of absolute sovereignty, it is agreed, can be embodied in a number of different constitutional arrangements. Pufendorf has no doubt that the second of his two covenants can either take the form of an agreement to establish a democracy (although this is held to present distinctive complications) or else an aristocracy or monarchy.[92] Heineccius reiterates that, when instituting the state, 'citizens or subjects may have submitted their will either to one, or many, or to the whole people'.[93] This in turn explains, Burlamaqui adds, why it is best to speak of sovereignty as 'a right conferred upon a person, and not upon a man' so that we are sure of understanding that 'this person may be not only a single man but likewise, and entirely as well, a multitude of men united in council'.[94] He is careful to remind us, however, that any grant of sovereignty must always give rise to an absolute form of rule. 'Let the form of government be what it will, monarchical, aristocratic, democratical or mixed, we must always submit to a supreme decision, since it implies a contradiction to say that there is any person above him who holds the highest rank in the same order of beings.'[95]

The way in which sovereigns exercise this supreme power is by enforcing obedience to the law. Here Pufendorf straightforwardly appeals to Hobbes's authority, arguing that we obey the laws 'not principally upon account of the matter of them but on account of the legislator's will'.[96] Heineccius agrees that 'civil laws are commands of the supreme power in a state' and are consequently expressions of the sovereign's will, to which 'the submission of all the members of a state' will at all times be due.[97] Burlamaqui, as so often, provides a succinct summary, declaring that 'the sovereign in a state is that person who has a right of commanding finally'.[98]

---

[88] Burlamaqui 1752, I. 3. 20, p. 21.   [89] Burlamaqui 1752, I. 3. 10, p. 14.
[90] Burlamaqui 1752, I. 3. 22, p. 21.   [91] Burlamaqui 1752, I. 4. 15, p. 28.
[92] Pufendorf 1729, VII. 2. 8, p. 640.   [93] Heineccius 1763, vol. II, 7. 128, p. 120.
[94] Burlamaqui 1752, I. 5. 4, p. 32.   [95] Burlamaqui 1752, I. 7. 4, p. 45.
[96] Pufendorf 1729, I. 6. 1–2, p. 59.
[97] Heineccius 1763, vol. II, 7. 128, p. 120 and vol. II, 8. 150, p. 152.
[98] Burlamaqui 1752, I. 5. 1, p. 31.

Hobbes had laid it down that the law primarily operates by threatening subjects with punishment for acts of disobedience.[99] Pufendorf similarly argues that the aim in punishing should be to deprive people 'of the power of doing harm', thereby providing 'sufficient caution for every man's security'.[100] Burlamaqui echoes Hobbes still more closely, speaking of the need for sovereigns to 'over-awe those who should be inclinable to disturb the peace'. He concludes that, without the threat of punishment and the power to impose it, 'the establishment of civil society and of laws would be absolutely useless', and there would be no possibility of living in safety and peace.[101]

The jurists end by spelling out how the law acts to secure obedience. One method, Pufendorf explains, is that threats of punishment can be used to 'constrain a man', contrary to his will, to act in conformity with the law by means of 'declaring and exhibiting a penalty'.[102] Generally, however, Pufendorf prefers to emphasise the power of law to stop or impede people from inflicting injury and violence, so that the contrast he likes to draw is between liberty and restraint. He refers to the ability of rulers to 'restrain evil and disobedient subjects',[103] and notes that 'the natural end of all punishment' is to dispose subjects to obey the law and 'restrain them from actions contrary to it'.[104] Heineccius likewise argues that 'all acts of wickedness may be restrained by punishments',[105] and Burlamaqui similarly speaks of how laws can be given 'a sufficient force to restrain the subject'.[106] With this account of how states limit freedom, the jurists complete their analysis of the character of sovereign power.

**********

While the jurists present their exposition of sovereignty with unwavering confidence, they are acutely aware of the strongly contrasting strand of argument that had originated with the monarchomach writers on popular rule. As we saw in Chapter 2, the monarchomach case had centred on the claim that, if the people subject themselves wholly to a sovereign whose will they are obliged to treat as law, they forfeit their standing as free persons capable of acting according to their independent wills and thereby reduce themselves to the condition of slaves. It is against this tradition that Pufendorf and his followers set themselves, and Pufendorf in particular responds ferociously. He opens his chapter on the properties of sovereignty by observing that 'many have taken the liberty to assert that

---

[99] Hobbes 2012, vol. 2, ch. 14, p. 216.    [100] Pufendorf 1729, VIII. 3. 12, p. 775.
[101] Burlamaqui 1752, I. 8. 4, p. 65.    [102] Pufendorf 1729, I. 6. 14, p. 73.
[103] Pufendorf 1729, VII. 2. 5, pp. 638–9.
[104] See Pufendorf 1729, VIII. 3. 24, p. 790 and cf. II. 1. 1, p. 96.
[105] Heineccius 1763, vol. I, 3. 84, p. 57.    [106] Burlamaqui 1752, III. 2. 3, p. 168.

the power of the prince neither can nor ought to be superior to that of all the people'.[107] These writers contend that, 'since the king is made for the people, not the people for the king, on that score the people must be superior to the prince'.[108] As a result, the term 'absolute' now 'bears a hateful sound in the ears of persons born under free governments'.[109]

Pufendorf responds with a scornful dismissal of this attempt to impose a vision of popular sovereignty that the monarchomachs have merely 'framed in their own fancy'.[110] (Barbeyrac in his accompanying note assures us that Pufendorf is here alluding to the *Vindiciae contra tyrannos*.[111]) By way of reply, Pufendorf promises to establish 'that absolute government is by no means so formidable a thing as these men are willing to fancy',[112] and more specifically that 'the desire of living under an absolute monarchy' is by no means an indication of 'a low and abject spirit' or a willingness to embrace a life of enslavement.[113]

Pufendorf begins his counter-attack by repeating that the ideal of natural liberty, and hence of independence from subjection to the will of others, is an absurd as well as a dangerous principle. The 'absolute liberty' for which the monarchomachs plead 'would be destructive to human nature', so that 'binding and restraining it with laws is highly conducive to the good and to the safety of mankind'.[114] Heineccius agrees that the error of the monarchomachs lies in refusing to recognise that there can be no question of retaining the freedom of the state of nature once we covenant to become subjects. Everyone must thereafter submit their will to those who have been vested with supreme power. These rulers can then be judged 'by none but God alone; and much less therefore can they be punished in any manner by the people'.[115] At this point he refers us to 'the doctrine of the monarch-killers, which makes the people superior to the king or prince', and specifically cites François Hotman's *Franco-Gallia* as well as the *Vindiciae contra tyrannos*.[116] The egregious mistake made by these and other monarchomachs 'lies in making the constituent superior to the constituted', a doctrine 'no less absurd than it would be to say that a servant who hath voluntarily subjected himself to a master is superior to his master'.[117]

Next Pufendorf argues that the monarchomachs commit a further and heinous error in claiming that, if we abandon our natural freedom from subjection to the will of others, we thereby reduce ourselves to a condition

[107] Pufendorf 1729, VII. 6. 5, p. 690.     [108] Pufendorf 1729, VII. 6. 6, p. 691.
[109] Pufendorf 1729, VII. 6. 7, p. 693.     [110] Pufendorf 1729, VII. 6. 6, p. 691.
[111] Pufendorf 1729, p. 691, note (e).     [112] Pufendorf 1729, VII. 6. 6, p. 692.
[113] Pufendorf 1729, VII. 6. 5, p. 690.     [114] Pufendorf 1729, II. 1. 2, p. 96.
[115] Heineccius 1763, vol. II, 7. 128, p. 120.
[116] Heineccius 1763, vol. II, 7. 128, p. 120n.
[117] Heineccius 1763, vol. II, 7. 128, pp. 120–1n. See also Burlamaqui 1752, I. 7. 13, p. 48.

of servitude. He expresses particular indignation at this suggestion, complaining that 'it seems by no means fair to compare the condition of subjects under an absolute monarch with that of slaves'.[118] What the monarchomachs forget is that the aims of any legal system will always be strictly limited. After the values of peace and security have been secured, there will still be a broad range of actions available to subjects in which the state takes no interest. Legally speaking, this is the area in which subjects are neither obliged to act nor to abstain from acting in any particular way, and consequently retain the right to act according to their own will and desires. Everyone reserves and secures 'so much of his former rights and privileges', and hence freedom of action, 'as is consistent with the nature of a civil state'.[119]

As he develops this argument, Pufendorf again speaks in terms reminiscent of Hobbes. He agrees that the extent to which, as subjects of sovereign power, we remain free to act is basically determined by what Hobbes had described as the silence of the law. Here Pufendorf is much more willing than Hobbes to admit that the liberty of subjects may be limited not merely by law but also by acts of illegal force and violence. He speaks of the shocking extent to which wicked men continue to bring 'so many evils and mischiefs on one another' even when 'they now live under the force of law, and under the fear of punishment'.[120] Apart from this, however, he writes largely in agreement with Hobbes. 'Since a man hath a power of doing all such things as can proceed from his natural abilities, except those which are forbidden by some law', we can say that 'those things which are not prohibited by such or such a law, we are said to have a right of doing by that law', and hence the liberty to do it.[121]

These considerations enable us, Pufendorf concludes, to 'state the notion of liberty in perfection and without alloy'.[122] The only liberty available to us is that which we enjoy as subjects of states, and this takes the form of an absence of 'outward impediment, whether natural or moral', and hence an absence of any hindrances of the kind produced by legal constraint or natural force.[123] Pufendorf is accordingly able to quote Hobbes with approval for the claim that 'liberty is nothing else but the absence of all impediments of motion', although he expands Hobbes's definition by adding that 'those impediments may be either natural and external, or moral and arbitrary'.[124] Where we encounter no such impediments, there we fully enjoy our liberty.[125] To be in possession of liberty is simply to

[118] Pufendorf 1729, VII. 6. 5, p. 690.    [119] Pufendorf 1729, VII. 7. 17, p. 704.
[120] Pufendorf 1729, II. 1. 6, p. 100.    [121] Pufendorf 1729, I. 6. 3, p. 59.
[122] Pufendorf 1729, II. 1. 2, p. 97.    [123] Pufendorf 1729, II. 1. 3, p. 97.
[124] Pufendorf 1729, VI. 3. 9, p. 620.    [125] Pufendorf 1729, VI. 3. 10, p. 621.

possess the power to move without being prevented by any 'rubs or hindrances' that 'may either prevent the motion or turn it another way'.[126]

Barbeyrac in his notes on this part of Pufendorf's text proposes that we should think of our liberty not simply as a matter of not being restrained or constrained by law, but also in a more positive way. 'The general notion of law', he suggests, must be understood to include 'not only an obligation to do or not do certain things, but also a liberty to do or not do others. So that liberty imports always a concession, either express or tacit, which is a positive thing.'[127] Pufendorf, however, prefers to follow Hobbes's simpler suggestion that the boundaries of freedom are marked by the extent to which the state takes no interest in the behaviour of its subjects, with the result that 'the subject hath the liberty to do or forbear according to his own discretion'.[128] Underlining Hobbes's dictum, Pufendorf concludes that 'whatsoever things the law permits, those it neither commands nor forbids, and therefore it really doth nothing at all concerning them'. To speak of the 'permission of the law' is consequently equivalent to speaking of 'every man's just liberty'.[129] The only liberty of which it makes sense to speak is this form of civil liberty.

Hobbes had rounded off his definition of liberty in *Leviathan* by repudiating the dictum in the *Digesta* to the effect that a free person is someone who is not a slave, not subject to the will of anyone else. When we speak of a free man, Hobbes retorts, we are merely saying that he is someone who is 'not hindered to do what he has a will to', and 'finds no stop in doing what he has the will, desire or inclination to do'.[130] By this stage in the argument Pufendorf feels ready to echo Hobbes almost word for word. Where I encounter no such 'stop or hindrance', there I am in possession of my liberty.[131] Burlamaqui was later to summarise by quoting a warning that Montesquieu had meanwhile issued in *The spirit of the laws*: 'we must have continually present to our minds the difference between independence and liberty'.[132] For Burlamaqui, as for Pufendorf, independence is a fantasy; liberty is nothing more than an absence of impediments or restraints.

### The Coming of the New View to Britain

Although Basil Kennett's translation of Pufendorf's *De iure naturae et gentium* went though four editions between 1703 and 1729, it seems

---

[126] Pufendorf 1729, II. 1. 2, p. 97.    [127] Pufendorf 1729, p. 73, n. 2.
[128] Hobbes 2012, vol. 2, ch. 21, p. 340.    [129] Pufendorf 1729, I. 6. 15, p. 74.
[130] Hobbes 2012, vol. 2, ch. 21, p. 324.    [131] Pufendorf 1729, I. 6. 15, p. 74.
[132] Burlamaqui 1752, I. 3. 17, p. 16. Cf. Montesquieu 1989, pt. 2, bk. 11, ch. 3, p. 155.

initially to have had little impact on British political debate.[133] Pufendorf's resolutely secular approach to questions about the origins of government sharply contrasted with Tory pieties, while his defence of absolute monarchy virtually guaranteed that he would be ignored during the heyday of Whiggism in the 1730s and 1740s. It is a mistake, however, to suppose that the view of liberty as independence remained 'more or less unchallenged in the English-speaking world' until the late eighteenth century.[134] We already find it challenged by admirers of the anti-monarchomachs as early as the 1730s, and by the middle years of the century the view that liberty simply consists in absence of restraint was beginning to gain widespread support.

One early example of this development can be found in the sermon preached by George Fothergill in 1737 to the University of Oxford on *The danger of excess in the pursuit of liberty*. Fothergill, who subsequently became principal of St Edmund Hall, was speaking at a time when Oxford was suspected of Jacobite sympathies, and goes out of his way to denounce the growing disregard for established authority and the refusal to recognise 'the great duty of submission to government'.[135] He sarcastically observes, with reference to the usual Whig pieties, that 'some late pretenders to great accuracy in disquisitions of this kind' have 'raised much clamour' against the suggestion 'that any of men's natural rights or natural liberties are receded from at their entrance into society'.[136] He responds that 'wheresoever authority is placed', the effect is to 'create a proportionable obligation to obedience' upon everyone, and thus 'a proportionable restraint upon the freedom of action they before enjoyed'.[137] The extent of the liberty of the subject must therefore be measured by the law.[138] As Fothergill explains, 'freedom is a term of relative import', which implies 'a respect to some obligations, restraints, inconveniences, burdens or the like, from which we are said, or supposed, to be free'.[139] It follows that 'the extent of our liberty in any capacity may best be adjusted by a view of the several restraints or obligations we lie under in that capacity'.[140] The liberty of subjects can only stem from an

---

[133] Ward 2004, pp. 105–51 takes a contrary view, seeing in Pufendorf the chief influence on James Tyrrell, whose *Patriarcha non monarcha* (1681) Ward treats as 'the voice of moderate whiggism'. But none of Tyrrell's views on the state of nature, the contract of government or the rights of subjects were peculiar to Pufendorf, whom Tyrrell cites in *Patriarcha non monarcha* solely to agree with his view that sovereignty cannot be divided. See Tyrrell 1681, pp. 130–1 and 236–7.

[134] Pettit 1997, p. 44.

[135] Fothergill 1737, pp. 5, 31. On Fothergill see *ODNB*, vol. 20, p. 533.

[136] Fothergill 1737, p. 12.    [137] Fothergill 1737, pp. 12, 13.    [138] Fothergill 1737, p. 13.

[139] Fothergill 1737, p. 7.    [140] Fothergill 1737, p. 7.

absence of restraint by law. This 'legal liberty' constitutes 'all that can be demanded', since to ask for more would be to demand 'a liberty to defeat the very ends of government'.[141] Fothergill concludes by calling for a ready acceptance of the need for submission to government and a refusal to consider any 'schemes of farther liberty'.[142]

A similar line of argument was pursued by another Oxford graduate of conservative leanings, Abraham Tucker. Rich and reclusive, Tucker devoted his life to his philosophical studies, beginning with the publication of *Freewill, foreknowledge and fate* in 1763.[143] Tucker opens his treatise with the claim that, if we are to understand the extent of the liberty available to us, it is essential to start by defining the concept itself. He then proceeds to offer his own analysis in the form of a critique of Locke.[144] Liberty, Tucker maintains, is 'a negative term, implying no more than a denial of restraint and force', so that 'when we say a man is free, we mean nothing else than that there is no hindrance', nothing that has the effect of stopping him from 'doing or forbearing' according to his will.[145] When we say of a man that he has lost his liberty, all we mean is that 'he is under a restraint which hinders him'.[146]

By the time Tucker published these anti-Lockean sentiments, a greatly increased interest in the legal and political writers who had originally argued in the same terms had already developed in Britain. In 1749 Kennett's translation of Pufendorf's *De iure naturae et gentium*, together with Barbeyrac's notes, was reprinted for the first time since 1729; in 1750 Hobbes's *Leviathan* was republished after an interval of more than fifty years;[147] and in 1752 Burlamaqui's *Principes du droit politique* made its first appearance in English. As British politics began to see a revival of Toryism after the accession of George III in 1760, these texts were soon welcomed into the mainstream of British legal and political debate.

One celebrated writer who declared himself at this juncture to be a deep admirer of Pufendorf was Laurence Sterne, who spoke of him in the opening volume of *Tristram Shandy* (first published in 1760) as one of 'the best ethic writers'.[148] Soon afterwards Thomas Bever – a Fellow of All Souls College who later became the Judge of the Cinque Ports – sought in his lectures at the University of Oxford to promote a re-evaluation of the entire continental school of natural jurisprudence.[149] Grotius and Pufendorf, he declared, 'were the ornaments of the last century and may

---

[141] Fothergill 1737, p. 13.     [142] Fothergill 1737, p. 36.
[143] See *ODNB*, vol. 55, pp. 489–90.     [144] [Tucker] 1763, pp. 7–12.
[145] [Tucker] 1763, p. 7.     [146] [Tucker] 1763, p. 8.
[147] After its first publication in 1651 *Leviathan* was republished only twice before 1750, first in c.1678 and again in c.1695. See Hobbes 2012, vol. 1, pp. 228–9, 262.
[148] Sterne 2003, p. 7.     [149] On Bever see *ODNB*, vol. 5, p. 585.

properly be called the fathers of modern jurisprudence'. Their only weakness stemmed from the fact that they were 'too often bewildered in the vast
variety and copiousness of their subject matter'. Fortunately, however,
'many of these perplexities have been cleared up by the learned notes of
Barbeyrac', while 'the labour of perusing such large works has been, of late
years, very agreeably shortened by Burlamaqui', whose special achievement has been to articulate the principles of Pufendorf 'in a very regular
and intelligible order', a service so useful that his works 'can never be
perused too carefully or too often'.[150]

By the time Bever was writing, some important English texts on law and
civil liberty had already been published in which the works of the continental European jurists played a major role in shaping the argument. One
was John Brown's *Thoughts on civil liberty*, first published in 1765.[151] We
have already encountered Brown as the author of a youthful tract on civil
and religious freedom, and he later gained widespread fame for his more
conservative and satirical *Estimate of the manners and principles of the times*
in 1757. Brown never ceased to think of himself as a Whig, and in his
*Thoughts on civil liberty* he attacked the Tories for their 'false principles
tending to despotism' no less vigorously than he attacked the radicals for
their willingness to 'inflame an ignorant and licentious populace'.[152] He
treats the accession of the Hanoverian dynasty as a moment of perfect
freedom, and believes that 'the just balance of divided power' established
by the mixed monarchy in Britain continues to provide the best security
for liberty.[153]

As soon as Brown turns, however, to consider the origins of the state, he
begins to echo the more absolutist views of Hobbes and Pufendorf.[154]
Quoting Hobbes's *Leviathan*, he characterises the life of 'natural liberty'
as 'solitary and savage', and speaks of 'this brutal state of nature'.[155] He
dismisses the ideal of natural liberty as nothing more than 'an unlimited
indulgence of appetite' that would amount to mere licentiousness if
carried over into the social state.[156] Hence the necessity that this natural
liberty should be given up. We shall otherwise have no prospect of
achieving what he repeatedly describes as 'public happiness',[157] which
can only be attained if we commit ourselves to the welfare of society,[158]
and thus to the promotion of public utility and the common good.[159] The

---

[150] Bever 1766, p. 35n.
[151] See Skjönsberg 2021, pp. 228–35. On Priestley's debate with Brown on liberty see
Canovan 1978.
[152] Brown 1765, pp. 106, 127.    [153] Brown 1765, pp. 94, 118.
[154] On Brown's increasing conservatism see Womersley 2019, pp. xxi–xxii.
[155] Brown 1765, p. 12.    [156] Brown 1765, p. 14.    [157] Brown 1765, pp. 10, 28, 39, 93.
[158] Brown 1765, pp. 13, 28, 118, 149, 167.    [159] Brown 1765, pp. 13, 161.

only means by which 'the necessity of curbing and fixing the desires of men' can be attained is by imposing 'such equal laws as may compel the appetites of each individual to yield to the common good', and it is 'from this salutary restraint' that 'civil liberty is derived'.[160] Civil liberty, the only liberty available to us, can thus be equated with that degree of freedom which is left to us after we have been 'swayed, impelled or induced' to behave in a properly sociable manner by 'the coercive power of human laws'.[161]

Of far greater significance was a further discussion of law and liberty that was first published in the same year and even more clearly reflected the same influences: William Blackstone's *Commentaries on the laws of England*, which appeared in four volumes between 1765 and 1769.[162] Blackstone opens with a general analysis of the nature of laws, after which his first chapter is entitled 'Of the absolute rights of individuals'.[163] The discussion begins with an examination of 'the natural liberty of mankind', which is held to consist in 'a power of acting as one thinks fit, without any restraint or control, unless by the law of nature: being a right inherent in us by birth, and one of the gifts of God to man at his creation'.[164] Natural liberty in part requires, that is, that we should not be restrained from acting at will by anyone else. But it also requires – and here Blackstone adopts Pufendorf's terminology – that we should not be controlled in such a way that it is within the power of anyone else to restrain us should they wish.[165] The state of nature is consequently one in which 'we are all equal' as well as being 'independent of any other', since we are 'without any other superior but him who is the author of our being'.[166]

We need to recognise, however, that this natural liberty cannot take the form of an inalienable right. The weaknesses and imperfections of human nature are so serious that life in the state of nature would be filled with wants and fears, and would allow us nothing more than a 'wild and savage liberty'.[167] The right to exercise our natural liberty must therefore be sacrificed. 'For no man that considers a moment would wish to retain the absolute and uncontrolled power of doing whatever he pleases, the consequence of which is that every other man would also have the same power, and then there would be no security to individuals in any of the enjoyments of life'.[168] As in Hobbes and Pufendorf, the requirement to

---

[160] Brown 1765, p. 13.     [161] Brown 1765, pp. 15–16.
[162] On Pufendorf and Blackstone see Lieberman 1989, pp. 37–9; Holland 2017, pp. 149–51.
[163] Blackstone 2016, pp. 33, 83.     [164] Blackstone 2016, p. 85.
[165] Blackstone 2016, p. 85.     [166] Blackstone 2016, pp. 33, 36.
[167] Blackstone 2016, p. 85.     [168] Blackstone 2016, p. 85.

renounce our natural liberty is treated by Blackstone less as a voluntary decision than an act of necessity.

This conclusion is reinforced with the warning that, unless we submit to control and restraint, we shall have no prospect of attaining the ends we chiefly seek. These ends are first described in largely individualistic terms. Our paramount aim is said to be that of achieving 'our own substantial happiness',[169] a goal that requires us to be able to live our lives in safety and convenience.[170] But in the ensuing chapter Blackstone goes on to stress that, if we are to achieve eventual happiness, we must be willing to pursue not merely our own well-being but the requirements of 'common utility' and 'public advantage'.[171] Only then will the greatest happiness eventually be achieved.

The liberty we are obliged to renounce is that of not being controlled by the will of anyone else. Within civil associations, no one is ever free from this form of dependence, since everyone is equally and wholly subject to the will of the state, which Blackstone characterises as 'a supreme, irresistible, absolute, uncontrolled authority' in which the rights of sovereignty reside.[172] Here again he closely echoes the vocabulary as well as the argument of Hobbes's *Leviathan*. Hobbes had argued that, when the members of a multitude agree to institute a sovereign to represent the state, they agree 'to confer all their power and strength upon one man, or upon one assembly of men', covenanting 'to submit their wills, everyone to his will, and their judgment to his judgment'. The outcome is that the sovereign acquires a duty of protection, while every subject acquires a corresponding duty of obedience. Blackstone agrees that the state is the name of 'a collective body, composed of a multitude of individuals, united for their safety and convenience, and intending to act together as one man' with 'one uniform will'.[173] Through the act of creating this political union, the members of the multitude 'submit their own private wills to the will of one man, or of one or more assemblies of men, to whom the supreme authority is entrusted' and thereby 'conform themselves to the will of the state'.[174] As in Hobbes's account, the outcome is a mutual relation between obedience and protection, although Blackstone prefers to present this conclusion as a claim about mutual rights: 'allegiance is the right of the magistrate, and protection the right of the people'.[175]

Blackstone never refers to Hobbes by name, nor does he refer to Pufendorf's similar analysis of the origins of the state, although he is

---

[169] Blackstone 2016, p. 35.     [170] Blackstone 2016, p. 42.
[171] Blackstone 2016, pp. 85, 86.     [172] Blackstone 2016, p. 39.
[173] Blackstone 2016, p. 42.     [174] Blackstone 2016, p. 42.     [175] Blackstone 2016, p. 84.

happy to cite Pufendorf on numerous occasions as an authority on specific laws.[176] Rather, he is intent on distancing himself from the accounts they give of how the powers of the state can be embodied in government. While they had conceded that sovereign authority can equally well be exercised by different types of regime, they had shown a marked preference for absolute monarchy. By contrast, Blackstone recurs to the Whig doctrine that no community can be said to be free unless its members possess the constitutional power to contribute to the making of the laws by which they are ruled. To deny them this right would be to leave them subject to the mere will of their rulers, and this would be to impose on them 'an arbitrary and despotic power' of the kind that subsists between masters and slaves.[177] Blackstone concludes that the best form of government must be a mixed form of monarchy in which a legislative assembly ensures that no laws are enacted without the consent of the people's elected representatives.

While the people must give their consent to the laws, Blackstone remains adamant that the law itself takes the form of the sovereign's will, by which the people are wholly controlled. Furthermore, the way in which the laws operate is that, 'by declaring and exhibiting a penalty against offenders, they bring it to pass that no man can easily choose to transgress the law, since by reason of the impending correction compliance is in a high degree preferable to disobedience'.[178] Blackstone concedes, however, that if the laws 'come armed with a penalty' to 'compel and oblige',[179] it might seem that, in abandoning the state of nature for a life of civil association, we have altogether forfeited our liberty. We lose our freedom from control when we subject ourselves to sovereign power, and we lose our freedom from constraint when we are subsequently coerced into obeying the law.

Blackstone's response is to invoke Florentinus's dictum in the *Digesta* about the nature of the *libertas* enjoyed by free persons within the *civitas* or state.[180] As we saw in Chapter 1, Florentinus had declared that this liberty consists in our having the power to act as we wish unless we are prevented by law or illegal force. Blackstone is willing to agree that our freedom of action may sometimes be limited by the exercise of force, but he is chiefly concerned with the restriction of liberty by law or right, and here he prefers to follow Florentinus in speaking not of constraining people to act against their will but rather of restraining them from exercising their will. He stresses that the state must always be careful not to

[176] Blackstone 2016, pp. 46–7, 158, 168, 288–9, 291.    [177] Blackstone 2016, p. 86.
[178] Blackstone 2016, p. 44.    [179] Blackstone 2016, p. 44.
[180] Blackstone 2016, p. 85 and n.

impose any 'wanton and causeless restraint of the will of the subject', which always constitutes 'a degree of tyranny'.[181] But he is no less emphatic that it will often be 'necessary and expedient for the general advantage of the public' for a law to be imposed 'which restrains a man from doing mischief'.[182]

Where subjects are neither restrained by law nor constrained by force, their remaining freedom can be spelled out as a list of rights that – as Blackstone notes – are generally characterised in the British constitution as liberties.[183] Among these there are 'three principal or primary articles', which are 'the right of personal security, the right of personal liberty and the right of private property'.[184] These and many other liberties 'it is our birthright to enjoy entire, unless where the laws of our country have laid them under necessary restraints'.[185] Where we encounter no such restraints, 'all of us have it in our choice to do everything that a good man would desire to do, and are restrained from nothing but what would be pernicious to ourselves or our fellow citizens'.[186] To speak of this zone of freedom is to speak of 'the civil liberty of mankind', which can be equated with the degree of liberty we enjoy when no one supposes that 'the public good requires some direction or restraint', and when we are consequently left unhindered from acting as we choose.[187] Blackstone cannot resist adding that 'the idea and practice of this political or civil liberty flourish in their highest vigour in these kingdoms, where it falls little short of perfection', and where the laws are 'peculiarly adapted to the preservation of this inestimable blessing even in the meanest subject'.[188]

After the publication of the opening volume of Blackstone's *Commentaries* to general acclaim in 1765, a number of legal and constitutional texts appeared in which his reworking of the natural-law theory of the state was paraphrased and reiterated. Among the most significant were Edward Wynne's *Dialogues concerning the law and constitution of England*, first published in four volumes in 1768 and reissued in 1774; Thomas Mortimer's *Elements of commerce, politics and finances*, first published in 1772 and likewise reissued in 1774; and an edited collection of laws concerning the freedom of subjects that appeared prefaced by *A general introduction on political liberty* in 1767.[189] These and other writers of the same period were now happy to announce their admiration for the continental writers on natural jurisprudence and their English followers. Mortimer makes a number of references to Barbeyrac and Burlamaqui as

---

[181] Blackstone 2016, p. 85.    [182] Blackstone 2016, p. 85.
[183] Blackstone 2016, pp. 87, 97.    [184] Blackstone 2016, p. 88.
[185] Blackstone 2016, p. 97.    [186] Blackstone 2016, p. 97.    [187] Blackstone 2016, p. 85.
[188] Blackstone 2016, p. 86.    [189] *A general introduction on political liberty* 1767.

well as to Blackstone and Hobbes.[190] Wynne more specifically directs us
to Heineccius as one of the most excellent writers on the connection
between law and fact,[191] as well as praising Burlamaqui for his analysis
of the powers of the state[192] and speaking admiringly of Blackstone's
*Commentaries*.[193]

The most important principle that all these writers take from the
continental European jurists is that, as the *General introduction* of 1767
phrases it, 'we must have continually present to our minds the difference
between independence and liberty'.[194] Here the author of the *General
introduction* appears to be quoting Burlamaqui, who had in turn taken the
dictum, as we have seen, from Montesquieu's *Spirit of the laws*.[195] Wynne
and Mortimer likewise speak of the state of nature as a condition of
independence, but Mortimer particularly stresses that it is indispensable
for this natural liberty to be resigned and given up.[196] No one can
otherwise be secured 'from the assaults of his own species' and hence
from a life of 'lawless rapine and violence'.[197] The only solution is to
surrender our liberty into the hands of one or more persons who are
thereby invested with authority to govern the rest and armed with
power to enforce their authority.[198] Once we submit to be governed in
this way, our natural liberty is replaced by 'a new creation', the extent of
which is determined by law. 'Whatever the law does not forbid is permitted, and on this permission are founded the rights of individuals in any
state' and hence the extent of their liberty.[199] Both Wynne and the author
of the *General introduction* had already arrived at the same conclusion. The
author of the *General introduction* defines liberty as 'a right of doing
whatever the laws permit',[200] and Wynne accepts that 'the only idea of
liberty in society is the power of acting as we please in all cases not
forbidden by known law'.[201] Everyone agrees that, whenever we speak
of the liberty we possess, we are never referring to anything other than the
absence of such impediments and restraints.

---

[190] Mortimer 1772, pp. 229, 230, 250, 373n.     [191] Wynne 1768, vol. 4, p. 24.
[192] Wynne 1768, vol. 4, pp. 24, 98, 163.     [193] Wynne 1768, vol. 4, pp. 24, 76, 172.
[194] *A general introduction* 1767, p. ii.
[195] Burlamaqui 1752, I. 3. 17, p. 16; cf. Montesquieu 1989, pt. 2, bk. 11, ch. 3, p. 155.
[196] Mortimer 1772, p. 243.     [197] Mortimer 1772, pp. 242–3.
[198] Mortimer 1772, p. 243.     [199] Mortimer 1772, pp. 243, 245.
[200] *A general introduction* 1767, p. ii.     [201] Wynne 1768, vol. 3, p. 52.

# 8 The New View Affirmed

## Liberty as Absence of Restraint

As the pro-imperial propagandists began to turn their fire on the defenders of the American colonists in the opening months of 1776, it was on the tradition of natural jurisprudence that they chiefly relied in formulating their rival account of civil liberty.[1] The earliest work in which this line of attack was deployed against Richard Price and his followers was published as a series of eight letters in *The Gazetteer* newspaper between March and April 1776. The author was John Lind, who had been educated at Balliol College Oxford, where he began a long association with Jeremy Bentham. Thereafter Lind trained as a lawyer at Lincoln's Inn and was called to the bar in 1776.[2] It was at this juncture that he produced his letters in criticism of Price, which he quickly expanded into a tract entitled *Three letters to Dr Price*, and soon followed with *An answer to the Declaration of the American Congress*, the earliest published attack on the Declaration of Independence.[3]

Lind's first complaint is that Price fails to offer a definition of civil liberty, thereby failing 'to settle what liberty is'.[4] Instead, Price opens his discussion ('preposterously') by outlining a fourfold division of allegedly different types of freedom.[5] Here Price's overriding concern, Lind notes, is with the concept of civil liberty, which he treats as a power of self-government and consequently takes to be 'something positive'.[6] Lind retorts that 'the truth is, sir, you set out with a capital mistake' in supposing liberty to be 'anything positive'. The consequence is that a confusion of ideas and an abuse of language run through the whole of the resulting book.[7]

---

[1] For a brief summary this development see Skinner 2024.　[2] See *ODNB*, vol. 33, p. 816.
[3] For contrasting discussions of Lind see Pettit 1997, pp. 42–4, 48–9 and Ghosh 2008, pp. 149–52. On Lind see also Avery 1978 and Miller 1994, pp. 385–97.
[4] [Lind] 1776, p. 8.　[5] [Lind] 1776, p. 8.　[6] [Lind] 1776, pp. 10, 15.
[7] [Lind] 1776, pp. 14, 65.

What then is the correct definition of liberty? Lind answers in terms almost identical with those used by the writers on natural jurisprudence, and most recently by Blackstone in his *Commentaries*. When we say that someone is free, what we mean is nothing more than that they are not being coerced.[8] Lind goes on to explain: 'I use the term coercion because it comprises constraint and restraint: by the former a man may be compelled to do, by the latter to forbear certain acts.'[9] He adds (invoking Pufendorf's terminology) that 'coercion may be physical or moral'.[10] 'I call physical coercion the operation of some extraneous physical cause or agent; which operation takes place during the time of another's doing or forbearing to do an act, and irresistibly compels that other to do or forbear it.'[11] By contrast, 'moral coercion I call the threat of some painful event to take place after and in consequence of our doing or forbearing to do certain acts', and 'it is this moral coercion that the legislator applies to make the subject obey his general commands'.[12] Lind concludes that this analysis not only provides us with 'a fair definition of liberty', but is also 'the only notion I can form to myself of liberty', the only definition that makes any sense.[13] Liberty is simply absence of restraint or constraint.[14]

A more considered argument along comparable lines was published in June 1776 by another lawyer, Richard Hey, under the title *Observations on the nature of civil liberty and the principles of government*.[15] Hey was a Fellow of Sidney Sussex College Cambridge who had been called to the bar in 1771 and became a member of the Middle Temple.[16] He opens his *Observations* by taking note of Lind's letters in *The Gazetteer*, to which he refers with respect, while at the same time stressing that his own approach is a different one.[17] He complains that Lind speaks stipulatively, even dogmatically, simply opposing one definition of liberty with another. Hey appeals to his readers to acknowledge that 'surely it is a pity to perplex a subject with arbitrary definitions of terms which in their common and received acceptation are already sufficiently determinate'.[18] The right approach, he suggests, must be 'to discover what idea is conveyed by the word in common conversation', thereby settling the meaning of liberty 'by examining the common use of the word'.[19]

---

[8] [Lind] 1776, p. 16.    [9] [Lind] 1776, p. 16.    [10] [Lind] 1776, p. 17.
[11] [Lind] 1776, p. 17.    [12] [Lind] 1776, p. 18.    [13] [Lind] 1776, pp. 19, 20.
[14] [Lind] 1776, p. 27.
[15] Hey 1776. For the date of publication see Elazar 2015, p. 428, a discussion to which I am much indebted.
[16] See *ODNB*, vol. 26, p. 941.    [17] Hey 1776, p. 9n.    [18] Hey 1776, p. 7.
[19] Hey 1776, pp. 7, 9.

Following his own advice, Hey imagines somebody being asked, 'Are you at liberty to walk to the Royal Exchange today?' Such a person would understand the question to be the same as if they had been asked, 'Does anything forbid or hinder your walking to the Royal Exchange today?'[20] Next he offers the example of a prisoner regaining their liberty. 'What do we understand by this? That a person who was confined within the walls of a prison is now not confined.'[21] We find, in short, that 'the common idea of liberty' is that it consists in 'the absence of restraint'.[22] 'Wherever you are not restrained, there you find what we call liberty.'[23] It cannot be doubted that this is to speak of 'the commonly received idea of liberty' and the 'obvious meaning' of the term.[24]

Hey then turns to Richard Price and his distinctions between natural, moral, religious and civil liberty.[25] Whereas Lind had dismissed the typology as preposterous, Hey has no objection to thinking about what he describes as different sorts of liberty, so long as we recognise that these terms can only refer to different forms of restraint.[26] This leads him to take issue with the way in which the distinction between natural and civil liberty had usually been drawn. As we saw in Chapter 7, most writers on natural jurisprudence had been willing to concede that, although it would be impossible to live in a state of natural liberty, such a condition would undoubtedly be one of complete independence. By contrast, Hey insists that even natural liberty must be understood as a condition in which we are not restrained. Just as moral liberty is restricted by moral constraints, and civil liberty by civil constraints, so the liberty of our natural condition would take the form of 'the absence of restraints imposed by the laws of nature'.[27] There is consequently nothing to prevent us from saying 'that physical, moral, religious, civil liberty is that liberty which physical laws allow, that which the laws of morality, the laws of religion, the laws of civil society allow'.[28]

When Hey turns to civil liberty, he accordingly concludes that our enjoyment of this form of freedom is 'greater as the restraints imposed on us by civil laws are fewer', and that 'the greatest degree of it would be to have no civil laws at all'.[29] He is unusually frank in adding that the freedom of citizens within civil associations is limited not only by law, but also by 'restraints imposed by the arbitrary violence of individuals'.[30] His response is to underline that 'there is one species of liberty which

---

[20] Hey 1776, p. 8. Here Hey uses the same example as Tucker had done in his very similar discussion of liberty as absence of restraint. See Tucker 1763, pp. 130–1.
[21] Hey 1776, p. 8.    [22] Hey 1776, p. 8.    [23] Hey 1776, p. 10.
[24] Hey 1776, pp. 10, 19.    [25] Hey 1776, p. 10.    [26] Hey 1776, p. 10.
[27] Hey 1776, pp. 15, 24.    [28] Hey 1776, p. 15.    [29] Hey 1776, p. 27.
[30] Hey 1776, p. 28.

cannot be too great', this being our freedom from the restraints imposed by any such illegal force.[31] As for the restraints imposed by law, his final word is that 'the point of perfection in civil liberty' is reached when the legislature manages 'to avoid, as much as possible, multiplying restraints upon the subject'.[32]

Throughout his analysis Hey is careful to limit himself to speaking of restraint as the exact antonym of liberty. This prompts him to offer a further criticism of Lind, who instead 'makes liberty to be the absence of coercion and observes that coercion comprises constraint and restraint'.[33] Hey objects that, if we return to common usage, we shall find that 'constraint is understood to include something more than a mere deprivation of liberty', and thus that it is Lind who is unhelpfully turning the concept of liberty into something positive.[34] Hey illustrates his objection with an example taken from Locke's *Two treatises of government*.[35] Suppose that 'a person by violence puts a pen into my hand, and then constrains or forces me to write certain words and sentences'. It is true that 'I am indeed deprived of the liberty of holding my hand still, or of moving it the way that I choose'. But it is also true that 'I am forced into one particular and determinate action' as the result of 'positive violence exerted upon me', so that something more than a mere deprivation of liberty is involved.[36] Hey accordingly concludes that 'I still am inclined to think that the common notion of liberty is merely absence of restraint'.[37]

These developments prompted the formidable figure of the young Jeremy Bentham to join the argument.[38] This is not to say that Bentham made any immediate contribution to the discussion in print.[39] He includes no explicit reference to this way of thinking about liberty in his *Fragment on government*, which was published in April 1776.[40] He planned a reply to Hey for inclusion in a revised version of Lind's *Three letters*, but in the event nothing appeared. Bentham's only immediate reaction took the form of a private letter to Lind of April 1776.[41] He recalls that, perhaps as much as a year before, he had communicated to Lind 'a kind of discovery I thought I had made, that the idea of liberty imported nothing in it that was positive: that it

---

[31] Hey 1776, p. 28.    [32] Hey 1776, p. 56.    [33] Hey 1776, p. 9.    [34] Hey 1776, p. 9.
[35] [Locke] 1690, para. 176, p. 398.    [36] Hey 1776, p. 9.    [37] Hey 1776, p. 9.
[38] Whatmore 2016, p. 110 argues that Price and Bentham were 'not in conflict about the nature of liberty', but I see Bentham as joining the argument on the side of Lind and Hey.
[39] Bentham made his sole published contribution to the debate in two letters published under the pseudonym 'Hermes' in *The Gazetteer and New Daily Advertiser* in July 1776. For the date, title and attribution see Elazar 2015, p. 427 and n.
[40] For the exact date see Bentham 2017, p. 309.
[41] For its importance see Long 1977, p. 54. On Lind and Bentham see Pettit 1997, pp. 42–4; and Elazar 2015, pp. 427–9.

was merely a negative one: and that accordingly I defined it *"the absence of restraint"'*. Referring to Lind's letters in *The Gazetteer*, Bentham concedes: 'I do not believe I then added *"and constraint"*: that has been an addition of your own.' But he adds that 'in the meantime I had discovered the defect: and had changed in my papers the word *restraint* into *coercion*, as that which would include both *restraint* and *constraint*. This new term I then communicated to you, and you have adopted it in preference to the other two.' Bentham concludes by asking Lind to ensure, when he republishes his letters as a pamphlet, to acknowledge that 'the idea you found occasion to give of liberty you took from a person who has not permitted you to give his name'.[42]

Lind had made a brief allusion to Bentham in his fifth letter to *The Gazetteer*, which had appeared on 29 March. But he went much further when he published his *Three letters* in July, in which the following footnote appeared:

That liberty is nothing positive, that it means only the absence of restraint, was an idea first suggested to me by a very worthy and ingenious friend, whose name I am not now permitted to mention. In turning this idea over in my mind I thought the definition imperfect. A man may be compelled to do as well as to forbear an act; liberty therefore I thought meant the absence of constraint as well as of restraint. I mentioned this some time after to my friend from whom I received the original idea. He had already perceived the defect, and had substituted the general term *coercion* to the partial one of restraint.[43]

As well as responding handsomely to Bentham's request, Lind here takes the opportunity to provide a summary of his own argument.

Recent scholars have been inclined to accept at face value Bentham's claim to have originated the view that liberty consists in absence of interference – whether in the form of constraint or restraint – and have spoken not merely of his 'innovative theory' but of what he rightly took to be his 'great breakthrough'.[44] But it is worth pausing for a moment to consider the relations between Bentham, Lind and Hey. Hey in his *Observations* claimed priority over Lind, assuring his readers that he initially read Lind's letters in *The Gazetteer* after he had already settled the definition of liberty in his own mind.[45] More strikingly, and by contrast with Bentham and Lind, Hey is anxious to disavow any claim to originality. He takes himself to be articulating the 'commonly received' definition of liberty,[46] and he specifically draws attention to the fact that Blackstone had already made use of it in his *Commentaries*. He quotes

---

[42] Bentham 2017, Letter 158, pp. 310–11.    [43] [Lind] 1776, pp. 16–17.
[44] Elazar 2015, pp. 418, 431; cf. Pettit 1997, pp. 42–3.    [45] Hey 1776, p. 9.
[46] Hey 1776, p. 29.

Blackstone's observation that 'different persons in the same community may enjoy different degrees of civil liberty', to which he adds Blackstone's comment on what it means to speak of such differences. Some people may be 'free from restraints' in cases where others are restrained, and when we refer to 'the absence of such restraints' we are speaking of what it means to be 'possessed of greater civil liberty'.[47]

It is possible that at this moment we come upon a considerable irony in Bentham's contribution to the debate. When Bentham assured Lind that the moment of epiphany about the meaning of liberty had come to him at some point in 1775, he was recalling the period when he was engaged in his close and forensic examination of the introduction to Blackstone's *Commentaries*.[48] Bentham notes in his *Fragment* that Blackstone begins by considering the law of nature, the law of revelation and the law of nations before turning to municipal law.[49] When mounting his attack on Blackstone's analysis, Bentham concentrates exclusively on the last of these categories. But in doing so he appears to forget that, when comparing the law of nature and revelation with human law, Blackstone had introduced the claim that, when thinking about law and liberty, the contrast we need to draw is with being restrained. As Blackstone had explained, there are many 'indifferent points' where 'both the divine law and the natural leave a man at his own liberty; but which are found necessary for the benefit of society to be restrained'.[50] Blackstone reiterates the contrast in the opening chapter of his *Commentaries*, in which he presents his definition of civil liberty. As we saw in Chapter 7, he concludes that 'the civil liberty of mankind' can be equated with the degree of freedom we enjoy when no one supposes that 'the public good requires some direction or restraint', and when we are consequently left unrestrained from acting as we choose.[51]

Richard Hey's *Observations*, as well as John Lind's *Three letters*, were both in print by July 1776. During the months that followed, the most remarkable feature of the ensuing war of words was the extent to which their view of liberty was instantly and extensively taken up.[52] A large number of writers not only echoed their claim that liberty consists in nothing more than absence of restraint, but took it to be unquestionable that, in doing so, they were using the word in its obvious and natural sense. The first to write in these terms was the author of *Experience preferable to theory*, one of the earliest and most careful dissections of

---

[47] Hey 1776, p. 30.
[48] For Bentham on liberty in 1774–6 see Elazar 2015, pp. 421–2, 427–31.
[49] Bentham 1988, p. 33.    [50] Blackstone 2016, p. 35.    [51] Blackstone 2016, p. 86.
[52] For an exceptionally full and helpful bibliography of the ensuing pamphlet war see Reid 1988, pp. 163–216.

Richard Price's argument.[53] 'I am far from thinking', the writer begins, that 'there is no such thing as civil liberty.'[54] But as subjects of sovereign power we can never be entirely free, if only because 'there is a certain degree of restraint necessary to the very being of government'.[55] Where we find the laws 'laying greater restraint than is necessary to answer the ends of government', there we may say that there is too little liberty. But 'where there are laws sufficient to answer this end and no more' we have reached 'the highest idea I can have of the liberty in a state of government' that any subject can hope to enjoy.[56] The extent of our liberty must always be measured by the extent to which we are or are not restrained.

This view was frequently repeated in the paper-war that quickly escalated. One of the most impressive tracts in which the same argument was laid out was published anonymously as *Civil liberty asserted*, in which the author identifies himself only as 'a friend to the rights of the constitution'. He mounts a savage but carefully argued attack on what he stigmatises as Price's anarchical principles,[57] beginning with a dismissal of Price's entire approach to the topic of civil liberty. He responds that 'civil liberty can extend no further than the laws of the society permit'. Here 'the will and power of individuals are limited by the general law' and 'the same law that lays a restraint upon him, and prevents his abusing others, protects him and his property'. As a result, the extent of our liberty can only consist in the absence of any such restraint.[58] Writing shortly afterwards, the author of *The duty of the king and subject* even more briskly affirmed that 'civil and restrained are synonymous'.[59] To live in a civil association is to be restrained by law, so that 'the full scope of liberty allowed by the constitution' is simply the degree of liberty left to us when we are not restrained.[60] Price's contrasting view of civil liberty as a matter of self-rule is dismissed as fanatical anarchy, and we are warned that it is 'importantly big with danger to civilisation'.[61]

A more moderate statement of the same claim was provided by the anonymous author of *Three dialogues concerning liberty*, which appeared later in 1776. The dialogues take the form of a series of questions from the author to a friend who is introduced as someone who possesses a good understanding as well as calmness of mind.[62] The friend begins by expressing surprise at the current disputes about liberty, since the subject

---

[53] Lind mentions it in *Three letters*, p. xvn.
[54] *Experience preferable to theory* 1776, p. 18.
[55] *Experience preferable to theory* 1776, p. 19.
[56] *Experience preferable to theory* 1776, p. 19.    [57] *Civil liberty asserted* 1776, title page.
[58] *Civil liberty asserted* 1776, p. 8.    [59] *The duty of the king and subject* 1776, p. 6.
[60] *The duty of the king and subject* 1776, pp. 8–9.
[61] *The duty of the king and subject* 1776, p. 3.    [62] *Three dialogues* 1776, p. 1.

is 'much more simple than was commonly imagined'.[63] 'The liberty or freedom of man', he declares, simply consists 'in a power of doing, or of forbearing to do, any action at his pleasure' so long as there is no impediment to the exercise of his power.[64] 'If there were any impediment either to his doing or not doing any action, he was in such case not free; he was confined on the one side or on the other.'[65] To be at liberty, in short, is to be unimpeded; it is when we 'suffer restraint' that liberty is taken away.[66] As the two speakers agree in the concluding dialogue, the political question that arises about individual liberty is consequently about the extent of the 'just restraint' that can be placed on its exercise.[67]

A year later John Gray wrote in similar terms, but much more vituperatively, in his tract entitled *Doctor Price's notions of the nature of civil liberty*. Gray had already risen to prominence as a commentator on the economic relations between Britain and America, and had aggressively supported the right of Parliament to tax the colonies. Price's attempt to stigmatise the latter policy as tyrannical is dismissed by Gray as a 'wonderful absurdity and confusion of ideas'.[68] Turning to the question of civil liberty, Gray notes that Price at first focuses on the idea of legislative independence, but then 'drops this first sense of the term' and 'always implies by it the legislative independence of individuals in respect to each other'.[69] He then proceeds to ridicule the latter view as absolute nonsense.[70] Fully matching what he takes to be Price's effrontery, he objects that 'it is altogether new, and may I think be termed an abuse of language', to speak in these terms.[71] The simple truth is that we enjoy 'the most perfect degree of civil liberty' when our personal freedom suffers 'the least abridgment' from the coercive force of law.[72]

It took only a few years for this understanding of liberty to pass beyond the realms of polemic and find its place in a number of general treatises in moral and political philosophy. Among these, one of the most popular was Thomas Gisborne's *Principles of moral philosophy,* first published in 1789.[73] By this time Gisborne felt able to pronounce with complete assurance that 'liberty and restraint are opposed each to the other', and that when we reach 'the limits of that restraint' we are left with liberty.[74]

---

[63] *Three dialogues* 1776, pp. 2, 4.    [64] *Three dialogues* 1776, p. 5.
[65] *Three dialogues* 1776, p. 5.    [66] *Three dialogues* 1776, p. 6.
[67] *Three dialogues* 1776, p. 102.    [68] Gray 1777, p. 4.    [69] Gray 1777, p. 3.
[70] Gray 1777, pp. 3, 4.    [71] Gray 1777, p. 8.    [72] Gray 1777, p. 9.
[73] Gisborne 1798. Gisborne published his *Principles* in 1789. The fourth edition (1798) included for the first time a separate chapter on civil liberty. See Gisborne 1798, ch. 19, pp. 343–56. An Anglican clergyman, Gisborne accepted a perpetual curacy in 1783 which he thereafter occupied until his death sixty-three years later. See *ODNB*, vol. 22, pp. 356–7.
[74] See Gisborne 1798, p. 345; and cf. p. 347, where he quotes Paley to the same effect.

By far the most influential of these general works was William Paley's *Principles of moral and political philosophy*, which first appeared in 1785 and went through fifteen editions before Paley's death in 1805.[75] Presenting his case in a manner that clearly influenced Gisborne, Paley begins by defining civil liberty as 'not being restrained by any law, but what conduces in a greater degree to the public welfare'.[76] He then argues that 'the degree of actual liberty' we enjoy as members of civil associations simply bears 'a reversed proportion to the number and severity of the restrictions' which have the effect of restraining us from acting at will.[77] Once again, the conclusion is that liberty is simply the absence of any such restrictions or restraint.

### Liberty as Independence: The Alleged Confusions

The critics of Richard Price were not merely intent on affirming their new view of liberty; they were also interested in identifying what they took to be the precise nature of the conceptual confusion underlying Price's rival account. One suggestion immediately put forward was that those who think of liberty as independence are confusing the possession of liberty with the enjoyment of security for the liberty we possess. John Lind already presents a statement of this distinction in his *Three letters* of July 1776. Addressing Price in his characteristically impatient tone, he asserts that 'very different are political liberty and security from power', and that Price's fundamental error is that 'these, sir, you are perpetually confounding'.[78] Whereas liberty 'is produced by a positive operation of the laws', it is impossible for security to be produced in the same way, because the security must be 'against those very persons in whose hands the power is lodged'.[79]

Lind's argument was immediately taken up by one of Price's most celebrated critics, John Wesley, the founder of Methodism, who published *Some observations on liberty* soon after the American Declaration of Independence in July 1776. Wesley is respectful of Price, and acknowledges that his *Observations* is 'certainly a masterpiece in its kind'.[80] But he completely rejects Price's claim that, even at the time when the colonists

---

[75] The *Principles* appeared in its fifteenth edition in 1804. All quotations are from the first edition of 1785. For details of Paley's life see O'Flaherty 2019, pp. 35–8, 77–80.

[76] Paley 1785, p. 441; later (p. 572) he makes the same point about religious liberty.

[77] Paley 1785, p. 443.    [78] [Lind] 1776, p. 74.

[79] [Lind] 1776, p. 88. According to Kelly 2001 Bentham agrees that there can be no liberty in the absence of security. But as Elazar 2015 points out (pp. 431, 437–9), Bentham speaks only of 'liberty by security'. He does not speak of liberty as requiring security from dependence.

[80] Wesley 1776, p. 3.

were enjoying their liberty and rights 'all quiet and undisturbed', the problem they already faced was that they had no security for any of their liberties, because 'the king and parliament can take them all away'.[81] No doubt they can, Wesley retorts, 'but they do not; and until it is done they are freemen'.[82] While it is true that 'the supreme power of my country can take away either my religious or civil liberty', it is equally true that 'till they do I am free in both respects', and am consequently 'free now, whatever I may be by and by'.[83] Price's mistake is to write as if it makes sense to say that 'I have no money now because it may be taken from me tomorrow'.[84] What he fails to recognise is that, when we ask whether the colonists are in possession of their liberty, 'we are not talking about what may be, but what is; and it cannot be denied that they are free' at the present time.[85]

The same argument was later given special prominence by William Paley in the chapter on civil liberty in his *Principles of moral and political philosophy*. Paley also appears to have Price specifically in mind,[86] although the proponents of this view of freedom whom he seems to have read with the closest attention were the English republicans of the previous century.[87] After explaining that liberty is nothing other than absence of restraint, Paley goes on to observe that 'there is another idea of civil liberty' which is 'neither so simple nor so accurate', although he admits that it agrees better with 'the usage of common discourse'.[88] 'This idea places liberty in security; making it to consist not merely in an actual exemption from the constraint of useless and noxious laws and acts of dominion, but in being free from the danger of having such hereafter imposed or exercised.'[89]

To underline his rejection of this view, Paley considers a recent political drama, the constitutional coup engineered by King Gustav III of Sweden in 1772. He notes that commentators 'are accustomed to say of Sweden that she has lost her liberty by the revolution which lately took place'. But he objects that 'we are assured that the people continue to be governed by the same laws as before, or by others which are wiser, milder, and more equitable'.[90] The loss suffered by the Swedish people is that the concurrence of their parliamentary assembly is no longer required in the making of laws. They have thereby 'parted with the security they possessed against any attempts of the crown to harass its subjects by oppressive and useless exertions of prerogative'.[91] But what has been altered is 'not their present burdens, but their prospects of future grievances'.[92]

---

[81] Wesley 1776, p. 5.    [82] Wesley 1776, p. 5.    [83] Wesley 1776, p. 5.
[84] Wesley 1776, p. 5.    [85] Wesley 1776, p. 8.    [86] As noted in O'Flaherty 2019, p. 190.
[87] See O'Flaherty 2019, pp. 190–1.    [88] Paley 1785, p. 444.    [89] Paley 1785, p. 444.
[90] Paley 1785, pp. 444–5.    [91] Paley 1785, p. 445.    [92] Paley 1785, p. 445.

Paley concedes that many people will wish to say that this alteration should be pronounced 'a change from the condition of freemen to that of slaves'.[93] But again he responds that those who speak in these terms 'do not so much describe liberty itself as the safeguards and preservatives of liberty'.[94] We need to recognise that the situation in which a man is 'governed by no laws but those to which he has given his consent, were it practicable, is no otherwise necessary to the enjoyment of civil liberty than as it affords a probable security against the dictation of laws imposing arbitrary and superfluous restrictions upon his private will'.[95] The question about liberty, in other words, is always a de facto one. Are you now being restrained from acting as you choose? If you are not, you are a free person. To Paley this seems so obvious that he takes the case against the prevailing way of thinking about liberty to be finally proved.[96]

**********

The objection that Price confuses liberty with security was perhaps the most searching criticism he had to face, but it was rarely emphasised until Paley gave special prominence to it. The cardinal mistake that Price was more usually held to have made was that of confusing the idea of civil liberty with our natural condition of independence and self-government. This is the juncture at which Price's critics begin to draw extensively on the tradition of natural jurisprudence developed by Pufendorf and his followers and later invoked by Blackstone in his *Commentaries*. Like the jurists, the critics of Price are generally willing – Hey is a rare exception – to ask themselves what life might be like without law, and hence to imagine a state of nature in which everyone is in possession of a natural right to act as they choose. The author of *Civil liberty asserted* speaks of 'the unbounded liberty' of our natural condition, 'in which indeed every man may be said to be his own legislator' with a right of 'following his own will' in everything.[97] John Wesley similarly envisages the state of nature as the original condition of humankind, speaking of 'the naked sons of nature'[98] and the universal right 'to be self-governed and independent' during the period before any civil societies were formed.[99]

The point on which these critics insist, however, is that it makes no sense to think of these natural rights as inalienable. Here they explicitly endorse the claim that Pufendorf and his followers had made about the need to relinquish all such rights if we are to have any prospect of living a happy life. The point of departure among those who develop this

---

[93] Paley 1785, p. 445.     [94] Paley 1785, p. 446.     [95] Paley 1785, pp. 446–7.
[96] On Paley's account of the alleged confusion between liberty and security see O'Flaherty 2019, pp. 227–31.
[97] *Civil liberty asserted* 1776, pp. 10, 15.     [98] Wesley 1775, p. 7.     [99] Wesley 1776, p. 10.

argument is the familiar contention that the basic aspiration of the state should be the promotion of happiness. John Wesley had already offered a patriotic restatement of this ideal and its relationship with liberty in his *Calm address* of 1775:

What civil liberty can you desire which you are not already possessed of? Do you not sit, without restraint, every man under his own vine? Do you not, every one, high or low, enjoy the fruit of your labour? This is real, rational liberty, such as is enjoyed by Englishmen alone, and not by any other people in the habitable world.[100]

A year later the Tory politician Henry Goodricke reiterated the argument in his *Observations on Dr Price's theory and principles of civil liberty and government*. Goodricke argues that the aim of government should always be 'to promote the happiness of the people'.[101] He cites Burlamaqui as his authority for this judgement, and describes him – along with Grotius and Pufendorf – as 'one of the most esteemed writers on government'.[102] Wesley and Goodricke were subsequently echoed by the author of *Republican letters* in his exceptionally forthright attack on the supporters of the colonial cause.[103] He laments the current danger to the greatest benefit we receive from 'our happy form of government', which is that we are able to 'sit with safety under our own vine and fig tree' and 'enjoy unmolested the fruits of our labour and industry' in a state of contentment.[104]

Some months after the appearance of Wesley's *Calm address*, Jeremy Bentham published *A fragment on government*. Although Bentham never explicitly speaks in this text of liberty as absence of restraint, he formulates the associated ideal that the promotion of happiness should be the goal of the state in a manner that exercised a widespread influence. Here again it is possible that his formulation owed more to Blackstone than he is ready to admit. Blackstone had already pronounced in the introduction to his *Commentaries* that 'the foundation of what we call ethics' lies in the precept 'that man should pursue his own true and substantial happiness'.[105] This raises the question of how the state can hope to contribute most effectively to this end. Blackstone had replied that the answer must be to ensure that laws are imposed only if they promote the

[100] Wesley 1775, p. 16.
[101] [Goodricke] 1776, p. 122. Goodricke's name does not appear on the title page, but at p. 60 he acknowledges his authorship. Goodricke was elected to Parliament in 1778, but his career was cut short by his premature death in 1784.
[102] [Goodricke] 1776, pp. 118, 127.
[103] The title page ascribes the tract to 'G. Usher', on whom I have been unable to discover any information.
[104] Usher 1778, p. 2.  [105] Blackstone 2016, pp. 34, 35.

public good, and hence serve some 'purpose of common utility'.[106] The aim must be to bring it about that every subject remains 'entire master of his own conduct, except in those points wherein the public good requires some direction or restraint'.[107] Bentham similarly contends that, in relation to actions in general, we need to recognise that 'the common end of all of them' is happiness, and that 'this tendency in any act is what we style its utility'.[108] The aim of government, in relation to any acts that may be said to be 'among the objects of law', must be to ensure the law's utility, and hence its tendency to promote instead of restricting our happiness.[109] The axiom by which everyone needs to be guided is that 'it is the greatest happiness of the greatest number that is the measure of right and wrong'.[110]

Responding to Price in his *Three letters*, Lind closely follows Blackstone and Bentham's arguments. The supreme duty of government is to make laws in such a way 'as may produce the greatest happiness of the greatest number'.[111] Our aim must therefore be to ensure that the powers of government are distributed in a manner that will 'best ensure the greatest happiness'.[112] Richard Hey speaks in similar terms in the section of his *Observations* on the perfecting of civil society. The point of perfection is said to be reached when every member of the community is 'allowed to pursue his own happiness in a manner consistent with that of the other members', with the result that the greatest happiness is achieved.[113]

These commitments soon began to be widely reiterated by other defenders of the new view of liberty. Goodricke in his *Observations* picks up Bentham's phrase about the duty to promote 'the greatest happiness',[114] while Gray in *Doctor Price's notions of the nature of civil liberty* expresses the same thought more rhetorically, asking to be informed 'what is the object of government but to make the most happy and the fewest wretched'.[115] Paley was later to provide one of his characteristically assured summaries. After declaring that 'it is the will of God that the happiness of human life be promoted',[116] he goes on to affirm that 'civil society conduces to that end'[117] and concludes that laws must therefore 'impose no restraints upon the private will of the subject but what conduce in a greater degree to the public happiness'.[118]

---

[106] Blackstone 2016, p. 86.    [107] Blackstone 2016, p. 86.
[108] Bentham 1988, pp. 25–6.    [109] Bentham 1988, pp. 26, 27–8.
[110] Bentham 1988, p. 3.    [111] [Lind] 1776, p. 88.
[112] [Lind] 1776, p. 73. Here Lind refers us to Bentham's *Fragment on government*.
[113] Hey 1776, p. 56.    [114] [Goodricke] 1776, pp. 106, 122.    [115] Gray 1777, p. 115.
[116] Paley 1785, p. 423.    [117] Paley 1785, p. 423.    [118] Paley 1785, p. 442.

With the articulation of this utilitarian ideal, the defenders of the new view of liberty arrive at the heart of their argument. If we are to attain the peace on which our happiness depends, it is essential that we should stop thinking in terms of inalienable natural rights. Price's cardinal error is not to see that this is imperative. As Pufendorf and his followers have already shown, the weaknesses of human nature are such that, if we were to attempt to live together in our natural state, in which everyone would have an equal liberty to act as they wished, the outcome would be a state of perpetual conflict and war. We have no option but to relinquish our natural liberty and submit ourselves to a sovereign power with an unchallengeable capacity to compel obedience if we are to have any prospect of achieving a happy life.

As the American colonies moved towards open war, this argument began to be widely invoked by outraged supporters of the British government. John Gray in his tract of 1774 on *The right of the British legislature to tax the American colonies* had already quoted a maxim from Pufendorf that he claimed was accepted by every civil lawyer. This lays down that 'whoever becomes a citizen resigns up his natural liberty and subjects himself to a governing power' which thereby gains complete power of life and death over him.[119] The rival theory of inalienable natural rights, so often associated with the almost sacred name of John Locke, is dismissed out of hand. 'How weak and inconclusive must the propositions of Mr Locke now appear!'[120] Ambrose Serle, an undersecretary for the colonies, supplemented the argument in his tract of 1775 on *Americans against liberty* with a much more religious-minded account of man's first disobedience as the underlying reason for the impossibility of retaining any natural rights.[121] There is so much evil in human nature that man is 'in a state of war with himself and with all about him'.[122] To maintain the 'absolute kind of freedom' characteristic of our natural condition would simply be to grant everyone 'the liberty of following the depravities of his nature'.[123] We have no alternative but to submit our wills to a government in which 'every individual member is a bondsman' if we are to have any prospect of escaping 'the wild excursions of private will'.[124]

Samuel Johnson, whose *Taxation no tyranny* also appeared in 1775, pays no attention to such theological niceties.[125] He simply offers

---

[119] [Gray] 1774, p. 5.    [120] [Gray] 1774, p. 5.
[121] [Serle] 1775. Attribution from BL catalogue.    [122] [Serle] 1775, p. 7.
[123] [Serle] 1775, p. 13.    [124] [Serle] 1775, pp. 6, 17, 19.
[125] Johnson's tract appeared anonymously, but he was immediately identified as its author. See *The pamphlet entitled taxation no tyranny* 1775, p. 1.

a dogmatically confident statement of the need to recognise that absolute submission to government is part of the order of nature:

> There must in every society be some power or other from which there is no appeal, which admits no restrictions, which pervades the whole mass of the community, regulates and adjusts all subordination, enacts laws or repeals them, erects or annuls judicatures, extends or contracts privileges, exempt itself from question or control, and bounded only by physical necessity.[126]

As Johnson acknowledges, the colonists will reply that 'liberty is the birthright of man, and where obedience is compelled, there is no liberty'.[127] But to this objection, he retorts, the answer is simple: 'Government is necessary to man, and where obedience is not compelled, there is no government.'[128]

Soon afterwards Jeremy Bentham took up a similar stance in his discussion of sovereignty and obedience in *A fragment on government.* Bentham has little to say about the idea of a state of nature, although he concedes that, if the phrase means anything, it must refer to the condition that men 'are in or supposed to be in, before they are under government'.[129] Like Johnson, he prefers to emphasise that government is an unavoidable necessity for humankind, so that 'governors, of some sort or another, we must have' if we are to fulfil our purposes.[130] Once we concentrate on this indubitable truth, we find that the relationship between states and their subjects can only be one of complete sovereignty and obedience. To speak of 'a supreme legislature' is always to refer to 'a set of men acknowledged to be absolute'.[131] To speak of a subject is to refer to someone who lives 'in a state of submission, or of subjection, with respect to governors' who are 'in a state of authority' over him.[132]

While these were important contributions, it is to the proponents of the new view of liberty, especially in their dispute with Price in 1776, that we need to turn for the fullest and most influential exposition of this neo-Hobbesian vision of sovereignty and obedience. From the outset, these writers agreed that, even if it makes sense to talk about natural rights, it is a fatal error to think of them as inalienable. This is the contention underlying Lind's attack on Price's attempt to derive the powers of the state from God-given rights of nature. Even if we concede that the laws of nature 'have established the right of liberty, still that right cannot be unalienable'. To live as the subject of a state is to live under the rule of law, and 'all laws are coercive; the effect of them is either to restrain or to constrain', and thus to take away liberty. So 'by what magic then is it that

---

[126] [Johnson] 1775, p. 24.    [127] [Johnson] 1775, p. 77.    [128] [Johnson] 1775, p. 77.
[129] Bentham 1988, pp. 38, 42.    [130] Bentham 1988, p. 60.    [131] Bentham 1988, p. 107.
[132] Bentham 1988, p. 42. See also pp. 46, 47.

you contrive to bestow on every member of society an unalienable right to be free from that restraint?'[133] Towards the end of his *Three letters* Lind refers his readers to a tract already published under the title *Cursory remarks on Dr Price's Observations*, in which the same point had already been made. The writer, who identifies himself as a London merchant, concedes that it makes sense to speak about 'the natural equality of all mankind', especially as this is a doctrine for which 'we can plead the authority of Pufendorf'. But he denies that it makes any sense to speak about 'the natural and unalienable rights of every man as a member of society' and rejects this line of thought as 'little to the purpose'.[134]

A similarly dismissive tone was sustained throughout the ensuing debate. The author of *Civil liberty asserted* complains about the vein of sophistry that runs throughout Price's work in consequence of his insistence on the false principle 'that there are certain rights of human nature which are unalienable'.[135] We need to recognise that 'he that is guided by his own will, with a competency of power, is too free for anyone else to be free', so that the state of nature would be a wild and lawless condition without any security or peace.[136] We cannot fail to acknowledge that 'it is essentially necessary to government that individuals should give up all right of being guided by their own will', which is so unruly as to be 'incompatible with civil liberty'.[137] Goodricke in his *Observations* on Price emphatically agrees that our anti-social desires beget 'not only an expediency but a necessity of subjection', and concludes that 'it is a plain and undoubted truth that the end of government is only to restrain an injurious exercise of private liberty'.[138] As John Gray summarises, Pufendorf is right to insist that 'whoever enters into civil society throws his natural liberty overboard'.[139] Human nature is such that it is only by a renunciation of natural liberty that civil liberty can be possessed.[140] As a further reminder, Gray places on his title page a quotation from Pufendorf to the effect that sovereigns must always be promptly obeyed.

**********

We have arrived at the moment when the proponents of the new view of liberty collide head-on with the theory of freedom and the state that had served as a ruling ideology in Britain and the colonies for much of the eighteenth century. According to the established view, to be subject to any unlimited form of power is what it means to be enslaved; what it means to be free is to be your own master, not subject to the arbitrary and

---

[133] [Lind] 1776, p. 24.    [134] *Cursory remarks* 1776, p. 2.
[135] *Civil liberty asserted* 1776, p. 38.    [136] *Civil liberty asserted* 1776, pp. 8, 10–11, 15, 30.
[137] *Civil liberty asserted* 1776, pp. 30, 32, 38.    [138] [Goodricke] 1776, pp. 85, 87.
[139] Gray 1777, p. 6.    [140] Gray 1777, p. 6.

absolute power of anyone else. While this is precisely the claim that the defenders of the new view wish to discredit, they are willing to make two concessions to it. They accept that the act of submitting yourself to unlimited sovereignty has the effect of rendering your liberty less than fully secure. This is because, as Lind admits, 'there are no bounds which can be set to the supreme power'.[141] They also accept that, in the act of subjecting yourself, you drastically limit your liberty. You are now subject to law, which not only imposes a duty of obedience but enforces it with threats of punishment. As Bentham observes in *A fragment on government*, from the perspective of liberty, law is always a mischief.[142] Hey also speaks about 'the mischief of restraints', which is why he concludes that a good and wise legislature should always 'avoid, as much as possible, multiplying restraints upon the subject'.[143]

Having allowed these concessions, the advocates of the new view of liberty proceed to offer a spirited rebuttal of the claim that their view of sovereignty leads to the enslavement of subjects. They first of all point out that, although law may be the enemy of liberty, it does not normally impinge extensively on our daily lives. Gray reminds us of this fortunate truth in his characteristically sarcastic style:

Do we in this island rest uneasily in our beds because we know that Parliament has a right to govern us in all cases whatsoever? Do we expect to be enjoined at what hour we shall rise in the morning, how many glasses of wine we may drink after dinner, how many cabbages we may plant in our garden, how often we shall wash our hands?[144]

The truth is that the law places very few restraints on our ordinary pursuits. But to be free from such restraints is precisely what it means to be in full possession of our liberty. Take the case, Lind suggests, of a legal restraint that has never been imposed. Then 'all the subjects would in this instance have been free'. Or suppose that an existing legal restraint is taken off. Then 'they would again become free'.[145] As soon as you recognise that the extent of your liberty depends on the silence of the law, you will come to appreciate that, as Hey puts it, you are as free as you can wish or desire.[146]

The other rebuttal offered by these writers is an almost paradoxical one. When we submit to sovereign power, the effect is not to enslave us but to enlarge and guarantee our liberty. Here again we catch an echo of Blackstone, who had already offered it as a maxim that 'laws, when prudently framed, are by no means subversive but rather introductive of

---

[141] [Lind] 1776, p. 71.    [142] Bentham 1988, pp. 26–7, 55–6.
[143] Hey 1776, pp. 54, 56.    [144] Gray 1777, p. 36.    [145] [Lind] 1776, p. 68.
[146] Hey 1776, p. 56.

liberty'.[147] Lind agrees that laws do not operate merely to restrain us, for 'the law which secures my property is a restraint upon you', just as 'the law which secures your property is a restraint upon me'.[148] Soon afterwards the author of *Civil liberty asserted* offered a fuller resolution of the paradox. When the laws 'operate indiscriminately on all orders and degrees of men', the effect is that 'the meanest individual is protected from the insults and oppressions of the great', and this is nothing less than the perfection of human liberty.[149]

These writers are adamant, however, that the extent of our liberty remains wholly subject to the will of the sovereign power under which we are bound to live, so that our liberty (as Hobbes had phrased it) will sometimes be more, and at other times less, 'according as they that have the sovereignty shall think most convenient'.[150] This contention in turn gives rise to a distinctive and deliberately circumscribed answer to the question of what it might mean to speak of having the right to enjoy one's liberty. As we have seen, two contrasting answers had dominated the constitutional debates of eighteenth-century England. One had come to be associated in particular with John Locke, and was unequivocally endorsed by Richard Price. Both speak of personal liberty, together with life and property, as natural rights that are granted to us by God as the author of nature, and are thus incapable of being alienated. These rights have the character of universal moral demands, and consequently have the status of entitlements. The other and very different answer had underpinned the official justification of the Revolution Settlement in 1689. Here the right to personal liberty – together with the right to life and property – are said to have been recognised over such a long period of time, and to be so fundamental to the fulfilment of the basic purposes of society, that they have come to be placed beyond debate. These rights have a local rather than a universal character, but they now enjoy the status – as the Bill of Rights puts it – of ancient and indubitable rights and liberties that even the law cannot be allowed to change or take away.[151]

By contrast with both these accounts, the defenders of the new view of liberty argue that our right to exercise our personal freedom is enjoyed wholly at the discretion of the sovereign power under which we live. How is it, Lind asks, 'that a man acquires a right to do or to forbear any act?' He does so 'by the declaration of the legislator that he may do or forbear it, joined to a promise of the legislator, express or implied, that he will restrain every other person from constraining him to forbear the one or

---

[147] Blackstone 2016, p. 86.     [148] [Lind] 1776, p. 24.
[149] *Civil liberty asserted* 1776, pp. 8, 17.     [150] Hobbes 2012, vol. 2, ch. 21, p. 340.
[151] Williams 1960, p. 30.

to do the other'.[152] Lind concludes that the concept of a right 'is a mere legal term'; our rights amount to nothing more than privileges allowed to us by the law, so that 'where no law is, there is no right'.[153]

This view was soon echoed by many other writers on the relationship between law and liberty. One notable instance can be found in the strikingly devout tract of 1776 entitled *Serious and impartial observations on the blessings of liberty and peace*. The writer argues that 'Christians are to consider true liberty, not as consisting in a right to say and do what they please, but in the peaceable enjoyment of all those privileges or rights given by the laws'. Such subjects will be 'desirous to be obedient, and yet free', and will 'look upon human laws, when judiciously framed and impartially executed, as the proper foundation of civil liberty'.[154] The same view was reiterated in *A constitutional defence of government* in 1782, in which the writer – who dedicates his work to the queen – insists that when we speak of having a right to act as we choose, this is merely a way of saying that the act in question is legally permitted. As he concludes, every citizen is subject to a constituted authority 'by which all his rights are established and all the enjoyments of civil liberty are secured'.[155]

### Liberty as Independence: The Unacceptable Implications

As well as pointing out Price's alleged confusions, the proponents of the new view of liberty denounce what they take to be the unacceptable implications of accepting that civil liberty consists in being independent rather than simply unrestrained. One line of argument they powerfully develop is that this mistaken view of liberty commits the colonists and their supporters to a no less mistaken view about the institution of slavery. Price had incautiously affirmed that 'to be free is to be guided by one's own will; and to be guided by the will of another is the characteristic of servitude', thereby implying that anyone living in dependence on someone else's will must be accounted a slave.[156] One problem with this definition was immediately noted by Adam Ferguson, whose *Remarks on a pamphlet lately published by Dr Price* was one of the earliest and most perceptive critiques of Price's argument.[157] As Ferguson observes, 'it does not appear that upon this idea of liberty any civil community can be formed without introducing slavery', for 'even where the collective

---

[152] [Lind] 1776, p. 21.    [153] [Lind] 1776, pp. 21–2 and n.
[154] *Serious and impartial observations* 1776, p. 64.
[155] *A constitutional defence of government* 1782, p. 5.    [156] Price 1991, p. 26.
[157] See [Ferguson] 1776, who speculates (pp. 26, 33) on whether the colonists will declare independence, thereby indicating a date of publication in the first half of 1776. On Ferguson as a defender of the imperial cause see Zeng 2022.

body are sovereigns they are seldom unanimous, and the minority must submit to a power that stands opposed to their own will'.[158] Wesley in his *Observations on liberty* more bluntly objects that, if we accept Price's definition, 'then there is no free nation in Europe'. We are left saying that 'all in every nation are slaves except the supreme powers', so that in the case of France we would have to say that everyone is a slave except the king.[159] As Goodricke sardonically concludes, Price's equation of dependence with slavery 'will be found to introduce slavery almost everywhere, and to make it absolutely necessary to the happiness of mankind'.[160]

An associated but much graver criticism was that Price's equation between dependence and enslavement fails to acknowledge the most distinctive and shocking feature of slavery. When we describe someone as a slave, we are saying that their life, and not merely their liberty, is wholly subject to the will of someone else. The colonists and their admirers are refusing to recognise the full repulsiveness of slavery, which is that slaves are the property of others, and as mere chattels are capable of being disposed of at will.

Blackstone had already emphasised in Book I of his *Commentaries* in 1765 that the distinctive mark of enslavement is that 'life and liberty' are both 'held to be in the master's disposal', so that 'an absolute and unlimited power is given to the master over the life and fortune of the slave'.[161] Granville Sharp may have had Blackstone in mind when he published his pioneering warning in 1769 against the introduction of chattel slavery into England.[162] The specific 'injustice and dangerous tendency' that Sharp singles out is that of 'admitting the least claim of private property in the persons of men'.[163] As he lays down at the outset of his argument, to enquire into the legality of slavery is equivalent to asking 'how far one man may lawfully be considered as the property of another'.[164]

Sharp was one of those who prompted and paid for the defence of the slave James Somerset in a test case adjudicated by Lord Mansfield in 1772. Somerset had been purchased in Boston by an English customs officer, who brought him to London in 1769. Somerset escaped, but was recaptured and imprisoned on a ship ready to carry him back to be sold in

---

[158] [Ferguson] 1776, p. 3. For Ferguson on popular participation see Skjönsberg 2019; for Ferguson on republicanism see Geuna 2002 and Oz-Salzberger 2002, pp. 198–211. See also Kalyvas and Katznelson 2008, pp. 51–87.

[159] Wesley 1776, p. 5.      [160] [Goodricke] 1776, p. 81.

[161] Blackstone 2016, pp. 272, 273.

[162] On Sharp see Olusoga 2021, pp. 121–4. On the abolitionist movement see Scanlan 2020, pp. 137–88.

[163] Sharp 1769, title page.      [164] Sharp 1769, p. 11.

Jamaica.[165] A writ of habeus corpus was successfully sought, and the case was tried before Mansfield in the Court of King's Bench.[166] The lawyer who appeared most prominently for the defence was Francis Hargrave, then a young member of Lincoln's Inn, who subsequently published his speech as *An argument in the case of James Somerset*.[167] Hargrave's general aim, as the full title of his speech announced, was 'to demonstrate the present unlawfulness of domestic slavery in England',[168] and he opens his case by expressing strong agreement with the thrust of Sharp's argument. Slavery not only involves 'an obligation of perpetual service' in which the life and limb of the slave can both be 'exposed to the arbitrary will of the master'. We also need to recognise that slavery is an institution which 'allows the master to alienate the person of the slave in the same manner as other property'.[169] Hargrave then proceeds to establish that no such institution is recognised in English statute or common law, and in his judgment Mansfield felt obliged to rule that Somerset must be freed and discharged.[170]

Several contributors to the attack on Price and the colonists in 1776 adopted a similar stance. The author of *Serious and impartial observations* speaks of slavery with an intensity of religious feeling rarely encountered in the debate. The *Observations* begins by noting that 'there is indeed still a remarkable violation of human liberty in several Christian states, which I cannot properly pass by unnoticed. I mean the slave trade carried on in the western world.'[171] The writer speaks of the grief that everyone should feel at the fact that 'several who call themselves Christians, and also, like the Romans, pretend to be great patrons of liberty, should show themselves to be the most cruel tyrants over great numbers of their fellow creatures'. The specific cruelty he singles out is that of 'buying and selling them as the ordinary cattle that till the ground'.[172]

Of all the critics of Price and the colonists in 1776, the one who devoted the fullest attention to the problem of slavery was John Wesley. He first raised the issue in his *Thoughts upon slavery* of 1774, in which he shows several signs of drawing on the speech that Hargrave had published two years before. Wesley begins by laying down three criteria that need to be met if we are to speak properly of slavery and servitude. The first is that 'slavery imports an obligation of perpetual service' which is at the same time coercive, since it is one that 'only the master can dissolve'.[173] Next,

---

[165] Olusoga 2021, p. 128.    [166] Olusoga 2021, pp. 128–9.
[167] Olusoga 2021, pp. 129, 131–2.    [168] Hargrave 1772, title page.
[169] Hargrave 1772, p. 15.
[170] Hargrave 1772, pp. 49–50. On Mansfield's judgment see Olusoga 2021, pp. 136–8.
[171] *Serious and impartial observations* 1776, p. 10.
[172] *Serious and impartial observations* 1776, pp. 10–11.    [173] Wesley 1774, p. 3.

slavery places the victim entirely at the mercy of the master. The master generally has 'an arbitrary power of any correction not affecting life or limb', and 'sometimes even these are exposed to his will, or protected only by a fine or some slight punishment too inconsiderable to restrain a master of an harsh temper'.[174] Finally, it is crucial that to be a slave is also to be the property of someone else, so that slavery 'allows the master to alienate the slave, in the same manner as his cows and horses', a power of disposal that 'descends in its full extent from parent to child even to the latest generation'.[175]

When he published *Some observations on liberty* two years later, Wesley restated his argument in much more polemical terms. He quotes Price as saying that 'I have no other notion of slavery but being bound by a law to which I do not consent'.[176] Wesley allows himself a note of derisive impatience in response. 'If you have not, look at that man chained to the oar. He is a slave. He cannot, at all, dispose of his own person.'[177] Wesley also quotes Price as saying that 'if the Parliament taxes you without your consent you are a slave'.[178] Here Wesley expresses even greater impatience. He reminds Price that slavery 'is a state wherein neither a man's goods, nor liberty, nor life, are at his own disposal', and that this is the condition of tens of thousands of people living in the American colonies. But we cannot possibly say that their masters are in the same state. 'Does anyone beat or imprison them at pleasure? Or take away their wives, or children, or lives? Or fell them like cows or horses? This is slavery: and will you face us down, that the Americans are in such slavery as this?'[179] Price's entire discussion of slavery is denounced as a moral disgrace.

Wesley here touches on a topic handled with memorable scorn by many other critics of the colonists and those who supported their revolutionary cause. Price and his admirers, as Lind points out, celebrate the American colonies as a land of liberty, but they neglect to mention that it is also a land in which 'men and cattle are offered to sale in the same advertisement', and in which 'one of their most distinguished champions was hanged in effigy, and would have been hanged in person could they have caught him, for proposing only gradual abolition of slavery'.[180] Speaking two years later of those who profit from the slave trade, the author of *Republican letters* similarly objects that 'our warmest patriots have never condemned this barbarous shocking custom'. Rather, 'they contend eagerly at the same time for the profits of buying human

---

[174] Wesley 1774, p. 3.    [175] Wesley 1774, p. 3.    [176] Wesley 1776, p. 34.
[177] Wesley 1776, p. 34.    [178] Wesley 1776, p. 5.    [179] Wesley 1776, p. 25.
[180] [Lind] 1776, p. 45.

creatures and of selling them again into slavery', thereby continuing to display 'abundant traces of hypocrisy, falsehood and cruelty'.[181]

Yet more disgraceful, these critics frequently add, is the hypocrisy shown by the colonists themselves. As the author of *Serious and impartial observations* reflects, 'no panegyric in praise of liberty can come gracefully from the mouths or pens of those who make no scruple to detain others in slavery'.[182] Writing two years later, the author of *An appeal to reason and justice* developed this indictment in a tract specifically targeting the patriots in the colonies. They 'pretend to be the most zealous champions of freedom; in practice they are the severest of tyrants'. They assert that 'all men are created equal; yet they shamefully make a property of their fellow creatures, whom they purchase for gold, condemn to the most servile and laborious employment, and render completely miserable by inflicting on them the most unjust and severe torments that ingenious cruelty can invent or unrelenting tyranny can practise'.[183] Paying no heed to the fact that it is 'impossible that a rebellion can have liberty for its object which has the proprietors of slaves for its leaders', the colonists 'make no scruple to purchase their fellow creatures for gold, to deprive them of happiness, of liberty, and in some instances even of life itself'.[184]

Of all these critics, none was more contemptuous than the redoubtable Josiah Tucker.[185] Before his appointment as dean of Gloucester in 1758 Tucker had served for twenty years as a curate and rector in Bristol, where his exposure to the realities of the slave trade had turned him into an early and active abolitionist.[186] He viewed the colonists not in the least as champions of liberty but as mere promoters of sedition fatally misled by the writings of John Locke, and he devotes one of his *Four letters* of 1783 to denouncing the evil consequence of Locke's principles.[187] Locke himself, we are assured, ended his political career as an anarchist, and his *Second treatise* consists of nothing more than 'the resolves of the Cromwellian Levellers worked up into a system'.[188] Worse still, Locke began his career as an apologist for tyranny and slavery. He 'first distinguished himself as a political writer by his famous laws of Carolina', in which he carried the defence of slavery so far, and allowed 'such powers to masters to put their slaves to death', that 'a completer system of baronage and vassalage never yet appeared in the world'.[189] This is the system that the colonists

[181] Usher 1778, pp. 85–6.    [182] *Serious and impartial observations* 1776, p. 10.
[183] *An appeal to reason and justice* 1778, p. 76.
[184] *An appeal to reason and justice* 1778, p. 79.
[185] On Tucker see Shelton 1968; Pocock 1985, pp. 157–91; Miller 1994, pp. 405–9.
[186] See *ODNB*, vol. 55, pp. 497–8.
[187] Tucker 1783, p. 89. For Tucker on Locke see Sakkas 2016, pp. 213–33.
[188] Tucker 1783, p. 96.    [189] Tucker 1783, pp. 92–3.

continue to uphold, and their leaders are in turn denounced by Tucker for their shocking hypocrisy in upholding Locke's theory of natural liberty while at the same time accepting his defence of chattel slavery.

Samuel Johnson had already drawn attention in his *Taxation no tyranny* of 1775 to the irony that the loudest yelps for liberty come from people who own slaves themselves.[190] Tucker in his *Treatise concerning civil government* of 1781 goes on to single out some especially embarrassing examples. The leading hypocrites are two of 'the greatest American champions for the unalienable right of mankind, one the generalissimo of the republican army, the other lately the President of the Congress'.[191] The first reference is to George Washington, who 'has several slaves now on his plantations'. The other is to Henry Laurens, who 'got his fortune by acting as a kind of broker in the slave trade, buying and selling his fellow creatures on commission'.[192] Both have demonstrated 'by their own example that they have no objection against slavery provided they shall be free themselves and have the power of enslaving others'.[193]

********

Price's critics no less loudly denounce the unacceptable constitutional implications of his attempt to equate liberty with independence and self-government. Price had argued that one implication of the equation was not merely that the American colonists have never been represented in the British Parliament, but that the British people will also continue to lack any fair representation until they manage to institute a system of universal suffrage. Josiah Tucker addresses this claim in the second of his *Four letters* of 1783, but he can hardly manage to take it seriously, and he ends by dismissing it as 'so very unreasonable that the bare mentioning of it is an insult to common sense'.[194] The famously abusive Tory journalist John Shebbeare had much more to say in his essay on 'national society', in which he claimed to have comprehensively refuted Price's argument.[195] Shebbeare's overriding objection to Price's call for universal suffrage is that 'an adequate representation does not consist in the number of the electors but in the sufficiency of the elected'.[196] Once this principle is recognised, we can see that 'the fairness and adequateness of representation, by whomsoever the members are elected, consist in the elected being of intelligence equal to the duty' and 'in being upright in the

---

[190] [Johnson] 1775, p. 89.      [191] Tucker 1781, p. 168.
[192] Tucker 1781, p. 168. For attempts by the American colonists to deploy their understanding of liberty to legitimise chattel slavery see Koekkoek 2022, pp. 147–51.
[193] Tucker 1781, p. 168.      [194] Tucker 1783, p. 55.
[195] Shebbeare 1776, title page. On Shebbeare see Avery 1978; Miller 1994, pp. 388–90; *ODNB*, vol. 50, pp. 143–6.
[196] Shebbeare 1776, p. 105.

discharge of it'.[197] The disastrous and unworkable suggestion that adequate representation is exclusively a matter of numbers fails to recognise that many will 'vote from their faith in other men's opinions' rather than from any understanding of the issues involved.[198]

The principal objection that most of Price's critics raised against his view of political representation was a more familiar one. They relied on the well-worn claim that virtual representation not only provides an adequate system, but is also the only one that is practicable. Here they generally revert to the claims that Thomas Whately had made at the time of the Stamp Act crisis in 1765. The anonymous author of *Cursory remarks*, one of the earliest attacks on Price, reiterates that we have no choice but to accept that 'a real consent, by a real representation, never was obtained in any kingdom under the sun', and that we need to content ourselves with virtual representation, which he takes to be 'the true genius of the English government'.[199] We need to recognise that 'when any member is chosen into the House of Commons, he is not to regard only the interests of a paltry borough, or even of a whole country, but is to look upon himself as the guardian of all Englishmen, of their lives, liberties and properties', whether these are in England or 'in East or West Indies, Africa and Europe'.[200]

Lind refers to this tract in his *Three letters* and goes on to develop the argument. He urges Price to take the word 'represent' in an extensive sense, acknowledging that what it basically means is to speak and act for others.[201] Once this is recognised, it becomes easy to see that it is possible for a single member of Parliament to represent an entire country and watch over its interests as a whole. This is the sense in which 'the House of Commons represents not barely the electors, but all the inhabitants of Great Britain'. So 'why should not the same House of Commons, in the same sense, represent the British subjects residing in America?'[202] By the time Shebbeare published his denunciation of Price a few months later he felt able to treat this argument as beyond dispute. While each member of Parliament is locally elected, they all become 'the representatives of every individual in the whole community'.[203] As a result, 'the town which sends no members, the meanest man who has no vote, have equally a right to be governed by just laws', and all of them equally enjoy that right. This alone,

---

[197] Shebbeare 1776, pp. 76–7.     [198] Shebbeare 1776, p. 92.
[199] *Cursory remarks* 1776, p. 11.     [200] *Cursory remarks* 1776, p. 12.
[201] [Lind] 1776, p. 120.
[202] [Lind] 1776, p. 121. For the same argument see *Experience preferable to theory* 1776, p. 20; *The duty of the king and subject* 1776, p. 9; *Civil liberty asserted* 1776, p. 75.
[203] Shebbeare 1776, p. 77.

Shebbeare concludes, is what it means to be fairly and adequately represented.[204]

Among the constitutional implications of Price's view of liberty, the most pernicious was held to be his apparent suggestion that, because there can be no liberty without self-government, there can be no prospect of upholding civil liberty except under some form of republican or democratic rule. Here his critics generally responded by objecting that this is to assign far too much significance to different forms of government. As the author of *The duty of the king and subject* impatiently put it, civil liberty is always the same 'whether in Paris, Madrid or London'.[205] The author of *Experience preferable to theory* sought to explain why this is so. We need to recognise that 'in all forms of government, so long as the powers exist, the degree of power is the same'. It follows that 'the degree of restraint depends upon the laws, not the form of government', so that 'it is absurd to say I am more free in a state where laws are established which are in a greater degree restrictive, because I consented to the appointment of the persons who made them, than I am where there are laws less restrictive, although I had no voice in such appointment'.[206] With his usual assurance, Paley later added what proved to be an influential summary. He first recalls that the liberty we enjoy as subjects always bears 'a reversed proportion to the number and severity of the restrictions' imposed on us.[207] From this it follows 'that every nation possesses some, no nation perfect liberty', and that 'this liberty may be enjoyed under every form of government'.[208] He ends with an ironic flourish. 'Were it probable that the welfare and accommodation of the people would be as studiously and as providently consulted in the edicts of a despotic prince, as by the resolutions of a popular assembly, then would an absolute form of government be no less free than the purest democracy.'[209]

While these writers reject the claim that it is possible to live as a free person only in a self-governing state, they remain interested in asking whether there is any particular form of constitution under which we may be said to have the best chance of preserving our liberties. Here they draw on the stridently patriotic answer that Blackstone had already given in the introduction to his *Commentaries*. Speaking of how 'the constitutional

---

[204] Shebbeare 1776, p. 77. For the same argument see *An Appeal to reason and justice* 1778, pp. 101–2; Murdin 1779, pp. 12–13.

[205] *The duty of the king and subject* 1776, p. 7.

[206] *Experience preferable to theory* 1776, pp. 10, 18–19. For the same argument see Gray 1777, p. 12.

[207] Paley 1785, p. 443.    [208] Paley 1785, p. 443.    [209] Paley 1785, p. 445.

government of this island is so admirably tempered and compounded', Blackstone had praised the mixed constitution and the separation of powers in unqualified terms. 'The executive power of the laws is lodged in a single person', so that we enjoy 'all the advantages of strength and dispatch that are to be found in the most absolute monarchy'. At the same time 'the legislature of the kingdom is entrusted to three distinct powers', so that 'there can no inconvenience be attempted by either of the three branches, but will be withstood by one of the other two'. The outcome is that sovereignty is 'lodged as beneficially as is possible for society', since 'in no other shape could we be so certain of finding the three great qualities of government so well and so happily united'. It is due to our supremely happy constitution, in short, that we are enabled to achieve our own happiness.[210]

Some of the most patriotic champions of the new view of liberty were content to reiterate that 'our constitution is the wonder and praise of every stranger',[211] and that 'our happy form of government distinguishes us from the rest of Europe and bestows on us a pre-eminence that has always been assumed by a free people'.[212] There were others, however, who followed Blackstone in seeking to explain the mechanics of the mixed constitution and its unique advantages. Ferguson maintains that the best way to uphold our liberty will always be to place the right to legislate 'in the hands of persons interested in the justice of the laws which they make' and at the same time to give 'all the different orders of the state a power to reject or amend every law that is likely to be grievous on themselves'.[213] Gray speaks yet more fulsomely of how 'the present happy constitution of liberty' enables the people to 'become the judges when it is proper to call forth the strength of the state', so that every act of the government 'in a manner appeals to the majority of the subjects for their approbation and receives its stamp of authority from their acquiescence'.[214] Like Blackstone, he has no hesitation in concluding that these arrangements make the British constitution 'the nearest approaching to perfection of any on the face of the globe'.[215]

It was unusual, however, for the defenders of the new view of liberty to express themselves in such self-congratulatory terms. Rather, they tend to sound a note of warning about such entrenched complacencies. Civil liberty, they once again remind us, takes the form of absence of restraint. But governments largely function by imposing the force of law, and every such imposition involves some form of restraint. We need to acknowledge

---

[210] Blackstone 2016, p. 41.     [211] *Remarks on Dr Price's Observations* 1776, p. 72.
[212] Usher 1778, p. 2.     [213] [Ferguson] 1776, p. 13.     [214] Gray 1777, pp. 22–3, 27.
[215] Gray 1777, p. 20.

that, even under the best constitution, the law will always be the prima facie enemy of liberty. As Bentham observes at the end of *A fragment on government*, we are faced with a task of no less intricacy 'than that of adjusting the claims of those two jealous antagonists, liberty and government', and we need to recognise that 'a more invidious ground is scarcely to be found anywhere within the field of politics'.[216] Rather than celebrating the existing body of English law in the manner of Blackstone and his admirers, we ought to be asking ourselves how any laws can possibly be justified.

It was at this juncture that Bentham exercised his most immediate influence on other defenders of the new view of liberty. As we have seen, he affirms in the preface to *A fragment on government* that 'the common end' of all actions is happiness, and that the tendency of any act to promote this end 'is what we style its utility', just as we style any divergence from that end its mischievousness.[217] On this basis Bentham argues that, in the case of existing laws, 'to point out to a man the utility of them or the mischievousness, is the only way to make him see clearly that property of them which every man is in search of; the only way, in short, to give him satisfaction'.[218] He concludes that 'the principle of utility is all-sufficient',[219] furnishing us as it does 'with that reason, which alone depends not upon any higher reason, but which is itself the sole and all-sufficient reason for every point of practice whatsoever'.[220]

Bentham was not the first to speak in these terms.[221] But he was exceptionally persuasive, and this view about how to justify or reject the necessity of any specific law was immediately taken up. The author of *The duty of the king and subject* argues that the fundamental obligation of all members of Parliament is to ask themselves 'what is of utility for the nation'.[222] Richard Hey in his *Observations* similarly insists that every member of society must 'pursue his own happiness in a manner consistent with that of the other members', thereby ensuring that no one is 'more free than the public good will allow'.[223] We must always ensure, in other words, that we 'argue on the ground of utility'.[224] The same appeal was echoed a year later by the author of *A letter to Dr Price*, who likewise concluded that the only rightful foundations for government are provided by considerations of public utility, and further revealed his intellectual allegiances by adding that the only work he has seen on this issue which lacks any fear 'of expressing sentiments that are not supported by prior

[216] Bentham 1988, p. 93.    [217] Bentham 1988, pp. 25–6.    [218] Bentham 1988, p. 26.
[219] Bentham 1988, p. 58, marginal gloss.    [220] Bentham 1988, pp. 58–9; cf also. p. 96.
[221] On pre-Benthamite utilitarians see Connolly 2021, pp. 393–8.
[222] *The duty of the king and subject* 1776, p. 9.    [223] Hey 1776, p. 56.
[224] Hey 1776, p. 49.

authority' is *A fragment on government*.[225] As so often, William Paley provided a resounding summary. We need to remember that civil liberty is the condition of 'not being restrained by any law, but what conduces in a greater degree to the public welfare'.[226] The test for any proposed act of legislation must therefore be how far it 'conduces to public utility'; that is, how far it 'contributes to the establishment of good laws' or 'secures to the people the just administration of these laws'.[227]

The general moral is said to be that, although the British constitution may be admirable, we need to stand continually ready to reform it in the name of more effectively fostering the greatest happiness of the greatest number. Bentham's foremost complaint against Blackstone is that he 'seems so hostile to reformation, and to that liberty which is reformation's harbinger'.[228] Blackstone stands accused of pronouncing 'with equal peremptoriness and complacency, that everything, yes, everything is as it should be', and absurdly concluding 'that the system of our jurisprudence is, in the whole and every part of it, the very quintessence of perfection'.[229] Bentham wishes instead to encourage 'free censure of established institutions' in line with 'the voice of reason and public utility'.[230] The project he wants everyone to contemplate is that of being open to any 'liberal plan of political discussion' and willing to encourage the promotion 'of true science and of liberal improvement'.[231] It was not long before this plea to look for a liberal pathway between conservative complacency and revolutionary radicalism began to be widely heard.

---

[225] *A letter to Dr Price* 1777, p. 14.    [226] Paley 1785, p. 441.    [227] Paley 1785, p. 487.
[228] Bentham 1988, p. 16; cf. also pp. 4, 20n., 29.    [229] Bentham 1988, p. 18.
[230] Bentham 1988, pp. 12, 13.    [231] Bentham 1988, p. 7 and p. 11n.

*Part V*

# The Rival Views in Contestation

## The Critics Criticised

The climacteric year of 1776 witnessed an immediate counter-attack against those who were denouncing the cause of colonial freedom and independence.[1] As we saw in Chapter 8, one of the arguments against the colonists and their supporters had taken the form of a renewed invocation of the high Tory doctrine that government is divinely ordained and can never be lawfully resisted. This was not, however, a view that Price and those sympathetic to his commitments felt any need to take seriously. Price himself noted that theories of divine right appeared to be reviving again, but simply dismissed them as pernicious and absurd.[2] Writing at the same time, the anonymous author of a fervently Whiggish tract on the origin of civil government expressed himself even more outspokenly. He begins by assuring his readers that he will waste no time in exposing 'the infamy of every prostituted priest' who is still attempting 'to support the tottering fabric of ecclesiastical domination' when it is obvious that the doctrines of divine right and passive obedience 'will shortly sink unnoticed into merited contempt'.[3]

Price and his allies preferred to devote their polemical energies to attacking those who were arguing that civil liberty amounts to nothing more than absence of restraint. Price himself in his *Additional observations* of 1777 was one of the earliest and most effective contributors to the debate.[4] He begins by putting forward an unyielding restatement of what he takes everyone to mean 'when they say of themselves or others that they are free'. What we mean is that we are 'masters of our own resolutions and conduct', so that we may be said to have a power of self-government.[5] He later underlines this definition in his *Two tracts* of 1778, in which he speaks with uncharacteristic bitterness of a sermon that William Markham, the Archbishop of York, had preached in the previous year

---

[1] On London supporters of the revolutionaries see Sainsbury 1987.
[2] Price 1991, pp. 86, 88.    [3] *A letter to the Rev. Dr Cooper* 1777, pp. 1, 3.
[4] Price 1991, pp. 76–100.    [5] Price 1991, p. 76.

on the glorious nature of liberty.[6] Markham had defined civil liberty as 'a freedom from all restraints except such as established law imposes for the good of the community'.[7] At the same time, he had sought to associate the most dangerous misunderstandings of liberty with the Dissenters, and had included some threatening remarks about the possibility of laying renewed restraints upon them if their principles proved 'dangerous to our civil interests'.[8] Price sarcastically notes that the good archbishop 'has given a definition of liberty which might as well have been given of slavery', since he thinks of liberty as compatible with living in subjection to someone else's arbitrary will and power.[9] As Price had by this time made abundantly clear, his own view is that to be subject to arbitrary power is precisely what it means to have forfeited your liberty.

Although Price's restatement of this view was quickly and widely echoed, this is not to say that everyone who wrote at this juncture about liberty as independence was reacting in a polemical vein. Some continued to deploy this familiar analysis without making any reference to the attacks that had lately been mounted on it. One particularly notable example is that of Adam Smith in *The wealth of nations*. When Smith speaks about freedom of trade he is generally referring to the fact that, under the mercantile system, trade is restricted by prohibitions and other restraints.[10] But in discussing civil liberty he speaks in very different terms. When he turns in Book III to consider the rise and progress of towns and cities after the fall of the Roman Empire, he examines in detail the extent of the liberty that many of their inhabitants came to enjoy. Here he contrasts their increasing freedom with the condition of being servile and equates it with living in independence. A majority of towns 'arrived at liberty and independency much earlier than the occupiers of land in the country'.[11] Their inhabitants gained the right to trade freely, and later the privilege of being able to dispose of their property at will. Smith comments that 'the principal attributes of villeinage and slavery being thus taken away from them', they came to be known as free burghers and 'became really free in our present sense of the word freedom'.[12] He takes it for granted that the present sense of the word refers to the condition of being a free person by contrast with a slave, and hence to those capable of living and acting with independence. This is how he speaks in the first edition of *The wealth of nations*, which was published in March 1776, but he saw no reason to make any subsequent changes to his account, even when he reissued his text with extensive revisions in 1784.[13]

---

[6] Markham 1777, p. 18.     [7] Markham 1777, p. 19.     [8] Markham 1777, p. 17.
[9] Price 1991, p. 17.     [10] Smith 1976, IV. ii and IV. iii, pp. 457, 472.
[11] Smith 1976, III. iii, p. 399.     [12] Smith 1976, III. iii, p. 400.
[13] See Smith 1976, vol. I, pp. 61–3. For Smith on liberty and free government see Elazar 2022b, pp. 692–4. Elazar persuasively questions the claim in Harpham 2000, p. 236 that

It was very unusual, however, for writers on freedom and government during these years to ignore the debate that had been sparked in the opening months of 1776. Price's enemies soon found themselves confronted with emphatic reaffirmations of the familiar view of liberty as independence. One of the earliest and most outspoken appeared in the anonymous tract of 1777 on the origin of civil government in which the author introduces himself as an advocate for the principles of Whiggism, and repeatedly insists that the basic contrast to be drawn when talking about civil government is between liberty and arbitrary power, liberty and dependence, liberty and bondage.[14] This view of what it means to live in freedom is said to have been 'uniformly maintained by the wisest and best men', so that it cannot be said of 'the great Dr Price and other modern writers of Whig principles' that they have introduced any novel refinements into their accounts of civil liberty. Rather, 'they have vindicated with a strength of reasoning sufficient to strike conviction into any but the most prejudiced minds the principles which were inculcated and practised by Locke, Russell, Sidney and Hampden and other illustrious patriots'. These are the principles that have been so ably restated in Dr Price's *Observations on civil liberty*, and they now need more than ever to be upheld.[15]

As the reaffirmations of this view of liberty gathered pace, one remarkable feature of the discussion began to emerge. A considerable number of those who wrote in agreement with Price's views were clergymen of the Church of England. Some were obscure figures, such as Cornelius Murdin, a vicar in Hampshire, who published *Three sermons* on liberty in 1779. Murdin contents himself with attempting to show that liberty is 'a most valuable blessing' by way of asking what it means to be deprived of it. He answers that it means 'to be at the will or caprice of any superior power', so that 'the highest species of tyranny' is 'to live at the mercy of our fellow creatures'.[16] Some eminent Anglicans were no less willing to speak in similar terms. One was Dr Richard Watson, the Regius Professor of Divinity at the University of Cambridge, who published *An essay on civil liberty* in 1776. Watson begins by noting that 'the principles maintained in the following essay have of late become generally unfashionable', but he insists that they are nevertheless 'founded in truth'.[17] The truth about human liberty is that we are all naturally independent agents. No one can

Smith 'lies outside and challenges the republican or neo-Roman tradition', showing that Smith supports and applies the ideal of liberty as independence. On Smith and republican liberty see also Winch 2002; Kelly 2011, pp. 159–72; Herzog 2013, pp. 143–6.

[14] *A letter to the Rev. Dr Cooper* 1777, pp. 1, 25–6, 35, 51, 53.

[15] *A letter to the Rev. Dr Cooper* 1777, pp. 29–31, 50–3.   [16] Murdin 1779, pp. 5–6.

[17] Watson 1776, p. v.

be said to suffer from 'any natural dependence or inequality', nor to have 'any right to dominion on the one hand or obligation to subjection on the other'. To fall into such a condition of subjection is what it means to forfeit your liberty.[18]

A yet more prominent Anglican supporter of Price's principles was the Reverend Peter Peckard, who published a sermon on *The nature and extent of civil and religious liberty* in 1783. Peckard was Master of Magdalene College Cambridge, but was at the same time a radical Whig commentator on the political scene.[19] Like Watson, he begins by deploring the current state of debate about freedom and arbitrary power. With a hostile nod in the direction of Pufendorf and his followers, Peckard speaks of the many voluminous treatises published some generations ago with the aim of proving 'that man hath not any natural right to liberty, and that all government is absolute'.[20] Despite the fact that these doctrines were 'solidly confuted and completely answered' by John Locke, we now find that 'arbitrary power is openly commended' again, and that some writers are seeking to persuade us that civil liberty amounts to nothing more than 'absence of coercion'.[21] We are in danger of losing sight of the fact that, under despotic and arbitrary forms of rule, there can never be anything more than an appearance of liberty. It is true that 'the slaves by the gracious good humour of the tyrant may be presented with a temporary and precarious freedom'. But these men are not free, because 'that is not liberty which hath any relation to, or any dependence upon tyranny'. Men are only 'properly speaking free when they enjoy their liberty not from the variable and fluctuating will of governors', but from being their own masters and living in a state of self-government.[22] 'There is an inherent independence belonging to every man, which sets him free from every other' and which 'arises from the rights of nature'.[23] It is an indispensable part of this natural liberty 'that every man should be master of his own judgment and determination' in religious as well as civil affairs.[24] Liberty essentially consists in the enjoyment of this condition of independence.

**\*\*\*\*\*\*\*\*\*\***

Having reaffirmed the meaning of liberty to their own satisfaction, Price and his allies next turn to comment on the specific criticisms that were being raised against their view of liberty as independence. Perhaps the most searching accusation against Price had been that his understanding of the concept rests on a confusion between what it means to possess your

---

[18] Watson 1776, p. 8.    [19] See *ODNB*, vol. 43, pp. 374–5.    [20] Peckard 1783, p. 2.
[21] Peckard 1783, p. 3 and n.    [22] Peckard 1783, p. 8.    [23] Peckard 1783, p. 9.
[24] Peckard 1783, p. 18.

liberty and what it means to enjoy security for the liberty you possess. Price himself felt obliged – perhaps with Wesley specifically in mind – to give serious attention to this objection, and he opens his *Additional observations* by answering it.[25] He begins by reiterating that we are free if we are 'masters of our own resolutions and conduct', and are consequently 'able to act or forbear acting as we think best'.[26] He takes it to follow that, if we wish to determine whether an individual or a community is free, all we need to find out is whether there is any will different from their own to which they are subject, and thus whether or not they are capable of self-government.[27] If you are instead subject to the will of someone else, then whatever actions you perform will always be the outcome not merely of your own will, but at the same time of the indulgence or permission of your master.[28] You will never be in a position to act or forbear from acting simply as you think best.

With these considerations Price takes himself to have answered the objection that he is confusing the question of whether someone is currently free to perform some particular action with the question of whether they will be secure from interference if they choose to perform it. He responds with studied moderation. A distinction needs to be drawn at this point, he suggests, 'which appears to me of considerable consequence'.[29] We can lack freedom because we are suffering from oppression and interference, but we can also lack freedom in the absence of any such hindrance or even any threat of it. If anyone is in a position to interfere with impunity, this is sufficient to take away our freedom to act at will. 'Individuals in private life, while held under the power of masters, cannot be denominated free however equitably and kindly they may be treated.' The reason is that 'if there is any human power which is considered as giving it, on which it depends, and which can invade or recall it at pleasure, it changes its nature and becomes a species of slavery'.[30] There is thus no confusion between liberty and security for liberty. Unless you are secure from interference you cannot be said to be in possession of your liberty. Liberty consists not in absence of restraint or interference but rather in the absence of any controlling will, and hence any danger of interference. We can only say that a citizen is a free person when 'the power of commanding his own conduct and the quiet possession of his life, person, property and good name are secured to him'.[31]

The other principal accusation that Price's critics had made was that his definition of freedom rests on a confusion between the idea of civil liberty

---

[25] Here I draw on Skinner 2024.    [26] Price 1991, p. 76.    [27] Price 1991, p. 76.
[28] Price 1991, p. 77.    [29] Price 1991, p. 77.    [30] Price 1991, p. 77.
[31] Price 1991, p. 82.

and the condition of independence that everyone would undoubtedly have enjoyed in the state of nature. As we have seen, they had argued that, if there is to be any prospect of living together in peace, we have no option but to relinquish the rights we would have possessed in our natural state and submit ourselves to sovereign power, resting content with whatever degree of liberty is left to us by the law. This is the objection to which Price and his allies chiefly address themselves, and once again it is Price in his *Additional observations* of 1777 who provides the fullest response.

This is the moment at which the religious premises underlying Price's political commitments surface most visibly, especially by contrast with the self-consciously secular approach favoured by his opponents.[32] The section he devotes to the value of liberty in his *Additional observations* begins by arguing that our natural rights are granted to us by God as the author of nature. As a result, no one is ever 'the vassal or subject of another', nor 'has any right to give law to him, or without his consent to take away any part of his property or to abridge him of his liberty'.[33] This being so, no lawful form of government ever infringes on our liberty, nor does it take away any of the God-given rights of mankind, but instead serves to ensure that they are protected and confirmed.[34] There is therefore no confusion between civil liberty and the freedom of the state of nature. They are one and the same, except that as citizens our rights are protected by law instead of by ourselves.

The same line of argument was followed by most of those who wrote in agreement with Price. Some were clearly indebted to his account,[35] but the best summary was provided by Richard Watson in his *Essay on civil liberty*, the publication of which preceded Price's *Additional observations* by almost a year. Watson begins with the reflection, echoed by Price, that 'mankind may be considered as one great aggregate of equal and independent individuals', all of whom are endowed by God with 'the great rights of nature'.[36] From this it follows that 'the just superiority of any one man, or of any order and succession of men in any community over the other members which compose it, must spring from their express appointment and free consent'.[37] This is to say that 'the authority of the supreme magistrate to restrain natural liberty, and to dispose of personal property', must depend upon 'the mere good pleasure of those who entrust him with it'.[38] Kings must never 'consider themselves as superior

---

[32] On the religious basis of Price's political thinking see Clark 1985; and Sakkas 2016, pp. 47–63, 83–92.
[33] Price 1991, p. 86.    [34] Price 1991, pp. 81–2.
[35] See, for example, Peckard 1783, p. 8, following Price 1991, pp. 76–8.
[36] Watson 1776, pp. 5–6.    [37] Watson 1776, p. 10.    [38] Watson 1776, p. 11.

to the laws or their subjects as slaves'. If they violate the terms of the covenant by which the people institute them in office, then the people can justly remove them.[39] The people, in short, never give up their natural and God-given rights; when they create civil associations, they merely entrust them to be protected by those whom they appoint for that purpose. As in Price's account, the independence of the state of nature is held to be continuous with the idea of civil liberty.

**********

As we saw in Chapter 8, Price's opponents were not merely keen to show that Price gives a confused analysis of liberty; they were no less concerned with what they took to be the unacceptable implications of his argument. One especially troubling criticism they advanced was that Price's mistaken account of liberty commits him to a no less mistaken view about the institution of slavery. He contrasts the condition of being free with that of servitude in such a way as to suggest that anyone who is unable to govern themselves by their own will must be accounted a slave. But he thereby fails to acknowledge the greatest horror of slavery. This is not that slaves are subject to the will of a master, but rather that they count as their master's property, so that their life as well as their liberty is wholly at the disposal of someone else.

This was an objection impossible to gainsay, and we find that, in reaffirming their view of liberty as independence, Price and his allies are careful to modify the terms of the debate. Price speaks in his *Additional observations* of different sorts of slavery;[40] of some people as being 'worse slaves' than others;[41] and of reducing people to living in circumstances sufficiently slavish to resemble enslavement.[42] He explicitly acknowledges that we need to distinguish slavery 'in its properest sense', a sense he now takes to include not merely a life of subjection but the condition of being owned by someone else, and thus susceptible of being 'disposed of as if he was a beast'.[43] Price is now willing, in short, to mark a distinction between chattel slavery and the 'political' form of slavery (as Wollstonecraft was to call it) which is suffered by those who live in subjection to arbitrary power.[44] Peckard writes in similarly chastened terms in his sermon on civil liberty in 1783. He too asks what it means to be 'a proper slave', and in this connection he specifically refers to being treated as someone else's property, and thereby reduced to 'an article of

---

[39] Watson 1776, pp. 11–12, 20.
[40] Price 1991, p. 78. For Price on the different species of slavery see Page 2011.
[41] Price 1991, p. 93.    [42] Price 1991, p. 84.    [43] Price 1991, pp. 81, 179.
[44] On the distinction between political and chattel slavery see Nyquist 2013, Koekkoek 2022. For Wollstonecraft on 'political' slavery see Wollstonecraft 1995, p. 262.

public commerce'.[45] He is anxious to emphasise that this is the form of servitude at which 'the blood of every man not absolutely hardened to cruelty would freeze with horror'.[46]

Price and his allies were more concerned, however, to establish that it is not their own view of slavery, but rather that of their opponents, which remains open to serious moral doubts. When the defenders of the new view of liberty spoke about slavery, they generally assumed – in line with their definition of liberty as absence of restraint – that what it must mean for slaves to lack liberty is that they are coerced and oppressed. When Richard Hey pleaded for 'the proper sense' of the word slavery to be distinguished from merely figurative usages, he concluded that no one can rightly be called a slave unless their obedience is exacted from them in 'oppressive and injurious' ways.[47] But this led some exponents of the new view of liberty to speak as if slavery amounts to nothing more than forced labour. William Paley defines slavery as 'an obligation to labour for the benefit of the master without the contract or consent of the servant'.[48] He is closely followed by Thomas Gisborne, who states at the outset of his tract *Of slavery and the slave trade* that slavery is nothing other than the condition of being 'compelled to labour at the will of another without any previous contract'.[49]

The effect of contrasting freedom and servitude in these terms was to leave open the possibility of mounting a partial defence of slavery. Both Paley and Gisborne were opposed to the slave trade, but their definition had the effect of turning enslavement into a matter of degree. This emphasis helped the opponents of abolition to mount what many observers felt to be a strong case in favour of retaining the institution of slavery while accepting that the slave trade ought to be outlawed. When William Wilberforce eventually persuaded the House of Commons to consider the abolition of the trade, this defence was ruthlessly pursued.[50] During the debate of 1792, Mr Baillie assured the House – speaking as a plantation owner in the West Indies – that the slaves there 'are in as comfortable a state as the lower orders of mankind in any country in Europe'.[51] Mr Vaughan, another plantation owner, spoke in warm agreement about the comfortable condition of the plantation slaves. The truth, he assured the House, was that they were scarcely oppressed at all. He had 'seen little if any of the cruelty' of which their owners stood accused. Rather, the slaves 'appear as happy as any other poor' and have 'as much cheerfulness'.[52]

---

[45] Peckard 1783, pp. 8, 10.    [46] Peckard 1783, p. 10.    [47] Hey 1776, p. 23.
[48] Paley 1785, p. 195.    [49] Gisborne 1792, p. 8.
[50] The speakers on this side of the debate appear to have been influenced by the defence of slavery in [Turnbull] 1786. On the life of plantation slaves see Scanlan 2020, pp. 63–104.
[51] Cobbett 1817, col. 1075.    [52] Cobbett 1817, cols. 1085–6.

This was also the time when Jesse Foot, a surgeon who had practised in the West Indies in the 1760s, published *A defence of the planters*, in which he argued that the condition of the West Indies slaves provides no reason for their slavery to be abolished.[53] While conceding that they work without contracts, Foot insists that the life of the typical plantation slave is such that 'his toil is so light that he feels it not' and 'his freedom is so indifferent to him that he will not buy it'. Wilberforce's campaign is dismissed as little more than a call to remove imaginary chains.[54]

Faced with these arguments, those who defended the idea of liberty as independence replied, often with high indignation, that these accounts wholly overlook the fact that one horror of slavery is undoubtedly that people are condemned to live in perpetual subjection and dependence. We already encounter this reaction among those who came to Price's defence in the paper-war of 1776,[55] and same argument was later developed in one of the earliest and most important treatises in favour of abolition, Thomas Clarkson's *Essay on the slavery and commerce of the human species*.[56] Clarkson had been an undergraduate at Cambridge when the Reverend Peter Peckard delivered his sermon on civil liberty, which Clarkson is very likely to have heard, and which he appears to quote in his book.[57] When Peckard became Vice Chancellor of Cambridge in 1784, one of his duties became that of deciding on the topics for prize essays in the university, and for the Latin essay prize of 1785 he chose the question 'Is it lawful to consign people to slavery against their will?'[58] Clarkson entered the competition and answered the question emphatically in the negative. He was awarded the prize, and went on to publish his submission in a much expanded form as his *Essay* in 1786.

Clarkson is largely preoccupied in his *Essay* with the iniquities of the slave trade, and thus with the fact that slaves are regarded as 'merchantable goods' capable of being bought and sold.[59] But he is also much concerned with the fact that slaves are persons who have lost their liberty. He is very far, however, from viewing their resulting predicament simply as one in which they are forced to act under compulsion and continually oppressed. This is all too likely to be their fate, but what it fundamentally means to lose your liberty is to forfeit your independence.[60] Clarkson goes on to argue that the possession of equal independence was the original and natural condition of mankind. Everyone enjoyed 'an equal right to

---

[53] See *ODNB*, vol. 20, pp. 245–6.     [54] Foot 1792, pp. 10, 32.
[55] See, for example, *A complete answer* 1776, pp. 8, 11, 23.
[56] On Clarkson see Scanlan 2020, pp. 161–9.
[57] See, for example, Clarkson 1786, p. 72, echoing Peckard 1783, p. 10.
[58] *An liceat invitos in servitutem dare?*     [59] Clarkson 1786, p. xiii.
[60] Clarkson 1786, pp. 56–7, 61, 76.

the soil and produce of the earth' and lived together in 'a state of universal liberty', from which we can infer that 'liberty is a natural and government an adventitious right'.[61] Once we appreciate these relations between freedom and government, we can easily arrive at the answer to the question posed by the university.[62] Given that all men are free by nature, and given that nature has 'made every man's body and mind his own', the institution of slavery must be contrary to the laws of nature as well as the laws of God, in consequence of which no one can ever be consigned to slavery without their consent.[63]

A similar line of argument was pursued by the radical Whig William Belsham in his *Essay on the African slave trade* in 1790.[64] Belsham addresses the claim that the injury done by the slave trade is slight, because those who are enslaved and transported 'enjoy a degree of happiness in their state of bondage little if at all inferior to that which they possessed in their native country'.[65] He dismisses these claims with disgust as those of haughty and unfeeling tyrants, who must be so much 'engrossed by one fatal passion, the rage of accumulating wealth', that they are unable to recognise that they are speaking of people who have been made 'subject to thy dominion' in violation of 'the common rights of humanity'.[66]

By this time a shocking first-hand account of slavery in the West Indies had been published by Olaudah Equiano, who had lived there as a slave in the 1760s. Equiano had originally been brought to England in 1757, but was sold by his owner and taken to the plantations, where he eventually managed to buy his freedom in 1766.[67] Returning to England as a free man in 1777,[68] he became a friend of several leading abolitionists, including Thomas Clarkson and Granville Sharp, and an active supporter of the cause.[69] He published *The interesting narrative of the life of Olaudah Equiano* in 1789, in which he provided extensive and harrowing details about the barbarities practised by the slave owners.[70] But at the same time he emphasised, very much in the manner of Clarkson, that a further horror of slavery lies in the fact that it violates 'that first natural right of man, equality and independency', and 'gives one man a dominion over his fellows' so that they are 'humbled to the condition of brutes', contrary to the laws of nature as well as of God.[71]

---

[61] Clarkson 1786, p. 66.     [62] Clarkson 1786, pp. 69–70.
[63] Clarkson 1786, pp. 68–9, 72.     [64] On Belsham see *ODNB*, vol. 2, pp. 43–4.
[65] [Belsham] 1790, pp. 10–11.     [66] [Belsham] 1790, p. 11.
[67] Equiano 1789, vol. 1, pp. 94, 103, 115, vol. 2, pp. 13–14.
[68] Equiano 1789, vol. 2, p. 214.
[69] Olusoga 2021, pp. 211–12. Clarkson and Sharp were both subscribers to the first edition of Equiano's book. See Equiano 1789, vol. 1, Sig. A, 1a.
[70] Equiano 1789, vol. 1, pp. 180–226.     [71] Equiano 1789, vol. 1, p. 224.

When the time at last came for the abolitionists to reply to their opponents in the parliamentary debates prompted by William Wilberforce in 1791 and 1792, these were again the arguments most frequently deployed. Mr Martin spoke of how slavery involves the exercise of despotic and tyrannical power 'without control and without law', thereby undermining the rights of nature and mankind.[72] Mr Francis agreed that the loss of liberty suffered by slaves takes the form of being made to live in subjection to an uncontrollable and despotic form of power.[73] Mr Whitbread at the conclusion of the second debate in 1792 referred satirically to the attempt of several speakers to claim that slaves on plantations pass their days 'in healthful easy labour', after which they retire to rest 'with bodies unfatigued and hearts at ease'.[74] Even if these allegations were true, which they manifestly are not, they would still miss the point, which is that slavery is an institution under which people are subjected to 'the arbitrary and uncontrolled will of a master' who possesses the power to exercise cruelty with impunity whenever he may choose.[75] To recognise that this is what loss of liberty entails is to understand why it is not merely the slave trade but the institution of slavery itself that must be abolished.

These acts of abolition eventually happened, but only after a campaign that lasted for a further generation. Wilberforce's Bill to outlaw the slave trade in the British Empire duly passed the House of Commons in 1792, but was immediately defeated in the House of Lords, and it was not until 1807 that it was finally enacted.[76] Nor did this lead to the abolition of the institution of slavery itself. It was only after forty years of further debate, and a promise to pay enormous sums in compensation to slave owners for the loss of their property, that the Slavery Abolition Act was finally passed by the British Parliament and gained the royal assent in 1833.[77]

**********

No less unacceptable to Price's opponents, as we saw in Chapter 8, were the constitutional implications of his attempt to equate liberty with independence and self-government. One outrageous implication was held to be that the American colonists were never represented in the British Parliament, and that the British people will continue to lack any fair representation until they institute a system of universal suffrage. A further and still more outrageous implication was said to be that, because there can be no liberty in the absence of self-government, there

---

[72] Cobbett 1817, cols. 285–6.    [73] Cobbett 1817, cols. 288–9.
[74] Cobbett 1817, cols. 1100–1.    [75] Cobbett 1817, col. 1101.
[76] Taylor 2020, pp. 23–4.    [77] Taylor 2020, pp. 270–2, 282–5.

can be no prospect of upholding civil liberty except under some form of republican or democratic rule.

Faced with intense hostility to both these lines of argument, Price and his allies found little to say about the relationship between liberty and republican government. It is perhaps not surprising that they largely evaded this question, if only because any direct attack on the institution of monarchy might have led to a charge of treason. By contrast, Price was positively eager to engage with the accusation that his understanding of liberty gives rise to a dangerously mistaken view of political representation. He offered a vigorous response in his *Additional observations*, in which he clarified his support for the principle of universal suffrage (although without responding to Lind's observation that, if this is what he wants, he will have to enfranchise women as well as men).[78] Price does not deign even to mention the idea of virtual representation, and instead insists that no community can count as free unless it allows a complete representation of the people in two senses of the term. One is that no part of the community must be left without representatives. 'No state, a part of which only is represented in the legislature that governs it, is self-governed.'[79] The other is that no state can count as self-governed unless it enjoys what he describes as 'the blessing of a complete representation', which alone 'can properly denominate a people free'.[80] As he summarises, 'every independent agent in a free state ought to have a share in the government of it, either by himself personally, or by a body of representatives in choosing whom he has a free vote'.[81]

By the time Price came to clarify his views on representation he was able to call on the powerful authority of John Cartwright. After beginning his career in the navy Cartwright left the service in 1771 and thereafter devoted his life to the cause of political reform.[82] One of his earliest and most influential pamphlets first appeared in October 1776 under the resounding title *Take your choice!* Price in his *Additional observations* enthusiastically recommends Cartwright's analysis to anyone who wishes to be convinced of the practicality of a complete representation of the people.[83] Cartwright had already called attention to the two senses in which representation is required. One is that no part of the country should lack any representation of its interests. But under current arrangements there are places with 'neither house nor inhabitant' which are able to send to Parliament 'as many members as your most opulent cities', while there is not a single representative for 'many towns of the first manufacturing

---

[78] See [Lind] 1776, p. 40. The same objection is raised in Tucker 1783, pp. 55–6.
[79] Price 1991, p. 78.    [80] Price 1991, p. 93.    [81] Price 1991, p. 80.
[82] See *ODNB*, vol. 10, pp. 400–3.    [83] Price 1991, p. 93n.

consequence'.[84] The other requirement is that everyone should have a vote in deciding who should represent them. But at the moment 'those who now claim the exclusive right of sending to Parliament the five hundred and thirteen representatives for about six millions consist of less than twenty thousand persons' – to which Cartwright adds that 254 of those representatives are elected by less than 6,000 voters.[85]

Cartwright next turns to consider the idea of virtual representation. He first warns that, because this system 'was so learnedly argued to extend to three millions of people beyond the Atlantic, we may expect that it will be most unmercifully crammed down the throats of poor Englishmen', who will be told that it is 'every whit as good, as wholesome and nourishing, as a real representation'.[86] But to these contentions the only appropriate response is 'we have tried your fare, and find it will not do'.[87] The truth is that 'the Commons of this kingdom have at the present time nothing better than a mock representation of so dangerous a nature that nothing short of the constant miraculous interposition of heaven in their favour can possibly save them from a speedy subjection to arbitrary power'.[88] The British people need as a matter of urgency to establish 'such a representation as, by the eternal principles of freedom in general, and the express doctrine of their own constitution in particular, they are entitled to'.[89]

What, then, are these eternal principles of freedom? First of all, everyone has been created free. 'Were it otherwise, neither virtue nor vice, right nor wrong, could be ascribed to their actions; and to talk of happiness would be to talk nonsense.'[90] From this it follows that 'they are doubtless under an eternal obligation to preserve their freedom to the utmost of their power'.[91] Next, 'The all-wise Creator hath likewise made men by nature equal, as well as free. They are all of one flesh, and cast in one mould.'[92] Here it follows that 'how much soever any individual may be qualified for or deserve any elevation, he hath no right to it till it be conferred upon him by his fellows'.[93] We find, in short, 'that it is liberty, not dominion, which is held by divine right'.[94]

The implications of these principles for a just system of government are then spelled out. If we consider the representation of the people, we find that

the first and most natural idea which will occur to any unprejudiced man is that every individual of them, whether possessed of what is vulgarly called property or not, ought to have a vote in sending to parliament those men who are to act as his

---

[84] [Cartwright] 1776, p. 39.    [85] [Cartwright] 1776, p. 44.
[86] [Cartwright] 1776, p. 48n.    [87] [Cartwright] 1776, p. 48n.
[88] [Cartwright] 1776, p. 37.    [89] [Cartwright] 1776, p. 37.    [90] [Cartwright] 1776, p. 2.
[91] [Cartwright] 1776, p. 2.    [92] [Cartwright] 1776, p. 2.    [93] [Cartwright] 1776, p. 3.
[94] [Cartwright] 1776, p. 3.

representatives; and who in an especial manner, are to be the guardians of public freedom; in which the poor, surely, as well as the rich have an interest.[95]

We then need to reflect that there is a crucial sense in which everyone is an owner of property. John Locke is admiringly quoted for observing that 'every man has a property in his own person', because 'the labour of his body and the work of his hands, we may say, are properly his'.[96] But if this is so, then 'no man can be without a right to vote for a representative in the legislature', and this right must be observed.[97]

Cartwright draws to a close on a boldly democratic note. He claims to have established that the poorest peasant in the land 'hath as high a title to liberty as the most illustrious nobleman', and thus that 'in justice, the voice of the peasant goes as far as that of the richest commoner towards the nomination of a member of a parliament'.[98] The signature of a peasant to a petition addressed to the crown or Parliament will likewise be just as valuable 'as that of any freeholder or borough voter whatever'. This is because 'it will be the signature of a freeman: of a man every way entitled to the protection of the laws, and competent to a share in the framing of them'. To vindicate this right is of supreme importance, 'for liberty, like learning, is best preserved by its being widely diffused'.[99]

### The French Revolution and the Right to Liberty

While these reaffirmations of liberty as independence built up into a formidable response, a much stronger stimulus to the revival of the ideal was provided by the outbreak of the French Revolution in 1789. The enemies of despotism at once began to dispatch messages of congratulation to France, some of which were also circulated in England. One of the earliest was produced by two lawyers from Lincoln's Inn, Robert and Hercules Cramond, and was published as *A letter to the National Assembly*. The authors rejoice in the fact that the glory of liberty 'now seems to have collected all its rays in France, where it has already dispelled the darkness of slavery, and hence its mild and lovely radiance promises long to illumine the admiring world' as well as promoting 'the general happiness of a generous nation too long and severely oppressed'.[100]

A similar message was sent by the London Revolution Society, which had been established in the previous year to commemorate the settlement of 1689. The society now turned its attention to the revolution in France. Speaking at the anniversary meeting in November 1789, Richard Price

---

[95] [Cartwright] 1776, p. 19.     [96] [Cartwright] 1776, pp. 20–1.
[97] [Cartwright] 1776, p. 21.     [98] [Cartwright] 1776, p. 88.
[99] [Cartwright] 1776, pp. 88–9.     [100] Cramond and Cramond 1789, p. 1.

proposed – and it was unanimously resolved – that the society should 'offer to the National Assembly of France their congratulations on the revolution in that country' as a means of expressing their joy 'in every triumph of liberty and justice over arbitrary power'.[101] They also spoke of 'the particular satisfaction with which they reflect on the tendency of the glorious example given in France to encourage other nations to assert the unalienable rights of mankind, and thereby to introduce a general reformation in the governments of Europe, and to make the world free and happy'.[102]

This meeting of the Revolution Society was also the occasion on which Price delivered his *Discourse on the love of our country*.[103] He took the opportunity to restate his earlier argument that civil government 'is an institution of human prudence for guarding our persons, our property and our good name against invasion, and for securing to the members of a community that liberty to which all have an equal right'.[104] He then turns to the reasons for celebrating the anniversary of the 1688 revolution: the fetters of despotism had been broken; the rights of the people were asserted; and their authority to frame their own government and treat its powers as a delegation from themselves was finally established.[105] Price ends by giving special thanks for the fact that, after the further glory of the American Revolution in 1776, he has been spared to witness yet another and no less glorious revolution in France, 'in which every friend to mankind is now exulting': 'I have lived to see thirty millions of people, indignant and resolute, spurning at slavery, and demanding liberty with an irresistible voice, their king led in triumph, and an arbitrary monarch surrendering himself to his subjects.'[106] Price rejoices that a light has been lit that, 'after setting America free', has now been 'reflected to France and there kindled into a blaze that lays despotism in ashes and warms and illuminates Europe'.[107]

This is by no means to say that every English political writer who endorsed Price's view of civil liberty was at the same time an enthusiast for the French Revolution. The most celebrated exception was Edmund Burke, who published his *Reflections on the revolution in France* in November 1790.[108] Burke begins with a mocking attack on Price's *Discourse* and a scornful dismissal of the Revolution Society to which it

---

[101] *Revolution Society* 1789, p. 10. On the Revolution Society see Claeys 2007, pp. 111–15; on Price and the society see Fitzpatrick 1991.
[102] *Revolution Society* 1789, p. 11.  [103] Price 1991, pp. 176–96.
[104] Price 1991, p. 184.  [105] Price 1991, pp. 189–90.  [106] Price 1991, p. 195.
[107] Price 1991, p. 196. On Price's development of this narrative see Elazar 2022a.
[108] Burke 2001, p. 68. For a comprehensive analysis of the *Reflections* see Bourke 2015, pp. 677–739. For Burke on the ancient constitution see Pocock 1971, pp. 202–32; for his Whig allegiances in the *Reflections* see Pocock 1985, pp. 279–84.

had been addressed.[109] Price is denounced for misusing the pulpit to speak, without any breath of moderation, about civil liberty and civil government.[110] Even if he were not attempting to promote unheard-of and fictitious rights,[111] he should recognise that he is meddling with matters irrelevant to his calling and entirely outside his range of knowledge.[112]

It is striking, however, that when Burke turns to speak about the concept of liberty he has no quarrel with Price about the meaning and application of the term. The basic contrast he draws is between living securely in liberty and being condemned to live in subjection to 'the headlong exertions of arbitrary power'.[113] When he voices his distrust of the unmediated power of the people, his objection is that they are no less capable than kings of deploying arbitrary power and exercising domination 'under a false show of liberty'.[114] Like Price, he contrasts the enjoyment of liberty with abject submission to a dominating will,[115] and especially with being condemned to live in a state of slavery and servitude.[116] On the one hand, we are assured that 'a brave people will certainly prefer liberty, accompanied with a virtuous poverty, to a depraved and wealthy servitude'.[117] And on the other hand, the defenders of the revolution in France are ridiculed and denounced for claiming that 'those who reprobate their crude and violent schemes of liberty ought to be treated as advocates of servitude'.[118]

When Burke shifts his attention to the situation in France, he speaks of the country as living in a condition of merely 'pretended liberty' which is really its opposite.[119] He repeatedly stigmatises the government of the National Assembly as 'an unheard of despotism',[120] and a form of tyranny willing to strike at 'property, liberty and life'.[121] With the abolition of the Parlements, the final bulwark against arbitrary power has now been removed.[122] If the National Assembly proceeds to establish the proposed state tribunal, the effect will be to 'extinguish the last sparks of liberty in France and settle most dreadful and arbitrary tyranny'.[123]

---

[109] Burke 2001, p. 153. On Price and Burke see Thomas 1977, 309–42.
[110] Burke 2001, p. 157.    [111] Burke 2001, p. 162.    [112] Burke 2001, p. 157.
[113] Burke 2001, pp. 176, 187–8. For Burke on liberty see Bourke 2015, pp. 16–24.
[114] Burke 2001, p. 258. Burke is here quoting Hobbes's *Leviathan*. See Hobbes 2012, vol. 2, ch. 21, p. 334.
[115] Burke 2001, p. 258.
[116] See Burke 2001, pp. 176, 251 on slavery; and pp. 175, 238, 412 on servitude.
[117] Burke 2001, p. 303.    [118] Burke 2001, p. 291.    [119] Burke 2001, p. 402.
[120] Burke 2001, p. 323; cf. also p. 291.
[121] Burke 2001, p. 277; for the repeated accusation of tyranny see pp. 271, 289–90, 307, 323.
[122] Burke 2001, p. 375.
[123] Burke 2001, p. 379; for the addition to this paragraph see p. 421.

Great Britain, by contrast, is neither a monarchical despotism nor a despotism of the multitude.[124] It is a free country in which the treasure of liberty is safely guarded, so that the people are able to enjoy security for their constitutional rights.[125] When speaking of British liberty Burke takes himself (as he several times avows) to be writing as a Whig, but one of his aims is to distance himself from two prominent strands of Whig thinking about the revolution of 1688. First he rejects the view, forcefully restated by Price, that the 1688 settlement was based on accepting the idea of the inalienable rights of man and the need for legitimate states to be grounded on recognising and inscribing those rights into law. Burke never speaks of inalienable rights, and when he refers to the rights of man he generally does so with heavy irony.[126] He also rejects the claim that the 1688 settlement constituted the first foundation of British liberty. He celebrates the settlement as the reaffirmation of a great inheritance of rights and liberties, tracing their descent in a line running from Magna Carta and the Petition of Right to what he takes to be their definitive codification in the Declaration of Rights in 1689.[127] The achievement of the 1688 settlement, he argues, was to settle for ever a number of fundamental laws and liberties,[128] which he also describes as 'the real rights of men'.[129]

Burke does not disagree with the believers in natural rights that the most essential among the real rights of men are life, liberty and property.[130] But he takes a very different view of their source and character. His *Reflections* may be said to carry us back to the debate about rights that had marked the defence of the 1688 revolution. On one side had stood the view that came to be associated in particular with John Locke, and that Richard Price and his allies were now reiterating. According to this account, everyone in the state of nature would have equally enjoyed the right to life, liberty and property, and these natural rights were subsequently embodied in a supposed contract upon which the state was originally grounded. On the other side stood the view that James Tyrrell, George Petyt and others had adopted and developed from Sir Edward Coke, and that Burke was now bringing back to the centre of the political stage. According to this rival account, the rights to life, liberty and property are the most salient of the liberties that have arisen out of the life of the state itself and have passed what Burke describes as 'the solid test of long experience'.[131] The only sense in which the state is based on a contract is that it is grounded on an agreement between the many

---

[124] Burke 2001, p. 291.     [125] Burke 2001, pp. 178, 211, 333.
[126] See, for example, Burke 2001, pp. 151, 217, 393.     [127] Burke 2001, pp. 163, 182–5.
[128] Burke 2001, pp. 163, 175, 177, 185.     [129] Burke 2001, p. 217.
[130] Burke 2001, pp. 277, 333.     [131] Burke 2001, p. 217.

generations of citizens who have come to recognise that these liberties are indispensable to our shared social life.[132] Echoing Coke's doctrine of the 'artificial' reason of the law, Burke concludes that the contention on which the English generally and correctly agree is that it is far safer to trust one's liberty to this general bank of ages than to the fallible and feeble reasoning of a single generation about the supposed rights of man.[133]

Burke's intervention was received with instant acclaim. It is true that some of the plaudits amounted to little more than words of adulation combined with contemptuous remarks about the need to consign the idea of natural rights to the region of nonsense.[134] If, however, we turn to Burke's admirers in Ireland, we come upon a much more careful analysis of the two rival views about the character of rights. The case was comprehensively restated in the *Vindication* of Burke published in 1791 by Thomas Goold, a Master in the Irish Court of Chancery. Goold notes that, according to Price, 'Mr Burke has been decrying popular rights'.[135] But rights must not be confused with powers.[136] What Burke has established, and what his critics have failed to comprehend, is that our rights as citizens arise out of developments in the law, and hence out of 'the long and approved experience of mankind'.[137] The egregious error of Burke's critics is that they 'seem to despise governments that come recommended by the collected wisdom and integrity of ages' and hence by 'the steady principles of good government'.[138]

Among Burke's early admirers, the one who came closest to him in language as well as outlook was the Reverend Jerom Alley of County Armagh, who published his *Observations on the government and constitution of Great Britain* in 1792. Alley fully accepts that one of the basic aims of the British constitution is to secure the fundamental rights of the people.[139] But he is emphatic that he is not talking about natural rights or the supposed rights of man. We need to understand that the British constitution is a historical construct, the value of which has been 'confirmed by experience'.[140] A right is a liberty of action established over time, the outcome not of speculative reasoning but of 'a rich and precious inheritance'.[141] The rights we now enjoy 'have gradually and slowly arisen' and reflect 'the accumulated sagacity and experience of various countries and ages'.[142] As a result, our laws 'harmonise with all the

---

[132] Burke 2001, pp. 181, 183, 185, 260–1.    [133] Burke 2001, pp. 185, 251.
[134] See, for example, Cooper 1791, pp. 6–9, 151, 156.    [135] Goold 1791, p. 27.
[136] Goold 1791, p. 83.    [137] Goold 1791, p. 79.    [138] Goold 1791, pp. 84, 85.
[139] Alley 1792, p. 59.    [140] Alley 1792, pp. 38–9.    [141] Alley 1792, p. 59.
[142] Alley 1792, pp. 62, 63.

established customs and habits of the people', which is why 'we will not part with them for the newborn theory of the rights of man'.[143]

**********

While the admirers of Burke lauded his incomparable combination of wisdom and eloquence,[144] many readers found the *Reflections* patronising as well as pernicious, and Burke was instantly subjected to a fierce barrage of attacks.[145] Some of these denunciations were largely personal, and included a bitter response from Price, who condemned Burke with uncharacteristic ferocity for his lack of candour and frantic zeal.[146] But the immediate responses to Burke also included some serious engagements with his line of argument about freedom and rights. One of the earliest was the work of Capel Lofft, a radical lawyer who had trained at Lincoln's Inn and later became a vocal opponent of the government.[147] Lofft first published his *Remarks* on Burke in December 1790, in which he repeatedly cites Price against Burke and grounds his own argument on a series of claims about the equal and natural rights of man.[148] He notes that Burke supposes 'a surrender of the whole rights of the individual to society',[149] but responds that 'man by uniting himself to civil society resigns no rights but such as are inconsistent with the ends of such society'.[150] Everyone remains 'his own governor by the right he has to share in the formation of those laws which are to govern the community of which he is a part', and everyone retains 'his right of determining what is just' in cases where the law cannot interfere.[151] Lofft concludes with a celebration of the revolution in France and the 'grand features of that ever memorable and unparalleled event'.[152] He singles out the vindication of liberty of conscience, the substitution of the representative will of the people for the arbitrary will of the king, and above all the recognition of the natural and civil rights of mankind. These changes have produced a diffusion of light, liberty and happiness, and accordingly form a just subject of joy and congratulation to all who want to end the horrors of servitude.[153]

Although Lofft's tract was reprinted in 1791 in an extended form, it was immediately overshadowed by the appearance of the two most important among the immediate responses to Burke. The first was Mary Wollstonecraft's *Vindication of the rights of men*, which appeared in

---

[143] Alley 1792, p. 66.    [144] See, for example, Cooper 1791, pp. 6–9; Goold 1791, p. 1.
[145] For a listing of attacks on Burke in 1790–3 see Boulton 1963, pp. 265–72.
[146] Price 1991, p. 177.    [147] See *ODNB*, vol. 34, pp. 295–7.
[148] On Price and Burke see Lofft 1790, pp. 9, 17, 71. For the date of publication see Lofft 1790, p. 79.
[149] Lofft 1790, p. 39.    [150] Lofft 1790, p. 37.    [151] Lofft 1790, pp. 37–8.
[152] Lofft 1790, p. 75.    [153] Lofft 1790, pp. 76, 79.

November 1790;[154] the second was Catharine Macaulay's *Observations on the Reflections*, which was also in print by the end of the year.[155] Burke's greatest weakness, they agree, lies in his perpetual tendency, as Wollstonecraft puts it, to inflame his imagination instead of seeking to enlighten his understanding.[156] Wollstonecraft finds in him 'a mortal antipathy to reason',[157] while Macaulay objects to his continual appeals to opinion and prejudice, and his associated refusal to base his arguments on any abstract principles.[158]

Wollstonecraft responds by laying out her views about the abstract principles that need to be invoked. We must begin by acknowledging the primacy of reason, and thus by recognising 'that there are rights which men inherit at their birth as rational creatures', so that custom and prescription 'can never undermine natural rights', which are not merely native but inalienable.[159] Macaulay arrives at similar conclusions when she turns at the end of her *Observations* to consider Burke's hostility to the rights of men. If, she suggests, Burke 'could have descended from the lofty strain of poetic imagination to the drudgery of close reasoning', he would have been obliged to admit that our only possible starting point in politics must be to acknowledge 'the native and unalienable rights of men' and their indefeasible character.[160]

To these assertions Wollstonecraft adds that our natural rights are also sacred in origin.[161] We receive them from God, which is why custom and prescription can never undermine them.[162] As she tersely explains, 'religion is included in my idea of morality'.[163] Here she continues to align herself with Price and his way of thinking about religion and political life. But this was an alignment that the revolution was beginning to question, and Macaulay tends to echo its more secular tone. Although she thinks of good laws as proceeding in part from a sense of sympathy we owe to the Author of our being, she never affirms in her *Observations* that our natural rights have been given to us by God.[164] She simply speaks of them as 'the native rights of the species'.[165]

Where Wollstonecraft and Macaulay fully agree is in the account they give of what it means to speak of having a right to liberty.[166] We are

---

[154] Tomaselli 1995, p. xxxi.    [155] Skjönsberg 2023, p. xxxiv.
[156] Wollstonecraft 1995, p. 7.    [157] Wollstonecraft 1995, pp. 6–7, 8.
[158] Macaulay 2023, pp. 262, 281.    [159] Wollstonecraft 1995, pp. 12–13, 33.
[160] Macaulay 2023, p. 299.    [161] Wollstonecraft 1995, pp. 7, 34.
[162] Wollstonecraft 1995, pp. 12–13.    [163] Wollstonecraft 1995, p. 7n.
[164] Macaulay 2023, p. 292.
[165] Macaulay 2023, p. 276. But for an emphasis on Macaulay's religious faith see Green 2018 and Skjönsberg 2023, pp. xxiii–xxv.
[166] For Macaulay on liberty see Green 2012; Green 2017; Coffee 2017; Whatmore 2023, pp. 99, 102–4. For Wollstonecraft on domination see Coffee 2013. For Wollstonecraft on rights and liberty see Coffee 2014; James 2016; Halldenius 2017; Hirschmann and Regier 2019.

referring to the condition in which we are free from subjection to the arbitrary will of anyone else, and are consequently in a position to use our reason to act independently and pursue our own ideal of happiness. Wollstonecraft always contrasts liberty with domination and submission,[167] and when speaking about 'the newly acquired liberty of the state' in France she stresses that this has in turn provided the people with a glorious chance to attain virtue and happiness.[168] Macaulay similarly contrasts liberty with subjection to bondage,[169] and the basis on which she commends the National Assembly is that its members have taken steps towards emancipating and securing the happiness of the entire population by acting as 'the friends and promoters of liberty' and granting equal freedom to all.[170] This is what makes the French Revolution the most important and astonishing event that has ever happened from the point of view of the dearest interests of mankind.[171]

Catharine Macaulay's *Observations* was the last work she was able to complete, but Mary Wollstonecraft went on to present a further affirmation of the ideal of liberty as independence in her *Vindication of the rights of woman*.[172] Here the right with which Wollstonecraft is chiefly concerned is that of women to receive an education capable of turning them into independent agents, thereby enabling them to engage in duties useful to society.[173] This concern again places the issue of liberty at the heart of her argument. She takes it for granted that what it means to be free is to be independent. To say that someone possesses their freedom is to say that they are not living in 'slavish dependence', not obliged to act 'according to the will of another fallible being'.[174] They are able to judge and act according to their own will and pursue their own idea of happiness.[175] The contrast is always with the predicament of slaves, who are obliged to live completely subject to, and dependent upon, the will of their masters, and are thereby wholly deprived of liberty.[176]

Turning to address the value of liberty, Wollstonecraft begins by putting forward a distinctive and pivotal argument. She proposes that independence is 'the basis of every virtue'.[177] You cannot hope to be virtuous

---

[167] See, for example, Wollstonecraft 1995, pp. 48–9, 60–1. But for a contrasting account, arguing that Wollstonecraft's understanding of liberty includes a 'positive' element, see Hirschmann and Regier 2019.

[168] Wollstonecraft 1995, pp. 41, 50.      [169] Macaulay 2023, pp. 265, 273.

[170] Macaulay 2023, pp. 258, 264, 266.      [171] Macaulay 2023, p. 257.

[172] Skjönsberg 2023, p. xxxiv; Tomaselli 1995, p. xxxi.

[173] Wollstonecraft 1995, p. 236.      [174] Wollstonecraft 1995, pp. 116–17, 120.

[175] Wollstonecraft 1995, p. 69.

[176] Wollstonecraft 1995, pp. 69, 80, 126, 155, 186. For Wollstonecraft on slavery and anti-slavery see Brace 2016.

[177] Wollstonecraft 1995, p. 67.

unless you are free.[178] Unless you are independent of the will of others you can never hope to exercise your reason, thereby judging for yourself which courses of action are right to pursue.[179] Freedom has the effect of strengthening reason, and it is only by these means that you can hope to be led to happiness and eventually to God.[180] But the fundamental problem is that women are not free. They are degraded from being rational creatures, condemned to acquire manners before morals and to live in dependence on men.[181] Some are entirely dependent, so that they are 'reduced to neglecting the duties that reason alone points out'.[182] They live under a yoke, in bondage and servitude, in slavish submission and obedience.[183] Wollstonecraft is careful to add that she is speaking here of slavery only 'in a political and civil sense'.[184] But she does not hesitate to affirm that men enslave women,[185] and she speaks with disgust of 'the slavery of marriage'.[186]

   The only way to resolve the problem is for women to be more rationally educated.[187] Rousseau is denounced for arguing 'that a woman should never, for a moment, feel herself independent', and his writings on education are dismissed as beneath contempt.[188] The great need is for women to be instructed in such a way as to give them an active desire for independence.[189] They will then be able to change their status, to take their place as free citizens capable of making a contribution to society in such roles as physicians, farmers and managers of shops, all supported by their own industry and all living an independent life.[190] It ought also to be made possible for women to become politicians, 'instead of being arbitrarily governed without having any direct share allowed them in the deliberations of government'.[191] Although Wollstonecraft never managed to fulfil the promise she makes to examine this further issue at a future date,[192] she leaves her readers with a suggestion about the reform of parliamentary representation that even the most radical supporters of that cause had hitherto ignored.

**********

---

[178] Wollstonecraft 1995, pp. 107, 230, 236.    [179] Wollstonecraft 1995, pp. 106, 206.
[180] Wollstonecraft 1995, pp. 68, 79; on rational religion see pp. 280–1.
[181] On women and manners see Wollstonecraft 1995, pp. 91–3. For her views on manners and civility see Davidson 2004, pp. 76–91; O'Brien 2009, pp. 173–200.
[182] For these claims see Wollstonecraft 1995, pp. 102, 122, 137–8, 218, 230.
[183] For these claims see Wollstonecraft 1995, pp. 105, 161, 202, 239–40, 246.
[184] Wollstonecraft 1995, p. 262.    [185] Wollstonecraft 1995, pp. 69, 91, 116.
[186] Wollstonecraft 1995, pp. 69, 248.    [187] Wollstonecraft 1995, p. 111.
[188] Wollstonecraft 1995, pp. 94, 113–14.    [189] Wollstonecraft 1995, pp. 111–12.
[190] Wollstonecraft 1995, pp. 239–40. For Wollstonecraft on liberty as the possession of a distinctive status see Halldenius 2015, pp. 23–4.
[191] Wollstonecraft 1995, p. 237.    [192] Wollstonecraft 1995, p. 237.

The opening months of 1791 saw the publication of many further protests against the tone as well as the arguments of Burke's *Reflections*. Some critics were merely vituperative,[193] but others attempted a serious engagement with his views on liberty and rights. These commentators included the prominent Irish lawyer Benjamin Bousfield,[194] as well as Joseph Priestley in his *Letters* to Burke. Priestley had been well known since the 1750s as a dissenting teacher and minister, and since the 1760s as a radical writer on politics.[195] He now stepped forward not merely to celebrate the French Revolution but to predict 'the general enlargement of liberty, civil and religious, opened by the revolution in France'.[196] He condemns Burke's wild declamation against the rights of man[197] and celebrates the revolution as a change 'from a most debasing servitude to a state of the most exalted freedom'. He ends by rejoicing in the fact that there is now a prospect of 'leaving all men the enjoyment of as many of their natural rights as possible', thereby enabling them to lead flourishing and happy lives.[198]

Priestley's *Letters* quickly went through two further editions, but even his contribution was overshadowed by the appearance in March 1791 of part I of Thomas Paine's *Rights of man*, which sold over 40,000 copies within the year.[199] Paine presents himself specifically as an enemy of Burke's views on the historical formation and development of civil rights.[200] Attacking what he condemns as these poisonous principles, he replies that 'every age and every generation must be as free to act for itself, in all cases, as the ages and generations which preceded it'.[201] He counters with an extensive discussion of the rights of man, which he first sets out in opposition to Burke, and later elaborates in his analysis of the National Assembly's Declaration of the Rights of Man and Citizen.[202]

Paine's resulting account closely resembles the one that Price and his allies had already given in response to the new view of liberty, and at the beginning of his treatise Paine refers to Price in admiring terms.[203] Like Price, he believes that our rights are granted to us directly by God as 'the maker of man'.[204] He goes on to explain that the rights to which he is referring are those which everyone would have possessed in the state of nature. 'Man is all of one degree', so that 'all men are born equal and with

---

[193] See, for example, [Scott-Waring] 1791, pp. 43–6.

[194] Bousfield 1791, pp. vi–vii, 54.      [195] See Miller 1993, p. xxix.

[196] Priestley 1791, p. 140. On Priestley's politics see Miller 1994, pp. 337–48.

[197] Priestley 1791, p. 151; and cf. p. xi.      [198] Priestley 1791, pp. 141, 142–3.

[199] Paine 2000, pp. 57–153. But the estimate is Paine's own boast (see Paine 2000, p. 159) and was probably an exaggeration. See Clark 2018, p. 233.

[200] For Burke and Paine see Claeys 2007, pp. 11–48; Whatmore 2023, pp. 223–51.

[201] Paine 2000, p. 63.      [202] Paine 2000, pp. 83–8, 123–7.      [203] Paine 2000, p. 61.

[204] Paine 2000, p. 85.

equal natural rights'.[205] We must recognise that 'man did not enter into society to become worse than he was before, nor to have less rights than he had before, but to have those rights better secured'.[206] It follows that 'every civil right has for its foundation some natural right pre-existing in the individual', and that no lawful power can be applied to invade or take away any of them.[207]

These claims are prefaced with a narrative of the outbreak of the French Revolution[208] in which the people of France are congratulated for having brought about a transformation 'generated in the rational contemplation of the rights of man'.[209] Paine provides an analysis of the new constitution created by the National Assembly, in the course of which he pursues the political implications of his account of natural rights.[210] Because these rights are inalienable, no government can have any claim to legitimacy unless it is willing to treat them as the foundations of the state. 'A constitution founded on the rights of man and the authority of the people' is based on 'the only authority on which government has a right to exist in any country'.[211] What then are these essential rights? Here Paine appeals directly to the Declaration of the Rights of Man. 'The end of all political associations is the preservation of the natural and imprescriptible rights of man', which are 'liberty, property, security and resistance of oppression'.[212]

Paine also produces a ringing reaffirmation of the ideal of liberty as independence.[213] When he narrates the origins and course of the French Revolution he maintains that before 1789 the people were wholly deprived of liberty, making it clear that by this he means that they were condemned to living in enslavement to a despotic form of power. He speaks of 'the hereditary despotism of the monarchy' and 'the ministerial despotism operating everywhere',[214] the effect of which was to make the people 'accustomed to slavery'.[215] Set against this background, the storming of the Bastille can only be viewed as 'an enthusiasm of heroism such as only the highest animation of liberty could inspire'.[216] Later, when describing the work of the National Assembly, he refers to France as 'a country regenerating itself from slavery', and ends by celebrating 'the extinction of despotism' in France and the establishment of a free state.[217]

This analysis leads Paine to conclude by reiterating the revolutionary claim he had already put forward in *Common sense*.[218] No government in which there is any element of despotic power can be legitimate, and all

---

[205] Paine 2000, p. 85.    [206] Paine 2000, p. 86.    [207] Paine 2000, pp. 86, 87.
[208] Paine 2000, pp. 66–83.    [209] Paine 2000, p. 70.    [210] Paine 2000, pp. 123–7.
[211] Paine 2000, p. 123.    [212] Paine 2000, p. 124.    [213] Paine 2000, p. 61.
[214] Paine 2000, p. 69.    [215] Paine 2000, p. 75.    [216] Paine 2000, p. 76.
[217] Paine 2000, pp. 93, 145.    [218] Paine 2000, pp. 127–38.

forms of monarchical government embody elements of despotic power.[219] He ends, as in *Common sense*, with a call to arms. We need to recognise that 'sovereignty, as a matter of right, appertains to the nation only and not to any individual', and thus that 'the romantic and barbarous distinctions of men into kings and subjects' has at last been 'exploded by the principles on which governments are now founded'.[220] What we have been witnessing in America and France is 'a renovation of the natural order of things'.[221] We are now living in an age of revolution, and the time has come for monarchical sovereignty, 'the enemy of mankind and the source of misery', to be brought to an end.[222]

Two months later, the young James Mackintosh produced a no less fervent celebration of the revolution in his *Vindiciae Gallica*. Mackintosh was an aspiring law student at the time, but his *Vindiciae* brought him instant fame.[223] His title alludes to the *Vindiciae contra tyrannos*, and he offers a similar defence of popular sovereignty, while at the same time execrating Burke for his scurrilous, intemperate and deluded attack on the new regime.[224] Mackintosh's narrative focuses on the despotism of Louis XVI and the reforms initiated by the National Assembly in its advance towards freedom and light.[225] He admits that some mistakes have been made along the way, but he is still intensely enthusiastic about the abolition of the privileges previously enjoyed by the nobility and their replacement by a unified and representative form of government. He hails the new constitution as grounded on the natural rights of man, and thus on the general principles of reason and freedom.[226] He believes that 'the shock that destroyed the despotism of France has widely dispersed the clouds that intercepted reason from the political and moral world',[227] and he ends by holding out the hope that 'freedom and reason will be rapidly propagated from their source in France'.[228]

Mackintosh also provides an account of the meaning and value of the freedom that the French have achieved. The government of Louis XVI was a wanton and bankrupt despotism[229] under which the feeble king 'affected to represent his will as the rule of their conduct',[230] while the people were made to endure 'a degrading and injurious subjection'.[231] Under the new constitution the people are living under the rule of law, the primary function of which is to protect their most sacred and

---

[219] Paine 2000, pp. 127, 131, 134, 137.     [220] Paine 2000, p. 150.
[221] Paine 2000, p. 151.     [222] Paine 2000, p. 151.
[223] See Haakonssen 1996, pp. 261–93; Winch 2006, pp. x–xvii.
[224] Mackintosh 2006, pp. 7, 39.     [225] Mackintosh 2006, p. 20.
[226] Mackintosh 2006, pp. 29, 91.     [227] Mackintosh 2006, p. 151.
[228] Mackintosh 2006, p. 161.     [229] Mackintosh 2006, pp. 14, 16, 24.
[230] Mackintosh 2006, pp. 23–4.     [231] Mackintosh 2006, pp. 21–2, 34, 79, 147.

imprescriptible rights.[232] Beyond the confines of the law the people are free to act as they choose, and are thus able to exercise a freedom 'which no power can impair or infringe'.[233] Summarising his central claim, Mackintosh concludes that the criterion distinguishing laws from arbitrary dictates is at the same time the criterion that distinguishes freedom from servitude.[234] John Locke is said to deserve immortal honour for having systematised and rendered popular this understanding of civil and religious liberty.[235]

In the writings of Paine and Mackintosh, as well as in the resolutions of the London Revolution Society, we find the ideal of liberty as independence reaffirmed with unparalleled self-confidence. Mackintosh expresses the conviction that 'the free and vigilant spirit of an enlightened age' will now prevail in France,[236] while Paine argues that, due to 'the enlightened state of mankind', we can expect that further revolutions brought about 'by reason and accommodation' will soon begin to make their way across Europe.[237] But what these writers were about to witness was not the triumph but the eclipse of their vision of enlightenment.[238] Rather than being finally realised, their hopes for a world in which citizens would be able to live in equality and independence were about to be destroyed.

---

[232] Mackintosh 2006, p. 98.    [233] Mackintosh 2006, p. 95.
[234] Mackintosh 2006, p. 147.
[235] Mackintosh 2006, p. 136. For Mackintosh's subsequent abandonment of his radical principles see Johnston 2013, pp. 205–23.
[236] Mackintosh 2006, p. 21.    [237] Paine 2000, p. 153.
[238] On the failed dream of enlightenment see Whatmore 2023.

# 10 The New View Entrenched

## The Conservative Response

By the beginning of 1792 the growing enthusiasm for the French Revolution was beginning to create anxiety in England about the stability of private property and monarchical rule. This was the year in which the conservative lawyer John Reeves founded his association 'for preserving liberty and property against republicans and levellers', which immediately began to issue a series of tracts in denunciation of the freedom and equality promised by the revolution.[1] This was also the year in which the Tory administration under William Pitt began to introduce draconian legislation to increase their control of the press, beginning with the Proclamation on Seditious Publications in May 1792. Condemning the growing number of wicked and inflammatory writings in circulation, the Proclamation commanded magistrates to prosecute the authors and printers of all such works, and to inform the government about everyone involved.[2]

One of the first victims of the new legislation was Thomas Paine, who had published part II of his *Rights of man* in February 1792.[3] He not only continued to extol the French Revolution, but went on to predict that there would now be 'a general revolution in governments'.[4] At the same time he dismissed, more vehemently than ever, the folly and farce of monarchy,[5] declaring that 'all hereditary government is in its nature tyranny',[6] and arguing that every form of prerogative power takes away liberty and replaces it with a species of slavery.[7] As soon as the Proclamation of May 1792 was issued, Paine was immediately arrested on a charge of seditious libel. He managed to escape to France, but was

---

[1] The first meeting took place in November 1792. See *Proceedings of the Association* 1793, p. 3.
[2] *By the king, a Proclamation* 1792. For a list of those tried for sedition and treason between 1792 and 1798 see Johnston 2013, pp. 329–30.
[3] Paine 2000, pp. 155–263.     [4] Paine 2000, pp. 163, 212, 256.
[5] Paine 2000, pp. 182, 254.     [6] Paine 2000, p. 172.     [7] Paine 2000, pp. 198, 201.

tried and convicted in absentia in December 1792 and thereafter never returned to England.[8]

A further reason for the increasing unease about events in France arose from the growing violence with which the revolution was being implemented. Catharine Macaulay had already warned that the people of France might end by subjecting themselves to a new tyranny,[9] and the Whig member of Parliament John Scott-Waring in his *Letter* of 1791 to Burke had expressed the prescient anxiety that, 'although the French have destroyed despotism', it could still rear its head in another form 'infinitely more horrible'.[10] By the second half of 1792 it was already beginning to seem to some English observers that such fears were proving well grounded. In August the Tuileries palace was stormed and Louis XVI was imprisoned; in September the National Assembly was replaced by the Convention, which immediately abolished the institution of monarchy; and in December the king was put on trial. He was executed in January 1793, and two weeks later France declared war on England.

By 1792, and in the years immediately following, these doubts and fears began to be increasingly reflected in discussions about the nature and extent of civil liberty. One response took the form of an almost panic-stricken reaction against the very idea that government can be limited.[11] As we have seen, a strand of high Tory argument about the sacred character of kingship had continued to resurface at moments of political crisis throughout the eighteenth century. During the early 1790s a new generation of clerical writers came forward to reiterate once more that, because our rulers are ordained by God, the extent of their authority can never be challenged or controlled. What this was taken to mean in practice was summarised by William Hales, a prominent Irish cleric and scholar, in his treatise on *The scripture doctrine of political government and political liberty*. Hales begins by contending that, if we wish to understand the first principles of government, we must turn 'to the sacred sources of original scripture' and 'oppose their authority to a host of popular opinions and popular prejudices, which madly strike at the root of all order and subordination' and thereby 'prey upon the vitals of the state'.[12]

A number of sermons and tracts written from this viewpoint specifically addressed the relationship between the powers ordained by God and the possession of civil liberty. It was widely agreed that a scriptural perspective requires us to begin by acknowledging that our duty to God is our

---

[8] Kuklick 2000, p. xxv. On the vilification of Paine in the 1790s see Davis 2016.
[9] Macaulay 2023, p. 300.
[10] [Scott-Waring] 1791, p. 5. Attribution from BL catalogue.
[11] On counter-revolutionary writing in the 1790s see Gilmartin 2007.
[12] Hales 1794, pp. 3–4.

most exalted obligation of all. Edward Salter, chaplain to the Duke of Gloucester, underlined the point at the outset of a sermon he preached in 1791 on *Obedience to God the measure of human liberty*. He appeals in particular to the authority of St Peter, who taught that 'the service which we owe to God must be the rule of Christian conduct at all times'.[13] William Agutter of Magdalen College Oxford, in a sermon of 1792 on *Christian politics*, in turn explained that we owe this service because 'all power and authority come from God', and cannot arise from any other source. In particular, 'power can no more originate from the people than the soul can originate from the body, or that heaven can originate from earth'.[14]

If we ask what obligations we owe to God in the political realm, we learn from the scriptures that His will, and hence our primary duty, is to follow the pathway of passive obedience. As Salter explains, this is 'the behaviour of the true servants of God'. 'They will not wish to violate His commandments nor transgress the laws of a well-ordered government.' They will always observe the duty to 'look up to those who are in authority over them', showing them the reverence due 'from the sons of freedom to the guardians of their sacred laws'.[15] The Reverend John Fawel, in a sermon on *Due subordination true freedom*, similarly underlined what he described as this 'necessity of legal subordination'. God's will in matters of government is that 'the head is naturally to rule, and be supreme; and the inferior parts in all their several degrees to obey and be subordinate'.[16]

We are also shown that these requirements were unwaveringly accepted by Christ and his Apostles. Charles Weston, prebendary of Durham, in a sermon of 1793 on *The authority of government and duty of obedience*, celebrated the figure of Christ as 'a pattern of submission'.[17] He agrees with Salter and Fawel that we must 'cheerfully and conscientiously cooperate with the exertions of government' and offer 'ready submission and obedience'.[18] This is one of the moments when Christ shows us the true way. 'He is all subjection; he interferes not with the jurisdiction of the laws'; rather, 'his own obedience and deference to authority' is unfailing.[19] Fawel and Hales both make use of an anachronistic but topical vocabulary to press home the point. Fawel assures us that Christ was 'a sincere friend to the civil rights of princes',[20] while Hales characterises him as 'a true and faithful patriot' as well as 'a sober and discreet reformer'.[21] This is the political moral we need to draw from the incomparable example of his life.[22]

---

[13] Salter 1791, p. 5. See also Churton 1790.    [14] Agutter 1792, p. 5.
[15] Salter 1791, p. 22.    [16] Fawel 1793, pp. 9, 16.    [17] Weston 1793, p. 10.
[18] Weston 1793, p. 19.    [19] Weston 1793, pp. 9–10.    [20] Fawel 1793, p. 7.
[21] Hales 1794, p. 5.    [22] Hales 1794, pp. 5, 16.

The duty of passive obedience is said to be further confirmed by the teachings of the Apostles. Fawel observes that, although they lived 'under the most arbitrary and tyrannical government', yet 'on all occasions they obey the decrees of those governments, and command others to do the same'.[23] Hales similarly notes that the Apostles as well as Christ exhort everyone 'from the highest to the lowest to be amenable to the lawful government in being'.[24] The Apostle most frequently cited in this context is St Paul, especially when he argues in the Epistle to the Romans that every soul should be subject to the higher powers, and that any who resist will receive damnation.[25] Hales even alters the wording of the Authorised Version to press home the relevance of St Paul's argument, quoting him as declaring that 'there is no sovereign power but from God', and that 'they that resist shall receive to themselves punishment from the magistrates'.[26]

If our primary obligation is to accept subordination, what becomes of our civil liberty? The answer we are given is that the best way of exercising our freedom is to discharge our duty of non-resistance. As Salter explains, 'where the spirit of the Lord is, there and there alone will be true liberty', so that 'human liberty, in relation to government, can be nothing other than obedience'.[27] James Wemyss, in a sermon of 1794 entitled *A scriptural view of kings and magistrates*, summarised the almost paradoxical conclusion to which these writers are led. To affirm that you are free is to say that you are 'at liberty to do all the good you are capable of to yourselves, your fellow-Christians and your fellow-creatures'.[28] The demands of the revolutionaries for freedom from subjection and the rights of man are consequently an impious violation of Christian principles. As Fawel had already argued, by contrast with 'the unparalleled mischief and ruin' that the French have brought upon themselves, the British live in a land that already enjoys real liberty, the defining feature of which is a willingness to 'submit ourselves to every ordinance of man for the Lord's sake'.[29]

### The Liberal Response

Although the conservative case was vociferously argued, it proved incapable of commanding much support – or even respect. Thomas Gisborne, although an Anglican clergyman, felt able to assure readers of his *Principles of moral philosophy* that all such doctrines are by now 'so

---

[23] Fawel 1793, pp. 4–5.    [24] Hales 1794, pp. 21–2.
[25] See, for example, Wemyss 1794, pp. 21–2. Cf. Romans 13.1–2.
[26] Hales 1794, pp. 20–1.    [27] Salter 1791, p. 13.    [28] Wemyss 1794, p. 34.
[29] Fawell 1793, p. 18. See also Weston 1793, p. 14.

generally exploded as not to require a particular discussion'.[30] During the early 1790s, however, a much more powerful line of attack on the rights of man and the ideal of liberty as independence began to develop. An extensive group of legal and political theorists came forward to reaffirm that liberty amounts to nothing more than an absence of impediments or restraint, and to deploy this claim as a means of shaping a middle way that was equally opposed, as its proponents liked to say, to the fanatical extremes of Paine as well as Burke.[31] These self-consciously middle-of-the road writers were far from regarding the British constitution as beyond criticism, but they were steadfastly opposed to any demands for radical reform. Picking up the terminology already used by Jeremy Bentham, they explained that what they wanted was neither revolution nor reaction, but a more liberal approach to moral and political life.[32] They saw themselves as living in a liberal age,[33] and as speaking in the name of liberty for a programme of piecemeal social reform designed to remove unnecessary restraints and free the people to pursue their happiness in their own way.[34]

The general outlook of this first generation of self-avowed liberals is well captured in a tract published in 1793 by the King's Chaplain in Scotland, Dr Thomas Somerville, under the title *The effects of the French Revolution*. Somerville sees the present age as one in which there has been an increasing diffusion of what he commends as liberal principles.[35] The French Revolution at first seemed the greatest instance of this social progress, as it was 'urged by the most pressing necessity and justified by the most honourable motives'.[36] But we now see, 'with grief and disappointment', that France is 'plunging at once into the deepest abyss of barbarism'.[37] The moral is that we must learn to chart a course between two extremes. There is no doubt that 'the consequences of the revolution

---

[30] Gisborne 1798, p. 289.

[31] See, for example, Williamson 1792, pp. 238–9. These writers might be said to include Jeremy Bentham in his *Anarchical fallacies* of *c*.1795, in which he denounced natural rights as 'nonsense upon stilts'. But Bentham's text remained unpublished in English until John Bowring's edition of 1843.

[32] Bentham 1988, p. 7 and p. 11n.      [33] See *Reasons for seeking a repeal* 1790, p. 7.

[34] The earliest uses of the term 'liberal', applied in this familiar modern sense, have generally been traced to the early decades of the nineteenth century. See, for example, the discussion in Clark 1994, pp. 143–6. But many of the writers from the 1790s whom I discuss already described themselves as liberals in this sense. Cookson 1982 also singles out a separate group from the same period, the 'friends of peace', who likewise described their stance as a liberal one. There is no overlap, however, between this group and the liberal political writers I discuss. The friends of peace on whom Cookson concentrates were mainly Nonconformist writers aiming to promote what they described as rational Christianity by contrast with superstition and with the views of the Anglican establishment. See Cookson 1982, pp. 2–4, 26–8, 87–8.

[35] Somerville 1793, p. 12.      [36] Somerville 1793, p. 13.      [37] Somerville 1793, p. 13.

in France have been fatal to the interests of liberty', and that the excesses associated with revolutionary change must at all costs be avoided.[38] But we must take care not to become 'hostile to every sober plan for the correction of abuse and the extension of public prosperity', thereby incurring the danger 'of obstructing liberal designs and retarding the progress of improvement'.[39]

Several academic writers played a forceful role in promoting this vision of political life. John Bartlam, a Fellow of Merton College Oxford, published *An essay on liberty* in 1794, and Robert Willis, a Fellow of Gonville and Caius College Cambridge, followed with his *Philosophical sketches of the principles of society and government* in 1795.[40] A still more prominent role was played by a number of legal commentators associated with the Inns of Court. One of the first to put forward the liberal case was Richard Hey of the Inner Temple, who had earlier helped to initiate the attack on Richard Price in 1776. Hey published a tract entitled *Happiness and rights* in 1792, in which he denounced Paine and other revolutionaries for playing the tyrant while purporting to defend the ideal of liberty.[41] A year later Charles Sheridan (elder brother of the playwright), who had studied at Lincoln's Inn and later became a member of Parliament, published his *Essay upon the true principles of civil liberty and free government*.[42] He too mounted a virulent attack on Paine,[43] while at the same time acknowledging the need for a number of reforms that, as he put it, require the most liberal attention from everyone.[44] Thomas Townshend of Gray's Inn similarly condemned the radical critics of the British constitution in his *Considerations on the theoretical spirit of the times*, in which he pleaded for 'liberal intentions' to be pursued instead of demands for revolutionary change.[45] Soon afterwards Charles Watkins, a leading expert on property law, produced his *Reflections on government*, calling on the unprejudiced and peaceable to renounce debate and explore the paths of utility and truth.[46] These years also saw the circulation of numerous anonymous works on rights and liberty with a markedly legal bent. They included *A plain and candid statement of facts* in 1790, *The two systems of the social compact* in 1793 and *The freeman's vade-mecum* in 1798, in which the author particularly called for political debate to be grounded on the exercise of our faculties in a more liberal style.[47]

---

[38] Somerville 1793, p. 42.    [39] Somerville 1793, p. 43.
[40] The first edition appeared anonymously, but when a second was issued in 1796 Willis's name and affiliation appeared on the title page.
[41] Hey 1792, p. 12.
[42] On Sheridan (and specifically his comments on the 1772 coup in Sweden) see Skjönsberg 2022.
[43] Sheridan 1793, pp. v–vii.    [44] Sheridan 1793, p. 80.    [45] Townshend 1793, p. 40.
[46] Watkins 1796, p. vi.    [47] *The freeman's vade-mecum* 1798, p. xix.

The years following the outbreak of the French Revolution also saw the publication of numerous treatises by clerical writers who likewise attacked the radicals in the name of a less destructive and more liberal approach to political life. Among these were several prominent Anglican spokesmen, including Robert Nares, chaplain to the Duke of York, whose *Principles of government* was published in 1792,[48] as well as Thomas Gisborne, who added a substantial chapter on civil liberty to the revised edition of his *Principles of moral philosophy* in 1798. A number of anonymous tracts also appeared in which the style and vocabulary strongly suggest a clerical authorship, notably *The true Briton's catechism* and *Equality no liberty*, both of which appeared in 1793. A yet more important contribution was made by clerical spokesmen from outside the established Church, and especially by a number of Scottish Presbyterian and English Dissenting ministers. The most prominent Presbyterians were John Young, whose *Liberty and equality* appeared in 1794, and James Roger, who published his *Essay on government* in 1797. Among the English Dissenting writers, the most formidable was David Williamson, a Dissenting minister in Cumberland, who issued his *Lectures on civil and religious liberty* in 1792, after which a number of similar works followed, including Thomas Wood's *Essay on civil government* of 1796 and George Watson's *Thoughts on government* of 1799.

One of the principal aspirations of all these self-styled liberal theorists was to discredit the allegedly enlightened principles that had been applied to defend the American Revolution and the yet more alarming revolution in France. Here they generally pursued two closely related lines of attack. One was directed against the belief that civil liberty consists in independence, and against the arguments about equality and the rights of man that had come to be associated with this vision of liberty. Their other assault was on the radical account of the relationship between freedom and government, and in particular on the contention of Paine and other revolutionaries that there can be no civil liberty except under a constitution in which all power remains in the hands of the people.[49]

Turning to challenge the first of these positions, the liberal theorists simply revert to the view of civil liberty that the enemies of the American Revolution had drawn from the tradition of natural jurisprudence stemming from Grotius, Hobbes, Pufendorf and their disciples.

---

[48] Nares also published an abridgment in 1793.

[49] For a different approach to the emergence of 'liberal' writers at this time see Cookson 1982 and Burrow 1988. Burrow's stated aim (pp. 2–6) is to uncover continuities between eighteenth-century Whiggism and nineteenth-century liberalism. But I argue that, in discussions about civil and political liberty, what we find is rupture rather than continuity. Neither Cookson nor Burrow discusses any of the figures I single out.

They accordingly begin in the usual style of the jurists by asking what life would be like in the absence of law. Among the legal writers, Bartlam particularly stresses that in this natural condition everyone would have been equally 'free and independent'.[50] Watkins also speaks of a time when 'men were by nature equal', so that 'no one could have had authority over another', and everyone had an equal freedom to act as they chose.[51] A number of the clerical writers express themselves in similar terms. Williamson argues that 'antecedent to the institution of society' men were 'under God the sole judges of their own actions and the only defenders of their own liberty',[52] while the author of *The true Briton's catechism* likewise speaks of the absolute rights that 'belong to individuals in a state of nature' and 'may be called the natural liberty of mankind'.[53]

Continuing to echo the jurists, the liberal theorists next declare that it makes no sense to claim that these rights are inalienable. On the contrary, it is essential that they should be alienated. Here the legal writers employ an appropriately juridical vocabulary, referring to the need for us to abridge, restrict and even resign them up.[54] The clerical writers prefer to speak in more spiritual terms. Williamson stresses the need for 'a general renunciation',[55] while the author of *The true Briton's catechism* describes how, 'when man enters into society, he makes a sacrifice of part of his natural right'.[56] The point on which they all agree is that, as Wood expresses it, 'every man, when he becomes the member of a civil community, alienates a part of his natural rights', which are then 'transferred to the laws and the magistrate'. He adds that 'this single consideration is sufficient to show that the right to civil liberty is alienable, though, in the vehemence of men's zeal for it, and in the language of some political remonstrances, it has often been pronounced an unalienable right'.[57]

The recognition that we need to relinquish our natural rights is said to stem from our understanding of human nature. Here the liberal theorists like to begin by reiterating the long-established Whig belief that our most rooted desire is for a life of happiness. As Willis affirms, a society is nothing other than 'an assemblage which has regard to the well-being and happiness of the existing members'.[58] The vital question, as Watkins puts it, is accordingly what will 'add strength to society and make the people happy and free'.[59] The issue is one that the clerical writers raise

[50] Bartlam 1794, p. 5.    [51] Watkins 1796, pp. 58, 59, 61.
[52] Williamson 1792, pp. 18, 57, 64.    [53] *The true Briton's catechism* 1793, p. 5.
[54] Bartlam 1794, p. 5; Willis 1795, pp. 15, 36; Watkins 1796, p. 61.
[55] Williamson 1792, p. 75.    [56] *The true Briton's catechism* 1793, p. 6.
[57] Wood 1796, p. 23.    [58] Willis 1795, p. 11.
[59] Watkins 1796, p. 3. See also Hey 1792, pp. 54, 61.

with particular emphasis. Nares calls for us to study the constitutions that contain the ingredients necessary to 'produce the happiness of men in society'.[60] Williamson agrees that, because the end of society is 'the protection and happiness of all its members', we need to determine what kind of constitutional order will promote their happiness.[61] Sheridan closely echoes these sentiments: we need to find out what form of state is best suited to ensuring 'the preservation of civil liberty and thus happiness'.[62]

The first answer they give is that there can be no prospect of happiness in the absence of security. But they also insist that there can be no security in our natural condition of life. The clerical writers particularly underline this point, and Williamson does so at considerable length. The happiest nations are 'those in which the greatest degree of freedom is united with the most perfect safety of individuals and of the whole collective body'.[63] But in the state of nature, in which our liberty and rights were unbounded, 'this was the very circumstance which excluded men from the greatest blessings of life, quiet and protection'. The natural condition of mankind was one in which 'the liberty of all was inconsistent with the safety of all'.[64]

To understand why this was so, we need only reflect on the springs of human action. Here the clerical writers are sometimes inclined to place a puritanical emphasis on man's inherent wickedness. This is particularly true of Nares, who likes to dwell on 'the imperfections of man', his liability to 'great perversion and depravity' and his tendency 'to be foolish and wicked'.[65] Usually, however, they prefer to follow the writers on civil liberty of the late 1770s, many of whom had already associated themselves with Hobbes's claim that man is not fitted by nature for a life of peace. Willis quotes on his title page Hobbes's claim in *De cive* that 'nature has given each man a right to all things',[66] adding that 'the right of the strongest is the only right which a state of nature confers'.[67] Williamson observes that, although in the state of nature 'the unlimited exercise of freedom allowed you to trample on some weak and pusillanimous man, it exposed you in your turn to the violence of some person whom nature had armed with superior strength'.[68] This being the nature of man, these writers agree with Hobbes that life in the state of nature would inevitably turn into a condition of endless war.[69] As Bartlam puts

---

[60] Nares 1793, p. 10.    [61] Williamson 1792, pp. 20, 145.    [62] Sheridan 1793, p. 53.
[63] Williamson 1792, p. 58.    [64] Williamson 1792, pp. 57–8.
[65] Nares 1792, p. 4 and Nares 1793, p. 10.
[66] Hobbes 1998, I. X, p. 28. Willis quotes from the original Latin version of the text: *Natura dedit uniquique ius in omnia.*
[67] Willis 1795, p. 23.    [68] Williamson 1792, p. 57.
[69] Hobbes 2012, vol. 2, ch. 13, p. 192.

it, 'the wildness of caprice and the fury of passion' would rule out any possibility of enjoying the blessings of peace.[70] If we were to live without law, Nares agrees, we would condemn ourselves to 'a state of savage wildness'.[71] Williamson concludes that the resulting condition of anarchy 'would be thus divided between the acting and the suffering of oppression', and everyone would ultimately be left defenceless.[72]

This explains why, if we are to have any prospect of security and happiness, we have no alternative but to surrender our rights to a sovereign power capable of keeping the peace. This pivotal change is described in a variety of ways. Some refer to the need for submission, others to the need for subordination, but generally they prefer to speak of the need to subject ourselves.[73] Bartlam lays much emphasis on 'the necessity of subjection to civil government', and how 'obedience becomes the indispensable duty of all'.[74] Watkins adds in explicitly Hobbesian terms that 'society therefore must, from its very nature, subject men to general laws, and man owes obedience in return for protection'.[75] The author of *Equality no liberty* draws the underlying moral with memorable briskness: 'sovereignty and subjection are correlative, so that sovereignty without subjection is a contradiction in terms'.[76]

If we subject ourselves to sovereign power, what becomes of our liberty? Following Hobbes once more, the liberal theorists respond that it now depends on the silence of the law.[77] As Bartlam explains, 'in societies which are regulated by general rules', liberty simply means 'not being restrained by any law'.[78] Richard Hey concludes that this enables us to supply an indisputable definition of the term: where I am 'not hindered or forbidden, I have liberty'.[79] Many other legal writers concur that 'liberty' 'will always be found in greatest perfection' where 'there are the fewest restraints upon speech and actions',[80] and conversely that liberty is destroyed whenever there is 'restraint of the will of the subject'.[81] The clerical writers generally speak in the same terms, and in doing so provide some of the most resounding summaries. Young takes it to be manifest that liberty must always consist in 'following the dictates of one's own will without any restraint'.[82] Gisborne agrees that 'liberty and restraint are opposed

---

[70] Bartlam 1794, p. 5.    [71] Nares 1792, p. 35.    [72] Williamson 1792, pp. 57, 58.
[73] On submission see Williamson 1792, pp. 58, 273, 274; on subordination see Watkins 1796, p. 4 and Watson 1799, p. 20.
[74] Bartlam 1794, pp. 6–7.
[75] Watkins 1796, p. 8. For Hobbes on protection and obedience see Hobbes 2012, vol. 3, A Review and Conclusion, p. 1141.
[76] *Equality no liberty* 1792, p. 17.    [77] Hobbes 2012, vol. 2, ch. 21, p. 340.
[78] See, for example, Bartlam 1794, p. 5.    [79] Hey 1792, p. 44.
[80] *The freeman's vade-mecum* 1798, p. 44.    [81] Watkins 1796, p. 62.
[82] Young 1794, p. 80.

each to the other', and that when we reach the limits of restraint we are left with liberty.[83] Nares sums up in his usual grandiloquent style. 'Liberty in the most extended sense of the word is the power of acting without any species of restraints.'[84] The presence of natural restraints, or else the imposition of moral constraints, are what take away liberty.[85] But wherever 'every man may do, without restraint, whatever may be pleasing or advantageous to himself and not injurious to other individuals or to the community, liberty is sufficiently established'.[86]

As the liberal theorists move towards this conclusion, it is striking that they have almost nothing to say about one aspect of natural rights theory that the radical writers of the previous two decades had almost always emphasised. They had generally argued (Catharine Macaulay was a rare exception) that one reason why the natural liberty of man must be inalienable is that our freedom is a natural right granted to us by God as the author of nature. The proponents of the new view of liberty appear to feel no obligation to engage with this argument. Rather than mentioning any theological grounds for speaking of inalienability, they focus entirely on the psychological grounds for concluding that it is indispensable for our natural liberty to be alienated. This is particularly noticeable in the contributions made by the academic writers from Oxford and Cambridge. The name of God is never so much as mentioned by Richard Hey in his tract on rights, nor by John Bartlam in his essay on liberty, nor by Robert Willis in his treatise on government.[87] With this silence, they begin to introduce an almost unprecedentedly secular tone into their accounts of the freedom of subjects and the powers of the state.

\*\*\*\*\*\*\*\*\*\*

The other line of attack mounted by the liberal theorists on the radicals and revolutionaries was directed against their accounts of the relationship between freedom and government. Bartlam sarcastically dismisses those who 'would lead us to suppose that the perfections of freedom are exclusively peculiar to a democracy',[88] while Willis condemns the view 'that right is coeval with man's existence' as 'a fatal delusion' now spreading itself over Europe.[89] The author of *The true Briton's catechism* denounces the fallacy and malignity of which Paine was guilty when he argued that we have no liberty unless we live in a free state,[90] while Sheridan deplores 'the absurdity, the falsehood and the danger' of supposing that civil liberty

---

[83] Gisborne 1798, p. 345.    [84] Nares 1792, p. 24.    [85] Nares 1792, pp. 26, 27.
[86] Nares 1792, pp. 29–30.
[87] God's name appears once in Bartlam 1794, but only in a quotation (p. 27) from Richard Hooker.
[88] Bartlam 1794, p. 11.    [89] Willis 1795, pp. 19, 21.
[90] *The true Briton's catechism* 1793, pp. 8, 40.

can be upheld only under a form of government in which everyone remains, as Price had put it, his own legislator on terms of equality with everyone else.[91]

The allegedly enlightened claim that liberty requires democracy is said to be doubly dangerous and mistaken. There is in the first place no reason to suppose that the establishment of a republican or democratic regime would offer any guarantee that the freedom of the people would be upheld. As Townshend observes, the ruinous path followed by the French Revolution has demonstrated the absurdity of any such belief. The people were at first informed 'in all the pomp of French wisdom that all men are equal', and that 'equality and liberty are the right of all'. But what ensued was 'bloody tyranny' and 'the present wreck of society in France'.[92] Roger speaks in yet more highly coloured terms of 'the late unhappy French revolution' in which turbulent and factious representatives took pleasure 'from the magnitude of political mischief they could produce', with the result that a murderous regime was established and 'the killers of royalty soon imbrued their hands in each other's blood'.[93] The moral is said to be that 'republics are fraught with danger and uncertainty' and 'bring us no promise of happiness'.[94]

Some of the clerical writers carry this argument much further, claiming that violence and tyranny are the only outcomes to be expected from any political movement grounded on the dangerously mistaken belief that freedom consists in independence. According to the author of *Equality no liberty*, what we are witnessing in France is 'an admirable example of republican liberty, which hath ever united within itself the two odious extremes of tyranny and licentiousness', and which merely serves 'to introduce confusion and anarchy'.[95] Nares in his *Principles of government* emphatically agrees that 'a popular assembly is the region both of prejudice and passion', and asserts that 'an Assembly of that nature cannot think'. The only possible outcome is that they will 'contrive that the laws shall be directed to their own individual advantage' and not to securing the liberty of the people. This, he concludes, 'has been the general history of democratic legislation', and shows why it must never be encouraged.[96]

The first objection is thus that democracy is no guarantee of liberty. The other and more fundamental objection is that it is equally possible to have liberty without democracy. Among the legal writers, Watkins is particularly explicit that, if a king derives his power from the laws, and if the laws are well suited to the society at large, then every subject will be

---

[91] Sheridan 1793, pp. 25, 28. Cf. Price 1991, p. 24.    [92] Townshend 1793, pp. 6, 8, 11.
[93] Roger 1797, pp. 22, 23, 25.    [94] Roger 1797, pp. 15, 19.
[95] *Equality no liberty* 1792, pp. 11–12.    [96] Nares 1792, pp. 42–3.

'equally free in such a monarchy as in a republic'.[97] Sheridan develops the same argument at greater length. He takes it to be obvious that, because everyone remains free as a subject so long as they are not restrained in the exercise of their lawful rights, civil liberty can in principle be equally well enjoyed 'under an Antoninus, an Aurelius or an Alfred', or as it was in Peru 'under the mild, beneficent and just government of their Incas'.[98] It is possible to 'enjoy the highest possible degree of civil liberty without possessing a shadow of political liberty' in the sense of having an active involvement in government.[99]

The clerical writers are no less eager to underline the point. Nares observes that 'every country not in a state of savage wildness has some established constitution of its government', and emphasises that under any constitution in which 'all the most important ends of equal law are fully answered' it will be possible for 'liberty, security and happiness' to be fully achieved.[100] Roger echoes Paley's suggestion that, under a wise and beneficent ruler, we might even discover that the best species of government for the maximising of individual liberty is unlimited monarchy.[101] This being so, as Bartlam summarises, the claim of the radicals and the revolutionaries that it is possible to live freely only in a so-called free state is nothing more than a dangerous error 'propagated by those who, seduced by the mere name of liberty, would impede its best enjoyments and destroy its most important ends'.[102]

Although the liberal theorists agree that individual liberty can in principle be enjoyed under any system of government, they are anxious to establish that one particular form is best suited to promoting happiness. The optimum arrangement will always be a mixed and balanced constitution embodying a separation of powers. The legislative needs to comprise a mixture of monarchical and aristocratic as well as democratic elements, so that different social and economic interests can be heard and reconciled. Each element will be able to check any encroachments from the other two, so that the whole system will be held in equilibrium. As Watkins summarises, the best system will thus be one based on 'a contrariety of interests which, by their mutual checks upon each other, preserve the safety and happiness of the whole'.[103] We need to recognise that 'it is jealousy of power which preserves the freedom of the state'.[104]

These criteria are said to be fully met by the existing structure of the British constitution. This patriotic tone of self-congratulation had already become popular in conservative circles as a means of dampening

---

[97] Watkins 1796, p. 7.     [98] Sheridan 1793, p. 48.     [99] Sheridan 1793, p. 49.
[100] Nares 1792, pp. 35–6.     [101] Roger 1797, p. 11.     [102] Bartlam 1794, pp. 11–12.
[103] Watkins 1796, pp. 10–11.     [104] Watkins 1796, p. 13.

enthusiasm for the experiments in France, and numerous pamphleteers had stepped forward to assure the British people that their constitution stood in no need of change.[105] Some liberal theorists speak in no less reactionary terms,[106] but most were eager to distance themselves from the enemies of all reform, and they sometimes ridicule Burke for what Williamson describes as his 'violent predilection for the government of England' and his refusal to recognise that in many respects it is indefensible.[107] They generally acknowledge that an intractable difficulty needs to be faced if a proper balance is to be struck between freedom and government. Watkins in his *Reflections on government* offers a forthright summary of the dilemma. Everyone 'is of right entitled to the highest possible degree of liberty', so that the aim of reformation needs to be that of maximising freedom from restraint.[108] But the law operates by means of imposing restraints, so that all laws, 'whether made with or without our consent', are prima facie destructive of liberty.[109] How, then, can the imposition of any law be justified?

No one ever proposes that, because liberty is the overriding political value, the answer must be that he governs best who governs least. This almost anarchical version of liberalism did not rise to prominence in Anglo-American political thinking until more than a generation later, when Herbert Spencer and William Sumner published their attacks on what Sumner was to stigmatise as 'state interference'.[110] The liberal theorists of the 1790s unequivocally reject this view of freedom and government, and no one more forcefully than Williamson in his lectures on civil and religious liberty. If, he argues, freedom means exemption from restraint, then there is little justice in the claim 'that nations are happy in proportion to the extent of their freedom'. Prior to the establishment of law, when liberty was unbounded, this was 'the very circumstance which excluded men from the greatest blessings of life'. It is not liberty itself, but liberty 'guarded by a vigorous exertion of equal laws', which 'constitutes the true happiness of nations'. 'Those are the happiest in which the greatest degree of freedom is united with the most perfect safety of individuals and of the whole collective body' under the rule of law.[111]

With this commitment Williamson already points to the solution offered by most of the liberal theorists to the dilemma they had raised. We simply need to ensure that the effect of imposing any given law will be

---

[105] See, for example, Cocks 1791; Jones 1792; Parsons 1793.
[106] See, for example, Bartlam 1794, pp. 25–6; Willis 1795, pp. 154, 159.
[107] Williamson 1792, pp. 263, 311.    [108] Watkins 1796, p. 64.
[109] Watkins 1796, pp. 62–3.    [110] See De Dijn 2020, pp. 304–7.
[111] Williamson 1792, pp. 57–8.

to contribute to the ultimate goal of promoting happiness. Bentham in his *Fragment on government* had already enunciated this cardinal principle in the form of the proposition that the greatest happiness of the greatest number must be treated as 'the measure of right and wrong', and had added that the tendency of any act to promote the greatest happiness 'is what we style its utility'.[112] The liberal theorists of the 1790s never speak about the greatest happiness, but they employ several formulations that come close to this way of expressing their central contention about the ends that law should serve. They frequently refer to the value of promoting the public good,[113] and Watkins quotes Beccaria to the effect that the test of any law should be whether it promotes 'the greatest good of the greatest number'.[114] They also speak of utility as the proper test of the value of a law. Bartlam reflects that mankind must have come to see that subjection to government was what 'pointed to general utility',[115] and Watkins offers it as a general principle that laws limiting liberty should do so only in the name of 'civil utility'.[116] Their usual preference, however, was to speak of the need to ensure that law promotes the general welfare. Here they appear to draw on the formula that Paley had used in his *Principles* of 1785, in which he had concluded that civil liberty can be defined as 'not being restrained by any law, but what conduces in a greater degree to the public welfare'.[117] Gisborne quotes this definition, duly attributing it to Paley,[118] while other clerical writers speak in similar terms about the welfare of society and the state.[119] The legal writers exhibit the same preference, and in several instances they too appear to rely on Paley's account. Townshend warns of the need to avoid any actions 'prejudicial to the general welfare',[120] and Willis agrees that what must above all be considered is 'the welfare of society' as a whole.[121]

As soon as the liberal theorists ask themselves what the general welfare requires, they feel obliged to recognise that the British constitution is far from perfect. They admit that Parliament is in need of being reformed. The rotten boroughs must be disenfranchised, the franchise ought to be extended to include small property holders, and the new industrial towns

---

[112] Bentham 1988, pp. 3, 25–6.
[113] On the public good see *A plain and candid statement* 1790, pp. 14, 20, 43; Hey 1792, p. 46; *The true Briton's catechism* 1793, p. 7. On the general good see Nares 1792, p. 12; Young 1794, p. 81.
[114] Watkins 1796, p. 33.     [115] Bartlam 1794, p. 6.
[116] Watkins 1796, pp. 27, 43. See also Williamson 1792, pp. 89, 116 on the test of public utility.
[117] Paley 1785, p. 441.     [118] Gisborne 1798, p. 347.
[119] See Nares 1792, p. 20; *Equality no liberty* 1792, p. 19; Wood 1796, p. 7.
[120] Townshend 1793, p. 26.
[121] Willis 1795, p. 40. On the need to 'look to the welfare of society' see also *The two systems of the social compact* 1793, p. 31; Bartlam 1794, p. 5.

should be represented.[122] They also concede that it would be in the public interest to abolish the penal statutes limiting eligibility for public office to members of the Church of England. Writing as a Dissenter, Williamson argues that such a reform is a requirement of justice. When a majority decides to 'make the approbation of their religious sentiments a necessary qualification for places of power and trust, they render the laws partial and by consequence they render them unjust'.[123] Watkins in his *Reflections on government* writes in more robustly secular terms. 'Society was instituted for the regulation and benefit of man in this world', so that the legal arrangements underpinning society have nothing to do with any other world.[124] If someone 'believes in transubstantiation, or in consubstantiation, or that the substance remains as before, what is it to anyone else?'[125] To interfere in religion 'cannot possibly be within the province of the civil magistrate', and all attempts to regulate religious observance ought to be given up.[126]

The liberal theorists are anxious to make it clear, however, that they are not calling for any revolutionary changes, and they remain implacably opposed to most of the major reforms that Richard Price and his followers had wished to see enacted. Apart from Williamson, they have nothing to say about the need to abolish the slave trade and the institution of slavery.[127] The question is never raised in any of the legal or academic tracts on civil liberty of the 1790s, and the only clerical writer to devote a work to the subject was Thomas Gisborne in his pamphlet *Of slavery and the slave trade* in 1792, in which he upholds a highly equivocal stance. He opposes the slave trade,[128] but he is willing and even anxious to defend the institution of slavery, arguing that there will always be two conditions under which, 'agreeably to natural justice, an individual may be reduced by force' to the condition of being a slave, one being indemnification and the other punishment.[129]

The liberal theorists are no less emphatically opposed to the demand for universal suffrage. Nares retorts that the proposal is 'neither requisite nor practicable',[130] while the author of *The true Briton's catechism* warns that it would be nothing less than fatal to accept such an intemperate demand for change.[131] As for the rights of women, they treat the idea of female suffrage – if they mention it at all – as an obvious *reductio ad absurdum*. Nares and Williamson both point out that to speak of every

[122] See, for example, Williamson 1792, p. 265; Nares 1792, pp. 51–2; *A plain and candid statement* 1790, p. 56.
[123] Williamson 1792, p. 273.    [124] Watkins 1796, p. 42.    [125] Watkins 1796, p. 42.
[126] Watkins 1796, p. 43.    [127] Williamson 1792, pp. 242, 251–3, 289.
[128] Gisborne 1792, p. 15.    [129] Gisborne 1792, pp. 6–7.    [130] Nares 1792, p. 48.
[131] *The true Briton's catechism* 1793, pp. 41–2.

individual having a right to vote is to say that this must be 'the right of one sex as well as of the other'.[132] Both take this conclusion to be so absurd that no more needs to be said. But what about the rights of women more generally? About this question they have nothing to say at all. The contributions of Mary Wollstonecraft and other feminist writers are never criticised; they are simply ignored.

The conclusion at which all these writers arrive is thus that no changes to the constitution should be contemplated unless they can be accommodated within its existing structure. While this makes them hostile to any encroachments of prerogative power, they are above all anxious to ensure that the project of reform never begins to slide in the alarming direction of democratic rule. Perhaps the most vivid summary of their fears can be found in a memorable cartoon published by James Gillray in April 1793. William Pitt is shown steering a small boat, with Britannia seated in the bow, towards an island on which a castle is flying a flag that reads 'Haven of public happiness'. On Pitt's left we see, arising out of a stormy sea, a towering rock on which the cap of liberty has been placed on a pole at its summit, while to Pitt's right we see a whirlpool in the shape of an inverted royal crown. The caption reads: 'Britannia between Scylla and Charybdis. The vessel of the constitution steered clear of the rock of democracy and the whirlpool of arbitrary power.' Pitt is managing to hold a straight course past the whirlpool, but the imminent danger remains of being dashed to pieces by democracy and its ideal of liberty as independence.

### The Liberal Victory

When the ideal of liberty as independence was challenged in the 1770s, this way of thinking was immediately and incisively reaffirmed. But after the renewed challenge in the 1790s there was no comparable response. This is by no means to say that the ideal was abandoned. But this was not because, as some have sought to argue, liberalism 'was born from the spirit of republicanism' and gave it a new direction.[133] The ideal of liberty as independence survived mainly because the Tory government's increasing authoritarianism helped to provoke a reaction from some of the earliest English socialists, all of whom were ardent proponents of the view that there can be no liberty in the absence of equality and self-government.[134]

---

[132] Nares 1792, p. 48n.; Williamson 1792, p. 270n.
[133] Kalyvas and Katznelson 2008, pp. 4, 14.    [134] Dickinson 1977, pp. 232–69.

One of the fiercest of these reactions came from the Scottish revolutionary John Oswald in his *Review of the constitution* in 1793. Declaring that 'liberty is only another name for equality', Oswald called for the violent overthrow of the British government, arguing that 'no nation unarmed ever rescued their liberty' and that 'it is force alone that can vindicate the rights of the people'.[135] Two years later Thomas Spence published *The end of oppression*, calling in a similar spirit for the forcible redistribution of property in the name of equal liberty. The essence of Spence's case is that the right to hold private property, far from being indispensable to the upholding of liberty, is a right that must be abolished if freedom from dependence and servitude is to be achieved. The people have been 'disinherited and enslaved for ages', and now need to reclaim 'the whole of their rights'.[136] They need to take possession, within each parish, of all landed property and put it to common use. If the landlords resist, 'let the people be firm and desperate, destroying them root and branch'.[137] The aim must be to establish a democratic form of government in place of the present enslaving tyranny, thereby making a transition 'to perfect freedom and felicity'.[138]

Within a generation, this emphasis on the control exercised by an enslaving ruling class was much expanded in the work of Engels and Marx. Both argued that, even before wage-slaves become subject to individual factory owners, they are already controlled by the capitalist class as a whole, whose ownership of the means of production leaves the wage-slave no alternative but to work for them.[139] As Engels was to summarise, they become 'not the slave of a particular individual, but of the whole property-holding class'.[140] A generation later the 'labour republicans' in America were to argue more specifically that co-operative production, with control by workers over the workplace, was a necessary condition of realising the ideal of liberty as independence.[141]

Conceptually these developments are of great importance. The socialist republicans added an economic dimension to the ideal of liberty as independence that had been lacking in earlier accounts. But historically the immediate effect of their call for a fully egalitarian society was to confine the discussion of liberty as independence to the radical margins of political debate.[142] Meanwhile the liberal view of liberty became so

---

[135] Oswald 1793, p. 52.    [136] [Spence] 1795, p. 4.    [137] [Spence] 1795, p. 7.
[138] [Spence] 1795, pp. 7–8. For earlier examples see Kennedy 2013.
[139] See Leipold 2022.    [140] As cited in Leipold 2022, p. 200.
[141] On this movement see Gourevitch 2015.
[142] For a survey of radical ideology in the 1790s see Dickinson 1977, pp. 232–69. On socialism in the 1790s and the marginalising of liberty as independence I am especially indebted to Philp 1985 and Philp 1998. On the beginnings in this period of 'the triumph of modern liberty' see De Dijn 2020, pp. 277–340.

widely accepted that the question of how to think about the relationship between freedom and government soon almost ceased to be discussed. There was some further preaching in the opening decades of the new century about the need for freedom to be subordinated to Christian obedience,[143] and there was some discussion about the proper extent of religious liberty in connection with the Catholic Emancipation Act of 1829.[144] But very few treatises on freedom and government of the kind that had proliferated in the 1790s were published during these years.[145] When James Mill issued his celebrated essay on government in 1820, the topic of civil liberty was barely mentioned.[146] No further works of any significance on the relations between liberty and sovereign power appeared until 1832, when John Austin published the lectures he had been delivering in the University of London under the title *The province of jurisprudence determined*.[147]

Austin's treatise has come to be seen as a founding and classic statement of the utilitarian view of sovereignty and law. But it is no less appropriate, and may perhaps be more illuminating, to view it as a summation of the liberal view of freedom and government that had first been widely articulated in the 1790s. Austin reiterates the tenets of the self-styled liberal theorists almost in the form of a series of slogans, and in a manner calculated to suggest that the claims he is making are by now beyond dispute. He no longer sees any need even to mention the belief that the antonym of liberty might be subjection rather than restraint. He simply assures his readers that liberty 'can mean nothing else but exemption from restraint'.[148]

Like the liberal theorists of the 1790s, Austin takes the paramount purpose of any independent political society to be the advancement of human happiness.[149] He suggests that, if prospective subjects consider this to be the motive for imposing sovereign power, they will obey for that reason alone. But he argues that the sole cause of obedience common to all political societies is a recognition that this is the only means to avoid the anarchy of the state of nature.[150] The suggestion that sovereign power arises out of an act of consent and an original covenant is dismissed not merely as false but superfluous. A sufficient reason for subjection will always be that of securing protection from the violence of our fellow

---

[143] See, for example, Fawcett 1808; Griffin 1809; Goddard 1819; Plowden 1824.
[144] See, for example, Pearce 1827; Parkin 1828; Fox 1829.
[145] The only significant exceptions are [Evans] 1810 and Montague 1819.
[146] Mill's essay first appeared in the *Encyclopaedia Britannica* in 1820; it was published in book form, together with other essays, in 1823.
[147] Rumble 1995, p. xxviii. On Austin's view of law and sovereignty see Lobban 2007, pp. 173–87. See also Rumble 1995, pp. vii–xxiv.
[148] Austin 1995, p. 160.     [149] Austin 1995, p. 254.     [150] Austin 1995, pp. 243, 247.

subjects.[151] Here Austin cites Hobbes with strong approval for arguing that, although we may fear that such unlimited power may bring bad consequences, the alternative would always be worse.[152]

Austin goes on to emphasise that the political power we establish over ourselves must necessarily be unlimited. Drawing our attention to the fact that he is 'borrowing the language of Hobbes',[153] he argues that law simply reflects and affirms the will of the sovereign, whose power is incapable of being legally limited, and can be used to alter or abrogate any law at pleasure.[154] We live in a state of complete subjection to law, which operates by compelling and restraining every refractory subject in such a way as to prevent them from acting in a manner contrary to public advantage.[155] The rights of subjects consequently amount to nothing more than creations of the law, and take the form of specific liberties from legal obligation allowed to us by our government.[156]

As Austin admits, however, there is an objection to confront at this point. 'Wherein (it may be asked) doth political liberty consist'?[157] He closely echoes the liberal theorists of the 1790s in characterising the dilemma that needs to be resolved: on the one hand, law operates by imposing restraints; but on the other hand, liberty 'can mean nothing else but exemption from restraint'.[158] Austin responds that the objection can easily be dismissed, and takes the opportunity to ridicule the ignorant and bawling fanatics who try to stun us with their pother about liberty.[159] They fail to understand that there is a clear principle in the light of which it is always possible to determine whether any given restraint on liberty is justified.[160] The test is whether the imposition of the restraint will act as a means of furthering the common weal.[161] This is what Austin describes as the justifying test of general utility.[162] If a law is useful in promoting public advantage, then it will ultimately be helpful in advancing human happiness, and will consequently be justified as a contribution to the ultimate purpose of government.[163]

One striking feature of Austin's argument is his readiness to appeal to the authority of Hobbes.[164] As we have seen, a number of liberal theorists in the 1790s had already invoked Hobbes's vision of the state of nature as a condition of war, his associated claim that we have no alternative but to subject ourselves to absolute sovereign power, and his inference that the

---

[151] Austin 1995, pp. 224–5, 246–7, 258, 279.    [152] Austin 1995, p. 228.
[153] Austin 1995, pp. 165, 282.    [154] Austin 1995, pp. 165, 188, 212, 218, 282.
[155] Austin 1995, pp. 160, 166, 171, 183, 212.    [156] Austin 1995, p. 224.
[157] Austin 1995, p. 223.    [158] Austin 1995, p. 160.    [159] Austin 1995, p. 224.
[160] Austin 1995, p. 224.    [161] Austin 1995, pp. 224, 226.
[162] Austin 1995, pp. 242, 260.    [163] Austin 1995, pp. 242, 260.
[164] For a comparison between Hobbes and Austin see Murphy 2016.

rights remaining to us take the form of privileges arising from the silence of the law. Austin reiterates all these quintessentially Hobbesian themes, but he is far more willing than the earlier liberal theorists to express his admiration for Hobbes. He warmly praises what he describes as Hobbes's masterly treatises on government, while insisting that Hobbes's overarching design has been 'grossly and thoroughly mistaken' by those who have tried to censure him.[165]

It might not be too much to say that the spirit hovering over the whole process of unmaking the ideal of liberty as independence was the spirit of Hobbes. It was he who, in his first political treatise, *The elements of law* of 1640, had put forward the earliest unambiguous formulation in anglophone political theory of the contention that the antonym of liberty is restraint:

The names *lex* and *ius*, that is to say law and right, are often confounded; and yet scarce are there any two words of more contrary signification. For right is that liberty which law leaveth us; and laws those restraints by which we mutually agree to abridge one another's liberty. Law and right therefore are no less different than restraint and liberty, which are contrary.[166]

As Hobbes was later to summarise in *Leviathan*, liberty amounts to nothing other than an absence of external impediments to motion.[167] These formulations eventually proved to be among the most resonant definitions of the concept in anglophone political philosophy. The claim that the antonym of liberty is restraint was eventually espoused by all the leading and self-avowed liberal political theorists of nineteenth-century England, including John Stuart Mill,[168] Herbert Spencer and Henry Sidgwick. More than a century after Sidgwick's death, this is the view of liberty that continues to a large extent to dominate debate.

---

[165] Austin 1995, pp. 181, 217n., 229n.    [166] Hobbes 1969, 2. 10. 5, p. 186.
[167] Hobbes 2012, vol. 2, ch. 21, p. 324.
[168] As noted in Lovett 2022, p. 19n. But while this is true of Mill in *On liberty* it is less clear in his later discussion in *The subjection of women*, in which he moves towards the view of liberty as independence.

# Conclusion: A Reckoning

I have sought to trace the fortunes of the belief that liberty consists in independence, and is forfeited whenever we find ourselves living in subjection to the arbitrary will and power of any other person or group. As I have attempted to show, this view was almost universally accepted in early modern anglophone political theory, but was displaced by the end of the eighteenth century in favour of the rival claim that liberty simply consists in non-interference, in absence of restraint. One large question that remains is whether this conceptual transformation can be regarded as an intellectual advance. Or are there instances of unfreedom that the view of liberty as independence serves to highlight and the view of liberty as absence of restraint tends to overlook or obscure?[1]

Some recent critics have attempted to dismiss these questions by arguing that the ideal of liberty as independence was so deeply associated throughout its history with misogynist, militaristic and hierarchical prejudices that we cannot hope to make any fruitful use of it.[2] The same could of course be said about the view of liberty as absence of restraint.[3] Both theories have undoubtedly been used to serve unjust ends. But it makes little sense for critics of the ideal of liberty as independence to object that it is 'fundamentally inegalitarian' and 'inherently conservative and elitist'.[4] The theory simply affirms the claim – the anti-elitist claim – that individual liberty is best understood as absence of subjection, and thus that liberty is conceptually connected with equality. The normative question that remains to be answered is whether there is anything to be gained from reconsidering this line of thought.

My answer is that, in common with many others who have recently raised this issue,[5] I believe that the ideal of liberty as independence has

---

[1] In what follows I partly draw on Skinner 2022, pp. 261–6.
[2] See Goldsmith 2000; Maddox 2002, pp. 425, 430; Goodin 2003, pp. 56–7, 61–2; McCormick 2003.
[3] As noted in Hesse 2014.   [4] MacGilvray 2011, p. 1; Maddox 2002, p. 430.
[5] See, for example, Bellamy 2007; Halldenius 2022; Honohan 2002; Lovett 2010; Lovett 2022; Maynor 2003; Laborde and Maynor 2008; Pettit 1997; Pettit 2001; Pettit 2012;

a great deal to contribute to current debates about the improvement of our moral and political world. One reason for preferring this view is that it helps us to think more sympathetically about our relations with fellow members of civil society. Consider, for example, the extent to which de-unionised workforces increasingly live at the mercy of employers with power to dismiss them at will.[6] Or consider how far the widespread economic dependence of women continues to limit their freedom of choice, leaving them vulnerable to partners whom they lack the resources to escape.[7] The loss of liberty suffered in these circumstances need not stem from any overt acts of coercion or interference; it already stems from the mere fact of living in subjection to the arbitrary and dominating will of others.[8] As these examples suggest, some of the most troubling subversions of civil liberty currently arise from these sources. But the defenders of the view of liberty as absence of restraint are not well placed to recognise them. They are committed to the belief that, although living in subjection may affect the security with which you enjoy your liberty, this does nothing to undermine your liberty itself. This makes it all too easy for them to conclude that 'the worker or wife is at liberty to dissolve a relationship that has become oppressive', without any acknowledgement that such a course of action might be dangerous or impracticable.[9]

The view of liberty as independence also seems to me to yield a morally preferable account of the relationship between government and the governed. There are several different aspects of this relationship that need to be considered. Perhaps the most obvious is that this view sees a close link between the securing of individual liberty and the upholding of democratic forms of government. One outcome of the victory won by the proponents of liberty as absence of interference was the weakening of this link. They believe that the question to ask about liberty under government is not so much who makes the laws as rather how many laws are made, and hence how much freedom from restraint is left to us. As Isaiah Berlin was happy to put it in his classic essay *Two concepts of liberty*, 'there is no necessary connection between individual liberty and democratic rule'.[10] The reason is that, because liberty consists in 'not being interfered with by others', it is 'principally concerned with the area of control, not

---

Pettit 2014; Viroli 2002. For a partly comparable approach see Malcolm 2017, pp. 99–135.

[6] On the dominating power of employers see Taylor 2017, pp. 46–63; Anderson 2017. On liberty and exploitation see Zwolinski 2018.

[7] See Hirschmann 2003, pp. 103–17; Taylor 2017, pp. 27–45.

[8] As emphasised in Halldenius 2014, pp. 90–4 and Taylor 2017. See also Tully 2005 on domination and exclusion and Cicerchia 2022 on the social creation of domination.

[9] Brennan and Lomasky 2006, p. 243. For a response see Taylor 2017.

[10] Berlin 2002, p. 177.

with its source'.[11] This being so, Berlin concludes, we might find ourselves suffering less interference, and thereby enjoying greater liberty, under some forms of autocracy than under a system of self-government.[12]

By contrast, the view of liberty as independence includes the claim that we can never hope to enjoy our freedom except under a constitution in which two conditions are satisfied. One is that we must be fully secured in the enjoyment of our essential rights. The other is that, by a fair process of representation, each of us must be able to make our voice heard equally with that of every other citizen in establishing and upholding the laws under which we live. Unless these conditions are fulfilled we shall remain subject to the mere will of our rulers and lose our standing as free citizens. A democratic form of representative government is the only form in which liberty as independence can be guaranteed. No democracy, no liberty.

This ideal of liberty also embodies what seems to me a more satisfactory way of thinking about the rights of citizens within and potentially against the state. This point seems especially worth underlining, if only because it is often objected that the ideal of liberty I have defended is insufficiently attentive to the significance of individual rights.[13] I have tried to establish that this criticism is unfounded, and in Chapter 2 I also showed how the defenders of this ideal engaged in a debate about how the concept of individual rights should be understood. I now want to suggest that, if we reflect on this debate, we may be able to learn something to our present advantage about government and the governed.

Among exponents of the ideal of liberty as independence in its heyday, a majority affirmed that the rights enjoyed by free persons take the form of universal moral claims that everyone can equally make on others, who in turn have a duty to recognise the demands being made on them. These are the rights we are said to enjoy simply in virtue of being human.[14] They are taken to be logically prior to any system of law and to stand wholly outside the political realm. They are, in a word, natural rights, and by the end of the eighteenth century they had also begun to be described as human rights, 'the common rights of humanity'.[15] If we ask who has conferred these rights upon us, we find that the dominant answer – from John Locke in the 1690s to Mary Wollstonecraft a century later – was that they are granted to us by God as the author of nature and that, as expressions of his will, they embody a universal standard of rightness. As we have seen, Locke frequently has recourse to this argument in the

---

[11] Berlin 2002, pp. 170, 176.    [12] Berlin 2002, p. 176.
[13] See, for example, Kalyvas and Katznelson 2008, p. 7; for further examples see Laborde and Maynor 2008, pp. 15–17.
[14] Halldenius 2022, pp. 223–4.    [15] [Belsham] 1790, p. 11.

*Second treatise,*[16] and Wollstonecraft continues to speak of natural rights both as our birthright and as a God-given inheritance.[17]

The assumption that rights are universal moral claims still underpins most contemporary discussions of human rights. As a number of philosophers have lately argued, however, this is not an illuminating way of thinking about the provenance and character of the rights that most concern us.[18] One problem is that the identification of human rights is still frequently made to depend on something akin to unsupported religious premisses.[19] For example, the Universal Declaration of Human Rights of 1948 begins by affirming that all human beings are endowed with reason and are born free and equal in rights, after which twenty-nine human rights in the form of universal claims are presented as self-evident truths. A further problem with the approach, which the Universal Declaration might also be said to illustrate, is that it becomes difficult to prevent such unargued lists of rights from inflating into an inventory of everything judged to be necessary for a good life.

I concede, in short, that this way of thinking about rights runs into several difficulties. The same is by no means true, however, of the alternative view of rights that we also encounter in the heyday of discussions about liberty as independence. As we saw in Chapters 1 and 2, many defenders of this view of liberty were careful to avoid any reference to natural rights, preferring instead to speak exclusively about what they characterised as fundamental rights. The rights on which they concentrate are taken to consist of legally grounded liberties that have grown up over time, thereby helping to shape the views of a particular society about what constitutional arrangements are most conducive to securing the liberty of subjects against any encroachments of arbitrary power. These rights are held to be fundamental in the sense of being essential to the preservation of our standing as free persons, and are described as liberties to indicate that we have no duty to abstain from exercising them. But they are never declared to be universal or fixed. They are merely said to reflect the considered views of a long-established legal and parliamentary system about what arrangements are most conducive to securing freedom from dependence.[20]

---

[16] [Locke] 1690, paras 6, 8, 11, 66, 135, 142, 195, pp. 222, 224, 227, 284, 355, 364, 416.

[17] Wollstonecraft 1995, pp. 7, 12–13, 33–4, 246.

[18] See, for example, Halldenius 2022, pp. 222–7; Pettit 2023, pp. 237–52.

[19] On the role of Christian thinkers in formulating the Universal Declaration see Moyn 2015 and Edelstein 2019, pp. 220–3.

[20] See Skinner 1998, pp. 18–21 and Lovett 2022, pp. 85–6. For a comparable but partly contrasting account of what he describes as 'institutional' rights see Pettit 2023, pp. 252–63.

As we saw in Chapter 2, this was the view of individual rights most fully articulated by a number of historically minded legal and political writers in the wake of the 1688 revolution. They rejected the idea of a contract between rulers and subjects to uphold some supposedly antecedent natural rights. The rights and liberties enjoyed by the people as free subjects are said to have been constructed within and by the state itself. They became established at an early stage in the history of the nation, and have subsequently proved their value and efficacy over the course of time. They remain the most basic of the rights that need to be secured if we are to live in liberty, and are thus the rights that every government has a duty to uphold against any encroachments of arbitrary or despotic power. As I have been intimating, this line of argument seems to me potentially more helpful than current appeals to the metaphysics of natural or human rights.

As well as helping us to think more effectively about the relations between states and citizens, there is a case for saying that the ideal of liberty as independence is no less useful when it comes to thinking about the relations between states themselves. There are many states that currently live to some extent in dependence on the arbitrarily wielded power of richer states.[21] A state or corporation that chooses to invest in an economically disadvantaged country will always be in a position to exact special privileges. These may include favourable tax rates, easy regulatory conditions and a lowering of environmental standards.[22] A sufficiently powerful state or corporation may never need to signal its desire for such favours; there can scarcely fail to be a mutual awareness that a sufficiently disadvantaged state will not be in a position to refuse. According to the view of liberty as non-interference, the freedom of action of the disadvantaged state will not be infringed unless coercion is employed. But this merely reveals the incapacity of this view to recognise how discretionary and hence purely dispositional power can undermine autonomous choice. It is the mere awareness that the investing state or corporation has the power to impose its will that has the effect of taking away the liberty of the disadvantaged state.[23] I conclude that, in the case of states no less than individuals, it is difficult to see how the requirements of justice can be met in the absence of a commitment to the ideal of liberty as independence.

---

[21] This is a claim that Philip Pettit has pursued with particular incisiveness. See Pettit 2010 and Pettit 2015. On republicanism and global injustice see also Halldenius 2010; Laborde 2010; Laborde and Ronzoni 2016. For a contrasting approach see Tully 2008. For a commentary on the two approaches see Bell 2014.

[22] Pettit 2015, p. 55.

[23] On contemporary corporations and arbitrary power see Hoye and Monaghan 2018.

# References

## Primary Sources

*A complete answer to Mr Wesley's observations upon Dr. Price's essay on civil liberty* (1776). Newcastle.

*A conference desired by the Lords ... concerning the rights and privileges of the subjects* (1642). London.

*A constitutional defence of government* (1782). London.

*A declaration by the representatives of the united colonies [on] the causes and necessity of their taking up arms* (1775). Philadelphia.

*A defence of the minority* (1764). London.

*A dialogue on the principles of the constitution* (1776). London.

*A general introduction on political liberty* in *British liberties* (1767). London, pp. i–lxxix.

*A letter to Dr Price* (1777). London.

*A letter to the Rev. Dr Cooper on the origin of civil government* (1777). London.

*A letter to the Rev. Dr Richard Price* (1776). London.

*A plain and candid statement of facts respecting the natural and civil rights of man* (1790). Norwich.

*A Proclamation* (1689). London.

*A supplement to the remarks on a pamphlet entitled Considerations on the late Bill for paying the national debt* (1754). Dublin.

[Adams, Samuel] (2003). *A state of the rights of the colonists* in *Tracts of the American Revolution 1763–1776*, ed. Merrill Jensen, Indianapolis, pp. 233–55.

Agutter, William (1792). *Christian politics, or the origin of power and the grounds of subordination*, London.

Alley, Jerom (1792). *Observations on the government and constitution of Great Britain*, Dublin.

Ames, Richard (1692). *Liberty or slavery*, London.

*An address to the electors of Great Britain* (1747). London.

*An answer to a letter* (1699). London.

*An appeal to reason and justice in behalf of the British constitution* (1778). London.

*An essay on liberty and independency* (1747). London.

*An excellent sermon in defence of passive obedience and non-resistance* (1733). London.

*An inquiry into the original and consequences of the public debt* (1753). Edinburgh.

[Anderton, William] (1693). *Remarks upon the present confederacy and late revolution in England*, London.

Arendt, Hannah (1968). 'What is freedom?' in *Between past and future: Eight exercises in political thought*, New York, pp. 143–71.

Aristotle (1598). *Aristotle's Politics or Discourses of government*, London.

[Arnall, William] (1731). *The case of the opposition stated between the Craftsman and the people*, London.

[Arnall, William] (1735). *Opposition no proof of patriotism*, London.

Astell, Mary (1996). *Astell: Political writings*, ed. Patricia Springborg. Cambridge.

[Atwood, William] (1690). *The fundamental constitution of the English government*, London.

Austin, John (1995). *The province of jurisprudence determined*, ed. Wilfrid E. Rumble, Cambridge.

Azo of Bologna (1966). *Lectura super codicem*, ed. Mario E. Viora, Turin.

Ball, Nathaniel (1746). *A sermon*, London.

Ballard, Reeve (1745). *The necessity of magistracy from the vices of mankind*, London.

Ballard, Reeve (1746). *The rule of obedience*, London.

Barclay, William (1600). *De regno et regali potestate adversus Buchananum, Brutum, Boucherium et reliquos monarchomachos*, Paris.

Barnard, Thomas (1743). *Tyranny and slavery in matters of religion cautioned against*, London.

Barr, John (1746). *A sermon*, Lincoln.

Barret, John (1678). *God's love to man, and man's duty towards God*, London.

Bartlam, John (1794). *An essay on liberty*, n.p.

Bate, James (1734). *The advantages of a national observance of divine and human laws*, London.

*Beauty's triumph, or the superiority of the fair sex invincibly proved* (1745). London.

Bedford, Arthur (1717). *The doctrine of obedience and non-resistance ... stated and vindicated*, London.

Bellinger, Charles (1746). *The duty of thanksgiving*, London.

[Belsham, William] (1790). *An essay on the African slave trade*, London.

Benet, Gilbert (1746). *Jotham's parable*, Lincoln.

Bentham, Jeremy (1988). *A fragment on government*, ed. J. H. Burns and H. L. A. Hart, introd. Ross Harrison, Cambridge.

Bentham, Jeremy (2017). *The correspondence, volume I, 1752–76*, ed. Timothy Sprigge, London.

Berlin, Isaiah (2002). 'Two concepts of liberty' (1958) in *Liberty*, ed. Henry Hardy, Oxford, pp. 166–217.

Bever, Thomas (1766). *A discourse on the study of jurisprudence and the civil law*, Oxford.

Blackstone, William (2016). *Commentaries on the laws of England: Book I: Of the rights of persons*, ed. David Lemmings, Oxford.

Blackwell, Thomas (1746). *The dangers of the late rebellion and our happy deliverance considered*, London.

Blount, Charles (1693). *King William and Queen Mary conquerors*, London.

Bodin, Jean (1962). *The six books of a commonweal*, ed. Kenneth Douglas McRae, Cambridge, MA.

Bolingbroke, Henry St John, Viscount (1752). *Remarks on the history of England*, Dublin.

Bolingbroke, Henry St John, Viscount (1997). *Bolingbroke: Political writings*, ed. David Armitage. Cambridge.

Bousfield, Benjamin (1791). *Observations on the Right Hon. Edmund Burke's pamphlet*, London.

Bracton, Henry de (1569). *De legibus et consuetudinibus Angliae libri quinque*, London.

Bradford, John (1746). *A sermon*, London.

Brekell, John (1746). *Liberty and loyalty; or, a defence and explication of subjection to the present government upon the principles of the revolution*, London.

Briscoe, John (1694). *A discourse on the late funds*, London.

Brown, John (1746). *The mutual connexion between religious truth and civil freedom*, London.

Brown, John (1765). *Thoughts on civil liberty, on licentiousness and faction*, Newcastle.

Burke, Edmund (2001). *Reflections on the revolution in France*, ed. J. C. D. Clark, Stanford.

Burlamaqui, Jean-Jacques (1752). *The principles of politic law*, trans. Thomas Nugent, London.

Burnet, Gilbert (1689). *A pastoral letter*, London.

*By the king, a Proclamation* (1792). London.

Carr, George (1746). *A sermon preached at the English chapel in Edinburgh*, Edinburgh.

[Cartwright, John] (1774). *American independence the interest and glory of Great Britain*, London.

[Cartwright, John] (1776). *Take your choice!* London.

Chandler, Mary (1738). *The description of Bath*, London.

Chandler, Samuel (1745). *The danger and duty of good men under the present unnatural invasion*, London.

Chandler, Samuel (1746). *National deliverances just reasons for public gratitude and joy*, London.

[Chapone, Sarah] (1735).*The hardships of the English law in relation to wives*, London.

Chauncy, Angel (1747). *A sermon*, London.

[Chudleigh, Mary] (1701). *The ladies defence*, London.

Churton, Ralph (1790). *The will of God the ground and principle of civil as well as religious obedience*, Oxford.

Cicero (1534). *The paradoxe*, trans. Robert Whitinton, London.

Cicero (1556). *Marcus Tullius Cicero's three books of duties*, trans. Nicolas Grimalde, London.

Cicero (1913). *De officiis*, trans. Walter Miller, London.

Cicero (1942). *De oratore*, ed. and trans. E. W. Sutton and H. Rackham, 2 vols., London.

*Civil liberty asserted* (1776). London.

Clarke, Joseph (1746). *Reformation of manners the best thanksgiving*, London.

Clarkson, Thomas (1786). *An essay on the slavery and commerce of the human species*, London.

Cobbett, William (1807). *The parliamentary history of England, volume 2: 1625–1642*, London.

Cobbett, William (1813a). *The parliamentary history of England, volume 15: 1753–1765*, London.

Cobbett, William (1813b). *The parliamentary history of England, volume 16: 1765–1771*, London.

Cobbett, William (1817). *The parliamentary history of England, volume 29: 1791–1792*, London.

Cocks, John Somers (1791). *Patriotism and the love of liberty defended*, London.

Coleridge, John (1777). *Government not originally proceeding from human agency but divine institution*, London.

Coney, Thomas (1731). *The happiness or misery of a nation dependent upon the principles and conduct of its governors*, London.

Cooper, Samuel (1791). *The first principles of civil and ecclesiastical government delineated*, Yarmouth.

Courtville, Ralph (1738). *Memoirs of the life and administration of William Cecil Baron Burleigh . . . including a parallel between the state of government then and now*, London.

Cramond, Robert and Hercules Cramond (1789). *A letter to the National Assembly*, London.

*Cursory remarks on Dr Price's Observations on the nature of civil liberty* (1776). London.

Dalton, Michael (1746). *The country Justice*, London.

Defoe, Daniel (1989). *Moll Flanders*, ed. David Blewett, London.

Defoe, Daniel (2001). *Robinson Crusoe*, ed. John Richetti, London.

[Dickinson, John] (1768). *Letters from a farmer in Pennsylvania*, Boston.

*Digesta* (1902). *Corpus iuris civilis*, vol. 1, ed. Paul Krueger and Theodore Mommsen, Berlin, pp. 1–873.

Dobson, Joshua (1747). *Religious gratitude explained and religious and civil liberty . . . recommended*, London.

Dodd, Charles (1777). *The Contrast: or Strictures on select parts of Dr Price's Additional observations*, London.

Dodsley, Robert (1730). *The footman's friendly advice to his brethren of the livery*, London.

[Drake, Judith] (1696). *An essay in defence of the female sex*, London.

Draper, Richard (1763). *An authentic account of the proceedings against John Wilkes, Esq*, London.

[Dulany, Daniel] (1965). *Considerations on the propriety of imposing taxes in the British colonies* in *Pamphlets of the American Revolution 1750–1776*, ed. Bernard Bailyn, Cambridge, MA, vol. 1, pp. 610–58.

Dupont, John (1747). *The peculiar happiness and excellency of the British nation considered and explained*, London.

*English liberty in some cases worse than French slavery* (1748). London.

*Equality no liberty* (1792). London.

Equiano, Olaudah (1789). *The interesting narrative of the life of Olaudah Equiano*, 2 vols., London.

[Evans, Robert] (1810). *Six letters of Publicola on the liberty of the subject*, London.

*Experience preferable to theory* (1776). London.

Fawcett, John (1808). *The nature and extent of Christian liberty*, London.

Fawel, John (1793). *Due subordination true freedom*, Wigan.

[Ferguson, Adam] (1776). *Remarks on a pamphlet lately published by Dr Price*, London.

Fielding, Henry (1999). *Joseph Andrews and Shamela*, ed. Judith Hawley, London.

Fielding, Henry (2005). *The history of Tom Jones, a foundling*, ed. Thomas Keymer and Alice Wakely, London.

Fletcher, Andrew (1997). *A discourse of government with relation to militias* in *Political works*, ed. John Robertson, Cambridge, pp. 1–31.

Foot, Jesse (1792). *A defence of the planters in the West Indies*, London.

Fortescue, Sir John (1616). *De laudibus legum Angliae (In commendation of the laws of England)*, trans. Robert Mulcaster, London.

Fortescue, Sir John (1997). *On the laws and governance of England*, ed. Shelley Lockwood, Cambridge.

Fothergill, George (1737). *The danger of excess in the pursuit of liberty*, Oxford.

Fox, William (1829). *The providence of God in the progress of religious liberty*, London.

Gisborne, Thomas (1792). *Of slavery and the slave trade*, London.

Gisborne, Thomas (1798). *The principles of moral philosophy investigated and applied to the constitution of civil society*, 4th ed., London.

Goddard, William (1819). *On the use and abuse of religious and civil liberty*, Andover.

[Goodricke, Henry] (1776). *Observations on Dr Price's theory and principles of civil liberty and government*, York.

Goold, Thomas (1791). *A vindication of the Right Hon. Edmund Burke's Reflections*, Dublin.

Goslicki, Wawrzynic (1598). *The counsellor*, London.

[Gray, John] (1774). *The right of the British legislature to tax the American colonies*, London.

Gray, John (1777). *Doctor Price's notions of the nature of civil liberty*, London.

Griffin, John (1809). *Briton's jubilee, or the duties of subjects to their kind and the blessings of liberty*, London.

Grotius, Hugo (1718). *De iure belli ac pacis*, London.

Hales, William (1794). *The scripture doctrine of political government and political liberty*, Dublin.

Halley, George (1689). *A sermon*, London.

Hargrave, Francis (1772). *An argument in the case of James Somerset*, London.

Harrington, James (1992). *The commonwealth of Oceana and a system of politics*, ed. J. G. A. Pocock, Cambridge.

Harris, Thomas (1745). *Popery and slavery displayed*, London.

[Harrison, Thomas ] (1690). *Political aphorisms*, London.

Head, Erasmus (1747). *Loyalty recommended on proper principles*, London.

Heineccius, J. G. (1763). *A methodical system of universal law*, trans. George Turnbull, 2 vols., London.

Henriques, Jacob (1749). *The petition and proposal . . . for paying the national debt*, London.

Herring, Thomas (1745). *A sermon . . . on occasion of the present rebellion in Scotland*, London.

[Hervey, John] (1730). *Observations on the writings of The Craftsman*, London.

[Hervey, John] (1732). *The public virtue of former times and the present age compared*, London.

[Hervey, John] (1734). *Ancient and modern liberty stated and compared*, London.

Hey, Richard (1776). *Observations on the nature of civil liberty and the principles of government*, London.

Hey, Richard (1792). *Happiness and rights*, York.

Hickes, George (1689). *A letter . . . in defence of the history of passive obedience*, London.

Hoadly, Benjamin (1745 [1708]). *The happiness of the present establishment and unhappiness of absolute monarchy*, Edinburgh.

Hobbes, Thomas (1969). *The elements of law natural and politic*, ed. Ferdinand Tönnies, 2nd ed., introd. M. M. Goldsmith, London.

Hobbes, Thomas (1998). *On the citizen*, ed. and trans. Richard Tuck and Michael Silverthorne, Cambridge.

Hobbes, Thomas (2012). *Leviathan*, ed. Noel Malcolm, 3 vols., Oxford.

Hooke, Andrew (1750). *An essay on the national debt*, London.

[Hopkins, Stephen] (1965). *The rights of colonies examined* in *Pamphlets of the American Revolution 1750–1776*, ed. Bernard Bailyn, Cambridge, MA, vol. 1, pp. 506–22.

Howard, Leonard (1745). *The advantages of a free people and ill consequences of licentiousness considered*, London.

Hume, David (1741). *Essays moral and political*, Edinburgh.

Hume, David (1742). *Essays moral and political, volume II*, Edinburgh.

Hume, David (1748). *Three essays moral and political, never before published*, London.

Hume, David (1752). *Political discourses*, Edinburgh.

Hume, David (1764). *Essays and treatises on several subjects*, 2 vols., London.

Ibbetson, James (1746). *Public virtue the great cause of the happiness and prosperity of any people*, York.

[Jefferson, Thomas] (2003). *A summary view of the rights of British America* in *Tracts of the American Revolution 1763–1776*, ed. Merrill Jensen, Indianapolis, pp. 256–76.

Johnson, Robert C. and Maija Jansson Cole (eds.) (1977). *Commons Debates 1628, volume 2*, New Haven.

Johnson, Robert C., Mary Frear Keeler, Maija Jansson Cole and William B. Bidwell (eds.) (1977). *Commons Debates 1628, volume 3*, New Haven.

[Johnson, Samuel] (1775). *Taxation no tyranny*, London.

[Jones, Erasmus] (1740). *Luxury, pride and vanity the bane of the English nation*, London.

Jones, John (1792). *The reason of man*, Canterbury.

Kerrich, Samuel (1746). *A sermon of . . . public thanksgiving*, Cambridge.

[Kettlewell, John] (1691). *Christianity, a doctrine of the cross*, London.

Lane, William (1746). *A sermon*, London.

Lay, Benjamin (1737). *All slave-keepers . . . Apostates*, Philadelphia.

*Liberty and property* (1745). London.

[Lind, John] (1776). *Three letters to Dr Price*, London.

Livy (1600). *The Romane history*, trans. Philemon Holland, London.

Livy (1919). *Livy I, Books I and II*, trans. B. O. Foster, London.

Livy (1922). *Livy II, Books III and IV*, trans. B. O. Foster, London.

[Locke, John] (1690). *Two treatises of government*, London.

Lofft, Capel (1790). *Remarks on the letter of the Rt. Hon. Edmund Burke concerning the revolution in France*, London.

[Logan, William] (1746). *Superiorities display'd: or, Scotland's grievance*, Edinburgh.

*Loyalty to our king the safety of our country* (1745). London.

Macaulay, Catharine (2023). *Catharine Macaulay: Political writings*, ed. Max Skjönsberg, Cambridge.

Machiavelli, Niccolò (1636). *Machiavel's Discourses*, trans. Edward Dacres, London.

Mackintosh, James (2006). *Vindiciae Gallicae and other writings on the French revolution*, ed. Donald Winch, Indianapolis.

Maddox, Isaac (1746). *A sermon*, London.

[Mandeville, Bernard] (1723). *The fable of the bees, or private vices publick benefits*, 2nd ed., London.

Markham, William (1777). *A sermon*, London.

May, Thomas (1690). *An epitome of English history*, London.

Mays, Christopher (1746). *A sermon*, Cambridge.

Milton, John (1660). *The ready and easy way to establish a free commonwealth*, London.

Milton, John (1953). *Commonplace book* in *Complete prose works*, ed. Don M. Wolfe, vol. 1: *1624–1642*, New Haven, pp. 362–513.

Milton, John (1991). *John Milton: Political writings*, ed. Martin Dzelzainis, Cambridge.

Milton, John (1998). *The complete poems*, ed. John Leonard, London.

[Molesworth, Robert] (1694). *An account of Denmark*, London.

[Molesworth, Robert] (1721). *Franco-Gallia: Or an account of the ancient free state of France and most other parts of Europe before the loss of their liberties*, 2nd ed., London.

Montague, Basil (1819). *Some thoughts upon liberty and the rights of Englishmen*, London.

Montesquieu, Charles Louis de Secondat (1989). *The spirit of the laws*, ed. and trans. Anne Cohler, Basia Miller and Harold Stone, Cambridge.

Morell, Thomas (1754). *Judas Macchabaeus: A sacred drama*, Oxford.

Mortimer, Thomas (1772). *The Elements of commerce, politics and finances*, London.

Murdin, Cornelius (1779). *Three sermons*, Southampton.

Mynors, Willoughby (1716). *True loyalty: Or non-resistance the only support of monarchy*, London.

Myonnet, John (1734). *The nature and advantages of civil liberty*, London.

Nares, Robert (1792). *Principles of government deduced from reason, supported by English experience and opposed to French errors*, London.

Nares, Robert (1793). *Principles of government adapted to general instruction and use*, London.

*National spirit considered as a natural source of political liberty* (1758). London.

Nedham, Marchamont (1656). *The excellency of a free-state*, London.

Nedham, Marchamont (1969). *The case of the commonwealth of England stated*, ed. Philip A. Knachel, Charlottesville.

Nichols, Nicholas (1746). *A sermon*, Hull.

Osborne, George (1735). *Subjection to principalities, powers, and magistrates, explain'd and enforc'd*, London.

Oswald, John (1793). *Review of the constitution of Great Britain*, London.

Otis, James (1965). *The rights of the British colonies asserted and proved* in *Pamphlets of the American Revolution 1750–1776*, ed. Bernard Bailyn, vol. 1, Cambridge, MA, pp. 419–82.

[Overton, Richard] (1646). *An arrow against all tyrants and tyranny*, n.p.

Paine, Thomas (2000). *Thomas Paine: Political writings*, ed. Bruce Kuklick, Cambridge.

Paley, William (1785). *The principles of moral and political philosophy*, London.

[Parker, Henry] (1642). *Observations upon some of his Majesty's late answers and expresses*, London.

Parkin, Thomas (1828). *An exposure of religious and civil despotism*, London.

Parsons, Lawrence (1793). *Thoughts on liberty and equality*, London.

Patrick, Simon (1689). *A sermon*, London.

Pearce, Samuel (1827). *The oppressive . . . nature and tendency of the Corporation and Test Acts exposed*, London.

Peckard, Peter (1783). *The nature and extent of civil and religious liberty*, Cambridge.

Pendlebury, William (1746). *The errors and mischiefs of popery and the fatal consequences of arbitrary and despotic power*, York.

Perceval, John, Earl of Egmont (1763). *An essay on the means of discharging the public debt*, London.

[Petyt, George] (1690). *Lex parliamentaria, or a treatise of the law and custom of Parliaments*, London.

Pickering, Danby (1765). *The statutes at large*, volume 19, Cambridge.

Piers, Henry (1746). *Religion and liberty rescued from superstition and slavery*, Bristol.

Plowden, Francis (1824). *Human subordination*, London.

Pope, Alexander (2011). *The rape of the lock and other major writings*, ed. Leo Damrosch, London.

Potter, Francis (1745). *A sermon*, London.

Price, Richard (1991). *Richard Price: Political writings*, ed. D. O. Thomas, Cambridge.

Priestley, Joseph (1791). *Letters to the Right Honourable Edmund Burke*, Birmingham.

Priestley, Joseph (1993). *The present state of liberty* in *Joseph Priestley: Political writings*, ed. Peter Miller, Cambridge, pp. 129–44.

*Proceedings of the Association for preserving liberty and property against republicans and levellers* (1793). London.

Pufendorf, Samuel (1729). *Of the law of nature and nations*, trans. Basil Kennett [with the notes of Jean Barbeyrac], 4th ed., London.

[Pulteney, William, Earl of Bath] (1727). *A state of the national debt*, London.

Pym, John (1641). *The speech or declaration of John Pym*, London.

*Reasons for seeking a repeal of the Corporation and Test Acts* (1790).

*Remarks on Dr Price's Observations* (1776). London.

*Remarks on the life of Mr Milton as published by J. T.* (1699). London.

*Resistance no rebellion* (1775). London.

*Revolution Society: At the anniversary meeting* (1789). London.

Richardson, Andrew (1746). *A free and an arbitrary government compared*, Edinburgh.

Richardson, Samuel (1985). *Clarissa, or the history of a young lady*, ed. Angus Ross, London.

Richardson, Samuel (2001). *Pamela, or Virtue rewarded*, ed. Thomas Keymer and Alice Wakely, introd. Thomas Keymer, London.

Roger, James (1797). *Essay on government*, Edinburgh.

Sallust (1608). *The two most worthy and notable histories*, trans. Thomas Heywood, London.

Sallust (1931). 'The war with Catiline' in *Sallust*, trans. J. C. Rolfe, London, pp. 3–129.

Salter, Edward (1791). *Obedience to God the measure of human liberty*, Winchester.

[Scott-Waring, John] (1791). *A letter to the Right Hon. Edmund Burke*, Dublin.

[Seller, Abednego] (1689). *The history of passive obedience since the Reformation*, Amsterdam.

*Serious and impartial observations on the blessings of liberty and peace* (1776). London.

[Serle, Ambrose] (1775). *Americans against liberty*, London.

Sharp, Granville (1769). *A representation of the injustice and dangerous tendency of tolerating slavery or of admitting the least claim of private property in the persons of men in England*, London.

Shebbeare, John (1776). *An essay on the origin, progress and establishment of national society*, London.

Sheridan, Charles (1793). *An essay upon the true principles of civil liberty and free government*, London.

Sherlock, William (1691). *The case of the allegiance due to sovereign powers*, London.

[Sidney, Algernon] (1698). *Discourses concerning government*, London.

Sidney, Algernon (1990). *Discourses concerning government*, ed. Thomas G. West, Indianapolis.

Smith, Adam (1976). *An inquiry into the nature and causes of the wealth of nations*, ed. R. H. Campbell and A. S. Skinner, 2 vols., Oxford.

Smith, Samuel (1742). *The mission and duty of civil governors and the deference due to them*, London.

Smith, Sir Thomas (1982). *De republica Anglorum*, ed. Mary Dewar, Cambridge.

Smollett, Tobias (1995). *Roderick Random*, ed. David Blewett, London.
*Some considerations offered against the continuance of the Bank of England* (1694). London.
Somerville, Thomas (1793). *The effects of the French Revolution*, Edinburgh.
Southcomb, Lewis (1735). *Subjection to the higher powers a necessary duty in every Christian*, London.
[Spence, Thomas] (1795). *The end of oppression*, London.
[Squire, Samuel] (1746). *A letter to a Tory friend*, London.
Sterne, Laurence (2003). *The life and opinions of Tristram Shandy, gentleman*, ed. Melvyn New and Joan New, London.
Stevenson, William (1746). *The true patriot's wishes*, London.
Stewart, James (1689). *Salus populi suprema lex*, Edinburgh.
*Strictures on a sermon entitled The principles of the revolution vindicated* (1776). Cambridge.
Swift, Jonathan (2003). *Gulliver's travels*, ed. Robert Demaria, London.
Sykes, Arthur (1746). *A sermon*, London.
Tacitus (1591). *The end of Nero and beginning of Galba. Four books of the histories of Cornelius Tacitus: The life of Agricola*, trans. Henry Savile, Oxford.
Tacitus (1598). *The annales of Cornelius Tacitus: The description of Germany*, trans. Richard Grenewey, London.
Tacitus (1931). *The histories Books IV–V*, trans. Clifford H. Moore and *The annals Books I–III*, trans. John Jackson, London.
*The Declaration of his highness William Henry ... Prince of Orange* (1688). The Hague.
*The duty of the king and subject on the principles of civil liberty* (1776). London.
*The effects of industry and idleness illustrated ... Being an explanation of the moral of twelve celebrated prints lately published and designed by the ingenious Mr Hogarth* (1748). London.
*The female advocate, or a plea for the just liberty of the tender sex* (1700). London.
*The footman's looking-glass* (1747). London.
*The freeman's vade-mecum* (1798). London.
*The herald or patriotic proclaimer* (1758). 2 vols., London.
*The law-suit* (1738). London.
*The national debt as it stood at Michaelmas 1730* (1731). London.
*The pamphlet entitled Taxation no tyranny candidly considered* (1775). London.
*The present state of the national debt* (1740). London.
*The price of the abdication* (1693). London.
*The state of the national debt as it stood Dec. 31 1742 and on Dec. 31 1743* (1744). London.
*The true Briton's catechism* (1793). London.
*The two systems of the social compact and the natural rights of man examined and refuted* (1793). London.
Thomson, James (1736). *Britain: Being the fourth part of Liberty, a poem*, London.
*Three dialogues concerning liberty* (1776). London.
Tillotson, John (1689). *A sermon*, London.
[Toland, John] (1698a). *The danger of mercenary Parliaments*, London.

[Toland, John] (1698b). *A complete collection of the historical, political and miscellaneous works of John Milton*, 3 vols., Amsterdam.

[Toland, John] (1699). *The life of John Milton*, London.

[Toland, John] (1700). *The Oceana of James Harrington and his other works*, London.

Toland, John (1701). *Anglia libera*, London.

Townshend, Thomas (1793). *Considerations on the theoretical spirit of the times*, Cork.

[Trelawny, Edward] (1746). *An essay concerning slavery*, London.

[Trenchard, John] (1698a). *An argument showing that a standing army is inconsistent with a free government and absolutely destructive to the constitution of the English monarchy*, London.

[Trenchard, John] (1698b). *Free thoughts concerning officers in the House of Commons*, London.

Trenchard, John and Thomas Gordon (1995). *Cato's Letters*, ed. Ronald Hamowy, 4 vols., Indianapolis.

Trott, Edmund (1746). *A sermon on the present rebellion*, London.

[Tucker, Abraham] (1763). *Freewill, foreknowledge and fate*, London.

Tucker, Josiah (1774). *The true interest of Great Britain set forth in regard to the colonies* in *Four tracts*, Gloucester, pp. 143–216.

Tucker, Josiah (1781). *A treatise concerning civil government*, London.

Tucker, Josiah (1783). *Four letters on important national subjects*, Gloucester.

[Turnbull, Gordon ] (1786). *An apology*, London.

[Tyrrell, James] (1681). *Patriarcha non monarcha*, London.

[Tyrrell, James] (1694). *Bibliotheca politica: Or an enquiry into the ancient constitution of the English government*, London.

Usher, G. (1778). *Republican letters*, London.

Vaughan, William (1600). *The golden grove*, London.

*Vindiciae contra tyrannos, a defence of liberty against tyrants* (1648). London.

Warburton, William (1745). *A sermon occasioned by the present unnatural rebellion*, London.

Warburton, William (1746). *A sermon*, London.

Watkins, Charles (1796). *Reflections on government*, London.

Watson, George (1799). *Thoughts on government*, London.

Watson, Richard (1776). *An essay on civil liberty*, 3rd ed., Cambridge.

[Webster, William] (1740). *The consequences of trade as to the wealth and strength of any nation*, London.

Wemyss, James (1794). *A scriptural view of kings and magistrates*, Edinburgh.

Wesley, John (1774). *Thoughts upon slavery*, 3rd ed., London.

Wesley, John (1775). *A calm address to our American colonies*, Bristol.

Wesley, John (1776). *Some observations on liberty*, London.

Weston, Charles (1793). *The authority of government and duty of obedience*, Durham.

[Whately, Thomas] (1765). *The regulations lately made concerning the colonies*, London.

Wiche, John (1745). *Englishmen urged to loyalty by their sense and love of liberty*, London.

*Wilkes and liberty* (1763). London.

Wilkes, John (1763). *The following speech was made by John Wilkes*, London.

Williamson, David (1792). *Lectures on civil and religious liberty*, London.

Willis, Robert (1795). *Philosophical sketches of the principles of society and government*, London.

Wilson, James (1774). *Considerations on the nature and the extent of the legislative authority of the British Parliament*, Philadelphia.

Wilson, William (1689). *A sermon [on] our deliverance from popery and arbitrary power*, London.

Wollstonecraft, Mary (1995). *A vindication of the rights of men with A vindication of the rights of women and Hints*, ed. Sylvana Tomaselli, Cambridge.

*Woman not inferior to man* (1740). London.

Wood, Thomas (1738). *An institute of the laws of England*, London.

Wood, Thomas (1796). *Essay on civil government and subjection and obedience*, Wigan.

Wynne, Edward (1768). *Eunomus, or Dialogues concerning the law and constitution of England*, 4 vols., London.

Yardley, Edward (1746). *A sermon*, London.

[Yonge, Sir William] (1731). *Sedition and defamation displayed in a letter to the author of the Craftsman*, London.

Young, John (1794). *Essays . . . VI: Liberty and equality*, Edinburgh.

## Secondary Sources

Anderson, Elizabeth (2017). *Private government: How employers rule our lives (and Why we Don't Talk about it)*, Princeton.

Ando, Clifford (2010). '"A dwelling beyond violence": on the uses and disadvantages of history for contemporary republicans', *History of Political Thought* 31, pp. 183–220.

Arcenas, Claire Rydell (2022). *America's philosopher: John Locke in American intellectual life*, Chicago.

Arena, Valentina (2012). *Libertas and the practice of politics in the late Roman republic*, Cambridge.

Armitage, David (ed.) (1997). *Bolingbroke: Political writings*, Cambridge.

Armitage, David (2000). *The ideological origins of the British Empire*, Cambridge.

Armitage, David (2002). 'Empire and liberty: a republican dilemma' in *Republicanism: A shared European heritage, volume II: The values of republicanism in early modern Europe*, ed. Martin van Gelderen and Quentin Skinner, Cambridge, pp. 29–46.

Armitage, David (2004). 'John Locke, Carolina, and the *Two treatises of government*', *Political Theory* 32, pp. 602–27.

Armitage, David (2007). *The Declaration of Independence: A global history*, Cambridge, MA.

Arnold, Samuel and John R. Harris (2017). 'What is arbitrary power?' *Journal of Political Power* 10, pp. 55–70.

Ashby, Thomas (2022). 'Democracy in Algernon Sidney's *Discourses concerning government*' in *Republicanism and democracy: Close friends?* ed. Skadi Siiri Krause and Dirk Jörke, Cham, pp. 81–111.

Atkins, Jed W. (2018). 'Non-domination and the *libera res publica* in Cicero's republicanism', *History of European Ideas* 44, pp. 756–73.

Avery, Margaret (1978). 'Toryism in the age of the American Revolution: John Lind and John Shebbeare', *Historical Studies* 18, pp. 24–36.

Bailyn, Bernard (ed.) (1965). *Pamphlets of the American Revolution 1750–1776, volume 1:1750–1765*, Cambridge, MA.

Bailyn, Bernard (1967). *The ideological origins of the American Revolution*, Cambridge, MA.

Baker, J. H. (1995). 'Personal liberty under the common law of England 1200–1600' in *The origins of modern freedom in the West*, ed. R. W. Davis, Stanford, pp. 178–202.

Beasley, Jerry C. (1982). *Novels of the 1740s*, Athens, GA.

Beiner, Ronald (1984). 'Action, natality and citizenship: Hannah Arendt's concept of freedom' in *Conceptions of liberty in political philosophy*, ed. Zbigniew Pelczynski and John Gray, London, pp. 349–75.

Bejan, Teresa (2019). '"Since all the world is mad, why should not I be so?" Mary Astell on equality, hierarchy, and ambition', *Political Theory* 47, pp. 781–808.

Bell, Duncan (2014). 'To act otherwise: agonistic republicanism and global citizenship' in *On global citizenship: James Tully in dialogue*, London, pp. 181–205.

Bellamy, Richard (2007). *Political constitutionalism: A republican defence of the constitutionality of democracy*, Cambridge.

Benn, S. I. and W. L. Weinstein (1971). 'Being free to act, and being a free man', *Mind* 80, pp. 194–211.

Bernasconi, Robert and Anika Mann (2005). 'The contradictions of racism: Locke, slavery and the *Two treatises*' in *Race and racism in modern philosophy*, ed. Andrew Valls, Ithaca, pp. 89–107.

Bonwick, Colin (1977). *English radicals and the American Revolution*, Chapel Hill.

Boralevi, Lea Campos (2002). 'Classical foundational myths of European republicanism: the Jewish commonwealth' in *Republicanism: A shared European heritage, volume I: Republicanism and constitutionalism in early modern Europe*, ed. Martin van Gelderen and Quentin Skinner, Cambridge, pp. 247–61.

Boulton, James T. (1963). *The language of politics in the age of Wilkes and Burke*, London.

Bourke, Richard (2015). *Empire and revolution: The political life of Edmund Burke*, Princeton.

Bourke, Richard (2016). 'Popular sovereignty and political representation: Edmund Burke in the context of eighteenth-century thought' in *Popular sovereignty in historical perspective*, ed. Richard Bourke and Quentin Skinner, Cambridge, pp. 212–35.

Brace, Laura (2016). 'Wollstonecraft and the properties of (anti-) slavery, in *The social and political philosophy of Mary Wollstonecraft*, ed. Sandrine Bergès and Alan Coffee, Oxford, pp. 117–34.

Brand, Paul (2010). 'The date and authorship of *Bracton*: a response', *Journal of Legal History* 31, pp. 217–44.

Brennan, Geoffrey and Loren Lomasky (2006). 'Against reviving republicanism', *Politics, Philosophy and Economics* 5, pp. 221–52.

Brett, Annabel (1997). *Liberty, right and nature: Individual rights in later scholastic thought*, Cambridge.

Brett, Annabel (2002). 'Natural right and civil community: the civil philosophy of Hugo Grotius', *Historical Journal* 45, pp. 31–51.

Brewer, Holly (2021). 'Creating a common law of slavery for England and its new world empire', *Law and History Review* 39, pp. 765–843.

Brewer, John (1976). *Party ideology and popular politics at the accession of George III*, Cambridge.

Brewer, John (1980). 'The Wilkites and the law, 1763–4' in *An ungovernable people: The English and their law in the seventeenth and eighteenth centuries*, ed. John Brewer and John Styles, London, pp. 128–71.

Brewer, John (1989). *The sinews of power: War, money and the English state 1688–1783*, London.

Broad, Jacqueline (2014). 'Women on liberty in early modern England', *Philosophy Compass* 9, pp. 112–22.

Broad, Jacqueline (2015). 'Sarah Chapone on liberty as non-domination', *The Monist*, 98, pp. 77–88.

Broad, Jacqueline (2017). 'Marriage, slavery and the merger of wills: responses to Sprint, 1700–01', in *Women and liberty 1600–1800: Philosophical essays*, ed. Jacqueline Broad and Karen Detlefsen, Oxford, pp. 66–81.

Browning, Reed (1982). *Political and constitutional ideas of the court Whigs*, Baton Rouge.

Buckle, Stephen and Dario Castiglione (1991). 'Hume's critique of the contract theory', *History of Political Thought* 12, pp. 457–80.

Burgess, Glenn (2004). 'Regicide: the execution of Charles I and English political thought' in *Murder and monarchy: Regicide in European history 1300–1800*, ed. Robert von Friedeburg, Basingstoke, pp. 212–36.

Burns, J. H. (1985). 'Fortescue and the political theory of *dominium*', *The Historical Journal* 28, pp. 77–97.

Burns, J. H. (1993). 'George Buchanan and the anti-monarchomachs' in *Political discourse in early modern Britain*, ed. Nicholas Phillipson and Quentin Skinner, Cambridge, pp. 3–22.

Burrow, J. W. (1988). *Whigs and liberals: Continuity and change in English political thought*, Cambridge.

Burtt, Shelley (1992). *Virtue transformed: Political argument in England 1688–1740*, Cambridge.

Calvert, Jane (2008). *Quaker constitutionalism and the political thought of John Dickinson*, Cambridge.

Canovan, Margaret (1978). 'Two concepts of liberty: eighteenth century style', *Price-Priestley Newsletter* 2, pp. 27–43.

Carter, Ian (1999). *A measure of freedom*, Oxford.

Caudle, James (2012). 'The defence of Georgian Britain: the anti-Jacobite sermon 1715–1746' in *The Oxford handbook of the British sermon, 1689–1901*, ed. Keith Francis and William Gibson, Oxford, pp. 245–60.

Celikates, Robin (2013). 'Freedom as non-arbitrariness or as democratic self-rule? A critique of contemporary republicanism' in *To be unfree: Republican perspectives on political unfreedom in history, literature and philosophy*, ed. Christian Dahl and Tue Andersen Nexö, Bielefeld, pp. 37–54.

Champion, Justin (2003). *Republican learning: John Toland and the crisis of Christian culture 1696–1722*, Manchester.

Champion, Justin (2005). '"Anglia libera": commonwealth politics in the early years of George I' in *'Cultures of Whiggism': New essays on English literature and culture in the long eighteenth century*, ed. David Womersley, Newark, pp. 86–107.

Chater, Kathleen (2011). *Untold histories: Black people in England and Wales during the period of the British slave trade c. 1660–1807*, Manchester.

Christie, Ian R. (1998). 'A vision of empire: Thomas Whately and *The regulations lately made concerning the colonies*', *English Historical Review* 113, pp. 300–20.

Cicerchia, Lillian (2022). 'Structural domination in the labor market', *European Journal of Political Theory* 21, pp. 4–24.

Claeys, Gregory (2007). *The French Revolution debate in Britain: The origins of modern politics*, Basingstoke.

Clark, J. C. D. (1985). *English society, 1688–1832: Ideology, social structure and political practice during the ancien regime*, Cambridge.

Clark, J. C. D. (1994). *The language of liberty, 1660–1832: Political discourse and social dynamics in the Anglo-American world*, Cambridge.

Clark J. C. D. (2018). *Thomas Paine: Britain, America and France in the age of Enlightenment and revolution*, Oxford.

Clark, J. C. D. (2023). '"Lockeian liberalism" and "classical republicanism": the formation, function and failure of the categories', *Intellectual History Review* 33, pp. 11–31.

Clarke, Michelle T. (2014). 'Doing violence to the Roman idea of liberty? Freedom as bodily integrity in Roman political thought', *History of Political Thought* 35, pp. 211–33.

Cleary, Thomas R. (1984). *Henry Fielding: Political writer*, Waterloo, Ont.

Coffee, Alan (2013). 'Mary Wollstonecraft, freedom and the enduring power of social domination', *European Journal of Political Theory* 12, pp. 116–35.

Coffee, Alan (2014). 'Freedom as independence: Mary Wollstonecraft and the grand blessing of life', *Hypatia* 29, pp. 908–24.

Coffee, Alan (2015). 'Two spheres of domination: republican theory, social norms and the insufficiency of negative freedom', *Contemporary Political Theory* 14, pp. 45–62.

Coffee, Alan (2017). 'Catharine Macaulay's republican conception of social and political liberty', *Political Studies* 65, pp. 844–59.

Colley, Linda (1982). *In defiance of oligarchy: The Tory party 1714–1760*, Cambridge.

Collins, Jeffrey (2009). 'Quentin Skinner's Hobbes and the neo-republican project', *Modern Intellectual History* 6, pp. 343–67.

Connolly, Patrick J. (2021). 'Susanna Newcome and the origins of utilitarianism', *Utilitas* 33, pp. 384–98.

Cookson, J. E. (1982). *The friends of peace: Anti-war liberalism in England 1793–1815*, Cambridge.

Cornish, Rory (2020). *The Grenvillites and the British press*, Cambridge.

Crimmins, James (1986). '"The study of true politics": John Brown on manners and liberty', *Studies on Voltaire and the eighteenth century* 241, pp. 65–86.

Cromartie, Alan (2016). 'Parliamentary sovereignty, popular sovereignty, and Henry Parker's adjudicative standpoint' in *Popular sovereignty in historical perspective*, ed. Richard Bourke and Quentin Skinner, Cambridge, pp. 142–63.

Cruickshanks, Eveline and Howard Erskine-Hill (2004). *The Atterbury Plot*, Basingstoke.

Davidson, Jenny (2004). *Hypocrisy and the politics of politeness: Manners and morals from Locke to Austen*, Cambridge.

Davis, Michael T. (2016). 'The vilification of Thomas Paine: constructing a folk devil in the 1790s' in *Liberty, property and popular politics: England and Scotland, 1688–1815: Essays in honour of H. T. Dickinson*, ed. Michael T. Davis and Gordon Pentland, Edinburgh, pp. 176–93.

Dawson, Hannah (2013). 'Natural religion: Pufendorf and Locke on the edge of freedom and reason' in *Freedom and the construction of Europe, volume I: Religious and constitutional liberties*, ed. Quentin Skinner and Martin van Gelderen, Cambridge, pp. 115–33.

Dawson, Hannah (2022). 'Liberty before licence in Locke' in *Rethinking Liberty before liberalism*, ed. Hannah Dawson and Annelien De Dijn, Cambridge, pp. 60–76.

Dawson, Hannah (2023). 'When reason does not see you: feminism at the intersection of history and philosophy' in *History in the humanities and social sciences*, ed. Richard Bourke and Quentin Skinner, Cambridge, pp. 229–59.

De Dijn, Annelien (2020). *Freedom: An unruly history*, Cambridge, MA.

Dewar, Mary (ed.) (1982). *De republica anglorum by Sir Thomas Smith*, Cambridge.

Dickinson, H. T. (1977). *Liberty and property: Political ideology in eighteenth-century Britain*, London.

Dickson, P. G. M. (1967). *The financial revolution in England: A study in the development of public credit 1688–1756*, London.

Douglass, Robin (2023). *Mandeville's fable: Pride, hypocrisy and sociability*, Princeton.

Draper, Theodore (1996). *A struggle for power: The American Revolution*, New York.

Dunn, John (1969). *The political thought of John Locke: An historical account of the argument of the 'Two treatises of government'*, Cambridge.

Dunn, John (1980). *Political obligation in its historical context: Essays in political theory*, Cambridge.

Dzelzainis, Martin (ed.) (1991). *John Milton: Political writings*, Cambridge.

Dzelzainis, Martin (1995). 'Milton's classical republicanism' in *Milton and republicanism*, ed. David Armitage, Armand Himy and Quentin Skinner, Cambridge, pp. 3–24.

Dzelzainis, Martin (2014). 'Harrington and the oligarchs: Milton, Vane and Stubbe' in *Perspectives on English revolutionary republicanism*, ed. Gaby Mahlberg and Dick Wiemann, Farnham, pp. 15–33.

Dzelzainis, Martin (2019). '"The vulgar only scap'd who stood without": Milton and the politics of exclusion' in *Democracy and anti-democracy in early modern England 1603–1689*, ed. Cesare Cuttica and Markku Peltonen, Leiden, pp. 239–59.

Edelstein, Dan (2019). *On the spirit of rights*, Chicago.

Ehrenberg, John (1999). *Civil society: The critical history of an idea*, New York.

Elazar, Yiftah (2015). 'Liberty as a caricature: Bentham's antidote to republicanism', *Journal of the History of Ideas* 76, pp. 417–39.

Elazar, Yiftah (2022a). 'The downfall of all slavish hierarchies: Richard Price on emancipation, improvement and republican Utopia', *Modern Intellectual History* 19, pp. 81–104.

Elazar, Yiftah (2022b). 'Adam Smith and the idea of free government', *Intellectual History Review* 32, pp. 691–707.

Farr, James (1986). '"So vile and miserable an estate": the problem of slavery in Locke's political thought', *Political Theory* 14, pp. 263–90.

Farr, James (2008). 'Locke, natural law, and new world slavery', *Political Theory* 36, pp. 495–522.

Ferguson, Moira (ed.) (1985). *First feminists: British women writers 1578–1799*, Bloomington.

Fink, Z. S. (1962). *The classical republicans*, 2nd ed., Evanston.

Fitzpatrick, Martin (1991). 'Richard Price and the London Revolution Society', *Enlightenment and Dissent* 10, pp. 35–50.

Fontana, Benedetto (2009). 'Ancient Roman historians and early modern political theory' in *The Cambridge companion to the Roman historians*, ed. Andrew Feldherr, Cambridge, pp. 362–79.

Foord, Archibald S. (1964). *His Majesty's opposition 1714–1830*, Oxford.

Forbes, Duncan (1975). *Hume's philosophical politics*, Cambridge.

Forbes, Duncan (1976). 'Sceptical whiggism, commerce and liberty' in *Essays on Adam Smith*, ed. Andrew Skinner and Thomas Wilson, Oxford, pp. 179–201.

Foxley, Rachel (2013). '"Due libertie and proportioned equalitie": Milton, democracy and the republican tradition', *History of Political Thought* 34, pp. 614–38.

Foxley, Rachel (2022). 'Liberty and hierarchy in Milton's revolutionary prose' in *Rethinking Liberty before liberalism*, ed. Hannah Dawson and Annelien De Dijn, Cambridge, pp. 79–99.

Foxley, Rachel (2023). 'The possibility of democratic republicanism: the Levellers, Milton and Harrington' in *Republicanism and democracy: Close friends?* ed. Skadi Siiri Krause and Dirk Jörke, Cham, pp. 57–79.

Gardiner, Samuel (ed.) (1906). *The constitutional documents of the Puritan revolution 1625–1660*, Oxford.

Garnett, George (ed). (1994). *Vindiciae contra tyrannos*, Cambridge.

Gerrard, Christine (1994). *The patriot opposition to Walpole: Politics, poetry and national myth 1725–1742*, Oxford.

Geuna, Marco (2002). 'Republicanism and commercial society in the Scottish Enlightenment: the case of Adam Ferguson' in *Republicanism: A shared*

*European heritage, volume II: The values of republicanism in early modern Europe*, ed. Martin van Gelderen and Quentin Skinner, Cambridge, pp. 177–95.

Ghosh, Eric (2008). 'From republican to liberal liberty', *History of Political Thought* 29, pp. 132–67.

Gilmartin, Kevin (2007). *Writing against revolution: Literary conservatism in Britain 1790–1832*, Cambridge.

Glover, Jane (2018). *Handel in London: The making of a genius*, London.

Goldgar, Bertrand A. (1976). *Walpole and the wits: The relation of politics to literature 1722–1742*, Lincoln, NE.

Goldie, Mark (1980a). 'The revolution of 1689 and the structure of political argument', *Bulletin of Research in the Humanities* 83, pp. 473–564.

Goldie, Mark (1980b). 'The roots of true Whiggism 1688–94', *History of Political Thought* 1, pp. 195–236.

Goldie, Mark (1993). 'Priestcraft and the birth of Whiggism' in *Political discourse in early modern Britain*, ed. Nicholas Phillipson and Quentin Skinner, Cambridge, pp. 209–31.

Goldie, Mark (2006). 'The English system of liberty' in *The Cambridge history of eighteenth-century political thought*, ed. Mark Goldie and Robert Wokler, Cambridge, pp. 40–78.

Goldie, Mark (2007). 'Mary Astell and John Locke' in *Mary Astell: Reason, gender, faith*, ed. Michal Michelson, London, pp. 65–86.

Goldie, Mark and Clare Jackson (2007). 'Williamite tyranny and the Whig Jacobites' in *Redefining William III*, ed. Esther Mijers and David Onnekink, Aldershot, pp. 177–99.

Goldsmith, Maurice (2000). 'Republican liberty considered', *History of Political Thought* 21, pp. 543–59.

Goodin, Robert (2003). 'Folie républicaine', *Annual Review of Political Science* 6, pp. 55–76.

Gourevitch, Alex (2015). *From slavery to the co-operative commonwealth: Labor and republican liberty in the nineteenth century*, Cambridge.

Green, Karen (2012). 'Liberty and virtue in Catharine Macaulay's Enlightenment philosophy', *Intellectual History Review* 22, pp. 411–26.

Green, Karen (2017). 'Locke, Enlightenment and liberty in the works of Catharine Macaulay and her contemporaries' in *Women and liberty, 1600–1800: Philosophical essays*, ed. Jacqueline Broad and Karen Detlefsen, Oxford, pp. 187–96.

Green, Karen (2018). 'Catharine Macaulay's Enlightenment faith and radical politics', *History of European Ideas* 44, pp. 35–48.

Greene, Jack P. (2010). *The constitutional origins of the American Revolution*, Cambridge.

Haakonssen, Knud (1996). *Natural law and moral philosophy: From Grotius to the Scottish Enlightenment*, Cambridge.

Haakonssen, Knud (2007). 'Republicanism' in *A Companion to contemporary political philosophy*, 2nd ed., ed. Robert E. Goodin, Philip Pettit and Thomas Pogge, 2 vols., Oxford, vol. 2, pp. 729–35.

Haakonssen, Knud and Michael J. Seidler (2016). 'Natural law: law, rights and duties' in *A Companion to intellectual history*, ed. Richard Whatmore and Brian Young, Oxford, pp. 377–401.

Haig, Robert Louis (1960). *The Gazetteer, 1735–1797: A study in the eighteenth-century English newspaper*, Carbondale.

Halldenius, Lena (2002). 'Locke and the non-arbitrary', *European Journal of Political Theory* 2, pp. 261–79.

Halldenius, Lena (2010). 'Building blocks of a republican cosmopolitanism: the modality of being free', *European Journal of Political Theory* 9, pp. 31–47.

Halldenius, Lena (2014). 'Freedom fit for a feminist? On the feminist potential of Quentin Skinner's conception of republican freedom', *Redescriptions* 17, pp. 86–103.

Halldenius, Lena (2015). *Mary Wollstonecraft and feminist republicanism: Independence, rights and the experience of unfreedom*, London.

Halldenius, Lena (2017). 'Mary Wollstonecraft and freedom as independence' in *Women and liberty, 1600–1800: Philosophical essays*, ed. Jacqueline Broad and Karen Detlefsen, Oxford, pp. 95–108.

Halldenius, Lena (2022). 'Neo-roman liberty in the philosophy of human rights' in *Rethinking Liberty before liberalism*, ed. Hannah Dawson and Annelien De Dijn, Cambridge, pp. 215–32.

Hamel, Christopher (2011). *L'esprit républicain: Droits naturels et vertu civique chez Algernon Sidney*, Paris.

Hamel, Christopher (2013). 'The republicanism of John Milton: natural rights, civic virtue and the dignity of man', *History of Political Thought* 34, pp. 35–63.

Hammersley, Rachel (2013). 'Rethinking the political thought of James Harrington: royalism, republicanism and democracy', *History of European Ideas* 39, pp. 354–70.

Hammersley, Rachel (2019). *James Harrington: An intellectual biography*, Oxford.

Hammersley, Rachel (2020). *Republicanism: An introduction*, Cambridge.

Hamowy, Ronald (1990). 'Cato's Letters, John Locke and the republican paradigm', *History of Political Thought* 11, pp. 273–94.

Hankins, James (2023). *Political meritocracy in Renaissance Italy: The virtuous republic of Francesco Patrizi of Siena*, Cambridge, MA.

Harpham, Edward J. (2000). 'The problem of liberty in the thought of Adam Smith', *Journal of the History of Economic Thought* 22, pp. 217–37.

Harris, Michael (1987). *London newspapers in the age of Walpole*, Toronto.

Harris, Tim (2006). *Revolution: The great crisis of the British monarchy, 1685–1720*, London.

Herzog, Lisa (2013). *Inventing the market: Smith, Hegel, and political theory*, Oxford.

Hesse, Barnor (2014). 'Western hegemony, black fugitivity', *Political Theory* 42, pp. 288–313.

Higgins, Ian (2005). 'Remarks on *Cato's Letters*' in *'Cultures of Whiggism': New essays on English literature and culture in the long eighteenth century*, ed. David Womersley, Newark, pp. 127–46.

Hirschmann, Nancy J. (2003). *The subject of liberty: Towards a feminist theory of freedom*, Princeton.

Hirschmann, Nancy J. and Emily F. Regier (2019). 'Mary Wollstonecraft, social constructivism and the idea of freedom', *Politics and Gender* 15, pp. 645–70.

Hoak, Dale (2007). 'Sir William Cecil, Sir Thomas Smith and the monarchical republic of Tudor England' in *The monarchical republic of early modern England: Essays in response to Patrick Collinson*, ed. John F. McDiarmid, Aldershot, pp. 37–54.

Holland, Ben (2017). *The moral person of the state: Pufendorf, sovereignty and composite politics*, Cambridge.

Honohan, Iseult (2002). *Civic republicanism*, London.

Hont, Istvan (2005). *Jealousy of trade: International competition and the nation-state in historical perspective*, Cambridge, MA.

Horne, Thomas (1980). 'Politics in a corrupt society: William Arnall's defense of Robert Walpole', *Journal of the History of Ideas* 41, pp. 601–14.

Hoye, J. Matthew and Jeffrey Monaghan (2018). 'Surveillance, freedom and the republic', *European Journal of Political Theory* 17, pp. 343–63.

Hunter, Ian (2001). *Rival Enlightenments: Civil and metaphysical philosophy in early modern Germany*, Cambridge.

Hunter, Ian (2023). 'Human nature, the state of nature and natural law' in *The Cambridge companion to Pufendorf*, ed. Knud Haakonssen and Ian Hunter, Cambridge, pp. 109–39.

Ivison, Duncan (1997). *The self at liberty: Political argument and the arts of government*, Ithaca.

Jacob, Margaret (1981). *The radical Enlightenment: Pantheists, freemasons and republicans*, London.

James, Susan (1997). *Passion and action: The emotions in seventeenth-century philosophy*, Oxford.

James, Susan (2016). 'Mary Wollstonecraft's conception of rights' in *The social and political philosophy of Mary Wollstonecraft*, ed. Sandrine Bergès and Alan Coffee, Oxford, pp. 148–65.

Jensen, Freyja (2012). *Reading the Roman Republic in early-modern Britain*, Leiden.

Johnston, Kenneth R. (2013). *Unusual suspects: Pitt's reign of alarm and the lost generation of the 1790s*, Oxford.

Jones, Howard (1998). *Master Tully: Cicero in Tudor England*, Nieuwkoop.

Kalyvas, Andreas and Ira Katznelson (2008). *Liberal beginnings: Making a republic for the moderns*, Cambridge.

Kapust, Daniel J. (2004). 'Skinner, Pettit and Livy: the conflict of the orders and the ambiguity of republican liberty', *History of Political Thought* 25, pp. 377–401.

Kapust, Daniel J. (2011). *Republicanism, rhetoric, and Roman political thought: Sallust, Livy, and Tacitus*, Cambridge.

Kapust, Daniel J. and Brandon P. Turner (2013). 'Democratical gentlemen and the lust for mastery: status, ambition, and the language of liberty in Hobbes's political thought', *Political Theory* 41, pp. 648–75.

Kelleher, Richard (2022). 'Paper revolutions' in *Defaced! Money, conflict, protest*, ed. Richard Kelleher, Cambridge, pp. 16–25.

Kelly, Duncan (2011). *The propriety of liberty: Persons, passions and judgement in modern political thought*, Cambridge.

Kelly, P. J. (2001). 'Classical utilitarianism and the concept of freedom: a response to the republican critique', *Journal of Political Ideologies* 6, pp. 13–31.

Kennedy, Geoff (2013). 'Freemen, free labor and republican discourse in early modern England', *Contributions to the History of Concepts* 8, pp. 25–44.

Kennedy, Geoff (2014). 'Cicero, Roman republicanism and the contested meaning of *libertas*', *Political Studies* 62, pp. 488–501.

Kenyon, J. P. (ed.) (1966). *The Stuart constitution 1603–1688: Documents and commentary*, Cambridge.

Kenyon, J. P. (1977). *Revolution principles*, Cambridge.

Keymer, Thomas and Alice Wakely (eds.) (2005). *Henry Fielding: The history of Tom Jones, a foundling*, London.

Koekkoek, René (2022). 'Liberty, death and slavery in the age of Atlantic revolutions, 1770s to 1790s' in *Rethinking Liberty before liberalism*, ed. Hannah Dawson and Annelien De Dijn, Cambridge, pp. 134–53.

Kramer, Matthew H. (2003). *The quality of freedom*, Oxford.

Kramer, Matthew H. (2008). 'Liberty and domination' in *Republicanism and political theory*, ed. Cécile Laborde and John Maynor, Oxford, pp. 31–57.

Kuklick, Bruce (ed.) (2000). *Thomas Paine: Political writings*, Cambridge.

Laborde, Cécile (2010). 'Republicanism and global justice: a sketch', *European Journal of Political Theory* 9, pp. 48–69.

Laborde, Cécile and John Maynor (eds.) (2008). *Republicanism and political theory*, London.

Laborde, Cécile and Miriam Ronzoni (2016). 'What is a free state? Republican internationalism and globalisation', *Political Studies* 64, pp. 279–96.

Larmore, Charles (2001). 'A critique of Philip Pettit's republicanism', *Philosophical Issues* 11, pp. 229–43.

Laslett, Peter (ed.) (1988). *John Locke: Two treatises of government*, Cambridge.

Lee, Daniel (2016). *Popular sovereignty in early modern constitutional thought*, Oxford.

Leipold, Bruno (2020). 'Marx's social republic: radical republicanism and the political institutions of socialism' in *Radical republicanism: Recovering the tradition's popular heritage*, ed. Bruno Leipold, Karma Nabulsi and Stuart White, Oxford, pp. 172–93.

Leipold, Bruno (2022). 'Chains and invisible threads: liberty and domination in Marx's account of wage-slavery' in *Rethinking Liberty before liberalism*, ed. Hannah Dawson and Annelien De Dijn, Cambridge, pp. 194–214.

Lieberman, David (1989). *The province of legislation determined: Legal theory in eighteenth-century Britain*, Cambridge.

List, Christian, and Laura Valentini (2016). 'Freedom as independence', *Ethics* 126, pp. 1043–74.

Lobban, Michael (2007). *A history of the philosophy of law in the common law world, 1600–1900*, Dordrecht.

Lockwood, Shelley (ed.) (1997). *Sir John Fortescue: On the laws and governance of England*, Cambridge.

Long, Douglas (1977). *Bentham on liberty: Jeremy Bentham's idea of liberty in relation to his utilitarianism*, Toronto.

Lovett, Frank (2005). 'Milton's case for a free commonwealth', *American Journal of Political Science* 49, pp. 466–78.

Lovett, Frank (2010). *A general theory of domination and justice*, Oxford.

Lovett, Frank (2012). 'What counts as arbitrary power?' *Journal of Political Power* 5, pp. 137–52.

Lovett, Frank (2018). 'Non-domination' in *The Oxford handbook of freedom*, ed. David Schmidtz and Carmen E. Pavel, Oxford, pp. 106–23.

Lovett, Frank (2022). *The well-ordered republic*, Oxford.

MacGilvray, Eric (2011). *The invention of market freedom*, Cambridge.

Maddox, Graham (2002). 'The limits of neo-Roman liberty', *History of Political Thought* 23, pp. 418–31.

Malcolm, Noel (2017). *Human rights and political wrongs: A new approach to human rights law*, London.

Marston, Daniel (2001). *The Seven Years' War*, New York.

Matthiessen, F. O. (1931). *Translation, an Elizabethan art*, Cambridge, MA.

Maynor, John (2003). *Republicanism in the modern world*, Cambridge.

McBride, Cillian (2015). 'Freedom as non-domination: radicalisation or retreat?' *Critical Review of International Social and Political Philosophy* 18, pp. 349–74.

McConville, Brendan (2007). *The king's three bodies: The rise and fall of royal America 1688–1776*, Chapel Hill.

McCormick, John P. (2003). 'Machiavelli against republicanism: on the Cambridge school's "Guicciardinian moments"', *Political Theory* 31, pp. 615–43.

McCrea, Brian (1981). *Henry Fielding and the politics of mid-eighteenth century England*, Athens, GA.

Mendle, Michael (1995). *Henry Parker and the English civil war: The political thought of the public's 'privado'*, Cambridge.

Miller, Peter N. (ed.) (1993). *Joseph Priestley: Political writings*, Cambridge.

Miller, Peter N. (1994). *Defining the common good: Empire, religion and philosophy in eighteenth-century Britain*, Cambridge.

Moen, Lars (2022). 'Eliminating terms of confusion: resolving the liberal–republican dispute', *Journal of Ethics* 26, pp. 247–71.

Monod, Paul (2005). '*Tom Jones* and the crisis of Whiggism in mid-Hanoverian England' in *'Cultures of Whiggism': New essays on English literature and culture in the long eighteenth century*, ed. David Womersley, Newark, pp. 268–96.

Moore, Lucy (2000). *Amphibious thing: The life of Lord Hervey*, London.

Moyn, Samuel (2015). *Christian human rights*, Philadelphia.

Murphy, Mark C. (2016). 'Hobbes (and Austin and Aquinas) on law as command of the sovereign' in *The Oxford handbook of Hobbes*, ed. A. P. Martinich and Kinch Hoekstra, Oxford, pp. 339–58.

Nelson, Eric (2004). *The Greek tradition in republican thought*, Cambridge.

Nelson, Eric (2011). *The Hebrew republic: Jewish sources and the transformation of European political thought*, Cambridge, MA.

Nelson, Eric (2014). *The royalist revolution: Monarchy and the American founding*, Cambridge, MA.

Norbrook, David (1999). *Writing the English republic: Poetry, rhetoric and politics, 1627–1660*, Cambridge.

Norton, Mary Beth (2020). *1774: The long year of revolution*, New York.

Nyquist, Mary (2013). *Arbitrary rule: Slavery, tyranny, and the power of life and death*, Chicago.

O'Brien, Karen (2009). *Women and Enlightenment in eighteenth-century Britain*, Cambridge.

O'Flaherty, Niall (2019). *Utilitarianism in the age of Enlightenment: The moral and political thought of William Paley*, Cambridge.

Olusoga, David (2021). *Black and British: A forgotten history*, London.

Oz-Salzberger, Fania (2002). 'Scots, Germans, republic and commerce' in *Republicanism: A shared European heritage, volume II: The values of republicanism in early modern Europe*, ed. Martin van Gelderen and Quentin Skinner, Cambridge, pp. 197–226.

Page, Anthony (2011). '"A species of slavery": Richard Price's rational dissent and antislavery', *Slavery and Abolition* 32, pp. 53–73.

Palladini, Fiammetta (1990). *Samuel Pufendorf discepolo di Hobbes. Per una reinterpretazione del giusnaturalismo moderno*, Bologna.

Palladini, Fiammetta (2008). 'Pufendorf disciple of Hobbes: the nature of man and the doctrine of *socialitas*', *History of European Ideas* 34, pp. 26–60.

Parkin, Jon (2007). *Taming the Leviathan: The reception of the political and religious ideas of Thomas Hobbes in England 1640–1700*, Cambridge.

Pateman, Carole (1988). *The sexual contract*, Cambridge.

Pateman, Carole (2002). 'Self-ownership and property in the person: democratisation and a tale of two concepts', *Journal of Political Philosophy* 10, pp. 20–53.

Patten, Alan (1996). 'The republican critique of liberalism', *British Journal of Political Science* 26, pp. 25–44.

Paulson, Ronald (1967). *Satire and the novel in eighteenth-century England*, New Haven.

Peltonen, Markku (1995). *Classical humanism and republicanism in English political thought, 1570–1640*, Cambridge.

Peltonen, Markku (2023). *The political thought of the English free state, 1649–1653*, Cambridge.

Pettit, Philip (1997). *Republicanism: A theory of freedom and government*, Oxford.

Pettit, Philip (2001). *A theory of freedom: From the psychology to the politics of agency*, Oxford.

Pettit, Philip (2002). 'Keeping republican freedom simple: on a difference with Quentin Skinner', *Political Theory* 30, pp. 339–56.

Pettit, Philip (2007). 'Free persons and free choices', *History of Political Thought* 28, pp. 709–18.

Pettit, Philip (2008). 'Republican freedom: three axioms, four theorems' in *Republicanism and political theory*, ed. Cécile Laborde and John Maynor, Oxford, pp. 102–30.

Pettit, Philip (2010). 'A republican law of peoples', *European Journal of Political Theory* 9, pp. 70–94.

Pettit, Philip (2012). *On the people's terms: A republican theory and model of democracy*, Cambridge.

Pettit, Philip (2014). *Just freedom: A moral compass for a complex world*, New York.

Pettit, Philip (2015). 'The republican law of peoples: a restatement' in *Domination and global political justice: Conceptual, historical and institutional perspectives*, ed. Barbara Buckinx, Jonathan Trejo-Mathys and Timothy Waligore, London, pp. 37–70.

Pettit, Philip (2023). *The state*, Princeton.

Philp, Mark (1985). 'Rational religion and political radicalism in the 1790s', *Enlightenment and Dissent* 4, pp. 35–46.

Philp, Mark (1998). 'English republicanism in the 1790s', *Journal of Political Philosophy* 6, pp. 235–62.

Plumb, J. H. (1967). *The growth of political stability in England 1675–1725*, London.

Pocock, J. G. A. (1971). *Politics, language and time: Essays on political thought and history*, New York.

Pocock, J. G. A. (1975). *The Machiavellian moment*, Princeton.

Pocock, J. G. A. (1977). 'Historical introduction' in *The political works of James Harrington*, Cambridge, pp. 1–152.

Pocock, J. G. A. (1985). *Virtue, commerce and history*, Cambridge.

Pocock, J. G. A. (1987). *The ancient constitution and the feudal law: A reissue with a retrospect*, Cambridge.

Pocock, J. G. A. (1994). 'England's Cato: the virtues and fortunes of Algernon Sidney, *The Historical Journal* 37, pp. 915–35.

Pocock, J. G. A. (2006). 'Present at the Creation: with Laslett to the lost worlds', *International Journal of Public Affairs* 2, pp. 7–17.

Podoksik, Efraim (2010). 'One concept of liberty: towards writing the history of a political concept', *Journal of the History of Ideas* 71, pp. 219–40.

Power, Henry (2015). *Epic into novel*, Oxford.

Rahe, Paul (1994). *Republics ancient and modern: Classical republicanism and the American Revolution*, Chapel Hill.

Reid, John Philip (1988). *The concept of liberty in the age of the American Revolution*, Chicago.

Riding, Jacqueline (2017). *Jacobites: A new history of the '45 rebellion*, London.

Robbins, Caroline (1959). *The eighteenth-century commonwealthman*, Indianapolis.

Robertson, John (ed.) (1997). *Andrew Fletcher: Political works*, Cambridge.

Robertson, Ritchie (2020). *The Enlightenment: The pursuit of happiness 1680–1790*, London.

Rosen, Frederick (2003). *Classical utilitarianism from Hume to Mill*, London.

Røstvig, Maren-Sophia (1954–8). *The happy man: Metamorphoses of a classical ideal*, 2 vols., Oxford.

Rumble, Wilfred E. (ed.) (1995). *John Austin: The province of jurisprudence determined*, Cambridge.

Runciman, David (2003). 'The concept of the state: the sovereignty of a fiction' in *States and citizens: History, theory, prospects*, ed. Quentin Skinner and Bo Stråth, Cambridge, pp. 28–38.

Sabbadini, Lorenzo (2016). 'Popular sovereignty and representation in the English civil war' in *Popular sovereignty in historical perspective*, ed. Richard Bourke and Quentin Skinner, Cambridge, pp. 164–86.

Sabbadini, Lorenzo (2020). *Property, liberty, and self-ownership in seventeenth-century England*, London.

Sainsbury, John A. (1987). *Disaffected patriots: London supporters of revolutionary America 1769–1782*, Kingston, Ont.

Sakkas, Evangelos (2016). 'Richard Price and his critics: Liberty, representation, and political obligation in England c.1760–1789'. PhD thesis, Queen Mary University of London.

Scanlan, Padraic X. (2020). *Slave empire: How slavery built modern Britain*, London.

Schwoerer, Lois G. (2019). *'No standing armies!' The antimilitary ideology in seventeenth-century England*, Baltimore.

Scott, Jonathan (2004). *Commonwealth principles: Republican writing of the English revolution*, Cambridge.

Sellers, M. N. S. (1994). *American republicanism: Roman ideology in the United States constitution*, New York.

Sellers, M. N. S (1998). *The sacred fire of liberty: Republicanism, liberalism and the law*, New York.

Shanks, Torrey (2019). 'The rhetoric of self-ownership', *Political Theory* 47, pp. 311–37.

Shelton, George (1968). *Dean Tucker and eighteenth-century economic and political thought*, New York.

Shuttleton, David (2003). 'Mary Chandler's description of Bath: a tradeswoman poet of the Georgian urban Renaissance' in *Women and urban life in eighteenth-century England: On the town*, ed. Rosemary Sweet and Penelope Lane, London, pp. 173–94.

Skinner, Quentin (1978). *The foundations of modern political thought*, 2 vols., Cambridge.

Skinner, Quentin (1990). 'The republican ideal of political liberty' in *Machiavelli and republicanism*, ed. Gisela Bock, Quentin Skinner and Maurizio Viroli, Cambridge, pp. 293–309.

Skinner, Quentin (1998). *Liberty before liberalism*, Cambridge.

Skinner, Quentin (2002a). 'John Milton and the politics of slavery' in *Visions of politics, volume II: Renaissance virtues*, Cambridge, pp. 286–307.

Skinner, Quentin (2002b). 'Classical liberty, Renaissance translation and the English civil war' in *Visions of politics, volume II: Renaissance virtues*, Cambridge, pp. 308–43.

Skinner, Quentin (2002c). 'Augustan party politics and Renaissance constitutional thought' in *Visions of politics, volume II: Renaissance virtues*, Cambridge, pp. 344–67.

Skinner, Quentin (2002d). 'A third concept of liberty', *Proceedings of the British Academy* 117, pp. 237–68.

Skinner, Quentin (2008a). 'Freedom as the absence of arbitrary power' in *Republicanism and political theory*, ed. Cécile Laborde and John Maynor, Oxford, pp. 83–101.

Skinner, Quentin (2008b). *Hobbes and republican liberty*, Cambridge.

Skinner, Quentin (2009a). 'On trusting the judgement of our rulers' in *Political judgement: Essays for John Dunn*, ed. Richard Bourke and Raymond Geuss, Cambridge, pp. 113–130.

Skinner, Quentin (2009b). 'A genealogy of the modern state', *Proceedings of the British Academy* 162, pp. 325–70.

Skinner, Quentin (2012). 'On the liberty of the ancients and the moderns: a reply to my critics', *Journal of the History of Ideas* 73, pp. 127–46.

Skinner, Quentin (2016). *Thinking about liberty: An historian's approach (The annual Balzan lecture)*, Florence.

Skinner, Quentin (2018). *From humanism to Hobbes: Studies in rhetoric and politics*, Cambridge.

Skinner, Quentin (2019). *Machiavelli: A very short introduction*, 2nd ed., Oxford.

Skinner, Quentin (2022). 'On neo-Roman liberty: a response and reassessment' in *Rethinking Liberty before liberalism*, ed. Hannah Dawson and Annelien De Dijn, Cambridge, pp. 233–66.

Skinner, Quentin (2024). 'Neo-Roman liberty: a genealogy' in *The Oxford handbook of republicanism*, ed. Frank Lovett and Mortimer Sellers (online ed., Oxford Academic, 23 January 2024), https://doi.org/10.1093/oxfordhb/9780197754115.013.10.

Skinner, Quentin and Martin van Gelderen (eds.) (2013). *Freedom and the construction of Europe*, 2 vols., Cambridge.

Skjönsberg, Max (2016). 'Lord Bolingbroke's theory of party and opposition', *The Historical Journal* 59, pp. 947–73.

Skjönsberg, Max (2019). 'Adam Ferguson on partisanship, party conflict, and popular participation', *Modern Intellectual History* 16, pp. 1–28.

Skjönsberg, Max (2021). *The persistence of party: Ideas of harmonious discord in eighteenth-century Britain*, Cambridge.

Skjönsberg, Max (2022). 'Charles Francis Sheridan on the feudal origins and political science of the 1772 revolution in Sweden', *Journal of the History of Ideas* 83, pp. 407–30.

Skjönsberg, Max (ed.) (2023). *Catharine Macaulay: Political writings*, Cambridge.

Smallwood, Angela (1989). *Fielding and the woman question: Fielding and feminist debate 1700–1750*, Brighton.

Sommerville, Margaret R. (1995). *Sex and subjection: Attitudes to women in early-modern society*, London.

Somos, Mark (2019). *American states of nature: The origins of independence 1761–1775*, Oxford.

Sowaal, Alice (2017). 'Mary Astell on liberty' in *Women and liberty, 1600–1800: Philosophical essays*, ed. Jacqueline Broad and Karen Detlefsen, Oxford, pp. 178–94.

Spector, Horacio (2010). 'Four conceptions of freedom', *Political Theory* 38, pp. 780–808.

Springborg, Patricia (1995). 'Mary Astell (1666–1731), critic of Locke', *American Political Science Review* 89, pp. 621–33.

Springborg, Patricia (ed.) (1996). *Astell: Political writings*, Cambridge.

Spitz, Jean-Fabien (1995). *La liberté politique: essai de généalogie conceptuelle*, Paris.

Stein, Peter (1999). *Roman law in European history*, Cambridge.

Straumann, Benjamin (2016). *Crisis and constitutionalism: Roman political thought from the fall of the republic to the age of revolution*, Oxford.

Talisse, Robert B. (2014). 'Impunity and domination: a puzzle for republicanism', *European Journal of Political Theory* 13, pp. 121–31.

Targett, Simon (1994). 'Government and ideology during the age of Whig supremacy: the political arguments of Sir Robert Walpole's newspaper propagandists', *The Historical Journal* 37, pp. 289–317.

Tavor, Eve (1987). *Scepticism, society and the eighteenth-century novel*, London.

Taylor, Charles (1991). 'What's wrong with negative liberty' in *Liberty*, ed. David Miller, Oxford, pp. 141–62.

Taylor, Michael (2020). *The interest: How the British establishment resisted the abolition of slavery*, London.

Taylor, Robert S. (2017). *Exit left: Markets and mobility in republican thought*, Oxford.

Thomas, D. O. (1977). *The honest mind: The thought and work of Richard Price*, Oxford.

Thomas, D. O. (ed.) (1991). *Richard Price: Political writings*, Cambridge.

Thomas, Peter D. G. (1987). *The Townshend duties crisis: The second phase of the American Revolution 1767–1773*, Oxford.

Thomas, Peter D. G. (1991). *Tea Party to independence: The third phase of the American Revolution 1773–1776*, Oxford.

Thompson, Michael J. (2018). 'The two faces of domination in republican political theory', *European Journal of Political Theory* 17, pp. 44–64.

Tierney, Brian (2014). *Liberty and law: The idea of permissive natural law, 1100–1800*, Washington, DC.

Tomaselli, Sylvana (ed.) (1995). *Mary Wollstonecraft: A vindication of the rights of men with A vindication of the rights of women and Hints*, Cambridge.

Tuck, Richard (1979). *Natural rights theories: Their origin and development*, Cambridge.

Tuck, Richard (1993). *Philosophy and government, 1572–1651*, Cambridge.

Tully, James (1980). *A discourse on property: John Locke and his adversaries*, Cambridge.

Tully, James (ed.) (1991). *Samuel Pufendorf: On the duty of man and citizen according to natural law*, Cambridge.

Tully, James (1993a). *An approach to political philosophy: Locke in contexts*, Cambridge.

Tully, James (1993b). 'Placing the *Two treatises*' in *Political discourse in early modern Britain*, ed. Nicholas Phillipson and Quentin Skinner, Cambridge, pp. 253–80.

Tully, James (2005). 'Exclusion and assimilation: two forms of domination in relation to freedom', *Nomos* 46, pp. 191–229.

Tully, James (2008). 'The agonistic freedom of citizens' in *Public philosophy in a new key, volume I: Democracy and civic freedom*, Cambridge, pp. 135–59.

Viroli, Maurizio (2002). *Republicanism*, trans. A. Shugaar. New York.

Walker, William (2006). 'Sallust and Skinner on civil liberty', *European Journal of Political Theory* 5, pp. 237–59.

Ward, Lee (2004). *The Politics of liberty in England and revolutionary America*, Cambridge.

Watkins, David J. (2016). 'Slavery and freedom in theory and practice', *Political Theory* 44, pp. 846–70.

Watt, Ian (1957). *The rise of the novel: Studies in Defoe, Richardson and Fielding*, London.

Whatmore, Richard (2016). 'Quentin Skinner and the relevance of intellectual history' in *A companion to intellectual history*, ed. Richard Whatmore and Brian Young, Oxford, pp. 97–112.

Whatmore, Richard (2023). *The end of Enlightenment*, London.

Wicksteed, Charles (1849). *Lectures on the memory of the just*, London.

Williams, E. Neville (ed.) (1960). *The eighteenth-century constitution 1688–1815: Documents and commentary*, Cambridge.

Wilson, Kathleen (1998). *The sense of the people: Politics, culture and imperialism in England 1715–1785*, Cambridge.

Winch, Donald (2002). 'Commercial realities, republican principles' in *Republicanism: A shared European heritage, volume II: The values of republicanism in early modern Europe*, ed. Martin van Gelderen and Quentin Skinner, Cambridge, pp. 293–310.

Winch, Donald (ed.) (2006). *Vindiciae Gallicae and other writings on the French Revolution*, Indianapolis.

Wirszubski, C. (1950). *Libertas as a political idea at Rome during the late republic and early principate*, Cambridge.

Womersley, David (2019). 'Introduction' in John Brown, *An estimate of the manners and principles of the times and other writings*, ed. David Womersley, Carmel, IN, pp. ix–xxvi.

Wootton, David (1994). 'Introduction: the republican tradition from commonwealth to common sense' in *Republicanism, liberty and commercial society 1649–1776*, ed. David Wootton, Stanford, pp. 1–41.

Worden, Blair (1994). 'Marchamont Nedham and the beginnings of English republicanism 1649–1656' in *Republicanism, liberty and commercial society 1649–1776*, ed. David Wootton, Stanford, pp. 45–81.

Worden, Blair (1995). 'Milton and Marchamont Nedham' in *Milton and republicanism*, ed. David Armitage, Armand Himy and Quentin Skinner, Cambridge, pp. 156–80.

Worden, Blair (2007). *Literature and politics in Cromwellian England: John Milton, Andrew Marvell, Marchamont Nedham*, Oxford.

Zeng, Elena Yi-Jia (2022). 'Empire and liberty in Adam Ferguson's republicanism', *History of European Ideas* 48, pp. 909–29.

Zook, Melinda S. (1999). *Radical Whigs and conspiratorial politics in late Stuart England*, Philadelphia.

Zwolinski, Matt (2018). 'Exploitation and freedom' in *The Oxford handbook of freedom*, ed. David Schmidtz and Carmen E. Pavel, Oxford, pp. 421–38.

# Index

Page numbers in bold refer to content in footnotes.